Holding
Up
Half
the
Sky

Holding Up Half the Sky

Chinese
Women
Past,
Present,
and
Future

Edited by Tao Jie, Zheng Bijun,
and Shirley L. Mow

Foreword by Gail Hershatter

Translated by Amy Russell

THE FEMINIST PRESS
AT THE CITY UNIVERSITY OF NEW YORK

Published by the Feminist Press at the City University of New York
The Graduate Center, 365 Fifth Avenue, New York, NY 10016
www.feministpress.org

First Feminist Press edition, 2004

09 08 07 06 05 04   5 4 3 2 1

Library of Congress Cataloging-in-Publication Data

Holding up half the sky : Chinese women past, present, and future / edited by Tao Jie,
Zheng Bijun, and Shirley L. Mow ; foreword by Gail Hershatter.— 1st ed.
     p. cm.
   Includes bibliographical references (p.   ).
   ISBN 1-55861-466-4 (library cloth : alk. paper) — ISBN 1-55861-465-6 (pbk. :
alk. paper)
   1. Women—China—History. 2. Feminism—China—History. 3. Women—
Legal status, laws, etc.—China—History. 4. Women—Employment—China—
History. I. Tao, Jie. II. Zheng, Bijun. III. Mow, Shirley L. IV. Tao, Jie. V. Zheng,
Bijun. VI. Title.
HQ1767.H643 2004
305.4'0951—dc22

                                                           2003027997

Publication of this book has been made possible in part by a grant from the Ford
Foundation. The Feminist Press would also like to thank Helene D. Goldfarb and
Florence Howe for their generosity in supporting this project.

Cover and text design by Dayna Navaro
Printed on acid-free paper by Transcontinental Printing
Printed in Canada

CONTENTS

Contents

FOREWORD

Holding Up Half the Sky presents work by some of China's most distinguished women scholars. In the past two decades, these authors and their colleagues—some writing from China, some from locations abroad—have created a new area of inquiry in China: women's studies. Gender, a subsidiary and somewhat suspect category of analysis during the period of Mao's leadership, exploded into visibility in the 1980s and 1990s. Physical characteristics, beauty, adornment, courtship, love, marriage, divorce, work relations, violence, childbearing, and child rearing all were reconceptualized in the popular press as important locations of difference and pleasure, as well as inequality and danger, sometimes all at once.

This new interest in gender's many dimensions has been reported extensively outside China. What has been less visible until the publication of *Holding Up Half the Sky* is the emergence of work by Chinese scholars addressing these questions. The twenty-one authors anthologized here concern themselves not only with the contemporary scene, but also with the recent and more distant past. Most have published extensively in China, and a glance at their notes reveals a world of richly documented investigation and debate about the lives of Chinese women from early times to the present.

In her wide-ranging introduction, Tao Jie sketches this long history and introduces contemporary realms of gender inequality. In some respects, the essays that follow offer an oblique challenge to the conventional narrative of gender relations in China. First formulated in the early twentieth century, that narrative highlights women's oppression under a protracted period of feudalism, and women's eventual liberation by the Chinese Communist Party. The essays in Part I, "Women in Early Chinese History and Culture," do not deny gendered hierarchy and subordination. But they suggest that women's lives were more variegated and dynamic than twentieth-century polemics generally acknowledged. Zheng Bijun, for instance, finds elite women in the twelfth and thirteenth centuries who were accomplished writers and mathematicians, and whose achievements were recorded in subsequent dynastic collections. As the imperial civil service examinations became the established route to power, she suggests, literate women who could assist their husbands and educate their sons were highly valued. At the same time, urban women figured prominently in silk production, woodblock printing, and entertainment, providing major sources of revenue for merchants and state authorities. Huang Yufu, in her essay on women in Peking opera, finds a steady, if often controversial, expansion of the role of women as actors and spectators in the early twentieth century. Zhao Liming summarizes decades of research (including her own significant contribution) about the script created by rural Hunan women, explaining how it worked to convey experiences and emotions specific to women. These ranged from bridal laments and songs about the plight of widows to professions of loyalty between sworn sisters and playful nonsense rhymes.

In a revisionist look at the canon of normative behavior for women, Xia Xiaohong takes up the posthumous career of Ban Zhao, a woman historian who lived in the Later Han dynasty. Almost 2,000 years later, Ban Zhao became a favorite target of early twentieth-century reformers, who excoriated her for articulating—in learned and flawless prose—a doctrine of women's submission to men. Xia Xiaohong refocuses our attention on how late imperial thinkers, many of them women, excerpted, adapted, and in some cases distorted Ban Zhao's writings to argue that women must be educated. In the first decade of the twentieth century, she tells us, Ban Zhao even had an unexpected afterlife as a repentant born-again feminist in an opera and a novel. Xia repositions one of the standard stories of women's history in China so that it becomes not only a tale about an oppressive ideology, but also an account of local resourcefulness, variability, and even humor.

Part II, "Women and Changing China," traces women's participation in political movements and governance across the twentieth century, documenting past contributions and formulating contemporary demands. Lu Meiyi's account of women's political activism in the 1910s and 1920s establishes that the 1919 May Fourth movement, sometimes described as the beginning of radical activity in China, was preceded by years of militant suffragism (supported by the American suffragist Carrie Chapman Catt) and by women's anti-imperialist demonstrations and communal living experiments. Lily Xiao Hong Lee offers illuminating biographical detail about the women who went on the Communist Party's Long March of 1934–1935, later becoming top-ranking officials responsible for mobilization work among women. Wang Qingshu offers a fact-filled, sobering account of women's political participation, with particular attention to contemporary problems under the economic reforms. She argues that, although women's participation in formal politics has shown some gains over the past half-century, it continues to be limited by lack of education, the feminization of agriculture, urban lay-off patterns, household burdens, and insufficient attention to recruiting and training women. Media portrayals of politically active women as "jargon-spouting bureaucrats" do not help. Wang makes a strong argument that "free-market competition" for political posts will not result in gender equality, since the social resources that enable political participation are already unevenly distributed across gender lines.

Each of the essays in Part III, "Women and Education," expresses the desire to effect institutional change. Ma Wanhua's essay on contemporary higher education describes the proliferation of regular universities, adult education facilities, nonstate institutions, and self-study courses during the past two decades. While she lauds the expansion of educational opportunities, Ma is disturbed by the evident tracking of women and the sense of inferiority expressed by many women university students. She calls upon the government to provide better funding for girls and young women who attend school, as well as for changes in admissions policies. Unequal access to education is widespread at the most basic levels, Danke Li discovers in her investigation of rural schools. The Chinese government has worked to extend rural schooling since 1949, and the Compulsory Education Law of 1986 mandated nine years of schooling; enrollment of girls has increased at all levels. Nevertheless, in the western interior, dropout rates for girls far exceed those for boys, and families consistently prefer to educate sons rather than daughters when resources are scarce. Knowing that daughters will marry out, parents prefer to send them to earn money working in township and village enterprises before marriage, rather than paying rising school fees for their education. Li calls upon the government to abandon gender-blind policies, which tend to perpetuate existing gender inequities, and to make the improvement of girls' access to schooling an explicit priority.

Departing from the realm of government policy, and from the theoretical work for which she is internationally known, Li Xiaojiang contributes an account of how she has begun to build a gender studies program at Dalian University. Since 2000, she has worked to involve faculty and staff across the university in gender studies teaching and research. She seeks to undo the "double marginalization" whereby gender studies is peripheral to academia, and academic research does not inform most economic development projects aimed at women. Li has designed faculty training, self-help action teams for students, and community outreach projects aimed at "permeating" the existing curriculum with attention to gender. Her account complements the calls for more thoughtful state policies, providing a vivid illustration of the work that can be done on gender issues without direct state involvement.

Part IV, "Marriage and Family," maps the changing interplay between legal regulation and social practice. As Chen Mingxia notes, the 2001 Marriage Law reflects the rising incidence of divorce in reform-era China. It specifies the scope of community property, the need for negotiating a property settlement, and the entitlement to assistance of "the party who contributes more to the family (usually the woman) and the party who is economically distressed (usually the woman)." Yet as Chen's analysis and those of Xiong Yu and Wang

Xingjuan make clear, women's equal legal rights are still at variance with current social practice. Many marriages are still arranged. Women have less say in household decision-making than do men, carry far more of the burden of domestic work, suffer high rates of domestic violence, and in rural areas are more likely than men to commit suicide, usually over marital and family problems. Chen points out that a divorced woman's right to a share of community property does not solve the housing problem, particularly in rural areas where women have moved in with their husbands' families. Wang comments that domestic violence laws, drawn up locally and provincially since the mid-1990s, are in a nascent state and need to be complemented by legal assistance and psychological counseling provided directly to women. Meanwhile, women who remain in abusive situations are glorified as self-sacrificing mothers, and domestic violence itself is often not recognized as a problem. In explaining these persistent problems, Chen, Xiong, and Wang emphasize the stubbornly persistent notion of male superiority. They argue that the laws protecting women's rights need to be more clearly formulated and thoroughly enforced, a process that will require gender training for legislators and law enforcement personnel alike. Like many of the other authors in this volume, they also point out that gender-neutral laws and policies, promulgated in an environment of gender inequality, will fail to solve the problems confronting women.

Liu Ying calls attention to a subgroup whose problems have not heretofore been framed by a gendered analysis in China: elderly women. Women over sixty are now more than one-tenth of the population, and are projected to become one-quarter in the next few decades. Liu's essay on Beijing suggests that, although many elderly women enjoy financial independence, the gender inequality that has marked their working lives does not abate with age. Their incomes and insurance coverage are less satisfactory than those of elderly men, and, at the same time, they carry the burden of providing care for aging spouses as well as working children and school-age grandchildren. Elderly women living separately from children, about one-third of the total, have little access to economic or physical support; many worry about their health as healthcare costs soar and access to healthcare rapidly deteriorates. For rural women, a much larger group outside the scope of Liu Ying's study, the situation is markedly more dire in all respects.

The essays in Part V, "Women and Work," establish that work environments for women have been altered radically by the past two decades of economic reform, although not in an easily summarized fashion. Jiang Yongping compares the employment of urban women in the Maoist planned economy and the reform era, rendering a mixed verdict on the success of Mao-era policies in promoting women's equality. By the late 1970s, more than 90 percent of urban women were employed, raising their incomes and their social status, but they were tracked into lower-ranking positions and lower-paying sectors of the economy. Jiang joins many other women's studies scholars in criticizing the assignment of women to heavy physical labor or dangerous working conditions, making a case for the importance of gender difference. In the reform era, women have more leeway to choose their own work, and new types of work have opened up to them, but at the same time she finds that "women are gradually becoming marginalized." By 2000 the employment rate for urban women had fallen to 72 percent, with the gap between men's and women's employment opportunities and incomes widening. The willingness and ability of work units to provide benefits for women who are pregnant or nursing have declined. Jiang assigns equal blame to the workings of the market and to what she calls "traditional patriarchal culture," which affects both policy-makers and individual employers.

Surveying the employment options for rural women in the reform economy, Jin Yihong is more sanguine. Rural women have moved into waged work and managerial positions in unprecedented numbers, especially in areas like Jiangsu and Zhejiang that are industrializing rapidly. Although male managers outnumber female managers, particularly in high-level positions, some women have prospered in husband-wife business partnerships, been elected to political office, or been promoted up the ranks of administrative cadres. Work as a village director of women's affairs can pay 10,000 yuan per year, a substantial sum. Jin notes many circumstances enabling young rural women to succeed. Most intriguing, perhaps, is the support young married women receive from their mothers-in-law. Whereas scholars writing about past and contemporary rural families generally describe relationships between these two generations as rivalrous and fraught, Jin finds older women who encourage their daughters-in-law to realize their own deferred dreams.

Han Jialing's essay on rural women in western China, however, reminds us that this upbeat scenario is not found everywhere in China. In Guizhou, for instance, county governments have been eager to invest in profitable industries, but have seen one project after another founder because of a lack of infrastructure or insufficient data about the market. Meanwhile, basic-level projects that would make an enormous difference to women—delivery of water and electricity, education, micro-loans—go begging for funds. Han's work provides a strong critique of development strategies that pursue prestigious projects without considering local needs and capabilities, particularly those of women.

Women who leave their impoverished home villages in search of work now total about 26 million, and Tan Shen provides a very useful summary of their circumstances, much of it based on her own groundbreaking research. Some work in factories and the service sector, including the sex trade, while others set up small businesses with their husbands. Tan notes the opportunities that migration provides—material gain, increased autonomy—while pointing out that most jobs available to women require few skills, offer little pay, and are full of physical and emotional hazards. Migrations may alter a woman's expectations about marriage and enlarge the number of potential mates, leading to practical problems (e.g., when a couple tries to decide where to settle or how to educate their children in the city) and other frustrations (e.g., when women encounter hostility from local people as interlopers in the marriage market).

Women and education, women and family, women and work—all are familiar pairings that have preoccupied scholars of China for some time. Women's representation in the mass media, however, is a newer topic whose discussion has been pioneered by scholars writing in the PRC. Part VI, "Women and the Future," presents some of their findings. Shou Yuanjun reports as both participant and observer. As one of the producers of *Half the Sky*, a television program for women first aired in 1995, she describes the difficulties in developing a "gender perspective" on topics including laid-off women workers, single mothers, cosmetic surgery, gender discrimination in the kindergarten curriculum, and the woman-unfriendly design of public restrooms. Bu Wei criticizes the mainstream media for ignoring women's media needs, promoting stereotypes, treating women exclusively as consumers, and deploying women's bodies to sell commodities. Focusing on the period since 1995, she describes the distressingly familiar pattern wherein women are one-third of all news professionals but less than 9 percent of top decision-makers. Women reporters are relegated to "soft" news, and the media seldom report on the gendered dimensions of health, poverty, unemployment, or violence. A small number of programs for women have been created, including *Half the Sky*, but most of them are not aired during prime time. Bu suggests that women's continuing domestic burden limits their access to both print and broadcast media. The needs and desires of rural women, she notes, are particularly opaque. Yet the research of scholars such as Bu, and the formation of a Women's Media Monitoring and Testing Network, serve both to gather information and to develop an activist agenda for media reform.

In the final essay of *Holding Up Half the Sky*, Dai Jinhua outlines an ambitious critique of the ways class and gender have been framed in contemporary China. Too often, she says, women have born the brunt of social crises, including recent waves of lay-offs from state-owned enterprises. Yet when such lay-offs are discussed in exclusively gendered terms—in soap operas or advertisements about women's role in the home, for instance, or stories detailing the rise of woman entrepreneurs from the ranks of the unemployed— emerging class divisions are obscured. Dai worries that new expressions of rebellious class consciousness—such as a popular recent play about Che Guevara—are too often full of unacknowledged gender bias, while analyses of social problems organized exclusively by gender mask vast class differences among women. Dai reminds her readers that "class divisions and the reconstruction of a gendered social order are the most prominent and harshest realities of Chinese society in the 1990s and beyond." Thus it is important to map their relationship carefully.

In making available this creative, forceful, concerned, and sometimes indignant ensemble of voices, *Holding Up Half the Sky* allows English-speaking readers to eavesdrop on an ongoing conversation. It also invites us to participate in a new one. Scholarship by Chinese women, about Chinese women, has been engaged in talking back to Mao-era formulations of "the woman question" and establishing women's studies as a new realm of inquiry. It is a body of work that closely attends to recent Chinese history and current local concerns. At the same time, many of the questions raised here—how scholarship and activism intertwine, how a government might be made more responsive, how a women's studies curriculum can establish itself without being segregated—have concerned researchers and activists in many other locations. For the readers of this volume, both the particularities and the commonalities will be instructive and will invite response. In her essay, Li Xiaojiang cautions that the wholesale adoption of Western feminist methods may create "the kinds of problems that happen when an exotic tropical plant is transplanted to a colder climate." Yet the issue here is less one of transplantation than of traveling theory and practice, and such travel is rarely unidirectional. These essays open up multiple pathways along which ideas, arguments, and visions of change can move.

Gail Hershatter
Santa Cruz, California
September 2003

PREFACE

We began thinking about editing an anthology on Chinese women when Florence Howe, then publisher of the Feminist Press, suggested that we put together such a volume modeled after the press's popular 1995 publication, *Japanese Women: New Perspectives on the Past, Present, and Future.* The book on women in Japan sought to close the gap between what Japanese write at home and what the world abroad reads. We believed that this gap also existed with regard to Chinese, particularly about women. Experiences and firsthand observations by Chinese scholars about various aspects of Chinese society are not widely available to non-Chinese-speaking audiences. Compared to the abundance of scholarly work that is translated from English to Chinese, what gets translated into English is minuscule.

Unlike the handful of students and scholars who are engaged in specialized study of China, most non-Chinese are quite uninformed about the current situation of Chinese women. Daily newspapers and a few magazines provide superficial reports. In July 2002, for example, the *New York Times* published a report called "China Juggles the Conflicting Pressures of a Society in Transition" that profiled six Chinese women and men, devoting two or three paragraphs to each person. This kind of journalism, while better than nothing, often offers only a partial, perhaps exaggerated or distorted, view. Chinese women in particular are still often portrayed as exotic, passive, and subservient, although, as this book will show, many women now hold positions of leadership in government, the media, and other fields. We rarely hear the voices of Chinese women. Even if we search for more definitive reading, we hear about Chinese women as seen through a Western lens of researchers and writers, not to mention journalists. As Jonathan D. Spence so vividly describes in *The Chan's Great Continent: China in Western Minds*, American and European views of China have been shaped by Western writers from the time of Marco Polo and his travels in the thirteenth century, the Jesuits' letters and reports in the sixteenth century and Lord Macartney, whose writings about his experiences in eighteenth-century China were sometimes deliberate fiction.

When we began this project we were aware of a rich and extensive body of scholarship on the history of Chinese women and on contemporary issues concerning women. Most of this work had developed in China during the past twenty-five years, some of it beginning in the late 1970s with the implementation of China's open door policy. Then, in the early 1990s, a major burst of scholarship occurred in preparation for the Fourth United Nations Conference on Women in Beijing in 1995. The research on women has continued and expanded to include such new areas of interest as violence against women, along with detailed examinations of other injustices, as well as explorations about the depths of prejudice against women. One can now say that Chinese women scholars have developed their own form of feminism and feminist analysis. We believe it is important for the West to hear these voices speaking for Chinese women.

This book, therefore, presents a collection of essays written by Chinese women, all authorities on the status of women in the workplace or with regard to education, marriage, family, or cultural life. There is much in the volume about class as well as gender, and about differences between urban and rural life in contemporary China. We intend the volume as a significant introduction to Chinese feminist scholarship.

We began this project with the assumption that many women in China would be interested in contributing to this volume. We expected that they would welcome the intellectual challenge, and we were not disappointed. All except two of the authors live in China and are well-published scholars, academics, activists, journalists, and public officials. For the most part, their scholarship is unknown outside China, though a few of their essays have been translated for Western journals. We have two regrets: first, that we were unable to include essays on minority women—Uighurs, Tibetans, Miao, and members of other minority groups. Their lives differ significantly from those of Han women politically and culturally; their voices remain largely unheard. Second, we were not able to capture the new scholarship that is only now emerging on lesbianism in China or to explore this important aspect of women's experience.

In the summer of 1999, two of the editors, Tao Jie and Shirley L. Mow, met in Beijing for the first time. They discussed a possible collaboration between the Feminist Press at the City University of New York and Peking University's Center for the Study of Women at Home and Abroad. They were excited about forging a link between a women's center at a major Chinese university and a not-for-profit feminist press in residence at a major university campus. Through the Feminist Press, writings by Chinese women would find a broad audience in the United States, among not only scholars but also general readers. The idea generated excitement among the women's center's faculty and led Zheng Bijun, former director of the center, to join as third co-editor. The three editors explored a range of research areas and identified scholars from various universities and research institutes who might contribute to the anthology.

The following fall, Tao Jie and Shirley L. Mow met again in Santa Cruz,

Preface

California, to flesh out an outline of the book. In China, Zheng Bijun and Tao Jie invited some thirty academics, journalists, activists, and public officials to contribute to the anthology, their intention being to include authors who could write from various institutional and regional locations as well as from different areas of expertise.

Funding from the Ford Foundation enabled the editors and authors to meet as a group on two occasions to share ideas. For the first workshop in May 2001, Shirley L. Mow and Florence Howe traveled to Beijing. Seventeen authors attended a two-day session at Peking University. Howe opened the workshop with a talk about women's studies in the United States and internationally. She emphasized the importance of this book for students, teachers, and researchers, not only in the United States, but worldwide, and she affirmed the Feminist Press's commitment to publishing women's voices. As a way to illustrate cultural differences and similarities, Dai Jinhua, professor and graduate advisor at the Institute of Comparative Literature Research at Peking University, spoke on women in Chinese literature, followed by Dorothee Greenberg, professor of English at Pace University, who spoke on women in English literature. We spent a day and a half listening, as each of the other Chinese authors presented a synopsis of the essays they planned to contribute. Discussion was always lively, even through interpreters.

Authors submitted their first drafts by the end of October 2001, in time for review at a second workshop at the end of November in Beijing. All but three of the twenty-one chapters were written in Chinese. Those present, editors and authors, worked first in small groups, each with a third of the essays. Before the meeting ended, they had each read all the essays and were discussing them in the larger group. The workshops allowed for a rich exchange of ideas. Moreover, the face-to-face discussions helped the editors solve problems about such matters as repetition. The editors and authors, moreover, derived great pleasure from working with one another in this way.

When the Chinese-language essays were later translated into English, the team made every effort to ensure that the work remained faithful to the original. The English-language translations of essays were reviewed for accuracy by the co-editors and by the contributors, in some cases, several times. Throughout the volume we employ the pinyin system of romanization for Chinese names and terms, except in instances where they are well established in English, such as Peking Opera and Peking University. In the case of personal names, we follow the Chinese tradition of placing the surname first, followed by the given name. Two of the contributors, who live in the United States and Australia, preferred to adopt Western name order: Danke Li and Lily Xiao Hong Lee.

We owe many people our gratitude for their assistance: the Ford Foundation for funding the project, Gerald Postiglione in Beijing, Janice Petrovich and Gertrude Fraser in New York for their helpful suggestions. We are grateful to Jean Casella, current publisher of the Feminist Press, for her support of this project; Amy Russell, who translated all but four chapters; Danke Li for compiling the bibliography and checking the accuracy of the translation of classical Chinese texts; and P. H. Chin, who also read the chapters on ancient China and made changes to the translations. We are indebted to Ivy Su for her help with pinyin and to Jean Murley for her assistance in preparing the manuscript for the copyeditor.

Livia Tenzer, our editor at the Feminist Press, coordinated the translation and editing schedule and had the final responsibility for preparing the manuscript for publication. Dayna Navaro designed the beautiful cover for the book after an adventure to New York's Chinatown in search of artistic materials. Florence Howe planted the idea for this book in our heads and worked with the editors throughout the process. She did the first edit of the volume and kept the project on track with regard to time. Without Howe, this project would not have become a reality, not only because of her commitment to making women's voices heard wherever they live and work and her deep interest in China, but also because of the direction, advice, and encouragement she offered.

This is a product of collaboration. We want to thank the authors who made this volume possible by writing brilliantly about their experiences and research. What comes through their essays is the striking clarity with which each author identifies not only the issues and accompanying problems, but the points at which government and activists need to work to improve conditions for women in China. They understand the importance of the strategic points for change—education and the media, for example. The authors emerge for us not only as scholars, but as activists who will spend their lives working on behalf of women's rights. And we are pleased to present them to an English-speaking audience worldwide.

Shirley L. Mow
New York City
September 2003

INTRODUCTION

In China's creation mythology, the universe begins in chaos and Pangu, a male god, grows very fast to separate the heaven from the earth. When he dies, every piece of his body transforms into something that we now find in nature, including rivers and mountains. The creation of human beings, however, is indebted to a female god, Nuwo. Legend goes that she uses clay to make man and woman, and all the gods come to help her add arms and legs, ears and eyes to these human beings. Another famous legend about her tells that she mends the sky with colored rocks and stones when one corner of it starts to fall and disaster becomes imminent. So it seems that, in the remote past, male and female were rather equal and the female's intelligence and resourcefulness were well acknowledged.

Life, unfortunately, is never that perfect and ideal. When China began as a slave society more than four thousand years ago, the emergence of private ownership and a family and class hierarchy initiated a patriarchal system that put into power the male as husband, father, and head of the clan and reduced women to the control of men. During the ensuing period of more than 1,800 years, there appeared many great thinkers and different schools of thought, such as Confucius and Confucianism, Laozi and Daoism. Ironically, what started as innocent philosophy soon became a means of oppressing women. Take the yin-yang theory as an example. At the very beginning, it was just about the duality of nature. Ancient philosophers believed that all natural phenomena had two opposites—light and shade, cold and heat. They believed that such complements or contradictions of opposites were inherent in all matters of the universe. As time went on, however, scholars began to use the theory to explain such social phenomena as the relationship between the monarch and his subjects, the emperor and the common people, the master and the slave, and men and women, especially husbands and wives. Women became victimized because of the idea that yang, associated with men, was superior to yin, associated with women.[1] As for Confucius, he established many rules and regulations about the management of the state and the family, almost none of them favoring women.

During China's long history of feudalism, women were always a marginal group deprived of political and economic rights. They were excluded from social life and confined to the household, reduced to a state of dependence on men. They were even denied the opportunity for education because of the belief that "a woman's virtue lies in her lack of knowledge or ability." Confucianism and the feudal society laid down a double-standard code of behavior for men and women. For instance, a woman had no freedom regarding marriage. She had to marry the man her parents chose whether she liked him or not. Actually she often had no way to know one way or the other, since she would not have set eyes on her would-be husband until the wedding night. Inside the family, a woman had to obey her father before marriage, her husband after marriage, and her son after the death of her husband. A man had the freedom to desert his wife, while a wife had no right to ask for divorce. A man was allowed to have more than one wife or concubine, while a woman had to devote her whole life to the man she was forced to marry. A remark by Confucius, the most respected philosopher in Chinese history, that "women are hard to deal with" forever doomed them to the status of inferiority, while popular sayings such as "man should deal with the outside world while woman's place is within the courtyard of her house" and "woman is the source of evil, her beauty may bring disaster to the kingdom" further strengthened this belief.[2]

In addition to all the real-life and spiritual restrictions, a new form of oppression was invented more than seven hundred years ago: Women were physically fettered with bound feet. As a result, a woman was "a prisoner all her life and a beast of burden half her life," as Qiu Jin, a feminist fighter at the turn of the twentieth century, described it.[3]

Ironically, a distinguished woman scholar, Ban Zhao (45–120?), mapped out this oppressive code of behavior for women in the interest of patriarchy. Her *Admonitions for Women* contains fewer than 1,600 characters but it lays down the basic rule of "three obediences and four virtues," admonishing a woman to wait upon her husband in the same way that humans worship the God of Heaven, commoners serve the emperor, or a filial son takes care of his father.[4] For a long time, this little book championed women's inferiority as it supplied the theoretical foundation of the feudal society's oppression of women.

This situation, however, never completely forestalled Chinese women from distinguishing themselves as men's equals. Ban herself provides a good example. She was the first woman historian in Chinese history, who, at the behest of the emperor, completed *The History of the Han Dynasty*, a chronicle of the Han dynasty left unfinished by her brother, Ban Gu. She was also good at writing poetry and essays, and her daughter-in-law collected her writings and published them in three volumes. She gave lectures at the royal library on *The History of the Han Dynasty* to male students, some of whom later became distinguished historians. She was so good a scholar that the emperor invited her to the royal court to teach the empress and other women.

The Tang dynasty (618–907), a time of renaissance of art and literature, hailed renowned male poets, such as Li Bai, Bai Juyi, Du Fu. However, *The Complete Works of Tang Poetry* also includes successful female poets, not only of the royal court or aristocratic families, but also from among Daoist nuns and prostitutes.[5] The Song dynasty (Northern Song [960–1127]; Southern Song [1127–1271]) was famous for its neo-Confucianism, which put extremely high demands on women.[6] Yet at this time men also emphasized the education of women so that they might be able to serve their husbands and raise their sons more effectively. Many matriarchs of officials or nobility proved capable of helping their spouses or clans to succeed in careers or business. Men, however, acknowledged these women's achievements only after their deaths and in their tombstone inscriptions. What is worse, the inscriptions idealized these women and their service to men as "faithful and helpful wives, dutiful mothers and filial daughters-in-law," thus turning them into role models for future generations of women, with higher demands and more restrictions.

In Chinese popular literature, especially in local operas, countless stories were told about the wrongs done to women and their miseries.[7] But there were also stories about women who fought for their own happiness or who came forward at times of national or family crises. For example, one poem celebrates Hua Mulan, who went to war in place of her elderly father and distinguished herself on the battlefield, although she had to disguise herself as a man. But, however courageous or resourceful the heroines were on battlefields or in the royal court, they still had to change back into women's clothing at the conclusion of their tasks and fall back into the female lives prescribed by a patriarchal society. Wu Zetian (624–705), the only woman to become emperor (r. 690–705), met with so much opposition that she had to order at her deathbed that nothing be inscribed on her tombstone, so that future generations would be free to decide whether she had been an evil woman or someone who had contributed greatly to the development of the Tang dynasty. The debate continues even today, as she is still often depicted in novels, movies, or television plays as a cold-blooded, nasty, cruel, and unscrupulous woman who ruined many men during her lifetime.

Some women created a written language known only to women so as to tell their own stories and share their grief with other women. When fiction was established as a genre in the Qing dynasty (1644–1911) and women became fiction writers, they tried to create competent and resourceful female characters. They often wrote stories in the form of local operas performed to audiences made up mainly of other women. Even though most of the writers were daughters of rich families or high officials and, consciously or unconsciously, advocated the feudal mores they received through education, the brilliance of their heroines, their superiority to men in thinking and action, and the happy endings they obtained through their intelligence, confidence, strength of spirit,

and even passion have won the hearts of generations of Chinese women readers.[8]

Chinese women saw some hope of equality with men during the time of the
Taiping (Heavenly Peace) Kingdom (1851–1865). At the beginning of this
peasant uprising, some people advocated theories that men and women were
equals because all human beings are sisters and brothers. The Land Law promulgated in 1853 stipulated that women were entitled to the same amount of
land as men. The leaders also emphasized that marriage should not be
arranged on the basis of wealth, that women should not be made to bind their
feet, and that they should be allowed to participate in politics and become soldiers. For the first time in Chinese history, large numbers of women took up
arms and fought side by side with men not only for the purpose of overthrow-
ing the Qing, but also for their own freedom and independence. Unfortunately,
the uprising became more and more affected by feudal ideas and its leaders
started to keep concubines, support polygamy, and lay down restrictions on
women. Finally, with the suppression of the Taiping rebellion, women's aspirations for emancipation were devastated.

Some Qing bureaucrats, however, initiated a Westernization movement in
the latter half of the nineteenth century to bring into China techniques of
bourgeois production with the purpose of reviving the tottering regime. The
movement was a total failure, as demonstrated by China's defeat in the Sino-
Japanese War of 1894–1895, launched by Japan to annex Korea and invade
China. But it gave people an opportunity to learn about the lives of women in
the West and to recognize the problems of Chinese women, especially the pernicious effects of footbinding and women's exclusion from education. Male
scholars involved in the Reform Movement of 1898, such as Tan Shitong
(1865–1898), Kang Youwei (1858–1927), and Liang Qichao (1873–1929),
believed that the status of women reflected a nation's power; they attacked
many feudal ideas that had been used for years to oppress women.[9] They made
great efforts to establish "natural foot" groups and to set up schools for girls.
Although they were more concerned with saving the country, their ideas and
practices were favorable to women at that time.

The first school for girls run by the Chinese themselves was set up in
Shanghai in June 1898, and by 1909, 308 schools had been established.[10] As a
result, a group of educated women soon began to ready themselves to battle for
women's rights. In the first decade of the twentieth century, more than forty
women's groups were formed and about forty newspapers were founded specifically for women. Campaigns were organized against footbinding and for girls'
education. Moreover, women joined the Northern Army, participated in the
1911 Revolution that overthrew the Qing government, and openly demanded
the right to be involved in national politics. Unfortunately, the effort to include

in the law women's equality with men and women's rights to participate in politics was twice thwarted by men in power, even though it was supported by Sun Yat-sen (1866–1925), leader of China's democratic revolution. The Beijing government, then headed by Yuan Shikai (1859–1916), the chieftain of the Northern warlords who usurped state power from the revolutionaries, closed down some girls' schools and women's clubs involved in these efforts and formulated laws to prohibit association between unmarried men and women, exerted restrictions on women's education, and advocated the cultivation of "sweet wives and gentle mothers."

Undaunted by failure, women activists continued their struggles in the New Culture movement (1915–1919), especially the May Fourth movement (1919), a political and cultural movement against imperialism and feudalism. They courageously challenged traditional ideology and feudal culture and won special victories in the battles for women's rights to education and freedom in marriage. They demanded that high schools and universities be opened to women. With the support of sympathetic men, the first female college student in Chinese history enrolled at Peking University in spring 1920, and other universities started to admit female students. As a result, more and more girls and women saw education as a means to realize their individuality. One famous and moving story tells of Ge Jianhao (1865–1944), who was brought up in the old ways, illiterate and with bound feet. Influenced by the new ideas, she went to a primary school at the age of fifty, left her rich husband because he intended to marry off their thirteen-year-old daughter to a businessman, and later went to France with her son, daughter, and daughter-in-law to work and study.

The struggle for freedom in marriage was already advancing when two events drew special attention to the issue. In November 1919, to protest a marriage forced on her by her parents, Zhao Wuzhen committed suicide inside the sedan that was carrying her to the bridegroom's house. A few months later, Li Xinshu, another young woman in a similar situation, took a different road. She published a statement in the newspaper proclaiming that her will as a human being should be respected and that she had decided to leave her home for school to improve herself. The two incidents opened an animated discussion in newspapers and magazines all over China, not only about the two girls, but also about the possibilities for women's lives. More and more young women ran away from arranged marriages and attended school to learn professions. In order to assert their independence and succeed in their careers, some of them even made up their minds to remain single.

Under the influence of new ideas and social modes, new professions opened up to women.[11] In 1916, the Bank of China in Beijing started to hire women; banks in Shanghai took up the practice a year later. Although the real reasons were self-serving—employers believed that women "are more careful" than men and "women can be hired at a lower salary"—the opportunity allowed women to use their education and demonstrate their abilities in jobs that were not lower paid or more menial than men's.[12] From that time forward, women began to engage in professions that used to be reserved for men, such as medicine, education, and even law and business.

The New Culture movement and the May Fourth movement were important periods in China's women's movement. For the first time in Chinese history, these movements succeeded in undermining feudal conventions and other ideas about women deeply rooted in Chinese culture. These movements fostered a type of "new women" who had high awareness and tried very hard to have their own careers and maintain their independence. The movements also initiated a flowering of women's literature. Women began to write poems, stories, and essays about their suffering and aspirations, not only for women's journals but also for prominent political journals and newspapers. Chen Hengzhe (1890–1976), Lu Yin (1898–1934), Ding Ling (1894–1986), Bing Xin (1900–1999), and many others started writing during this period and enriched the history of Chinese literature.[13]

Women's movements, however, have never had smooth sailing in China. There were always ups and downs. For example, when Chiang Kai-shek started the New Life movement in 1934, he reverted to Confucian rhetoric and once again advocated traditional customs and older ideas about gender. On the other hand, Chinese women never stopped their struggles to escape the restrictions imposed on them and often persisted in forging careers outside the home.

The founding of the People's Republic in 1949 brought another great, if not the greatest, change in the lives of Chinese women. The government took as policy that women's rights and interests had to be protected. In 1950 the government adopted a Marriage Law that prohibited arranged marriages, rescued many women from misery, and gave them the freedom to choose their spouses. Ever since then, a woman has been able to keep her maiden name even after marriage, so that she never becomes "so-and-so's wife" without even a name of her own. She could now be an independent person with her own identity. In the early 1950s, the government encouraged women to train as tractor drivers, airline pilots, electricians, and engineers, trades that used to be for men only. Besides granting them equal job opportunities and equal pay for equal work with men, it also gave girls and women the opportunity for education, making literacy classes, primary and middle schools, and even colleges free of charge. In 1958, during the Great Leap Forward, the government again called upon women to leave their households to participate in productive labor. And in the early 1960s, Mao Zedong, then the highest authority in the country, praised women for being "an important force in production, holding up half the sky."

Introduction

In those days, newspapers and magazines often carried reports or feature stories about the achievements of women workers, peasants, or professionals. Posters showing healthy women working happily could be found on billboards in cities and the countryside. There were even songs, local operas, and movies depicting inspiring images of women. The best known were the opera *Liu Qiao'er* in the 1950s about a girl who fights against all odds for the freedom to marry the man she loves, and *Li Shuangshuang* in the 1960s about a woman who replaces her husband as the head of their village and succeeds in producing wonderful changes in that village.

Because of such government policies and representations in the public sphere, Chinese women seldom suspected that there was any gender discrimination in their society. Their self-complacency began to break down in the late 1970s when China entered its era of reform and ended its state of isolation. In its eagerness to modernize the country, the Chinese government began to send people to study abroad and to invite foreigners to teach and work in China. The returned students and foreign experts brought into China new ideas and theories that opened people's eyes to their own shortcomings and forced women into serious reflection. They came to understand that they had depended too much on the government to give them equal status with men. As a result, they lacked the self-awareness and confidence to compete as men's equals.

More important still, reality forced Chinese women in this age of the market economy to see not only prejudices against women but also injustices. For instance, it was the government's policy in the past to have some women as heads or deputy heads at every level of government institutions. When a new policy began in the mid-1980s of conferring positions through open elections rather than by appointment or nomination from the authorities, women discovered that they had lost their advantages because of men's prejudice.[14] Statistics reveal such injustices: In 1986, in a small county in Sichuan province, 323 women were cheated out of their houses, which were sold to men who lived thousands of miles away. When reform started in state-owned factories in the late 1980s, women were always the first to be laid off. At one point in the early 1990s they made up 70 percent of those who were told to go home and wait for employment. Another statistic shows that in 1989, women were only 33.7 percent of the total enrollment of students at colleges or universities and women professors held only 9.2 percent of faculty positions. Furthermore, college women graduates do not enjoy the same job opportunities as their male counterparts. In addition to such statistics, old ideas and old sayings, such as "woman is inferior to man," came back, and from time to time there was even discussion about women going back home to be good housewives so as to give men a better environment at home and therefore more opportunity to meet challenges at work. Commercial advertising, a new industry emerging with reform and opening up, was filled with prejudice against women as shown by its female images.[15] Evidence of such regression in the status of women during the last two decades of the twentieth century could fill volumes.

Faced with new prejudices and encouraged by the achievements of women in other countries, the All-China Women's Federation and women scholars began to reconsider women's status and women's issues, to speak out about their views, and to make suggestions to the government for improvements.[16] In the meantime, the government announced measures to forestall this decline in women's social status and lack of social welfare. For instance, in 1987 when the number of women leaders fell, the All-China Women's Federation together with the Ministry of Personnel held a seminar to call attention to the low percentage of women leaders in government institutions (6.18 percent at the provincial or ministry level, 6.85 percent at the regional or bureau level, and 8.12 percent at the county or department level) and the training of women cadres.[17] Efforts were then made to create a kind of "think bank" of capable women cadres who had already achieved some recognition and who were then recommended as candidates during elections.

The decision of the United Nations to hold the Fourth World Women's Conference in Beijing in 1995 gave momentum to the women's movement in China. Women's studies, a new program, had begun to emerge on university campuses and in research institutes in the mid-1980s, but then developed very quickly before and after the Beijing Conference. The All-China Women's Federation called upon small groups of women's studies scholars to help prepare for the Beijing Conference. Chinese women organized more than fifty workshops, all important to the conference. Since then, women's studies groups have carried out research projects related to social problems involving women, such as girls' education, unemployed women, sexual harassment, and domestic violence, as well as projects concerning the writing of women's history, women's literature, women and psychology, and women and sociology.

One of the legacies of the Beijing Conference is that Chinese scholars had an opportunity to hear new theories and viewpoints, including the use of the term "gender consciousness," an understanding of the differences between "biological sex" and "sociological gender." Scholars also have begun to broaden their fields of research into such areas as women and poverty, women and the economy, women and the mass media, women and the environment, and violence against women, all mentioned in the Platform of Action adopted by the Beijing Conference. Some women journalists in Beijing have established a monitoring network and begun writing special columns in *China Women's News* called "Media Observations" and "Readers' Comments on the Media," which publish criticisms of gender bias in newspapers and magazines as well as on radio or television programs. Studies of advertisements and commercials have also revealed the heavy use of stereotypes that demean women. The establishment of a program for women at the Central China Television Station, the biggest and most influential television station in China, is one special achievement worth mentioning.

In preparation for the Beijing Conference, the Chinese Government put out a Program for Women's Development in China (1995–2000) in July 1995 to promote women's right to participate in politics; their equality in job opportunity, labor protection, education, health, family, and marriage; their economic status; and other spheres. As the government continues to carry out this program, one can note achievements. Shortly before the Beijing Conference, this program laid down as its first article that women should be encouraged to participate in the decision-making and management of state and social affairs, that there should be women in leading positions at government institutions at all levels, and that the percentage of women in such positions should be further increased. Statistics show that, by the end of 1996, the number of women leaders at the level of town, county, provincial, and national government or party institution had increased to 50.9, 38.7, 22.6, and 13.9 percent respectively.[18]

One can also point to the participation of women in producing policies to control such formerly neglected areas as sexual harassment and domestic violence against women. Sexual harassment was not mentioned in the Law for the Protection of Women's Rights and Interests adopted and enacted in 1992. The Red Maple Center for Women's Psychological Counseling, a women's hotline founded in 1992, first noticed this problem because of the phone calls it received for advice about situations of sexual harassment. In order to raise public the concern, the center proposed ways of revising the law and organized the only nongovernmental organization (NGO) workshop on sexual harassment run by Chinese women. As for violence against women, although the Law for the Protection of Women's Rights and Interests of 1992 laid down several articles prohibiting violence against women, it did not attract much attention. Domestic violence was practically ignored, as it was often considered the private affair of a couple and supported by a traditional saying that "scolding or beating the wife are expressions of love." The Beijing Conference made a big difference in the study of these two issues. Chinese scholars started to re-examine them in a new light, tracing their causes to a male-centered social culture and the unequal gender-relation patterns within the family system, as well as the deficiency of effective laws or other legal regulations. Such research and investigations have encouraged battered women to fight for their rights and show government institutions that new and more relevant laws should be adopted.

Needless to say, government decrees are a great help in improving women's situation. For example, the Regulations for the Control of Advertisements issued by the State Council on 26 October 1987 made no mention of gender bias, and the advertisement law adopted by the Standing Committee of the Eighth National Party Congress on 27 October 1994 and enforced on 1 February 1995 has only one article that prohibits "any content that is prejudiced against any race, ethnic groups, religion or gender." However, section 10, "Politics and Measures," of the Program for Women's Development, suggested by the All-China Women's Federation and approved by the State Council on 27 July 1995, prohibits "any description in movies, TV programs, and publications that is demeaning or insulting to women's images." This speaks eloquently about the changes in the minds of decision-makers. The results should eventually be favorable to women in China.

Although there are many ways to examine the improvement in Chinese women's levels of awareness, the best examples may be found in women's literature, since literature reflects life. In recent years, a large number of women writers have become more and more influential. They have not only revealed the disadvantages of women under the market economy but have also created brilliant female characters who turn out to be more intelligent and resourceful than men.[19]

The women's movement for equality in China has not been carried out by protests or demonstrations. But, in its own way, it has made much progress in the past twenty-five years. However, that does not mean that gender discrimination has disappeared in Chinese society. As the popular Chinese saying goes, the future is bright but the road to get there is still long and winding.

This anthology is made up of twenty-one essays about different aspects of women's lives in China. Several of the authors provide historical perspective. Xia Xiaohong's account about how it took ten years to subvert the authority of Ban Zhao's *Admonitions for Women* is another demonstration of the rugged and tortuous path Chinese women walked to realize their liberation. Historians have viewed the Song dynasty as a time of transition and neo-Confucianism. Although during this period social, economic, and cultural elements were adopted from the Tang dynasty, new characteristics brought on by the growth of commerce and an urban population also emerged. As the Song dynasty elite paid more attention to women's education for the purpose of enabling them to serve their spouses and clans, they gave women space in which to use their talents. Zheng Bijun's essay describes the achievements of many women in official or aristocratic families, based on her research into more than a thousand inscriptions on women's tombstones. During the Song dynasty the development of commercial economy and the emergence of towns and cities also allowed women to work in the silk and food industries or as folk artists or even prostitutes. Such changes in the patterns of women's lives, however, did not foster the breakdown of the deeply rooted idea of male superiority. Feudal mores and conventions still restricted the lives of Song women. This was the fate of women in the old days. Interestingly, Huang Yufu suggests that women's inferior social status during this period, and at other times in early Chinese history, can be viewed through the Peking Opera. Women were not allowed to perform on stage or even attend performances as part of the audience until the twentieth century.

Zhao Liming describes one form of women's rebellion that was not as obvious as the changes in the cities but is still worthy of our special attention. In one county in Hunan province and some neighboring counties in Guangxi province, women invented a special writing system, the source and timing of which scholars still debate. Gender was the unique characteristic of a method of writing taught only by women to their best friends or by mothers to daughters. Most of the writing in this special script was in the form of songs, written on beautifully ornamented paper, books, fans, or handkerchiefs. Women in this region would go to fairs in honor of female goddesses or turn the annual bull-fighting festival attended only by men into an opportune "day of the female" when they would meet and read their writing to each other. They would invite friends to prewedding parties to sing women's script songs, and during the wedding ceremony this written discourse was sung openly by the bride herself as a farewell speech and by her female friends as gifts. Very often examples of the writing were buried with women after their death. Most of the narratives describe their dreams, lament the collapse of these longings, and express contempt for male aspirations for fame and wealth. What could be behind this mysterious discourse against the dominant customs and conventions but a strong desire to be man's equal?

The cliché that "where there is oppression there is rebellion" contains some truth. Lu Meiyi's article reports on the first wave of the women's movement in China at the turn of the twentieth century. Led by a group of educated women, it fought for women's right to an education, marital choice, and political participation. Through ups and downs, successes and failures, even sacrifices, the women's movement left a far-reaching impact on successive generations of women. Lily Xiao Hong Lee's essay describes a unique moment in the women's movement in more modern times: about thirty women participated in the Long March of 1934–1935, which, in many ways, laid the foundation for the success of the Chinese Communist Party.

Struggle brings about improvement. Most of the essays in this anthology depict improvements in women's lives as well as problems still waiting to be solved. Over the years, Chinese women succeeded in winning certain rights and liberties, including education, freedom in marriage, the abolition of footbinding, and even some participation in political affairs. Lu Meiyi and Wang Qingshu describe some of these changes, the most important of which came about after the founding of the People's Republic, and then again especially after 1979 when China opened up and began its economic reforms.

Education has long been important to women. The Chinese government has done much in this realm, as exemplified by the literacy classes in the early 1950s and the efforts today to make sure that girls have an equal opportunity to go to school. Danke Li's article describes both the improvement in female access to schooling and the continuing gender inequality in education, especially in rural areas, while Ma Wanhua traces the history of higher education for women, explicates the different patterns for men and women at the present moment, and describes the problems confronting women in furthering their studies.

In the mid-1980s, women's studies appeared in China and developed rapidly because of the United Nations Fourth World Women's Conference. It benefited from the theories and experience of women's studies scholars outside China. However, Chinese women had to take their own road, rather than imitating others. Li Xiaojiang, a pioneer in bringing women's studies to China, delineates her attempts at Dalian University to integrate women's/gender studies with higher education reform. Her efforts to establish women's studies as a separate discipline that can expand its influence to other fields or disciplines in institutions of higher education may, someday, prove significant to women all over China.

Chen Mingxia's essay about the marriage laws promulgated in 1950, 1980, and 2001 describes the struggle of Chinese women to win equality with men within the household. Xiong Yu gives more detail about the changes in women's status at home and in marriage. For instance, women now have more say in matters concerning marriage, sex life, and the possession and distribution of property. However, legal equality differs from actual equality. Chen Mingxia discusses the obstacles: remnant feudal ideas in society, weaknesses in the language of legislation, and the lack of a gender perspective in lawmaking itself. Wang Xingjuan delineates specifically the phenomena of domestic violence, long ignored and only acknowledged since 1990. She also describes the actions taken by the government and NGOs to deal with violence, as well as impediments and possible solutions.

Only lately has attention also been paid to elderly women, now a growing population in China. Liu Ying's essay outlines the characteristics of elderly women's lives, their needs and difficulties, including the lack of communication between them and their descendants and their need for financial support and healthcare.

Because of the new market economy and economic reforms, China is now in a transitional period. Jiang Yongping describes employment issues under a market economy as compared to those under a planned economy—and their different effects on women's development. While a planned economy gave women the right to work and thus their economic independence, which freed them somewhat from the absolute male authority in the family, women had little choice about the work they did. Furthermore, the planned economy also led women to depend too much on the state or the work institution, making it more difficult for them to compete successfully under other conditions. Now that a market economy prevails, women face many difficulties finding jobs they like, and they are usually laid off before men. Jiang sees the complexities of these two economic systems as they affect women; she also sees possibilities in the new market economy for women to avoid marginalization.

Many changes are taking place in both rural and urban areas, including large migrations of village people into cities. Jin Yihong gives an account not only of the causes behind the achievements of such women, but also the difficulties along their roads to success. Han Jialing offers a case study of women in a county in Guizhou province, one of the most backward rural regions in China. Women who stay behind in the countryside may gain an opportunity to enter administration and become decision-makers. According to Tan Shen, one-third of the migrants are women. She analyzes the impetus behind female migration and the changes it brings to women's lives and viewpoints. She also raises questions about such issues as labor protection rights, sexual harassment, prostitution, and the education of migrants' children.

The United Nations' Fourth World Women's Conference was an important stimulant for the development of the women's movement in China. Shou Yuanjun describes how she and her colleagues started the *Half the Sky* women's program at the Central China Television Station (CCTV) at a time when all China was preparing for the conference. She discusses the workings of this program and believes its survival depends on the gender awareness of its editors and producers. Bu Wei also discusses the influence of the conference on the field of communication science and explores the relationship between Chinese women and the mass media. Her description of an NGO organization—the Female Monitoring Network of the Mass Media—is worth special attention, as it proves that women are becoming more than an audience and are making their voices heard despite all challenges.

As a mirror of reality, literature in China must inevitably be affected by changes wrought under a market economy. Many women writers have begun to write not only about the tough battles women have to fight with men or about general social injustice, but also about their personal experiences and aspirations, even about sexuality, formerly a taboo subject. As a result, mainstream critics have labeled some women's writing as "small women's writing" or "body writing." Dai Jinhua points out that attacks on women's writing are sometimes being used to cover up more serious social issues.

China is a vast country, and situations vary from region to region. Generalizations can thus be dangerous. Indeed, our own plans to include work on minority women in China were not possible to pursue in time for publication, and we did not include any material on the issue of lesbianism in China. For a long time, homosexuality was a taboo subject in China. It was not until 1994, when Zhang Beichuan's *Tongxing'ai* (Same Sex Love) was published as the first book discussing homosexuality in China, that the issue was openly recognized. In December that same year, at a seminar on AIDS and Special Sex Issues, another scholar, Qiu Renzong, presented a proposal on support for homosexuals to be submitted to government and legal institutions (though researchers seemed to focus more on male homosexuals than on lesbians). Then, at the beginning of 1998, a health project targeting homosexuals, both male and female, called *Pengyou* (Friends), was initiated, involving both scholars and homosexuals themselves. The seminar chaired by Qiu Renzong in 1999, "Women in the Face of the Twenty-first Century: Dialogues Between Women Studies (Feminist) Scholars and Lesbians," may have been the first such seminar specifically on female homosexuals and meant to challenge women scholars working on women's issues. Since then there have been reports in newspapers, and even more discussion on websites, about lesbians and their activities. However, we did not even think of an article on this topic when we were planning this book, in part through ignorance on the topic and perhaps through prejudices internalized in our culture. This shows that women scholars working on women's issues have to broaden their scope of knowledge and open their minds to new issues (lesbianism is new in the sense that it was not publicly discussed before) and to changes in life and society.

We hope there will be chances for us to redress these regrets even though we do not see ourselves as the sole authorities on women's issues in China. We sincerely hope that this book, as it is, will still arouse some curiosity among our readers and encourage them to learn more about our country and the women here.

Tao Jie
Beijing
September 2003

NOTES
1. See the entry on yin-yang in Xia Zhengming et al., eds., *The Sea of Words* (Shanghai: Shanghai Dictionary Press, 1999), 507.

2. See chapter 17 of *Analects* by Confucius. The whole sentence is "Girls and inferior men are hard to raise. If you get familiar with them they lose their humility; if you are distant, they resent it."

3. Qiu Jin, "To My Sisters," in *Jindai Zhongguo nuquan yundong lishi ziliao:*

1840–1911 (Historical Records of the Recent Women's Movement in China: 1840–1911) (Taipei: Taipei Biographical Literature Press, 1975), Vol. 1, 434. Qiu Jin (1875–1907) was one of the first feminists in China. In 1907 she helped to found *Zhongguo nubao* (Chinese Women's Newspaper), one of the first newspapers for women. Later that year she was executed because of her effort to overthrow the Qing government.

4. The three obediences refer to obedience to one's father before marriage, to one's husband after marriage, and to one's son after the death of the husband. The four virtues are female morality, female speech, female appearance, and female accomplishment. According to Ban Zhao, a woman does not have to be brilliant but should know how to behave herself; a women does not have to be sharp-tongued but should know how to speak and what to say; a woman should not pay too much attention to being beautiful but should take care to be clean and fresh; and a woman should not strive for supreme achievement but should know how to weave and sew and cook and entertain.

5. This work was edited during the Qing dynasty in 1705 and first published in 1707. It includes almost 40,000 poems by 2,200 poets.

6. The following saying epitomizes one notorious principle for women: "It is a small matter to die of starvation but a serious matter to lose one's moral character or virginity." A woman was even encouraged to commit suicide at the death of her husband or her intended.

7. The most famous is *Injustice to Dou'e* by Guan Hanqing, a dramatist of the Yuan dynasty (1271–1368). The play is about a helpless widow who is wrongly executed by a corrupt official. To call attention to the wrongs done to her, her ghost calls upon heaven to cause snow in June.

8. For example, see "Zaishengyuan" (Love Reincarnate), "Bishenghua" (Elegant Words of the Brush). "Elegant Words of the Brush" was written by Qiu Xinru (1805?–1873?) and published in 1857. It is about a young woman who has been engaged to the son of an official since childhood. In order to escape from persecution by a family enemy, she disguises herself as a man, excels at the court examination, and has great successes in battles against foreign intruders. Finally she reveals her true identity and marries her betrothed with the emperor's permission. "Love Reincarnate," written by another female, Chen Duansheng (1751–1796?), tells a similar story. Meng Lijun, a brilliant woman, disguises herself as a man, works her way up to the royal court, wins the favor of the emperor, and finally marries the man to whom she had been engaged. There were many such stories during the Qing dynasty, especially after the mid-1850s. They were often written by women writers and told by folk artists to the accompaniment of string instruments or performed for the stage as local operas in different regions of China. They were extremely popular among the common people, especially female audiences. Although they depict women of great talent and express women's hopes of breaking out of patriarchal restrictions, they are often limited by the author's outlook on life. Almost invariably, the heroines are still supporters of the feudal norms and their final ideal is still to be a faithful wife and gentle mother.

9. For instance, Liang Qichao remarked in his article "On Women's Education," in "Selected Writings," *Yinbingshi Collected Works*, Vol. 1 (Beijing: China Bookstore, 1989) 38–44,

The country that pays the greatest attention to girls' education is the strongest in the world. It can subdue others without taking up arms. That is the United States. Countries that pay less attention to girls' education are less strong. They are Britain, France, Germany and Japan. If girls' education is neglected, then the mothers' education is lost, people have no idea for careers, there are not many intelligent people and very little power for the country to survive. India, Persia, Turkey are good examples.

10. The first school for girls was set up in 1844 by one Miss Aldersay, an English missionary.

11. Women started to work outside the home in the early 1870s. They were mainly uneducated women forced to go to factories to do unskilled labor because of family financial difficulties. Later, in the early 1910s, some women students found careers running their own newspapers.

12. See "There Will Be Female Tellers in Banks," *Shanghai Times*, 20 December 1916, 4.

13. Amy D. Dooling and Kristica M. Torgeson, eds., *Writing Women in Modern China*, is a good anthology of Chinese women's literature of the period discussed here.

14. or instance, in one county in Henan province during an election in 1987, all eight women who had formerly been deputy county governors or township mayors lost their positions.

15. One small example: A commercial for a drug to promote women's health called upon men to buy it because "it will give you a new wife every day."

16. For instance, beauty contests were forbidden in China because of protests by the All-China Women's Federation. Unfortunately, such contests have been in vogue since the 1990s.

17. Feng Yuan, "Successes of Women in the 1990s: A Brief Account of Chinese Women's Participation in Politics," *People's Daily*, 19 August 1997.

18. Ibid.

19. For example, Xu Kun's "Encounter of Love" and "The Kitchen" depict women who are eager to succeed in business but fail to find real love. Chi Li's "Good Morning, Miss" tells a story of the friendship among three women who form an alliance to punish the man who looks down upon them.

Part I

Women in
Early
Chinese
History
and
Culture

NEW MEANINGS IN A CLASSIC: DIFFERING INTERPRETATIONS OF BAN ZHAO AND HER *ADMONITIONS FOR WOMEN* IN THE LATE QING DYNASTY

Xia Xiaohong

In Chinese history Ban Zhao attained a level of renown rarely accorded women, especially as the author of the influential *Admonitions for Women.* The most authoritative account of Ban Zhao's life can be found in the *Lienü zhuan* (Biographies of Eminent Women) within the *Hou Han shu* (History of the Later Han Dynasty) compiled by Fan Ye. That biographical account—like those provided for other women in the volume—briefly summarizes her main achievements:

> [Ban Zhao,] wife of Cao Shishu of Fufeng, was the daughter of Ban Biao of the same district. Her personal name was Zhao, styled Huiban, alias Ji. She displayed profound erudition and talent of a high order. After the early death of her husband, Ban Zhao observed the canons of widowhood.
>
> Her elder brother Gu wrote the *Han shu* [History of the Han Dynasty], in which the "Eight Tables" and "Treatise on Astronomy" were not finished at the time of his death. Thereupon Emperor He summoned Ban Zhao to the Dong-guan Library and commanded her to complete the work.
>
> Often the emperor summoned Ban Zhao to the palace, where he ordered the empress and the ladies of honorable rank to treat her as a teacher. They addressed her accordingly in terms of respect. Every time there was a presentation of tribute or of unusual gifts the emperor commanded her to compose commemorative verses for the occasion.
>
> When the Empress Deng became regent [106 C.E.] she conferred with Ban Zhao concerning affairs of state. . . .
>
> At the time when the *Han shu* first appeared, most of the scholars could not comprehend it. Ma Rong, a native of the same district as Ban Zhao, was allowed as a special favor to go to the library, where he studied under her. Later Ma Rong's elder brother Xu was ordered to

continue and complete Ban Zhao's work. . . .

[Ban Zhao also] wrote *Admonitions for Women* in seven chapters, [a treatise that] affords assistance in the education of married women.

When [Ban] Zhao was over seventy years old, she died. The empress lamented loudly and wore mourning clothes for her and appointed an official to help take care of the funeral.

The literary works [of Ban Zhao] included . . . in all [enough to fill] sixteen books. Her daughter-in-law, of the Ding family, collected and edited her works.[1]

Usually, *Biographies of Eminent Women* summarizes women's lives in two to three hundred characters. The biography of Ban Zhao, thus, is quite remarkable because it includes her seven-chapter *Admonitions for Women*. Uniquely, the *Biographies of Eminent Women* gives *Admonitions for Women* three times more space than the account of Ban's life. Without the inclusion of the *Admonitions*, the biography of Ban would be equal to those of other women in the volume. Seemingly, then, writing the *Admonitions for Women* was the most important achievement of her life. The titles of its seven chapters—"Humility," "Husband and Wife," "Respect and Caution," "Womanly Moral Character," "Whole-hearted Devotion," "Implicit Obedience," and "Harmony with Younger Brothers- and Sisters-in-law"—convey the theme of "womanly virtue" as compliance. In male-dominated traditional Chinese society *Admonitions for Women* became required reading for women. Not surprisingly, the dramatic rise and fall of opinions about Ban have centered on views of her *Admonitions for Women*.

The achievements that gave Ban her place in history cannot be divorced from her literary talent. Her three most celebrated accomplishments are her continuation of the *Han shu*, her education of the women of the imperial court, and her composition of the *Admonitions for Women*. As values began to shift during the late Qing dynasty (1644–1911), the discussions of her merits and shortcomings all took *Admonitions* as their point of departure.

A MODEL FOR WOMEN'S EDUCATION

The reinterpretations of Ban Zhao and the *Admonitions for Women* began with the initiation of education for women on a social scale in China. In November 1897, modern reformers in Shanghai formally drew up plans for a girls' school. At the end of May in the following year the first girls' school founded by Chinese nationals—the China Girls' School—was born. It would have far-reaching effects. On 24 July 1898, the periodical *Nüxue bao* (Chinese Girl's Progress), which was founded by female instructors from the China Girls' School and female members of its board of directors, began publication. This paper was unique in that "the writers were all women." Hence, it received public acclaim for having "started a new trend."[2] The paper published a list of its writers. The top two were Xue Shaohui and Qiu Yufang. [3] It was by no means a matter of coincidence that they both showed great interest in Ban Zhao and the *Admonitions for Women*.

After the Shanghai *Xinwenbao* (News Gazette) published the "Summary Articles of the Trial Establishment of the Girls' School" on 18 November 1897, Xue Shaohui quickly wrote her "Opinions and Narrative on the Founding of a Girls' School," taking issue with the Summary Articles.[4] The first article read, "The school is to be established on the basis of Confucianism—our sacred religion [*shengjiao*], and a posthumous tablet will be dedicated to Confucius." Pointing out the special nature of the girls' school, Xue proposed substituting Ban Zhao for Confucius. She reasoned that Ban "continued work on the *Han shu*, instructed the ladies of the imperial court, and owing to her virtue and scholarship deserves to be a model for all ages. She also wrote the *Admonitions for Women*. . . . She continued the "Nei ze" [Inner Principles], and of all virtuous women past and present, there is none superior to her."[5] For this reason "sacrifices should be made to her in the school, that she may serve as a model for women." Xue believed that female sages of the past would naturally be more encouraging to female students. Moreover, Xue's selection of Ban as the one who should be enshrined in the girls' school indicated the importance she attached not only to Ban's virtue but also to her outstanding scholarship. The school had established a curriculum for ethics and morals, and the basic means of imparting information was to be through written texts. Ban, who had continued work on the *Han shu* and written the *Admonitions for Women*, works that had been passed down through generations, was more qualified to serve as a model for female students than a woman of virtue who had left no written record. This reasoning was key to the reformation of Ban's reputation during the late Qing dynasty.

Expecting more than the veneration by which female students would consciously model themselves after Ban Zhao, in her "Opinions and Narrative on the Founding of the Girls' School" Xue also directly suggests that *Admonitions for Women* be included as required reading in the Chinese-language curriculum, to "serve as an introduction to women's enlightenment, so that they will follow the path of women's virtue all their lives and fulfill their duty of women's work." Subsequently, the curriculum of the Chinese Girls' School contained the *Nü sishu* (Four Books for Women), including the *Admonitions for Women*.[6] In this way the school accepted Xue's suggestion.

Some people were disappointed that the first new girls' school founded by Chinese nationals retained traditional readers for teaching womanly virtue. On the other hand, were educators to reveal new interpretations of the ancient classics, as Qiu Yufang did, the results might be dramatically different.

In May 1898, with the reform movement developing vigorously, the *Wuxi Vernacular Gazette* was founded. It used the vernacular language as a tool to "enlighten the people." Qiu Yufang published her *Nüjie zhushi* (Annotations on *Admonitions for Women*), in this paper as a series of articles.[7] This work, which brought the author some fame, offered a completely different interpretation from older annotated texts. On the surface, annotating the *Admonitions for Women* (while not critiquing it) could easily be seen as adhering to tradition, but, in fact, Qiu's annotations centered on practical topics in the struggle for women's right to an education. This approach was totally incompatible with the position held by staunch conservatives who opposed the establishment of a girls' school. In her discussion of the preface to *Admonitions for Women*, Qiu sets out her view:

> I don't know what confused, unenlightened person said, "a woman without talent is bound to be virtuous." This statement has done great harm to all women of the world. . . . If Lady Cao [Ban Zhao] had adhered to the notion that "a woman without talent is bound to be virtuous," the *Han shu* would never have been continued, and the *Admonitions for Women* would never have been written. How would anyone today know about Lady Cao, let alone admire her and respect her? It can be seen that for a woman, education is a necessity.

Qiu makes clear that she has her own new reason for valuing *Admonitions for Women*. She and others hold in high esteem Ban Zhao's scholarly talents. Without those talents, they hypothesize, Ban would not have enjoyed the renown she did. This view departs dramatically from the historical view that Ban Zhao's reputation rested on her *Admonitions for Women*, which emphasizes womanly virtue. The new interpretation emphasized education instead. Furthermore, in Qiu's view, education is obviously the root of virtue. Women lacking education—"not reading books and not understanding the world"—will not be compliant to their husbands and in-laws, as required by the *Admonitions for Women* (ch. 6, "Implicit Obedience"). Although the book "teaches women the principles of how to get along with others" (*Annotations*, introduction), "to be a woman," Qiu Yufang insists, one must first study and be educated.

The novel topic of a "girls' school" was thus drawn from the *Admonitions for Women*. Qiu Yufang's method was to pick and choose certain sentences that supported her argument and highlight them, while ignoring the main themes of the work that contradicted these ideas. Her annotation of *Admonitions for Women*'s second chapter, "Husband and Wife," contains a good example of her method. Ban Zhao repeats often: "If a husband does not control his wife, then the rules of conduct manifesting his authority are abandoned and broken. If a wife does not serve her husband, then the proper relationship [between men and women] and the natural order of things are neglected and destroyed" (84). This is Ban's core idea but Qiu ignores it completely. Instead, in her discussion of chapter 3, "Respect and Caution," she proposes that "Husbands and wives are the same as friends."

In order to allow women to understand the principles of proper behavior, Ban follows the idea laid down in earlier texts that "It is the rule to begin to teach children to read at the age of eight years, and by the age of fifteen years they ought then to be ready for systematic cultural training," arguing that "according to this principle," this requirement should also apply to girls and rejecting the idea that "only boys should be educated and not girls" (84–85). Qiu seizes on this last sentiment and brings it to the fore, amplifying it in the process and ignoring Ban's belief that girls should be educated to serve men:

> Prior to the period of the Three Dynasties [Xia (2205–1766 BCE), Shang (1766–1122 BCE), and Zhou (1122–770 BCE)] in China, there were many rational, educated women. Women had governesses from childhood, and these governesses were female teachers. I believe that in ancient times there were also schools for girls. Later, the custom of regarding men as superior to women grew stronger as time went on, and women were not allowed to know the principles and learning of the world. All the women in the world were deliberately kept ignorant, considered to be outside civilized culture and learning. The root cause of this disease was the treatment of women as inferior. Actually, women's lack of knowledge and ignorance of reason caused no end of trouble for men everywhere. If all women were taught to read and understand reason, this would be a great benefit to both the nation and to families. Therefore, a girls' school is a necessity. (ch. 2)

"The nation" has no place whatsoever in *Admonitions for Women*, and the Confucian classics require that "Women not speak of affairs outside the home." Women were confined to the family. Thus the extended meaning developed by Qiu Yufang broke the pattern established for women by the "Nei ze" (Inner Principles) section of the *Li ji* (Book of Rites). The discussion of girls' schools focused on events of the time, and the *Admonitions for Women* was turned into a footnote for the ideas of the annotator.

This was not a unique occurrence. In 1906 the Sichuan Girls' School was founded in Beijing, and in a speech made during the school's opening ceremony, a seventeen-year-old female instructor, Liu Shurong, used the same method to fit Ban Zhao and *Admonitions for Women* to her own scheme. In her speech she cited Ban as a model for women's education. She also referred to a passage from the *Admonitions for Women*: "Yet only to teach men and not to teach women—is that not ignoring the essential relation between them?" (84). To prove her argument that China and Japan are "opposites in terms of strength," she stated that in Japan education for girls was well developed while China did not have it at all. "Although our population numbers four hundred million, we only use half of it," so how can we be anything but weak?[8] This linking of women's education and the fate of the nation was a contemporary topic and the use of the *Admonitions for Women* as a reference to bolster this argument was actually imposing additional meanings on the text.

In opposition to the belief held by Ban that "men are superior to women," Qiu Yufang and Liu Shurong promoted the concept of "equality between men and women." Naturally, they vigorously criticized the corrupt custom of "denigrating women." By examining how Qiu took a passage from the first chapter, on humility, in *Admonitions for Women* and put a positive spin on a negative text, we can gain insights into the skills the late Qing scholars used to interpret the classics.

The original text of Ban's *Admonitions for Women*, chapter 1, states clearly, "On the third day after the birth of the girl the ancients . . . placed the baby below the bed, . . . which indicated that she is lowly and weak, and should regard it as her primary duty to humble herself before others" (83). Faced with this passage that undeniably belittles women, Qiu takes a novel approach by "turning something rotten into something magical." She starts by stating that "although the text of the chapter 'Humility' advises women to be modest at all times, it does not say that women should be denigrated." She quickly disposes of Ban's discourse and moves on to another topic, leveling her criticism at the stubborn notion that "men are superior to women":

> I did not expect that in the world today there is not one man who does not disparage women. . . . Women are quite accustomed to being disparaged by men, and not only are they unaware they are being disparaged by men, but they also believe this is how it should be. If someone speaks of educating women, the women protest that this is the domain of men, and how could one go about talking about teaching us women? This is self-abasement, not the humility that Lady Cao spoke of. (ch. 1, "Humility")

Although Ban advocated that women should study, the purpose was to serve their husbands. Ban still belonged to an ethical system of male domination over women in which "the husband is the guiding force for his wife." In establishing her argument, Qiu ignores this tradition and changes the concept of "humility" into "modesty." Having separated Ban from the notion of male superiority, Qiu can now use her as she pleases. In Qiu's hands, the modern concept of education for women based on "gender equality" was thus skillfully married to the decaying body of *Admonitions for Women*. It is not overstating the case to say that *Annotations on the "Admonitions for Women"* had the effect of deconstructing the *Admonitions for Women*.

The two supporters of the Chinese Girls' School, Xue Shaohui and Qiu Yufang, were not the only ones who liked to pay tribute to Ban Zhao to promote girls' education. In 1906, Xu Dingyi published *Zuguo nüjie weirenzhuan* (Biographies of Great Women of the Motherland) in Japan, in which he held up Ban as "a person of greatness not seen before or after in the motherland" and "a sage of the highest order among women." Xu gave her particularly high praise because "Ban Zhao had qualifications both as an educator and as a writer."[9] Differing slightly from the views of Xue and Qiu, Xu's view of Ban directly affirmed her status as an "educator." There were quite a few women writers in Chinese history, though rarely could they continue work as Ban Zhao had on the *Han shu*. What was even rarer was a female writer who also distinguished herself as an educator. Ban did not achieve this designation only for writing the *Admonitions for Women*, but for her education of the ladies of the imperial court, her taking on the "famous Han dynasty Confucian" Ma Rong as a pupil, and her influence on her daughter-in-law, a refined woman from the Ding family. Thus Ban herself could be considered a pioneer in women's education. This revelation brought her and the new schools for girls even closer together.

People of the late Qing elaborated on the classics to interpret Ban in a positive way, first as a model for female students and later as an example of a scholarly woman. Most of these new interpretations, however, had emerged prior to the Reform Movement of 1898. During this early period, the idea of equality of the sexes was just beginning to gain support in China, although its proponents were constrained by the social atmosphere and frequently could not speak openly. For this reason, it was very popular to use the classics as a cover for ideas of equality. Qiu Yufang's hard work to annotate the *Admonitions for Women* makes clear how difficult it was to bridge the gap between the ancient classics and these new interpretations. But this was how the revolutionary ideas that broke the old patterns were born.

THE CHIEF CULPRITS OF MALE SUPERIORITY

Modern ideas about equality between the sexes stand in direct contradiction to the teachings of Ban Zhao's *Admonitions for Women*; there is no possibility for reconciling the two views. Qiu Yufang's *Annotations on the "Admonitions for Women"* thus had to distort the text in order to interpret it and could not adhere faithfully to the original. By the beginning of the twentieth century, as the concept of "women's rights" was introduced in China, calls for women's independence increased dramatically. Discussions about Ban no longer had to treat her as they had before, either holding her in great reverence or pretending to revere her while covertly disagreeing with her ideas. It was now possible to take a fairer attitude and discuss her strengths and weaknesses openly.

In 1905, Yan Bin, a female student studying abroad in Japan, wrote about her early experience studying the *Admonitions for Women* with a friend her own age. Her views illuminate the impact of Western ideas in the late Qing period. When Yan, who was born in 1870, was about ten years old, she was at school with her good friend Luo Ying: "Every time we read the histories we both became indignant over the unfairness in human affairs. Every time we read Ban Zhao's *Admonitions for Women*, we were in particular disagreement with her. To our way of thinking, women are also human beings, and so why should they be humble? Is that not absurd?" However, the two girls' doubts about the classics immediately earned them a scolding from Luo's father: "How dare little girls slander the ancients?" he asked. After that, Yan wrote, "We did not dare to speak openly about it." If not for the transmission of ideas about the equality of the sexes and women's rights after the Reform Movement of 1898, Yan's and Luo's questioning of the *Admonitions for Women* would have remained buried. Fortunately the two girls were born at the right moment. Yan was thus able to claim proudly in 1907 that "advocating theories in later years, supporting women's rights, striving for other women's happiness—these thoughts were already in my mind."[10]

In February 1907, in the premiere issue of *Zhongguo xinnüjie zazhi* (New Chinese Women's Magazine), which she edited, Yan Bin published a piece titled "Appraisal of Women's Rights." She begins by refuting chapter 1 in *Admonitions for Women*:

> Since the beginning of the discussions on humanism, the arguments for women's rights have grown stronger every day. Those who disapprove of [women's rights] think it a strange idea and consider it to be heresy, and they argue against it strongly. They believe that for men to be strong and women soft, and for men to be superior to women, are immutable principles. When women are chiefly concerned with being humble, what rights do they have? Alas! Those who say this are like "summer insects who cannot understand ice" or those with the perspective of a frog at the bottom of a well who cannot understand how vast the heavens are.

New Chinese Women's Magazine had as its primary goal to "present the newest scholarly ideas concerning women," and it vigorously advocated women's rights.[11]

After the beginning of the twentieth century, although Ban Zhao did not lose her status as a classic writer, she became a historical personage who could be evaluated, no longer a "female saint" immune from criticism. In 1907 an author named Ya Hua wrote six "Odes to Women in History," in which the poem to Ban reads,

> She completed the tables of the *Han shu* left by Ban Gu;
> Her appeal moved the emperor to summon back Ban Chao.
> Lamentable that she passed down the *Admonitions for Women*;
> "To be humble and weak," she has misled us for centuries.[12]

This poem recounts Ban's merits and demerits in clear terms, applauding her talents and learning—including the appeal that brought her aged brother, Ban Chao, back from China's western border to be reunited with his family—but severely castigating her *Admonitions for Women* for having poisoned and repressed women for two thousand years.

More and more scholars began viewing Ban in part positively, in part negatively. The advocate of women's education and champion of women's rights, Jin Yi, composed the "Song for Female Students Entering School," in which he praises "our teacher Ban Zhao."[13] But in the book *Nüjie zhong* (Women's Bell), which discussed ideas about women and won him the reputation as the "Rousseau" of Chinese women's studies, he openly criticizes the *Admonitions for Women:*

> Civilizations around the world are progressing, so education for women, like that for men, should also go through transformation. The experiences of reading books, going to school, and making friends, and traveling are all ways in which women can cultivate their knowledge and increase their morality. Morality and knowledge are God-given birthrights, and there is no distinction between men and women.[14]

The themes here emphasize "God-given human rights," equality of the sexes, and the advancement of the times. Women as well as men should seek an education and travel, and the home should not become a cage for women.

While acknowledging that the *Admonitions for Women* had long served as a textbook for Chinese women, progressive thinkers at the beginning of the twentieth century evaluated the nature of that text differently than the writers of the Reform Movement of 1898 period. The lectures of Ye Han, to take another example, an ethics educator at the Shanghai Patriotic Girls' School, are the most convincing. In the classroom he told students that "China's *Admonitions for Women* and the *Four Books for Women* are books that teach women how to be dependent, immature, and submissive to men. They make immature people even more immature, and submissive people even more submissive, and thus the character of Chinese women is quite predictable."[15] The differences between his views and Qiu Yufang's comment that "*Admonitions for Women* is the first good book for educating women" are extreme.[16] Not surprisingly, at the Patriotic Girls' School, *Admonitions for Women* lost its credentials as part of the curriculum and was considered valuable only for criticism.

At the same time, those who argued most forcefully against the *Admonitions for Women* were women. In 1907, He Zhen, who founded the Women's Rights Recovery Association in Japan and published *Tian yi* (Natural Justice) magazine, which promoted anarchism, prepared a long treatise entitled "Argument for Women's Revenge." Her text attacks Ban Zhao and the *Admonitions for Women* using extremely provocative language, calling her "Traitor Ban" and "Traitor Zhao." This attack is unparalleled in its time for its ferocity. Although He concedes that "Ban Zhao's scholarship is superior to anyone's past or present," her text quickly shifts to criticism: "What she advocates is completely absurd." She is particularly sharp about the passage about humility, submission to the husband and women's "chastity [as] her virtue and her appearance":

> Alas! As soon as this idea became widely known to the public, women began to accept that their fate was controlled by men. It purports to be teachings on Confucian ethics, but is actually nothing but shamefulness. It purports to be ethical principles, but is actually shamelessness. Is this not the so-called "way of the wife"? Traitor Ban was a woman, but she was confused by the evil teachings of Confucianism and killed her own kind. She left a legacy of shame to womankind, teaching women to be the servants of men. She is a great traitor to women.

Next, He continues her attack, turning her attention to the chapter on "Devotion":

> Traitor Zhao says that husbands have the right to remarry, but that it is not written that wives may remarry. She speaks of husbands as of Heaven, believing that, just as one cannot run away from Heaven, a woman cannot leave her husband. Alas! I can hardly believe that such words came from a woman's mouth, and it is even more incredible to me that these words were passed down through the generations.

In summary, He believes that "the reason women's rights have not been justified in subsequent generations is that women always passed on the writings of traitor Ban, considering the words that had been written before to be author-itative."[17] Ban thus became a pest and chief culprit for advocating "men's supe-riority to women."

Although He hates Ban bitterly, it is mostly "hating iron for not being steel," for being a woman to herself but acting as an accomplice to "the evil teachings of Confucianism." In fact, "Argument for Women's Revenge" con-siders men to be the true target of that revenge. Tracing the problem back to its origins, He finds that the primary actors in suppressing women for thou-sands of years were men. Thus He understands that, as detestable as *Admonitions for Women* may be, the perpetrator is still a victim: "Traitor Ban wrote as she did because of her adherence to Confucian texts, taking what had been written before as the authority. In this way, Traitor Ban's crime had its inception in Confucianism."[18] The Confucian classics that represent male domination should bear the brunt of the responsibility for the doctrine of "male superiority over women" that poisoned the culture for millennia, accord-ing to He. Seen in this light, the criticisms of Ban and the *Admonitions for Women* can also be extended to the Confucian classics.

In a period that began by casting doubt on the authority of the classics, even Confucius, who had been revered throughout the ages as a "sage," faced chal-lenges. A fourteen-year-old student at the Suzhou Jinghai Girls' School com-posed "Three Poems Expressing Indignation." In the chapter of the *Analects* about Yang huo in which Confucius states that "Only women and petty men are difficult to handle" is her first target. She criticizes Confucius for this out-rageous statement, writing

> You are so mistaken, Confucius, and crazy!
> Advocating heresies and scattering poison.
> You despise women and petty men, sorrowing us forever,
> Alas, even your mother also suffered from your accusation.[19]

Even in the imperial capital of Beijing, a woman pen-named "Confused Woman" took issue with Confucius: "You are a sage, but you look down on women. Why don't you protest to Heaven for allowing women to exist? Of course, ten fingers cannot be of the same length, and we admit that many among women do not work hard to improve themselves. But it's all your fault, because you did not approve of education for women. If you equate us with petty men, I will be the first not to let you get away with it!"[20] This "Confused Woman" is obviously an already enlightened New Woman.

Because the "sage" was the main culprit in the crime of "respecting men and suppressing women," literary works of the late Qing frequently cast Ban Zhao in the role of an ancient person who could be reformed. In the traditional opera *Shei zhi zui xiqu?* (Whose Guilt?), there is a scene of the trial of Ban Zhao held in heaven after Qiu Jin is killed for "advocating equal rights," and she is ordered to reform her ways. On trial, Ban admits her guilt and expresses her intention to become a new person. Qiu then pronounces her sentence: Ban is ordered to amend for her crime by doing good works and "is reincarnated to promote women's rights."[21]

The novel *Bu tian shi* (Patching the Sky with Stones) by Wa Hun (suspected to be the pen name of Yan Bin) tells the story of how Nüwa, who according to legend patched the sky with stones, sends Ban into the world to save and help all women. Ban is to set an example with her own life, using her repentance for past behavior as an example to strengthen the persuasiveness of her message:

> When I lived in the past, although I knew something of Confucian ethics, my incomplete learning allowed me to become trapped by society, and made me believe that women should be obedient. For this reason, although the seven chapters of the *Admonitions for Women* were adhered to by later generations, when I think about them now, I regret what I said. I blush with shame at the terrible legacy I left. . . . Women and men alike are citizens and all have the same duties, and so they should all enjoy equal rights. Men do not obey women, and naturally women should not obey men. The societies of the world were created by men and women together, after all. Any prejudice is not humanism.[22]

The plot of the novel is designed to have Ban repent on her own, which much more effectively removes her pernicious influence. If even the author of the *Admonitions for Women* acknowledged the absurdity of the doctrine of "humility" and enshrined the doctrine of "equal rights for men and women" in its place, blind adherents of the old ways would have had less ground to cling to. This is the real reason writers of the late Qing repeatedly, in their creative writings, made Ban express repentance.

The differences between the praise of Wu Fu, who wrote in the 1898 preface to Qiu Yufang's *Annotations on the "Admonitions for Women"* that "Lady Cao was the Confucius of women,"[23] and He Zhen's 1907 diatribe against Ban Zhao as "the great traitor to women" are extreme, although both commentators take as their reference the classic text on womanly virtue, the *Admonitions for Women*. In the space of ten years, appraisals of the woman and her writings shifted dramatically, from approval to censure and criticism. Reinterpretation of Ban Zhao and the *Admonitions for Women* during the late Qing was part of the general fate of the traditional classics during a period of social transformation and a manifestation of the awakening of women's consciousness.

NOTES

1. The translation quoted here (and in other places noted in the text) comes from Nancy Lee Swann, *Pan Chao: Foremost Woman Scholar of China* (Ann Arbor: Center for Chinese Studies, University of Michigan, 2001), 40–41.

2. *Nüxue bao* (Chinese Girl's Progress), *Xinwenbao* (News Gazette [Shanghai]), 30 July 1898.

3. See *Chinese Girl's Progress*, Vol. 1, 24 July 1898, list of eighteen "staff editors."

4. Xue Shaohui, "Chuangshe nüxuetang tiaoyi bing shu" (Opinions on the Founding of a Girls' School), *Qiu shi bao* (International Review), Vols. 9–10, December 1897.

5. "Nei ze" (Inner Principles) is the title of a chapter in the *Li ji* (Book of Rites), which prescribes morals in the speech and behavior of women in the home.

6. See "Shanghai chuangshe Zhongguo nüxuetang ji" (Record of the Establishment of the Chinese Girls' School in Shanghai), *Wanguo gongbao* (Chinese Globe Magazine), Vol. 125, June 1899.

7. Qiu Yufang, *Nüjie zhushi* (Annotations on *Admonitions for Women*), originally published in *Wuxi baihuabao* (Wuxi Vernacular Gazette), Vols. 3–18, May–August 1898. Also recorded in Qiu Tinglian, ed., *Baihua congshu* (Collected Vernacular Works), Vol. 1, 1901. All citations from *Annotations on the "Admonitions for Women"* are taken from this book.

8. "Remarks Made at the Opening of the Sichuan Girls' School," *Shuntian shibao* (Shuntian Times), 10 May 1906.

9. Xu Dingyi (Master of Juxuelu), "Cao dajia, Cao feng, Ding shi" (Lady Cao, Cao Feng, Madame Ding), *Zuguo nüjie weirenzhuan* (Biographies of Great Women of the Motherland) (Yokohama, Japan: Xinminshe, 1906).

10. Yan Bin, "Luo Ying nüshi zhuan" (Biography of Luo Ying), *Zhongguo xinnüjie zazhi* (New Chinese Women's Magazine), Vol. 5, June 1907.

11. Yan Bin, "Benbao wuda zhuyi yanshuo" (Remarks on the Five Main Principles of This Newspaper), *New Chinese Women's Magazine*, Vol. 2, March 1907.

12. Ya Hua, "Dushi yong nüshi" (Odes to Women in History), *New Chinese Women's Magazine*, Vol. 1, February 1907.

13. Jin Yi, "Nüxuesheng ruxuege" (Song for Female Students Entering School), Part Three, *Nüzi shijie* (Women's World), Vol. 1, January 1904.

14. Jin Yi, *Nüjie zhong* (Women's Bell), 1903, 15–16. See also Lin Zongsu, "*Nüjie zhong* shu" (Discussion of *Women's Bell) Jiangsu*, Vol. 5, August 1903.

15. Ye Han (Ye Haowu), "Wen Zhongguo nüzi renge yiyong hezhong yangchengzhi fa fang ke wanchuan" (Questions on What Methods Are Most Suitable for Cultivating the Character of Chinese Women), *Jingzhong ribao* (Daily Clarion), 21 April 1904.

16. Qiu Yufang, *Annotations on the "Admonitions for Women,"* introduction, in *Collected Vernacular Works*, Vol. 1, 1901.

17. He Zhen (He Yinzhen), "Nüzi fuchoulun" (Argument for Women's Revenge), *Tian yi* (Natural Justice), Vol. 3, July 1907.

18. Ibid.

19. Jing Qun, "Yifen sanshou" (Three Poems Expressing Indignation), *New Chinese Women's Magazine*, Vol. 2, March 1907.

20. Hutu nüzi (Confused Woman), "Gen laoshengren taitaigang" (Taking Issue with the Old Sage), *Beijing nübao* (Beijing Women's Gazette), 12 January 1909.

21. Bei Qiu, *Shei zhi zui xiqu?* (Whose Guilt?), Nos. 2–3, December 1908.

22. Wa Hun, *Bu tian shi* (Patching the Sky with Stones), *New Chinese Women's Magazine*, Vols. 2–3, March–April 1907.

23. Wu Fu, "Preface to the *Annotations* on Ban Zhao's *Admonitions for Women*," in *Annotations on the "Admonitions for Women*," in *Collected Vernacular Works*, Vol. 1, 1901.

CHARACTERISTICS OF WOMEN'S LIVES DURING THE SONG DYNASTY

Zheng Bijun

The Southern Song dynasty (1127–1271) saw the development of neo-Confucianism. It is often assumed that this development led to an increase in the oppression of women. But any society must give women some space to express themselves, even as it is oppressing them, or else the society will not survive. The Song dynasty was no exception. The question is how to explain the coexistence of women's oppression and expression. The Song dynasty, as a period of transition, inherited the socioeconomic and cultural features of the previous society but acquired new characteristics of its own through the growth of commerce, art, and handicrafts, and the rise of an urban population. Neo-Confucianism in these times did not increase the sufferings of women; on the contrary, this period repositioned women and introduced new social mores, making it possible for some women to acquire prominence. This essay focuses on women from two different social classes: the nobility and the urban working population.

This study is based on the examination of primary sources not previously used by Western scholars, including, for example, *Si ku quan shu* (Complete Library of the Four Branches of Literature), an authoritative archival encyclopedia of books, compiled during the early Qing dynasty (1644–1911). This study also complements Patricia Buckley Ebrey's 1993 findings that during the Song period women lived active, meaningful, and satisfactory lives, to the full extent that circumstances allowed.[1] In her studies of elite women in the seventeenth and eighteenth centuries, Dorothy Ko reveals that in their secluded inner chambers elite Chinese women not only lived in freedom and dignity but also actively functioned as moral educators. This study argues that as early as the Song dynasty, elite women were already living in that manner.[2]

ARISTOCRATIC WOMEN

In the 180 volumes of the *Si ku quan shu* on the Song dynasty, one can find records of over a thousand short biographies of mostly aristocratic women. Notable politicians, writers, or philosophers of the times wrote laudatory epitaphs about such women, reflecting the writers' views of women's positions

17

within the ruling class. A statistical analysis of the epitaphs reveals a remarkable portrait of these Song dynasty women.

Two-thirds of these women had been educated and were literate, a much higher percentage than that among women of preceding dynasties.[3] From the lavish praise granted to them for their devotion to study, one can conclude that men had encouraged women to study. The great minister of the Northern Song dynasty (960–1127), Sima Guang, writes in *Family Rules*: "No one should be exempt from study, men and women alike. Women at home should not omit to study the *Book of Filial Piety*, *The Analects*, as well as the *Classic of Poetry* and the *Book of Rites* and acquire a general understanding of these subjects."[4] According to him, a woman's education would improve her self-discipline, her support of her husband, and her contribution to the education of her children. Hence he adds, "Such skills as fancy embroidery and flute songs are not suitable for women's education."[5]

Compared to Sima Guang, Li Kefei—father of the famous poet Li Qingzhao—is much more liberal in his attitude toward women's education. 'The Biography of Li Kefei" in *History of the Song Dynasty* makes special mention of the education of women in his household: "His wife, neé Wang, the granddaughter of a distinguished scholar, was well versed in poetry, not to mention his daughter Li Qingzhao, famous for her writings in prose and verse."[6] Li Kefei once referred to a man who "had a daughter of whom he could be proud."[7] Although he was ostensibly describing Cai Yan, the famous learned woman of the Eastern Han dynasty (25–202 CE), he was in fact referring to his own daughter, revealing fatherly pride in his daughter's accomplishments.

The learning acquired by educated women in the Song dynasty far exceeded the texts named by Sima Guang. Nothing was beyond their grasp: prose and poetry, history and fiction, astronomy and geography, Confucianism, Daoism, the writings of such famous authors as Bai Juyi, Su Shi, and Huang Tingjian, as well as popular fiction. They also studied music, chess, and the arts.

The *ci* form of poetry, special to the Song dynasty, was both read and practised by women. *Ci* is a form of poetry written to accompany certain tunes using strict tonal patterns and rhyme schemes in fixed numbers of lines and words. It originated in the Tang dynasty (618–907) and developed fully in the Song. Li Qingzhao, for example, was so famous for her *ci* that her husband, Zhao Mingcheng, a noted scholar, was jealous. Once Li made a *ci* poem to the form of *zui hua yin*, the beautiful flower melody, and sent it to her husband, who was away from home. Her husband knew that it was superior to his own writings, but he did not want to concede that fact. He shut himself up for three days and wrote fifty verses. Mixing Li's *ci* among them, he showed the whole group to his friend Lu Defu. Lu looked them over and said that there were only three good lines: "Say not that one is not touched to the soul, / the curtain flaps in the west wind, / the person wastes away like the yellow chrysanthemums." All turned out to be Li's.[8]

Science and technology advanced remarkably during the Song. Of the three great inventions of ancient China—papermaking, gunpowder, and the art of printing—all except papermaking were developed during that time. Song women were great mathematicians and probed the secrets of the heavens and the earth. Hu Wenrou, the granddaughter of Hu Su, famous minister of the Song dynasty, was outstanding for her learning. As her epitaph reveals, the scientist Shen Kuo, author of *Notebooks of Mengxi*, sought her advice when he had a question in mathematics. Written by her husband, Li Zhiyi, the epitaph states that she was "especially talented in mathematics," and that "Shen Kuo during his lifetime, was my mentor; but whenever he had something to clarify, he would ask me to relay the question to [my wife] Wenrou. And he often lamented: if only she were a man, Wenrou would be my friend."[9] This testimony to Hu's high accomplishments as a mathematician also reveals the discrimination against women that condemned them to obscurity.

Over a long period in the Song dynasty, "Buddhism spread throughout the land, and the Confucianists secretly believed in its essence while publicly rejecting it."[10] Upper-class women of the Song dynasty, who studied the Confucian classics, also read the Buddhist sutras and the works of Laozi. In Li Shi's epitaph for a titled lady named Xue, he wrote, "the two families of Xue and Yang were for generations followers of Confucianism, but [the lady Xue] did not confine herself to studies of female filial piety. She also studied the classics, biographies, philosophic writings, histories, as well as the writings of Du Fu, Bai Juyi, and Su Shi. She observed Confucian rites but supplemented these with the study of Daoism."[11] The case of the Lady Xue was quite typical of educated women of the times.

Another social change helps to explain Song's emphasis on women's education among the upper classes.[12] The imperial examination system expanded rapidly to reach its peak of development during the Song, passing the highest number of graduates thus far in Chinese history.[13] The establishment of schools of learning and the printing of books also grew enormously. While only a fraction of the educated population could pass the imperial examinations, the reforms themselves increased energies for study among many in the society. Hong Mai of the Song describes the social climate of the region of Rao in Jiangxi province thus: "As a father or an elder brother, men are regarded as mean if they do not support their sons or younger brothers in study; as a wife or mother, women are regarded as shameful if they do not support their husbands or sons in their studies."[14] Preparing for the imperial examination became critical to a scholar and his family because it determined the rise or fall of the family fortunes. The imperial examination system also broke through the caste system, where heretofore commoners and gentry had been "as far apart as heaven and earth."[15] Now ordinary people might be able to enter the ranks of the intelligentsia. Aristocratic families were thus faced with unprecedented political, economic, and cultural challenges. To support husbands and sons in their studies became the prevailing pressure on women in these families.

From the more than one thousand extant epitaphs about women, one may conclude that women's lives combined traditional demands with responses to a society in flux. In arranging a marriage for a son, for example, a family would expect the daughter-in-law to conform to the traditional virtues of supporting her husband and educating her sons, but the parents would also wish her to carry out these responsibilities as an educated person and so help her sons enter the ranks of the intelligentsia. They would also want her to be able to manage the family property and elevate the social standing of the family as a whole. Such notable men of the Song dynasty as Sima Guang, Wang Anshi, Shen Kuo, Su Shi, and Zhu Xi lavished special praise on elite women who were able to support their husbands and educate their sons in part through the women's own cultural accomplishments.[16]

How were these women able to satisfy these additional demands? Clearly they drew not only on women's traditional virtues, but also on the advantages of education. Thus their responsibilities—no longer limited to the house-hold—could stretch to include giving opinions and problem-solving. For example, on one occasion Mei Zhuang offended the emperor in offering exhortations and was therefore very worried. His wife advised him that, as an official, he was bound to be a virtuous person, and if the two were incompatible, then he should give up being an official and be content to be a virtuous person. She said,

> As an official you have enjoyed royal favors. If his Majesty has faults you should point them out. If His Majesty ignores your exhortations you should leave. Do not waver on my account. If you have offended by straightforward talk, I am willing to join you in exile and I will have no regrets, even if I were to die there. I wish to be the wife of an honorable man rather than the wife of a high official.[17]

Another example of an elite woman whose education affected her role in her family is Lady Su Xun, mother of Su Shi and Su Che. That Su Xun and his two sons could become famous literary figures at the same time was a rare phenomenon in Chinese history, one possible only because of Lady Su, neé Cheng. To help her husband in his studies, Lady Su sold all her dowry and took up the whole family burden.[18] In his epitaph for his wife, Su Xun wrote with great feeling, "When I was young I never settled down to study; though you were silent I knew you were unhappy. I knew your heart, that you were anxious that I would not leave a name for posterity. Since you are gone, I have lost a good friend. Alone all day, who is there to remind me when I lapse?"[19] Su Xun was away from home most of the time and so Lady Su was responsible for their sons' early education and ethical training. Sima Guang wrote in his epitaph for her: "Lady Su loved reading, and was a good woman. Su Shi and Su Che were young at the time, and she taught them personally, and often encouraged them with examples from the illustrious ancients, saying, 'If you were to die an honest and moral man, I would not be overcome by grief.' Her two sons passed the examinations in the same year and won honored positions."[20]

The writers of these epitaphs never diminished these women's exceptional gifts; on the contrary, they highlighted their talents with myriad examples, a sure sign that these women were in step with the ideals of the times. As Sima Guang wrote in his epitaph for Lady Su, "A woman's gentleness could make the clan harmonious; her wisdom could bring order to the family, a true sign of virtue."[21] Without education, women could accomplish little. Here Sima Guang points to the important influence of educated women on the family and beyond, to the country as a whole.

One-fourth of the aristocratic families of the time included in their domain several hundred to a thousand family members. To keep the family together in harmony and stability was a basic requirement of the head of the family, and sex was not a consideration. The epitaph of Lady Shao, for example, says,

> When her husband was living, he ruled the household strictly; he guided his children in studies and was looked up to in the community. His wife worked in harmony with him and never indulged herself. The children competed in studies and won places at the imperial examinations. Shao was widely respected, and so was his wife. When Shao was deceased, his wife, Lady Shao, was aged. She called the household together and laid down the rules so that the family could continue in harmony. No one was to usurp her rule. In order that her husband's rules not be forgotten, she had them carved on a screen.[22]

In some cases, when family situations demanded, women who had been married could be remarried. In the Sun family five generations lived under one roof, its members numbering two hundred. A woman named Shi, "known for wisdom, at age seventeen married a man named Hu, who died a year later. The Sun family sought a second wife, but, seeking high and low, could find no one as good as the woman Shi and took her forcibly to wife." The woman Shi ran the family for sixty-eight years, practicing frugality and filial piety among old and young. She loved reading when young and kept it up in old age, having a general knowledge of the *Six Classics* and the *Four Books* of Confucius[23] and Mencius. In her old age, she passed on Sima Guang's *Family Rules* to all of her descendants. Thus the younger generation kept up the style of their forebears: They either passed the examinations to serve as officials in court or remained as scholars.[24]

Another example was Lady Cai. In his epitaph to her, Zhen Dexiu quotes Lady Cai's words to her son: "I have seen many people in my life, the rich and powerful, but where are they now? The important thing is to stand on one's own two feet."[25] Her view reflected the social reality of the time and echoes the advice of other educated women to their male family members. Clearly education allowed some women during the Song dynasty to become more than the virtuous wife inscribed in prior traditions.

WORKING URBAN WOMEN, "PROSTITUTES," AND ENTERTAINERS

Important aspects of Song society in transition included the development of its economy, certain handicrafts, and its cities. Business areas in the cities changed; the old handicraft system broke down; commerce expanded.[26] In the development of commerce, the rise of the city, and a new urban culture, ordinary women were important, though they still held a lowly place in the society.[27]

Silk production, printing, and pottery, well developed during the Song dynasty, stimulated both commerce and culture. Women were an important part of the workforce in many industries. Under the pressures of this urban economy, the traditional divisions of labor between men and women changed. Many privately owned silk plantations hired women. One surviving artifact from the Song dynasty, "Picture of Silk Weaving," illustrates a silk plantation with a scene of many women workers. To judge by their apparel, the forty-one women workers in the painting were commoners. Their clothing was varied in style, some without belts, while others actually showed their bosoms.[28] During the Song, woodblock printing reached a peak. Women also worked in that industry. According to *Notes from Rong Zhai*, the woodblock for printing "Picture of Silk Weaving" was carved by women. With regard to pottery, an integral part of Song handicraft, during the Southern Song, of five kilns in Ji county, now belonging to Jiangxi province, the best was considered that of Old Man Shu, thanks to his daughter Shu Jiao. She was a superb pottery artisan and her products, including toys, were among the best in the industry.[29]

Two of the most common occupations for women were prostitution and entertainment. In order to increase the tax income, the government national-ized the sale of wine and hired women to lure customers into singing houses, wine shops, and tea shops.[30] Wang Mao, in his *Series of a Wild Traveler*, reports: "Nowadays prostitutes are used to sell wine; it is called setting up a means." During the Southern Song dynasty, an official's promotion or demo-tion might depend on his ability to collect revenue on wine sales. Thus, raising a daughter to become a prostitute or entertainer became a way of making money for some families.[31] Chen Yu records that, in the south, families insisted that their daughters learn music, the arts, and the art of entertaining. From 1004 to 1048, the revenue from the wine tax increased fourfold and ranked third in the national revenue, following closely after the agriculture tax of sum-mer and fall and the salt tax.[32] Thus, the government, the wine merchants, and the family colluded to make women a means of income, and these women sac-rificed themselves to make this special contribution.

Women entertainers, though sometimes prostitutes, were singers and dancers and occasionally poets or actresses. Some of them were highly edu-cated and could write poetry or play musical instruments. Each had her own specialty. Some verses written by men were publicized through the singing of prostitutes, who thus contributed to the popularity of the *ci* form of poetry. Liu Yong, for example, was regarded as an intimate friend by prostitutes who were singers because of his ability to probe into their innermost feelings. He was widely known for his verses on love and lovemaking and on the women's long-ing for love. One of the lines in his famous poem "The Goose Goes Up to Heaven" says, "I would rather exchange worldly vanities for wine and song." There is a story that, when he went to take the imperial examination, the emperor said, "Why bother with worldly vanities? Just go and indulge in wine and song." In self-mockery, he gave himself a title, "Liu the verse maker by order of the Emperor" and spent the rest of his life writing poems.[33]

Because the Confucian theorist Lu Xiangshan's protégé Xie Ximeng often mixed with prostitutes, Lu reproved him, saying, "As a scholar, mixing with prostitutes, are you not a disgrace to your studies?" Xie did not agree. On the contrary, he built a mandarin duck tower for prostitutes and dedicated a verse to it: "The spirits of heaven and earth do not dwell with men, but reside in women."[34]

Women entertainers and prostitutes survived in the space allotted to them in an environment of neo-Confucianism and commercialization. Some of them were as young as thirteen or fourteen when they began their trade.[35] But, unlike other periods in which one views prostitutes through male eyes, the Song era included women sufficiently educated to reflect on their own feelings of degradation. In the *Complete Collection of Song Ci*, one-third of the poems were written by so-called prostitutes.[36] The *ci* by the famous courtesan Yan Rui is a good example. Yan was skilled in the arts and musical instruments, in singing and dancing, calligraphy, and painting, poetry, and *ci*. She was also a favorite of Tang Zhongyou, the magistrate. When falsely accused and imprisoned, she suffered tortures during an interrogation, almost to the point of death. A new magistrate, taking pity on her, ordered her to write a poem that would state her case. Yan recited an improvised *ci* right on the spot:

It is not for love of dalliance, but a case of predestined mismatch.
Flowers blossom and wilt in their own time, according to the
    goddess of spring.
If it is time to go, I must go. How can one stop the flow?
When wild flowers cover my head, ask not where I have gone.[37]

The poem reflects her spirit of revolt and her longing for life. One characteristic common to both the male poet Liu Yong and the female poet Yan Rui is their defiance of traditional ethical values and, with that, their avowal of a new philosophy of life. This departure from traditional views explains how *ci* reached a new peak of achievement in the literature of the Song.

Still another form of employment opened up to women in this age of thriving commerce. Streets and lanes filled with shop fronts large and small, crowded together door to door. Zhu Shuzhen describes the scene in the capital: "Strains of song and flute wafted from behind the gates of the rich and affluent, while the street market rocked with boisterous sounds of commerce."[38] Small shopkeepers who needed help from the family provided opportunities for women. Many stores and foods were named after women. Yuan Jun in *Readings by the Maple Window* writes, "In the capital there are many such labels for food and shops. Take cuisine, for example, and such brand names as Plum Blossom Dumplings from Jade Tower, or Grandma Cao's meat-filled pancakes, and others well known at the time." A book on food published during the Song tells how "Song Family Fifth Sister-in-law's Fish Cake were often patronized by the emperor, and thus customers flocked to the store, and the owner prospered." In the food business, women were not only part of the workforce but also took part in managing the family finances.

In the Song dynasty popular entertainment became an important part of the economy. Members of the growing bourgeoisie wanted entertainment that reflected their own wishes and interests, and thus men and women talented in singing and dancing began to put on dramatic performances and variety shows, and offer storytelling with musical accompaniment. Urban entertainment districts known as *wa zi* and areas for performing known as *goulan* appeared.[39] Records indicate that some theaters in the capital of the Northern Song could hold as many as several thousand people. No matter what the weather, the theaters were filled daily.

In the Southern Song city of Lingan, the largest *wa zi* was the Northern Wa, with thirteen *goulan* in the environs. Actresses of the Southern Song exceeded in numbers those of the Northern Song era.[40] According to records, there were fifty-five different categories of popular entertainment, at least twenty of them using female performers. The Zhang, Song, and Chen young women were well known: Lu Miaohui and Lu Miaojing for their recitals and exposition of scriptures; Shi Huiying for storytelling; Second Aunt Li and Black Mama for their puppet shows; and Grandma Xiao for her impromptu singing. Clearly, many women worked as entertainers during this period.

Storytelling was an important part of entertainment in the *wa zi*, and there were many women among the actors. On stage they impersonated such commoners as craftsmen, shopkeepers, and handymen, thus directly reflecting the daily life of urban people. The short story "The Jade Guanyin Bodhisattva," describing the love between a man and a woman who defied feudal proprieties, was a favorite. The female actors were somewhat educated, the most famous among them being Shi Huiying, Young Madam Zhang, Young Madam Song, Young Madam Chen, Lu Miaohui, and Lu Miaojing.[41]

The comic show, a branch of comic opera, also used female actors. According to records, some women could invent impromptu poetry on any designated subject over dinner. The point was to cause laughter. In some cases, women performed for the emperor and transmitted hidden messages in their acts. The emperor, it is said, enjoyed the show and ignored the messages.[42]

Another novelty of Song culture was wrestling. Sima Guang writes, "During the Lantern Festival, January 15 of the lunar calendar, his Highness the Emperor called upon all entertainers to display their skills and rewarded them with silver and silks. Among them were female wrestlers, who were likewise rewarded." Sima Guang continues, "With his Highness sitting above and the populace below, with Empress and concubines at the Royal side and aristocratic ladies in full view, it is unsuitable for female performers to expose themselves. It is a violation of the rites."[43] Although he petitioned the emperor to proclaim an edict prohibiting such displays in public, they continued.

Women in Song society, whether by choice or by force, broke through traditions that would have kept them confined to domesticity at other times. Women left home and were integral to the development of the Song economy. They also helped to create and develop an urban working-class culture.

NOTES

1. See Patricia Buckley Ebrey, *The Inner Quarters: Marriage and the Lives of Chinese Women in the Sung Period* (Berkeley: University of California Press, 1993).

2. See Dorothy Ko, *Teachers of the Inner Chambers: Women and Culture in Seventeenth-Century China* (Stanford: Stanford University Press, 1994).

3. Zheng Bijun, *Liangsong guanshen jiazu funü-qianpian guanshen jiazu funü muzhiming yanjiu* (Women from the Gentry Class in the Song Dynasties: A Study of a Thousand Epitaphs for Women of the Gentry Class), *Guoxue yanjiu* (Chinese Studies), 1999, 6. The women from the gentry class in this context were women from families of landlords, the bureaucracy, as well as a small percentage of hereditary officials and royal families.

4. Sima Guang, *Jiafan* (Family Rules), Vol. 6, *Si ku quan shu* (Complete Library of the Four Branches of Literature—the Classics, history, philosophy and collected literary works). *The Book of Filial Piety* is not a classic. It is believed to have been compiled and assumed its present form during the Han dynasty (202 BCE–220 CE). There is no information about the author. Three versions exist in China: the Han, Tang, and Qing. The *Analects* is a collection of conversations between Confucius and his disciple. It is considered the most important book of Confucian doctrine. *The Classic of Poetry* is one of the Confucian classics, an anthology of some three hundred poems dating mostly from the early, or Western, Zhou (c. 1025–771 BCE). Some of these are folksongs from various feudal states of early Zhou, while others are songs used by the aristocracy in their sacrificial ceremonies or at banquets or other functions. Confucius is supposed to have selected and edited these poems from a much larger body of materials, and though this tradition is open to question, there seems no reason to doubt the authenticity of the songs themselves. *Book of Rites* is another Confucian classic. It is a collection of texts covering a vast range of subjects from the broadest philosophical pronouncements to the most minute rules for the conduct of everyday life. It is uncertain when the collection assumed its present form, though the texts themselves appear to date from middle or late Zhou down to the early Han. Again Confucius is said to be the compiler and editor.

5. Ibid.

6. "Li Kefei zhuan" (Biography of Li Kefei), in *Song shi* (History of the Song Dynasty), Vol. 444 (Beijing: China Bookstore, 1959), 13–121.

7. Qian Qianyi, "Jin shi lei" (Notes to the Category of Archaeology and Cultural Relics), in *Jiang yun lou shu* (Jiang yun lou Catalogues), (Commercial Press, 1935), 1st edition, Vol. 4, 91, *Congshu jicheng chubian*.

8. *Wai zhuan* (Unofficial Biography) *Langhuanji* (quoted from *Critical Biography of Li Qingzhao* by Chen Zhumei, Nanjing University Press, 1995, Chapter 4, 147).

9. Li Zhiyi, *Gusu Jushi qian* (Collected Works of Gusu Jushi, part I), Vol. 50, *Si ku quan shu* edition.

10. Yuan Fu, "Tairuren bianshi muzhiming" (Epitaph for Lady Bian), in *Meng zhai ji* (A Collection from Meng Zhai), Vol. 18, *Si ku quan shu* edition.

11. Li Shi, *Fangzhou ji* (A Collection from Fang zhou), Vol. 17, *Si ku quan shu* edition.

12. Zheng Bijun, "Liangsong guanshen jiazu funü—qianpian guanshen jiazu funü muzhiming yanjiu" (Women from the Gentry Class in the Song Dynasties: A Study of

a Thousand Epitaphs for Women of the Gentry Class), *Guoxue yanjiu* (Chinese Studies), 1999, 6.

13. Zhang Xiqing, "Lun songdai kejuqushi zhiduo yu rongguan de guanxi" (On the Relationship Between the Enrollment in the Song Imperial Examinations and Bureaucratic Redundancy), *Beijng daxue xuebao* (Journal of Peking University), 1987, 5. According to this essay, during the 290–year reign of the Tang dynasty, there were 268 enrollment lists with a total of 20,619 people who passed the exams. During the 320-year reign of the two Song dynasties, there were 139 enrollment lists with a total of 115,427 people who passed the exams, five times the number during the Tang dynasty. In comparison, the enrollment number in the Song dynasties is thirty times that of the Yuan dynasty, four times that of the Ming dynasty and 3.4 times that of the Qing dynasty.

14. Hong Mai, "Raozhou fengsu" (Customs of Raozhou), in *Rong zhai si bi* (The Fourth Book Written at Rong zhai), Vol. 5 (Shanghai: Shanghai Press of Ancient Books, 1996), 665.

15. See Yuan Cai, "Fujia zhichan dangcun renxin" (The Wealthy Should Show Mercy in the Accumulation of Property), in *Yuanshi shifan* (Yuan's Rules for the World), Vol. 2 (Tianjin Press of Ancient Books, 1995), 162–163; and Zhang Zai, "Jingxue liku—zongfa" (Patriarchal Clan System), in *Interpretations of Confucian Classics*, from *Zhuangzi quanshu* (Complete Works of Zhuangzi*)*, Vol. 4, *Si ku quan shu* edition.

16. Zheng Bijun, "Liangsong guanshen jiazu funü, 6.

17. Yao Yi, "Meizhuang furen muzhiming"(Epitaph for Lady Mei Zhuang), in *Xue po ji*, Vol. 50, *Si ku quan shu* Edition.

18. Sima Guang, "Chengfuren muzhiming" (Epitaph for Lady Cheng), in *Chuanjia ji*, Vol. 78, *Si ku quan shu* edition.

19. Su Xun, *Jia youji*, Vol. 15, *Si bu cong kan* (Collection of the Classics, History, Philosophy and Literary Works) edition

20. Sima Guang, "Chengfuren muzhiming" (Epitaph for Lady Cheng), in *Chuanjia ji*, Vol. 78, *Si ku quan shu* edition.

21. Ibid.

22. Zhu Xi, "Tairuren Shaoshi muzhiming" (Epitaph for Lady Shao), in *Hui'an ji*, Vol. 90, *Si ku quan shu* edition.

23. At the heart of the Confucian canon are the *Six Classics* and the *Four Books*. The *Six Classics* include the *Book of Changes*, the *Book of History*, the *Classic of Poetry*, the *Book of Rites*, the *Spring and Autumn Annals*, and the *Classic of Music*, which was lost during the Han. The *Four Books* were brought together as a group by the neo-Confucian scholar Zhu Xi (1130–1200).

24. Wang Zao, "Lingren Shishi muzhiming" (Epitaph for Lady Shi from Ling), in *Fuxi ji*, Vol. 8, *Si ku quan shu* edition.

25. Zhen Dexiu, *Xishan wenji*, Vol. 45, *Si ku quan shu* edition.

26. Meng Yuanlao, "Dongjiaolou xiang" (Dongjiaolou Lane), in *Dongjing Menghua lu*, Vol. 2, "Puxi" (Shop Fronts), *Dongjing Menghua lu*, Vol. 3 (Beijing: China Bookstore, 1962); see also Zhou Baozhu and Chen, *Jianming Song shi* (A Concise History of the Song Dynasty) (Beijing: People's Press, 1985) Section 3 of Chapter 3 and Section 3 of Chapter 12.

27. "Xiongwei zhuangli de Jingshishi" (The Grand City of Jingshi), in *Marco Polo Youji* (Travels of Marco Polo), Chapter 76, Vol. 2 (Fuzhou: Fujian Press of Science and Technology, 1981). In *Nie Zheng Zhuang* (Biography of Nie Zheng), Vol. 86 of *Shiji* (Historical Records), Sima Qian says: "Zheng is among the shi jing people" (one of the townspeople). In *Notes to Historical Records*, it is stated: "In ancient times where people gathered together to draw water from the wells, they would often do buying and selling; hence the appearance of fairs. They left the place after trading." That was how the term "shi jing" (fair-well or marketplace) came about. The "shi jing women" in the two Song dynasties were women involved in business and commerce.

28. Lin Guiying and Liu Fengtong, "Canzhi tu" (A Preliminary Study of 'Picture of Silk Weaving,' Song Dynasty), *Wenwu* (Cultural Relics), no. 7, 1984, 31–32.

29. Zhu Yan, *Tao shuo* (On Pottery). This is a book of six volumes about the history, manufacturing, varieties, kilns in different locations, etc. of pottery and porcelain, first published during the Qing dynasty. The photocopy edition was published in 1988 by Tianjin Classical Literature Press.

30. Zhou Mi, "Jiu lou" (Wine Shops), in *Wulin jiushi* (Recollections of Wulin), Vol. 6; Guan pu nai de weng, "Jiusi" (Wine Shops), in *Ducheng jisheng* (Views of the capital), in *Dongjing Menghua lu*, Vol. 2.

31. Quoted in the Economics Volume in *On the Song Dynasty*, 21: 17. *Song hui yaoshihuo* (A Collection of Articles on the Song Dynasty), vol. 137 (Beijing: China Bookstore, 1957), 5152.

32. Li Tao, "Xin you, the ninth year of da zhong xiang fu" (Under the Rule of Emperor Zhen), *Xu zizhitongjian changbian* (Long Sequel to *Historical Events Retold as a Mirror for Government*), Vol. 86 (Beijing: China Bookstore, 1990); Qi Xia, "A Form of Revenue from Sales of Liquor in the Song Dynasties," Appendix 5, *Liangsong caizhengshi* (History of Finance of the Two Song Dynasties), Vol. 2 (Beijing: China Bookstore, 1995), 705–708

33. Liu Yong, *Yuezhang ji* (Songs and Verses*)*, Vol. 2, *Si ku quan shu* edition.

34. Pang Yuanying, *Tansou* (Miscellanies), quoted from "Xie Ximeng," in *Songren Yishi Huibian* (A Collection of Anecdotes from the Song Dynasty by Ding Chuanjing), Vol. 16 (Beijing: China Bookstore, 1981), 898.

35. Weng Mai, "Lumingyan zeng genji" (To the Singing Prostitute of *Luming* Banquet), in *Quan song shi* (The Complete Collection of Song Poetry), Vol. 875 (Beijing: Peking University Press, 1991), 10181.

36. Zheng Bijun, *Quan song ci* (The Complete Collection of Song Ci) (Beijing: China Bookstore, 1965). The conclusion is derived from statistics about female poets in *Quan song ci*.

37. Zhou Mi, "Taiji yanrui" (Courtesan Yan Rui from Taizhou), in *Qidongyeyu*, Vol. 20, *Si ku quan shu* edition.

38. Zhu Shuzhen, "Shop Fronts,"in *Mengliang Lu*, Vol. 13 (Shanghai: Shanghai Press of Classical Literature, 1956), 239–241; Zhu Shuzhen, *Zhu Shuzhen jizhu* (Notes to the Collected Works of Zhu Shuzhen), Vol. 2 (Zhejiang Press of Ancient Books, 1985).

39. Meng Yuanlao, "Jingwa jiyi" (Wa Zi Entertainers in the Capital), in *Dongjing Menghua lu*, Vol. 5 (Shanghai: Shanghai Press of Classical Literature, 1956), 29–30.

40. Xihu laoren (Old Man from the West Lake), "Xihu laoren fanshenglu—washi" (Wa Zi, Places of Entertainment), in *Records of Numerous Visits to Public Places*, Dongjing Menghua lu et al. (Shanghai: Shanghai Press of Classical Literature, 1956), 123–124.

41. Ibid.

42. Zhou Mi, "Zhu seji yiren" (A Variety of Entertainers and Performers), in *Recollections of Wulin*, Vol. 6 (Shanghai: Shanghai Press of Classical Literature, 1956), 453–466.

43. Sima Guang, *Wenguo wenzheng Simagong wenji* (Collected Works of Master Sima Guang), Vol. 21, *Si bu cong kan* edition.

CHINESE WOMEN'S STATUS AS SEEN THROUGH PEKING OPERA

Huang Yufu

Peking opera is an important part of Chinese traditional culture. After the Four Big Anhui Troupes came to perform in Beijing in 1790, Peking opera gradually took shape and developed into a highly complex artistic form.[1] Like other art forms, Peking opera reflects life. In fact, almost every significant social change and major social custom in Chinese history has found its expression on the Peking opera stage. Various social values have been advocated in its plays, including prevailing views that see men as superior to and stronger than women. The changing social status of Chinese women has also been reflected not only in the plays, but also in relations between men and women in Peking opera circles, as well as among actors and actresses and their families and friends. Such characteristics make it possible to use Peking opera as a window on the changes in the social status of Chinese women.

This essay reviews the period from the birth of Peking opera in 1790 to the beginning of the War of Resistance Against Japanese Aggression in 1937. It will focus only on Beijing, where Peking opera began and where outstanding artists played female roles. As we will see, those artists were initially male, but later Peking opera included female performers.

PEKING OPERA IN ITS EARLY DAYS—A WORLD OF MEN

In 1790, as part of the celebration of the eightieth birthday of the Emperor Qianlong (1736–1795) in the Qing dynasty (1644–1911), the Four Big Anhui Troupes came to perform in Beijing. By combining artistic elements drawn from northern Kunqu opera in that city, Clapper opera that originated in Shanxi and Shaanxi provinces, and Han opera from Hubei province, they gradually developed a new type of opera with special characteristics of the capital that came to be called Peking opera. Soon this new opera form became popular throughout China.

All those involved in the creation and staging of Peking opera, whether playwrights or performers, musicians or makeup artists, were men. Traditional theater training schools did not enroll female students, nor did actors accept

30

female apprentices. Women were generally excluded from Peking opera, except as members of the audience—and there, too, their presence was limited.[2]

Performances often took place at the Forbidden City before emperors and their entourage, which might include a few royal women. People of imperial lineage, high officials, and rich merchants might hold private functions and banquets at which troupes were invited to play. Here, among the audience, there might also be women. Likewise, every year at religious festivals, troupes might be invited to perform at temples with stages. Women who attended made donations that were an important source of temple revenue. As for popular theaters, women were permitted to enter prior to 1735, but after that date, it was declared an offence against decency for women to attend the theater.[3] Initially, then, since few women were allowed to enter the Forbidden City or to attend private functions, and because performances in temples were limited, the great majority of women rarely saw Peking opera.

Female characters in early Peking opera occupied mostly minor roles. Among leading female characters in the plays performed between 1845 and 1861, about 34 percent were "silly women," evil or licentious women, or sirens who bewitched men, thus promoting the view of women as troublemakers. Another 31 percent of female characters were *qingyi*: virtuous wives, wise mothers, or young women ready to die to preserve their chastity—the ideal women for whom the rule was "not to show their feet while walking, nor to show their teeth while smiling." Male actors played these roles wearing *qiao*, stiltlike shoes that gave the impression of small, or bound, feet. A small percentage of plays, perhaps 20 percent, featured women characters with outstanding military skills but of very low social origins. Called *wudan*, these female characters were originally played by male actors, whose performances featured martial arts and typically neglected characterization.[4]

EARLY TWENTIETH CENTURY

In the late nineteenth and early twentieth centuries, spectacular changes in the status of women in Peking opera broke the monopoly of men. These changes reflected a new social environment as the Chinese women's movement began to appeal for the equality of men and women.

In 1900, when the Eight-Power Allied Forces (Austria, Britain, France, Germany, Italy, Japan, Russia, and the United States) occupied Beijing, women could, for the first time since 1735, go to theaters to see Peking opera performed. The theaters were opened to women by the foreigners, who found it inconceivable to bar them, though women were seated in a separate area, away from men. For more than a year, ordinary women enjoyed Peking opera—women from elite families did not attend. When the Allied Forces withdrew from the capital in 1902, women were once again forbidden to enter theaters, a ban that prevailed until the founding of the Republic of China in 1914.[5]

When restrictions on women's attendance were lifted in 1914, women in the capital crowded into theaters with great enthusiasm and soon became an important part of the audience. With the construction of the First Stage, the first Western-style theater, women were allowed to sit with men in the boxes and, after 1930, throughout the theater. Although they could not quite understand the finer points of the acting of Peking opera, they took great interest in the beautiful appearance and colorful costumes of the women characters. Over time, the enlarged female audience led to the development of the art of female acting.

The first training school for actresses was established in 1916, and the first coeducational institution of the Peking opera—the China Theater Training School—in 1930.[6] Most theater schools, however, remained closed to women, and they had even more difficulty finding actors who would accept them as students. The first to accept actresses as students was Wang Yaoqing (1881–1954), a highly creative actor who played female roles. In 1927, he accepted his first female student, Li Huiqin, breaking down the old convention that had existed for more than a century.[7] Wang had many women students during his lifetime, including a number who became outstanding actresses. Other actors soon followed his example and began to take actresses as their students.[8]

As early as 1874 a few women began to act in Peking opera. Unable to earn much money, a second-rate actor of clown roles named Li Mao'er bought some girls from poor families in Anqing, taught them pieces of Anhui and Peking opera, and had them perform in teahouses and private functions in Shanghai. This was the first female troupe performing Peking opera. Only in 1912, however, did women begin to act in Beijing. In the dismal days after the 1911 Revolution, in order to calm public feeling, the official then in charge of internal affairs partly lifted the ban on performances by female actresses. A man named Yu Zhenting used this as an excellent opportunity. He hired actresses in order to attract audiences, and he built a theater at Xiangchang in Beijing where actors and actresses both began to perform.[9]

The appearance of actresses on the stage shocked the world of Peking opera. Many people thought it offensive, while the curious flocked to see it. For several months in 1912 and 1913 some actors and actresses in Beijing acted together, but such troupes were soon prohibited. The stated reason for this new restriction was the supposed offence against public decency. Actually the ruling reflected the conflicts and competition between men and women in the field of Peking opera. Since audiences tended to attend for the good looks of actresses rather than their artistic skills, actors, finding their own status slipping, persuaded the authorities to ban women, using the pretext of supporting public decency.

Despite such prejudice and discrimination, women's entry into Peking opera had become irresistible. By the 1920s, actresses had made considerable progress; many studied hard and achieved artistic success. The outstanding skill of some actresses gradually won recognition. In 1930, the authorities lifted the ban on women and men acting together, and many actors, including some renowned ones, were by then willing to act with women.

Women in Peking opera also began to develop a competitive relationship with men. By the 1930s, some actresses—such as Xue Yanqin (1906–1986), Zhang E'yun (b. 1912), Xin Yanqiu (b. 1910), and Meng Xiaodong (1907–1977)—were enjoying great popularity. They endeavored to perfect their skills, learned from others modestly, and made great efforts to stage new plays of their own, creating new artistic styles. Their popularity matched that of their male counterparts.

CHANGING IMAGES OF WOMEN IN PEKING OPERA

Although women's status in Peking opera circles was greatly improved in the early twentieth century, women's image on the stage was also changing. First, the importance of female roles increased in the Peking opera repertoire. Even by the early twentieth century, Wang Yaoqing's popular acting and singing of female characters had improved the status of female roles in the repertoire. With the appearance of the Four Famous *Dan*—actors who played female roles—headed by Mei Lanfang, the importance of certain female roles increased further. The leading roles in most new plays created in the early twentieth century were female.

Second, during the early twentieth century, the kinds of women portrayed onstage changed greatly.[10] On the whole, women characters seemed to exude perfection. They were either beautiful and affectionate, sensible and wise, with supreme talent and learning, like Xishi in *A Story of Xishi*,[11] or they were highly skilled in the military arts like Hongxian in *Hongxian Steals the Box*.[12] As for the goddesses created on the stage of Peking opera in this period, they embodied beauty, as for instance, the Goddess in *The Goddess of the Luo River*.[13] Many new plays also voiced protests against the maltreatment and persecution of women, as in *The Jade Hair Clasp*.[14] In addition, and for the first time in the history of Peking opera, a woman's search for love was depicted as something beautiful instead of licentious, in *Face and Peach*.[15]

The third and most striking change in Peking opera was that more and more actresses walked on natural feet instead of using *qiao*, a set of props worn on the feet of performers playing certain female roles, in order to imitate

Chinese women's bound feet.[16] Since the late Qing dynasty, footbinding, a prevalent social custom long practiced in Chinese society, found its expression on the stage of Peking opera. In the early twentieth century, some actors playing female roles ventured to abandon *qiao* in their performance. This change served not only as a significant reform of this ancient art but also as a reflection of the energy of the women's movement.

Still, all actresses had brief careers, for several reasons. Before 1949, while the social status of male actors was low, that of actresses was lower still. Actresses were sometimes forced to be the concubines of warlords, officials, gangsters, or rich men. Some yielded to the pressure and gave up their careers. Others fought bitterly for their right to act. Some were driven from the stage in order to preserve their reputation and dignity.

When an actress married, she was generally expected to renounce acting and become a virtuous wife and mother. Generally speaking, a husband would not allow his wife to continue her career as an actress. Many actresses regarded being a good wife and wise mother as an ideal goal. In spite of their deep love for acting, the uncertainty of such careers led many actresses to choose an uninteresting but comparatively safe course through life. Many sought a decent husband while still young and pretty, and it was quite common to find that, as soon as an actress began to enjoy success, she married and retired from the stage. In addition, aging, marriage, childbearing, and breast-feeding all posed problems for an actress's long-term career, although the effects of these physiological factors might vary from person to person.

Since the founding of the People's Republic of China in 1949, Chinese women's status in Peking opera has improved. All theater schools are now coeducational; girls and boys have equal opportunities to learn Peking opera. Most female roles are performed by actresses while few senior actors still play female roles. Women are active not only as actresses but also as playwrights, musicians, and makeup artists. Some of them have become leaders of national theaters. Actresses have also been selected as deputies to the National People's Congress.

The first reform carried out in Peking opera after 1949 was to ban the pornographic performances that were quite popular in traditional plays. Plays advocating polygamy, superstition, or other antirevolutionary ideology were also forbidden. Since the 1960s, many new plays with idealized female characters have been produced. These female characters are so intelligent, brave, resolute, and beautiful that even the male characters pale beside them. In some of these plays, the heroines are portrayed mainly as genderless revolutionaries, as in the "revolutionary model plays" during the Cultural Revolution, in which female characters might be leaders or soldier-mothers or daughters who participated in the revolution. Love and family life are simply absent from the

Peking opera stage in these plays.

In 1950, acting with *qiao* as a symbol of footbinding was officially banned. In the 1980s *qiao* reappeared on the stage of Peking opera, used by a young actress who was too short to play leading roles. The technical dimensions of *qiao* helped to disguise her defect, but the prop's symbolic functions had disappeared. Thus, even symbolic functions change as the social environment changes. In contemporary China, artists now enjoy more freedom to control their careers. Today, the early forms of Chinese opera, especially Kunqu, are being revived. Still, Peking opera remains the most popular and widely performed. As in the past, social and political changes in China will continue to find their way to the Peking opera stage.

NOTES

1.   Anhui opera is popular in Anhui province of China. In 1790, four troupes playing Anhui opera came to play in Beijing and their excellent performances were warmly welcomed in the capital. They are called the Four Big Anhui Troupes.

2.   Although women were completely excluded from the world of Peking opera as playwrights and performers, and had hardly any right to attend performances, it was impossible to remove female roles from the stage completely—though they remained minor in the early years of Peking opera. The following table shows changes in women's presence among the audience.

SEX COMPOSITION OF AUDIENCE IN THEATERS IN BEIJING (1790–1937)

Time	1790–1900	1900–1902	1902–1912/3	1912/3 or 1914	1914–1937
Audience	M.	M.F.a.	M.	M.F.a.	M.F.b.

Key: M.—male only; M.F.a.—male and female audience seated separately (usually women's seats were on the second floor while men's were on the first floor); M.F.b.—male and female audience seated together.
Sources: (1) Editorial Committee of Qi Rushan's Works, 1961, 1644–1648. (2) Takeo Tsuji, 1930. (3) Ma Shaopo et al., 1990, Vol. 1, 186–187.

3.   The First Stage was different from the traditional theaters, with a line of "boxes" in the front row on the second floor, which were convenient for the audience. "Boxes" were separated groups of seats for families and their friends, with five or six seats in each group. After 1930, men and women could sit together outside the boxes.

4.   The female acrobatic roles in Peking opera called *wudan* include sirens or brave and heroic young women skilled in martial arts.

5.   Editorial Committee of Qi Rushan's Works, 1961, 1646.

6. SEX COMPOSITION OF MAIN THEATER TRAINING SCHOOLS OF PEKING OPERA IN BEIJING

1790–1880	1880–1917	1917–1937
?–? Shuangqing (m)	1882–post-1888 Xiaorongchun (m)	1917–1930 Binqing (m)
?–? Xiaohechun (m)		1930–1937 China Theater Training School (m + f)
?–? Xiaofusheng (m)	1889–? Xiaojili (m)	1912–1948 Fuliancheng(m)
?–? Xiaojinkui (m)	1889–? Xiaodangui (m)	
1862–1873 Quanfu (m)	1889–? Xiaoyucheng (m)	1914–1916 Zhengle (m)
?–1877 Deshengkui (m)	1889–? Xiaofushou (m)	1916–1919 Chongya Society (f)
?–post-1880 Sizhentang (m)	1904–1907 Changchun (m)	
	1904–1912 Xiliancheng (m)	
	1909–1914 Sanle (m)	

Key: m—male students only; f—female students only; m + f—coeducation.
Sources: (1) Zhang et al., 486. (2) Ma et al., Vol. 2, 47–51. (3) Su, 204–209. (4) Wu and Zhou, 286–290.

7. Author interview with Professor Cheng Yujing, 2 December 1994.

8. For instance, in 1927, Mei Lanfang (1894–1961) accepted Xin Yanqiu (b. 1910) as his first female student; she was voted one of the four best actresses in 1930.

9. Zhang, 1930, 9–10.

10. FEMALE LEADING ROLES IN THE 83 PLAYS CREATED BETWEEN 1917 AND 1937

Characteristics of the Female Leading Roles	Number of Plays	Percent
women seeking love or happiness	28	34
wise mothers, virtuous wives, or ladies prepared to die in order to preserve their chastity	24	25
heroines	10	12
persecuted women	7	8
silly women, vicious women, or sirens	6	7
goddesses	5	6

11. Plot of *A Story of Xishi*: Xishi is a well-known beauty in Yue Kingdom, which is conquered by Wu Kingdom. She decides to save her country by marrying the king of Wu and making him live in wanton luxury. Finally the Wu Kingdom is overthrown by Yue. First acted by Mei Lanfang in 1923.

12. Plot of *Hongxian Steals the Box*: A young maid, Hongxian, steals a box from the camp of the enemy and puts it under a general's pillow. She does this to show the enemy that there are people with excellent military arts in her army. The enemy is frightened and retreats. First acted by Mei Lanfang in 1920.

13. Plot of *The Goddess of the Luo River*: Prince Cao Zijian sleeps in an inn by the Luo River and dreams of the goddess of the Luo River. The two meet by the river and express their admiration for each other. After a long talk, the goddess goes away. First acted by Mei Lanfang in 1923.

14. Plot of *The Jade Hair Clasp*: A young lady, Zhang Yuzhen, receives a marriage proposal from her cousin but refuses. On Zhang's wedding day, the cousin forges a love letter and puts it in the bridal chamber. The lady is suspected of being unfaithful to her husband and is maltreated. She is physically injured and mentally affected before the whole truth comes out. First acted by Cheng Yanqiu in 1930.

15. Plot of *Face and Peach*: A young scholar meets with a lady. They admire each other and are reluctant to part. The next spring, when the scholar visits the lady's house, she is not at home. The scholar writes a poem on her gate and leaves. When the lady finds the poem, she is so distressed that she dies of sadness. The scholar visits her house once again, only to find that the lady has passed away. He is so sad he becomes choked with tears. His crying brings the lady back to life and the loving couple marries. First acted by Ouyang Yuqian in 1920.

16. There are two types of *qiao*—hard and soft. Since the latter appeared much later and was much less popular than the former, in this article, when we talk about *qiao*, we mean hard *qiao* only.

REFERENCES

Anonymous. "Hope to the Co-acting of Actors and Actresses," *Shuntian Times*, 6 February 1930.

Chen Dongyuan. *A History of the Life of Chinese Women*. Taibei: Taiwan Commercial Press, 1975.

Chuiyun Gezhu. "Anecdotes Concerning Actresses," *Theater Monthly*, Vol. 3, no. 12, 1932.

Editorial Committee of Qi Rushan's Works, ed. *The Complete Works of Qi Rushan*. Taibei, 1961.

Jiang Shangxing. *What I Saw and Heard of Peking Opera in the Past Sixty Years*. Shanghai: Xuelin Publishing House, 1986.

Kang Youwei. *A Memorial to the Throne in 1898*. 1898.

Li Xin, ed. *A History of the Republic of China*. Beijing: China Books, 1982.

Ma Shaobo, Zhang Lihui, et al., eds. *History of Peking Opera*. Beijing: China Theater Publishing House, 1990.

Mei Society, ed. "A New Era of Peking Opera," *Mei Lanfang*, 1918.

Su Yi. *A Survey of the Two Hundred Years of Peking Opera*. Beijing: China Theater Publishing House, 1989.

Takeo Tsuji. "A Pioneer of Coacting of Actors and Actresses," *Shuntian Times*, 28 January 1930.

Wangxi Gezhu. "History of the Co-acting of Actors and Actresses," *Ten Days Theater*, no. 55, 1939.

Wu Tongbin and Zhou Yaxun. *A Dictionary of Peking Opera Knowledge.* Tianjin: Tianjin People's Publishing House, 1990.

Xingshi [pseud.], "A Short History of Actresses' Coming to Beiping," *Theater Monthly*, Vol. 3, no. 1, 1930.

You Tian. "A New Trend in Peking Opera," *Beiyang Pictorial*, 7 March 1928.

Zeng Bairong. *A Dictionary of Plays of Peking Opera.* Beijing: China Theater Publishing House, 1989.

Zhang Geng, Zhao Jinshan, et al., eds. *Traditional Opera and Chinese Folk Art Forms, Encyclopaedia Sinica.* Beijing: China Encyclopaedia Publishing House, 1983.

Zhang Kai. "A Chronicle of Events of Actors and Actresses in Beiping," *Theater Monthly*, Vol. 3, no. 1, 1930, 9–10.

Zhou Mingtai. *A Chronicle of Events of Peking Opera Since Daoguang and Xianfeng's Reigns.* Beiping: Jiliju Theatrical Series, 1932.

Zhucun [pseud.]. "The Masculinized Actress Xue Yanqin," *Beiyang Pictorial*, 20 July 1929.

THE WOMEN'S SCRIPT OF JIANGYONG: AN INVENTION OF CHINESE WOMEN

Zhao Liming

Nüshu, women's script (also translated as "women's language"), a form of women's writing, has existed in the Xiao River region of Jiangyong County, Hunan, for a very long time. Socially, what sets the women's script apart from other forms of writing is that it is neither an official nor a religious form of writing. The creators of the women's script and its users were ordinary rural women. In feudal society, women, particularly rural women, were not allowed to read as men did. The keepers of the women's script used their own form of writing and literary works to strive for the right to their own culture, a form of resistance for Chinese women.

Works in the women's script were generally songbooks of seven-character poems, written on fine cloth handicrafts such as wedding gifts, fans, handkerchiefs, and strips of paper. These crafts were called "third-day letters" (a reference to the custom of sending a congratulatory note to the bride and groom on the third day of their marriage), "song fans," "handkerchief letters," and "paper writings." Some texts were embroidered on handkerchiefs, which were called "embroidered words." Women in this area frequently gathered together to do needlework in the singing hall, while singing, exchanging, and passing on the women's script. Singing halls were also places where a bride's best friends would sing with her for several days before her wedding. Singing songs written using the women's script was referred to as "reading papers," "reading fans," or "reading handkerchiefs," and these activities created the special culture of the women's script. Men paid no attention to the women's script, considering it to be an affair of the women not worthy of their concern. The keepers of the women's script say proudly that men have men's characters (Chinese characters), men's script, and men's literature, and women have women's characters, women's script, and women's literature. In this way, although the men and women of this area spoke the same language, they wrote it using different characters—one spoken language with two written forms.

The themes of works written in the women's script are mainly life's hardships (often relayed in autobiographical accounts), exchanges with old friends (sworn sisters), marriage and third-day congratulations, historical narratives, worship, modified traditional Chinese stories, and playful folk motifs and rhymes. Songs of grief dominate the literature of the women's script, but it is also a literature of self-enjoyment and entertainment.

Women who were fluent in the women's script were called "noble women." They were also referred to as "song leaders." These women, who could sing, write, and compose in the women's script, were few in number. They were the teachers and transmitters of the women's script. The range of the script was defined by where these women moved after marriage. They enjoyed high prestige locally. With these women as the core, and the women's script as the soul, groups of women—sworn sisterhoods—formed. Their venues were the sewing rooms of people's homes, and their social interactions included writing the women's script, singing songs written in the women's script, and learning needlework from each other. Every time someone started singing a song written in the women's script, young girls, married women, and old women all gathered around to sing it together. In areas where the women's script was used, not all women could write the women's script, but nearly everyone could sing the songs written in it. Such works were shared, and even if they were autobiographical or letters to friends, they were sung for all to hear. Everyone joined in the singing. The literature of the women's script was a type of popular singing folk literature. The culture of the women's script was a kind of singing-hall culture.

As popular women's literature, the women's script literature differs from the lonely and mournful literature of palace ladies and young upper-class ladies. It also differs from the romantic songs of courtesans in the pleasure quarters and from the women's literature that longs for a husband who has been taken away because of war or strife. As folk songs, the songs in the women's script also vary from field and mountain songs intended to be sung outdoors. Instead, the women's script songs are a type of singing-hall literature intended to be sung indoors.

Typology of Women's Script Songs and Literature

The literature of the women's script is mainly a way of venting one's grief; such feelings of grief make up its core. The women's script literature can be divided into three types, from the most personal to the most public—the primary type, the secondary type, and the reproduction type.

The primary type includes widows' laments and exchanges between sworn sisters. This category represents the main corpus of the women's script culture. The works are to a certain extent private. Most of these are biographical, primarily concerned with venting grief. Many are lengthy autobiographical poems, generally written by older women. Those who could not write asked others to write for them, as the titles "The Pitiful Story of So-and-So" and "A Written Narrative of So-and-So's Sorrows" indicate (see Zhao Liming, *Zhongguo nüshu jicheng* [Collection of the Chinese Women's Script], hereafter abbreviated *Jicheng* [Collection]). Personal life experiences are also sometimes expressed in letters to friends and third-day letters. They often bound their works in handsome booklets to be read aloud. "Yang Huanyi in Her Own Words" writes on a fan:

> I am writing this in my own hand on a fan,
> Writing on a fan to be circulated everywhere.
> I am sitting in an empty room, picking up a pen to write.
> Before I write, I first weep.
> In an empty room I am thinking of the topic of this poem.
> I will tell the pitiful story of my life.
> When I think of my sorrows I grow anxious,
> I have never passed a day with any brightness from the sun.
> I was born a daughter in the Yang [sun] family,
> And I ended up in the village of Erdu Heyuan.
>
> (*Jicheng*)

The secondary type includes bridal laments, narratives, playful songs, folk rhymes, and songs for worship. This category of works records the shared culture of the region and is more public than the primary type. It is a regional and marginal form of the women's script literature.

From the more than six hundred works written in the women's script we have collected, one can see that the content of women's script literature is in fact extremely diverse. In addition to the themes we have already mentioned, such as autobiography, exchanges with sworn sisters, factual accounts, narratives, marriage and worship songs, translations, and so on, there are also examples of lighthearted playful songs and folk rhymes:

> The little duck has a yellow, yellow bill,
> And before he ate any grain he slid down the bank,
> When he slid down the bank, he didn't know whether the water was
>   deep or shallow,
> When he sang a song he didn't know where to start,
> When he sang the beginning he forgot the end,
> When he sang the middle part he left out the beginning and the end,
> I'm a bird from the mountains,
> I can flap my wings but I can't sing,
> When I sing loud everyone laughs,
> When I sing low nobody hears
>
> ("Seventy-eight," *Jicheng*)

These clever and lively songs are full of strong local flavor. The "Weaving Song" provides one example of their cleverness: "I'm sitting in Nanjing / My feet are in Beijing / My hand grasps a Suzhou ax / And my eyes are looking at Changsha." The word "Changsha" is a homophone for "long threads." Whether they were describing landscapes or crafting witty folk rhymes, the keepers of the women's script, molded by both Han and Yao cultures, endowed their work with full emotions. Each of these folk songs is like a tableau, letting us see scenes of daily life from different angles.

The reproduction type includes Tang poems and popular literature, such as the story of Liang Shanbo and Zu Yingtai. This is a recreation of traditional culture and is accessible to the general public. Works written in the women's script include many songbooks translated from "men's writing" into the women's script such as *The Story of Meng Jiangnü*. There are also many Tang poems and classics like the *Sanzi jing* (Three-Character Classic) and the *Sizi nüjing* (Four-Character Women's Classic). Some reach several hundred sentences, or five to six thousand characters, in length. These high-quality works, which show a maturity of skill, are related to the circulation of librettos of Peking opera, the neighboring Qi opera (the local opera of the Qiyang area of Yongzhou), "fishing drums," and other folk ballad songbooks.

Although these rural women were stripped of their right to culture under the old dominant writing system, they revered culture, strove for civilization, and yearned for a spiritual life. Yet, as they pursued culture, they had no choice but to accept traditional cultural values. Works such as "Woman Xiao" and "Woman Luo" praise the Confucian values of chastity and filial piety. "Record of Three Maidens" is basically a moral treatise on feudal ethics. These borrowed works clearly show that the traditional culture and feudal ideas of propriety were the fundamental values of the women's script culture.

MARRIAGE CUSTOMS AND WOMEN'S SCRIPT LITERATURE

The types of women's script culture can be viewed in terms of marriage customs. The most representative "classics" of women's script literature are the "third-day letters" sent as wedding gifts, and the most representative songs are those about marriage. The most solemn and grandest occasion was the wedding, which followed a prescribed ritual. Wedding festivities could go on for several days or even weeks, with the women friends keeping each other company day and night as they did needlework and sang the women's songs. The bride, her maid of honor, and everyone else wore their best clothes, a display of the women's skill at needlework. Weddings form the heart of the women's script culture. At the same time, the unique wedding customs of the area where the women's script was used provided fertile cultural soil for the growth of the women's script up to modern times, a social arena for its presentation, and its main motivation.

Wedding culture is not solely the culture of women but is an important component of Chinese traditional culture as a whole. Both in imperial palaces and among the public, the act of marriage has given rise to a series of programmatic rituals and customs that reflect to a certain extent the values of the larger cultural background.

Marriage customs in the Shangjiangxu region of northeastern Jiangyong, where the women's script was used, are in some ways similar to those of other parts of Jiangyong, but in other ways are unique. Prior to 1949, women of this area faced the same fate as women all over China—they were subject to the will of their parents and marriages were basically arranged in the feudal tradition. Parents ordered a girl to marry the person the matchmaker had chosen. Girls whose feet had been bound since childhood into "three-inch lilies" did not go outdoors and were the "upstairs girls" who learned needlework. When girls were still small children or teenagers, their parents would ask a matchmaker to find a spouse for their daughter. Some matches were even made when the girl was in utero. During the course of the engagement there were certain required procedures, such as going to a fortune teller to have the horoscopes of the betrothed investigated to determine whether the match was suitable. Anguished sentiments of helplessness, such as "my time of birth got me matched up with him, and even the eight hundred pieces of silver cannot revoke the arrangement," often appear in women's script literature. After the engagement, the girl was not allowed to see her betrothed until they were married.

On the third day after a girl married, the bride's family would present a chest of gifts to the groom's family. The chest contained edible delicacies made by the bride's family and friends, and third-day letters written to wish the newlyweds well and to congratulate the groom's family. The groom's family held a huge feast at which they entertained the guests from the bride's family in grand style, a custom known as "eating on the third day." The bride's family invited everyone to sample the delicacies and sweets and to view the handicrafts made by the bride's family. At this time, a number of exquisite third-day letters were shown and sung to display the talent and refinement of the bride's family. Celebrating the third day of a marriage is a custom common to the local area, but third-day letters are unique to the area where the women's script culture was practiced. The third-day celebration was in fact a performance of the poetry and song written in the women's script. This was the moment when words and letters composed by women were presented in grand public settings, and the men had to listen carefully. The women used the opportunity presented in the wedding ceremony to display women's literary talent before male society. These victims who had no status or rights under the old system could openly air their grievances about their fates, express their own thoughts, and criticize social inequities. The difference between third-day letters and other works in the women's script is that they are a type of open letter that provide women with a platform for airing their views.

Although the culture of the women's script is related to the customs of local minorities, the basic messages expressed reflect traditional Han culture in which men till the soil and women weave, a culture in which men are superior to women, and women do not have freedom in marriage.

ORIGINS OF THE WOMEN'S SCRIPT

The first legend explaining the origins of the women's script suggests that "clever girls created words in their needlework." According to this story, when girls living along the banks of the Xiao River in Shangjiangxu, Jiangyong County, did weaving or embroidery, they often gathered together to work. In order to record their personal sufferings and to write letters to their sisters, they created types of characters based on embroidery patterns.

The second legend is that of the "imperial concubine from the Hu family in Jingtian who wrote letters home." It also circulates in the Shangjiangxu area. According to the story, a girl named Hu Yuxiu (some versions call her Hu Xiuying) from the Hu family in the village of Jingtian became an imperial concubine. She was not well received at court and in seven years spent only three nights with the emperor. She was very sad about this and wanted to write a letter home to her family. Afraid that the palace eunuchs would discover her writing, she invented the women's script. She used the script to write letters on handkerchiefs, telling her mother and friends of the hardships she suffered in the palace. She then asked people to take the handkerchiefs back to her home village. She told her relatives the secrets to deciphering the letters: First, they should be read on a slant. Second, the characters should be read using the local pronunciation in order to understand them. This was how the script began to be passed around among the women of her home village. To this day the village of Jingtian has a site called "Hall of the Emperor's Calligraphy," with elaborately carved beams. It is said that the emperor himself wrote the words "Yuxiang Hall" inscribed there. The site remained in existence until the early 1960s, and many people in the village remember it clearly. The *Yongmingxian zhi* (Gazetteer of Yongming County) includes this record:

> During the reign of Emperor Zhezong (r. 1086–1101 C.E.) of the Song dynasty there was a scholar named Hu Xianhe who was an imperial degree holder and was appointed to an imperial office. His older sister, Yuxiu, was a woman of surpassing talent and scholarship.

Word of her reached the imperial court, and she was presented with a gift of calligraphy written by the emperor and given a stipend. For this reason, her family built a building to house the emperor's calligraphy.

Among the extant works in the women's script is "Yuxiu Writes a Letter Home." According to the Jingtian "Genealogy of the Hu Clan," the Hu clan moved from Qingzhou, Shandong, during the Song dynasty (960–1271).

The third legend is that of "buying books at the altar." The women of Jiangyong often went to the Niangniang Temple to pray for good luck. It is said that there is women's script on the altar. After burning incense and paper money, one could pick up a book to take home and read (this was called "spending money to buy a book"). After reading it, the woman could bring it back to exchange for another. According to the legend, the earliest women's script on the altar was not written with a brush but embroidered with silk floss on silk fabric and stored in rolls.

Legends are the traces of history. From the legends surrounding women's script we can learn the following: First, the form of the women's script is related to patterns in women's needlework. Second, the form of the women's script is related to Chinese characters. It is a variation not intended to be understood by everyone. Third, the women's script records the local dialect. Fourth, the women's script was created by women out of necessity to protect their own interests. Fifth, the social value of the women's script was to give women a way of exchanging feelings. These legends provide important information and references in investigating the origins and creation of the women's script.

Research shows that the women's script may have been the creation of one or a number of women in ancient times with a certain level of education who simplified and modified Chinese characters, blending in aspects of women's embroidery to create characters with a female flair. The women's script modified and simplified Chinese characters, incorporating the linguistic features of the local dialect. It was probably developed after Chinese characters were standardized.

CONSTRUCTION OF THE CHARACTERS IN THE WOMEN'S SCRIPT

The external form of the characters in the women's script is characterized by an oblong shape, which is higher on the right and lower on the left. The characters are slanted and spare, with no superfluous lines. They appear at first glance to be oracle bone script, yet they are completely different. Initially they look indecipherable, but upon closer scrutiny, one can discern the traces of many familiar Chinese characters. The women's script borrows many Chinese characters and other Chinese-style dialectical characters, but is different from the written language of ethnic minorities. The script was created not by merely cutting and pasting elements from existing characters but by creating new characters based on Chinese characters. The orthography, strokes, and components of Chinese characters were actively modified, as were some of the principles of creating characters to organically combine Chinese characters into the women's script system. The creators of the women's script strove for simplicity, ease of writing, and phonetic flexibility in the characters. Chinese characters were borrowed in the following ways:

1. Borrowing of the entire character and changing the layout from square to slanted. There are approximately one hundred of these characters, such as *tian* (field), *ri* (sun), *jia* (shell), *wang* (to flee), *ping* (flat), *dao* (knife), *xiao* (small), and *nan* (man). Some of these borrowed characters are reversed and written on a slant, such as *da* (large), *chun* (spring), *qi* (seven), *tian* (heaven), and *fu* (husband). Many of the characters are simplified, such as *ya* (inferior), *lai* (to come), *hao* (name), *shuang* (a pair), *bian* (to change), *sheng* (saint), *fen* (tomb), *dan* (to carry on the shoulders with a pole), and *dou* (dipper).

2. The orthography of the character has been slightly modified, but the original Chinese character from which it was borrowed is still discernable. There are approximately one hundred of these characters, such as *zuo* (yesterday), *ku* (to cry), *wu* (five), *zuo* (to do), *nü* (woman), *ni* (you), *dan* (thin), *wen* (written language), *jian* (to fry), *cha* (tea), *you* (to be), *ying* (hero), *chu* (kitchen), and *xiu* (to repair).

3. Characters have been greatly modified but still contain recognizable traces of Chinese characters. There are approximately two hundred of these characters, such as *yang* (sheep), *ting* (to hear), *wei* (to do), *qi* (wife), *qu* (to go), *yu* (fish), *lian* (to join), *guang* (light), *he* (to combine), *xiang* (each other), *duo* (many), *jiao* (scorched), *zu* (ancestor), and *wu* (none).

4. Characters have been created by modifying Chinese characters or borrowing elements from them to serve as phonetic symbols. These phonetic symbols comprise 130 groups of homophones, with approximately ten words per homophone group.

Together, the first three types comprise more than 50 percent of the women's script characters. The remainder of the characters are the phonetic symbols of the fourth type.

The women's script typically uses a one-character phonetic symbol to record a series of homophonous (or nearly homophonous) words. This is the primary means of recording the language using the women's script and is also the reason for its simplicity and ease of use. For example, in the women's script the character *fu* (father) also represents the homophonous words for "woman," "deputy," "to pay," "to carry on one's back," "to congratulate," "rotten," and so on. The character *wang* (king) represents the words for "round," "first," "original," "source," "edge," "garden," "whole," and the surname Yuan. When new inventions appear and new terms are coined for them, the women's script does not need to create new characters but can represent a word like "government" by using the existing characters. For example, the modified character *tian* (field) can represent the words for "sweet," "to fill," "electricity," "pad," "palace," and so on. The modified form of the character *shi* (to be an official) represents the words for "scholar," "to be," "clan," "market," "test," "to look at," and "to grant." To represent the word for "television" the women's script uses the characters *tian* and *shi*.

Many of the characters in the women's script are related to patterns found in women's needlework. The influence of needlework on the script is twofold. First is the geometric features of the graphs, including symmetry. This use of geometric forms relates to weaving and cross-stitch embroidery, as symmetrical designs are well suited to fabric with a warp and woof. Second is the beautiful curve of the lines, which is related to embroidery, painting, and paper cutting. The beauty of these designs gives the characters of the women's script a uniquely feminine style. Even today, these designs can still be found on fabrics and quilts made by local women. Some of them are clearly incomplete characters in the women's script—most women no longer know what they mean. However, the fact that women's script characters, Chinese characters, and in recent years even English letters are still used in needlework is a testament to the value these local women place on culture and the written word.

The heavy use of phonetic loan characters in the women's script is what makes it diverge fundamentally from Chinese script, developing instead into a phonetic system of writing. Although the women's script is a syllabic system of writing, it is different from Japanese *kana*. Each symbol of Japanese *kana* represents a syllable but generally not an entire unit of meaning. One special feature of the women's script is that a single character is sometimes used to represent homophones of different tones. One symbol in the women's script represents a rough grouping of homophonous (or nearly homophonous) Chinese words with different meanings. It is this feature of the women's script that gives it a unique place in the chain of development of written Chinese. The women's script can be considered linguistically significant for its simplification of the Chinese writing system, representing the most revolutionary and thorough simplification of Chinese characters ever attempted.

The women's script contains many simplified characters (characters written with fewer strokes) that have been used informally by the public since the Song and Yuan (1271–1368) dynasties. This proves that the women's script was a regional, gender-specific modification of Chinese characters that occurred *after* the standardization of written Chinese. The script could not have been created before the Tang (618–907)–Song transition, though some of the characters were created later, after the Song and Yuan dynasties. The development of the women's script reached its peak during the Qing dynasty (1644–1911). Since the beginning of the twentieth century, and particularly after 1949, the popularization of new types of schools meant that women could obtain an education, and the women's script gradually began to fade from the lives of women in Jiangyong.

Based on the slanted appearance of women's script characters, we can see that the script is a transplantation, modification, and reformulation of Chinese characters. The script is a "female" version of Chinese characters.

WHAT LANGUAGE DOES THE WOMEN'S SCRIPT RECORD?

According to census data, the population of Jiangyong County, Hunan province, was 230,000 in 1990. The ethnic Han population numbered 100,000, and the Yao nationality population numbered 116,000. The population of other minorities numbered approximately 4,000. The Yao language is generally spoken in areas with the greatest concentration of Yao people. Most Yao people living in areas where the population is mixed speak the dialect of the local Han Chinese and southwestern Mandarin. The other minorities generally speak the same dialect of Chinese as the local Han population.

Comparisons of phonology show that the dialect of Hunan historically has many corresponding phonological features with other Chinese dialects. It is a dialect of Chinese and not an ethnic minority language. The Chinese dialect spoken in Jiangyong County is roughly divided into southern and northern variants, which are not mutually intelligible. The southern variant of the dialect is mainly distributed in the Tao River region. The northern variant is mainly found in the Yongming River region. The northern variant recorded by the women's script can also be divided into two subdialects. One subdialect is spoken in suburban areas and is known as the "upper street language." The other subdialect, spoken in the town of Shangjiangxu and in the Tong Mountains, is known as the "lower road language."

The differences between these local dialects and subdialects are considerable, and this raises an important question: Did the pronunciation of the women's script change based on the location where it was read, or was there one general phonological model? And if there was only one model, then which area of Jiangyong County served as the standard? We believe this question has significance in determining the origins of the women's script. Our investigations have shown that, just as Beijing pronunciation is now used as the phonological standard for modern Mandarin, the women's script of Jiangyong had a clear model as well: the suburban dialect, or "upper street language." In the Shangjiangxu area and others where the women's script was used, when the local pronunciation of a word differed from its pronunciation in the suburban dialect, the local women generally preferred to use the suburban pronunciation of the word to read the women's script and not the local pronunciation. They believed that "it sounds better this way."

Several factors point to the origin of the women's script. Based on the cultural categories of the works written in the script, the relation of the women's script characters to Chinese characters and their place in the development of written Chinese, the relationship between the women's script and the dialects of Jiangyong, and the standard pronunciation of the women's script, we can conclude the following: The women's script could not have originated among ethnic minorities. The women's script could not have predated oracle bone script. The women's script did not originate in the rural areas of Jiangyong. It must have developed from the dialect spoken in the suburban areas of Jiangyong County.

FUNCTION OF THE WOMEN'S SCRIPT

Thanks to historical progress, women today can learn to read just as men do and use the form of writing common throughout society. The women's script is no longer necessary, and only a very few people can still read it. However, there must be a reason why the women's script was passed down until modern times. The script must have had a social function in the lives of lower-class women under the old system.

The women's script served as a tool for social interaction within a group and as a cohesive force. Use of the script was limited, however, to an isolated geographic area and to specific groups of women living there. The geographic range in which the women's script was used had a radius of less than a hundred miles, and the users of the women's script included only women living in a predominantly agricultural sphere. It was not a tool for communicating with the entire society but, rather, a device used only by ordinary rural women, united by status, fate, emotions, and cultural yearnings. The psychological and cultural traits common to these women, who were all part of the lower classes of society, gave the women's script a tremendous cohesive power. The special cultural power of the women's script brought women of modest means scattered throughout small villages together in sworn sisterhood groups whose activities included writing and singing works in the women's script. The cohesive force of the script greatly increased women's self-awareness and group consciousness.

The women's script also functioned as entertainment and as a psychological coping mechanism. The appreciation of culture, amusement, venting one's feelings, relieving psychological burdens, sympathy, exchange, and balance are all basic human psychological needs. Under the old feudal code of propriety, the social mores expressed in the sayings "a woman without talent is virtuous," "women are to be subservient," "the husband is the guiding force for his wife," and "in giving and receiving men and women should not touch each other" limited the sphere of women to the home. Their only opportunities to get out were to return to their parents' homes or to visit relatives. Excluded from the political, economic, and cultural life of the society, women had no freedom of movement or social interaction. However, "reading papers and reading fans," the sung literature of the singing hall, served as a type of folk art in which groups of women participated, performed for each other's enjoyment, and learned to appreciate themselves. It was in this way that they sang stories of the past and present and sang narratives of people's lives. In this way they could fully vent their grief and speak out against unfairness. Friendships with sworn sisters brought them sympathy and understanding, and they found solace in the beautiful spiritual world that they constructed for themselves. This unique world created by women was a world of freedom for women. Only in these closed, single-gender communities could women enjoy equality, freedom, and a type of refinement. The women's writings, women's songs, female friendships, and needlework constituted the culture of the women's script, giving women a way to cope socially and psychologically by expressing and affirming themselves. These free interactions and activities allowed the women to vent their feelings of bitterness, depression, and even hopelessness, and to achieve a kind of balance. They could then face their fates bravely, bear the hardships of their lives, and continually strive for new lives. Thus the functions of entertainment and coping served as a kind of aesthetic force.

The women's script also had customary and ritual functions as an embodiment of culture. For example, only the culture of the women's script has the third-day congratulatory letter, which not only served as a marker of the bride's status and that of her family but also became an indispensable part of local wedding celebrations. Rituals are social values manifested in a standard, programmatic, systematic form. The consolidation of certain rituals and customs allowed the women's script to develop from an expression of women's needs into a necessity for the entire community. This point is especially important because it means that the community recognized the women's script and affirmed its social value. The ritual function of the women's script was one of the driving forces behind its longevity.

In the culture of motherhood, the women's script also had a pedagogical function that was expressed not only among the groups of women but also in the early education of children. Under the old system in which culture was monopolized by a small number of people, the masses of working people, particularly women, did not have the right to an education. Their social history, knowledge, life skills, and moral training could only be obtained orally from the older generation, through their own experiences, and through the appreciation of folk arts. The women's script served as a writing system and a literature, allowing women's intelligence and talents to flourish and nurture others. The varied themes of works in the women's script allowed women to gain knowledge and a sense of morality as they passed on the culture of the women's script. The women's script functioned as a kind of moral, aesthetic, and intellectual education.

This educational function is revealed in many lively folk riddles and rhymes, such as: "If we don't plant in the spring / there will be no blooms all year long. / At certain times beans bear fruit / At other times watermelons bear fruit" ("The Moon," *Jicheng*). The women's script literature includes folk wisdom on agriculture, such as "The Twenty-Four Divisions of the Lunar Calendar"; admonishments to filial piety like "Ten Months of Pregnancy"; and songs against gambling and other vices. The women in the singing halls not only entertained each other and relieved their grief; they also passed on information and conducted a simple form of moral counseling.

As visible symbols of a language, the women's script, like other forms of writing, served the function of substantiating and storing the language. The written characters allowed women to write down songs in the women's script, converting an oral literature to a written one. This raised the quality of the women's cultural lives and provided them with enjoyment. Older women who still remember the women's script are frank about their creative motivations: "to write women's literature to be circulated everywhere." They were not willing to be swallowed up by society without a sound. Third-day letters, song fans, and song handkerchiefs written in the women's script were used as gifts and cherished for a lifetime. When women who could read and write the women's script died, any women's script items that had not been given away to family and friends were buried with the woman for her use in the next world. The women's script literature is a special kind of female expression that uses a visible, tangible form of substantiation to record the fates and struggles of women. The script stores their ideals and strivings, and preserves the affection and comfort shared among sworn sisters.

It is for these reasons that the women's script was valuable and necessary and passed down continuously from generation to generation for hundreds of years. We can also see here the limitations of the women's script—it did not constitute a threat to the old system of male domination over women. The functions of the women's script were limited to the cultural and spiritual spheres.

REFERENCES

Huang Xuezhen. *Jiangyong fangyan yanjiu* (Study of the Dialects of Jiangyong). Beijing: Shehuikexue wenxian chubanshe, 1993.

Lin Huixiang. "Lun changzhu niangjia fengsudi qiyuan ji muxizhi dao fuxizhidi guodu" (Discussion of the Custom of Brides' Remaining in Their Parents' Homes and the Transition from a Matrilineal to Patrilineal System), *Xiamen daxue xuebao*, Vol. 4, 1962.

Shi Jinbo, Bai Bin, and Zhao Liming. *Qitedi nüshu* (The Mysterious Women's Script). Beijing: Beijing yuyan xueyuan chubanshe, 1995.

Zhao Liming. "Nüshu di wenzixue jiazhi" (A Philological Study of the Women's Script), *Huazhong shifandaxue xuebao* (Academic Journal of the Huazhong Normal University) (1989); reprinted *Xinhua wenzhai* (Xinhua Abstracts), Vol. 3, 1990.

———. *Nüshu yu nüshu wenhua* (The Women's Script and the Culture of the Women's Script). Beijing: Xinhua chubanshe, 1995.

———. *Zhongguo nüshu jicheng* (Collection of the Chinese Women's Script). Beijing: Qinghua daxue chubanshe, 1992.

Zhao Liming and Li Lan. "Jiangyong tuhuadi neibu chayi yu nüshudi guifan duyin—nüshu qiyuan xintan" (The Internal Differences in the Dialects of Jiangyong and the Standard Pronunciation of the Women's Script—A New Exploration of the Origin of the Women's Script). In Zhao Liming and Huang Guoying, eds., *Hanzidi yingyong yu chuanbo* (The Application and Transmission of Chinese Characters). Beijing: Huayu jiaoxue chubanshe, 2000.

———. "Lun nüshudi qiyuan" (A Discussion of the Origins of the Women's Script). In City of Fanyu Gazetteer Committee, *Fanyuxian zhi, fengsu* (Gazetteer of Fanyu County, Folk Customs). Guangzhou: Guangdong renmin chubanshe, 1995.

Part II

Women
and
Changing
China

The Awakening of Chinese Women and the Women's Movement in the Early Twentieth Century

Lu Meiyi

Chinese society saw unprecedented and diverse changes in the early twentieth century. The intellectual world was more active than ever before, and many new ideas emerged. The main thrust of these new ideas was the pursuit of bourgeois democracy. The development of democratic thought, the deepening struggle of anti-imperialist patriotism, and the rise of a bourgeois democratic revolution propelled the women's liberation movement in China to new heights. Forward-thinking intellectual women formed the backbone of the women's liberation movement.

INTELLECTUAL WOMEN OF THE EARLY TWENTIETH CENTURY

In the early twentieth century, a new group of women appeared in China—intellectual women. Their emergence was a product of the modernization of China's educational system and an important indication that Chinese women's lives were changing. Education for women began late in the Qing dynasty (1644–1911). Initially introduced by Western missionaries, schools were later founded privately by Chinese groups and then by the government as the educational system became public. China's earliest school for girls was the Ningbo Girls School, founded in 1844 by one Miss Aldersay of the British Oriental Society for the Advancement of Girls' Education. In June 1898, at the height of the Reform Movement of 1898, the first girls' school founded by Chinese, the Jingzheng Girls School (also known as the China Female Students Association School), opened in Shanghai. In 1907 the Qing regime promulgated the charter for China's first public girls' schools, and education for girls took its initial steps toward a formal legal status. Due to the development of education for girls, a corps of intellectual women numbering in the tens of thousands emerged in China at the beginning of the twentieth century.[1]

The development of this group of intellectuals coincided with the rise in popularity of Western doctrines of democracy, which were being introduced in China at the time. Enlightening Western theories, including Charles Darwin's theory of evolution and Jean-Jacques Rousseau's theory of people's rights, were widely translated and circulated throughout China. The history and theories of the women's movement in the West, such as Herbert Spencer's doctrine of women's rights, Madame Roland's heroism in the French Revolution, efforts made by the leader of the Russian nihilist school, Sophia Perowskaja, and others were introduced to China. The viewpoints of Karl Marx and Friedrich Engels on women's issues were published in various periodicals. People in China who were concerned about women's issues began to study them from the perspective of bourgeois doctrines and wrote treatises advocating women's rights, such as *Nüjie zhong* (Women's Bell, published 1903). The traditional notion of men's superiority over women was called into question, and bourgeois ideas about marriage and the family, the anarchist "revolution to destroy the family," and other ideas came to the fore. Nurtured by democratic ideas, many intellectual women gained not only new knowledge but also new ideas and new ways of thinking. Public remarks such as "Since people like us have been born into this world, we should enjoy the right to freedom. The right to freedom is sacred and inviolable" show the awakening of Chinese women.[2]

Some intellectual women consciously linked the pursuit of women's liberation with the struggle to overthrow the Qing dynasty. These women constituted the backbone of the women's movement and were followers of the bourgeois democratic style of revolution. Approximately two hundred women intellectuals participated in the anti-Qing revolutionary group the Tongmenghui (United League, or Revolutionary Alliance), led by Sun Yat-sen. Qiu Jin (1875–1907) is one of their most outstanding representatives. In 1904 she left her husband, a bureaucrat in the Qing government with whom she shared neither values nor affection, and went to Japan as a student. She wrote many poems and articles championing women's rights and founded women's publications and schools to promote women's liberation. Qiu also served as a chief organizer of the United League's Zhejiang province branch and as a coordinator of the Xing Ming hui (Restoration Society). While helping to organize an uprising in Anhui and Zhejiang provinces, she was arrested and executed. She was only thirty years old. She has been hailed as a model for contemporary Chinese revolutionary women. Some women intellectuals actively participated in the practical work of the women's movement but, for various reasons, were not directly involved in political struggles. Lü Bicheng and her sisters, for example, worked on education for girls.[3] Some intellectual women, many of them the wives of officials, did not participate directly in the women's movement at all but still held views that supported women's liberation. Shan Shili and others who followed their husbands on diplomatic trips to Japan and Europe belonged to this category of women.[4]

THE RAPID DEVELOPMENT OF THE WOMEN'S MOVEMENT

The women's movement in China, which began at the end of the nineteenth century during the Reform Movement of 1898, grew rapidly during the first decade of the twentieth century.[5] First, women's groups began to emerge. Many women believed that: "If we don't form groups, women's rights cannot succeed, and if women's rights do not succeed, we will always be repressed by the family."[6] Between 1901 and 1911 more than forty women's associations and groups formed (Lü and Zheng, 1990, 170–173). Many were well organized, had clear guiding principles, and conducted regular activities. There were several types of organizations, and most of the groups that favored agitation for women's liberation were also keen on political struggle. Other groups focused exclusively on the goal of women's rights, while some concentrated on improving society or doing charitable work. The Public Benevolence Society, the Society to Ensure Education for Girls, the Hygiene Society, and the Chinese Women's Society were all representatives of the different types formed during this period. Once women had formed their own groups, they began to participate in social life and to strive for their own benefits.

The number of women's publications also increased rapidly, with nearly forty new journals appearing during this ten-year period. Women were involved in planning finances, writing articles, editing, and distributing these periodicals. *Nüxue bao* (Chinese Girl's Progress) by Chen Xiefen, *Zhongguo nübao* (China Women's Gazette), and many others created by women who went to study abroad in Japan had a tremendous impact on women. Beginning in 1907, *Zhongguo xinnüjie zazhi* (New Chinese Women's Magazine), which was founded in Tokyo, was published in Japan and China and had a circulation of up to five thousand copies per volume. Subsequently, because the magazine advocated assassination as a means of furthering the women's revolution, the Japanese government halted its publication. Women's publications played an important role in publicizing the idea of women's liberation, in transmitting new knowledge, and in communicating with society and expressing women's own demands.

The founding of schools for girls and the campaign against footbinding were the most successful activities of the women's movement of the early twentieth century. These campaigns targeted the outmoded notion that "a woman without talent is bound to be virtuous" and the Chinese custom of footbinding, which hobbled women both spiritually and physically. The missionaries were the first to lobby on these issues, and the Chinese women's movement took its point of departure from them.[7]

The campaign against footbinding first manifested itself as an increase in awareness. More and more people came to realize that footbinding was not only detrimental to women's health and the physical quality of the nation's people but also violated the rights of women who were "the mothers of the people." As the influence of the campaign began to spread, local governments in eighteen provinces promulgated directives banning footbinding. Groups opposed to footbinding spread from the cities to rural areas. The Natural Feet Society, founded by a British woman named Mrs. Alicia Bewicke Little (1845–1926), distributed more than 100,000 pamphlets across the nation and held many mobilization meetings attended by thousands.[8] The number of women who did not bind their feet grew rapidly, and, according to some accounts, 80 to 90 percent of the women in Guangzhou and other large cities stopped binding their feet. However, the practice of footbinding proved to be extremely stubborn, and it was not completely eliminated until decades later.

The development of education for girls began with the founding of private girls' schools and was then followed by a wave of publicly founded girls' schools. Well-known girls' schools such as the Shanghai Patriotic Girls' School, the Wuben Girls' School, and the Tianjin Northern Girls' School were founded at this time. Progressive thinkers considered the education of girls to be a precondition for saving the nation and promoting women's rights, and women were directly involved in these efforts. In 1906, Hui Xing, principal of the Zhenwen Girls' School in Hangzhou, committed suicide because of difficulties in finding money for the school, sending shock waves through the community. By 1909, there were 308 girls schools (not including those set up by missionaries), which were either elementary or secondary schools, and a total of 14,054 female students (Chen Yilin 100). In addition, some female students studied abroad. The development of education for girls created the conditions for the general improvement in the quality of women's lives and their integration into all aspects of society.

The great successes achieved by the antifootbinding campaigns and the girls' education movement were due in part to the active participation and support they received from the revolutionary factions, reform factions, and the Qing government. Although these three groups differed in their political inclinations, they constituted a united force that propelled these movements forward.

DEVOTING THEIR LIVES TO THE ANTI-IMPERIALIST PATRIOTIC STRUGGLE

One of the main topics of contemporary Chinese politics has been how to save the nation. During the Reform Movement of 1898, intellectual women made the resounding statement: "Women also bear some responsibility for the rise and fall of the world."[9] Real action, however, did not take place until the beginning of the twentieth century.

The Women's Movement in the Early 20th Century

Between the beginning of the twentieth century and the revolution of 1911, progressive women, mostly intellectuals, actively participated in a series of patriotic campaigns. In some people's opinions, participation in these activities was the duty of women and a political right. In order to resist the designs of czarist Russia to seize the northeastern section of China, between 1901 and 1905 the Chinese staged many campaigns against Russia. The women of Shanghai joined in this effort by founding the Anti-Russia Society of Women Comrades and made it known that they were "willing to go to the battlefield" when it became necessary. Chinese women studying abroad in Japan also formed organizations, circulated petitions, raised funds, and conducted other activities. Some students abroad even enlisted in militias to resist the Russians and were prepared to return home to join the battle.[10] In 1905, an anti-American patriotic campaign started to oppose American mistreatment of Chinese laborers and to demand the nullification of treaties that were unfavorable to the Chinese. Women in Shanghai, Guangzhou, and some cities in the provinces of Jiangsu and Zhejiang began a boycott of American products. During the Rights Recovery Campaign of 1907, the Shanghai Women's Society of Comrades to Protect the Railway sent representatives to Beijing to present a petition and raised funds of nearly 100,000 yuan, contributing to the effort to regain control of the Shanghai-Hangzhou-Ningbo Railway.

The emergence of women in the anti-imperialist patriotic campaigns proved that they were a political force that could not be ignored. One article in *Nüzi shijie* (Women's World) that displayed women's intense patriotic fervor stated that women had to prove with actions that "the will of the Chinese people does not die, and the will of Chinese women does not die either."

THE HEROISM OF INTELLECTUAL WOMEN DURING THE TURBULENCE OF THE 1911 REVOLUTION

During the 1911 Revolution, a watershed moment in Chinese history ending thousands of years of absolute monarchy, many women joined together under the banner of the United League. In the midst of armed uprisings, these women ran secret gatherings and networks, provided cover for their comrades, raised funds, transported weapons, made bombs, and did other tasks to help the cause. After the Wuchang uprising on 10 October, women members of the United League all over China joined in the struggle to overthrow the Qing dynasty. Zhang Mojun (Zhang Zhaohan) participated in secret gatherings during the liberation of Suzhou, writing banners and drafting announcements to prepare for the uprising. Yin Ruizhi and her sister Yin Weijun participated in the battles to take Shanghai, Hangzhou, and Nanjing. They threw bombs and joined in the assault on the provincial Zhejiang governor's office building.

Students from the Practical Girls' School in Hong Kong joined in the rebellion to liberate Guangdong. Women in the north, who up to that point had been more reserved, also started secret networks and printed leaflets. Under the leadership of the faculty and students of the First Girls' School, women in the north carried satchels packed with explosives and boarded trains to deliver weapons to their destinations. Women also took care of those injured in battle and raised funds to pay the soldiers. The director of the Shanghai Hospital, Zhang Jujun, personally led a group of 120 members of the Red Cross (54 of whom were women) to Wuhan, where they braved gunfire to rescue 1,300 wounded fighters. Zhang was wounded during the rescue mission. In early 1912, during the most difficult time for the newly founded Republic of China, the Shanghai Women's Assistance Society sent a delegation to Nanjing to present interim president Sun Yat-sen with funds they had raised.

During this period, the sudden rise of women's revolutionary militias created the greatest impact on society. After the rebels took over the three towns that make up Wuhan, a nineteen-year-old woman named Wu Shuqing repeatedly petitioned to join the military and received the approval of the military government. She organized the "women's revolutionary army," and several hundred young women enlisted. They were involved in pitched battles with the Qing army near Hankou and earned a sensational reputation. Women members of the United League in Guangdong organized the Guangdong Women's Northern Expeditionary Army, numbering nearly one hundred. After a brief period of training, these women followed the Northern Expeditionary Army to the frontlines in Xuzhou. A number of women's armies formed in Shanghai, including the Northern Expeditionary Women's Dare-to-Die Corps, the Women's Militia, and the Shanghai Women's People's Army. Each of these armies consisted of dozens or even hundreds of volunteers. Although most of these women's armies were not directly involved in actual combat, these women recruits were widely praised in society. Many newspapers lauded them as "the purest" and "the most tenacious" of China's four hundred million people. Sun Yat-sen praised the contributions made by women during the 1911 Revolution, saying that their "dauntless efforts in national affairs" showed a spirit "on par with the heroes of every province."[11]

THE FIRST WAVE OF WOMEN'S PARTICIPATION IN POLITICS

In the process of establishing a new political regime after the 1911 Revolution, some intellectual women took the "suffragist" movement in Britain as their model, giving rise to a wave of political participation by women. These women believed that the contributions made by women during the revolution had earned them the right to participate in politics.

The Women's Movement in the Early 20th Century

In November 1911, many women's political groups appeared in Shanghai, Nanjing, and other locations. The primary organizations included the Women's League for Political Participation, the Shenzhou (Divine Land) Women's Political Participation League, and the Shenzhou Women's Republican Society. Representatives from the women's communities paid repeated visits to President Sun Yat-sen and organized petition drives demanding that the "Provisional Constitution" affirm women's right to political participation. In his letter responding to this demand, Sun Yat-sen wrote, "There is no disparity between men and women in terms of God-given rights, . . . In the future, women's right to participate in politics is inevitable."[12] However, the Provisional Constitution amended by the interim legislature did not include language guaranteeing equality of the sexes or women's right to political participation, a fact that women bitterly resented. Beginning on 19 March 1912, the radicals, represented by Tang Qunying, repeatedly stormed into the legislature, where they engaged in heated debates with the legislators and got into scuffles with the security personnel posted at the doors, angrily smashing the glass doors in the process.[13] An uproar in public opinion ensued on whether women had the ability to participate in politics, what the natural vocation of women was, and whether women's participation in politics would be detrimental to the family and society. Newspapers carried a lively debate on the subject. Most people at the time either had doubts about women's participation in politics or rejected the idea altogether.

In February 1912, the political maverick Yuan Shikai took over as interim president in Beijing, and with his ascension to office the bourgeois republic died an early death and a pall was cast over the women's movement. In April, women's political organizations from every province held a conference in Nanjing, where they formed a unified Women's League for Political Participation. They decided to go north to continue their struggle. In August, the Guomindang (Nationalist Party) held a conference in Beijing at which the party was formally founded. Its political platform also failed to include language on equality of the sexes, which so incensed Tang Qunying and others that they twice came to blows with the chairman of the conference. Sun Yat-sen, who by that time had resigned from the office of president, was powerless to do anything about the situation. In his "Letter to the Women of the League for Political Participation," he wrote, "On the issue of equality of the sexes, I have always advocated it and was the first to put it into practice. . . . With regard to the issue of the omission of equality of the sexes in the party platform, this is the consensus reached by the majority of the men, and not something a minority can change." He admonished the women: "Do not rely on men to make efforts on your behalf, so that you will not be used by men."[14]

International women's organizations tried to help the struggling Chinese women. From August to September 1912, the president of the recently founded International Woman Suffrage Association, the American Carrie Chapman Catt, and the president of the Dutch branch of the association, Aletta Jacobs, made a trip to China. They met with leaders of the women's political participation movement in Shanghai, Nanjing, Tianjin, and Beijing, and attended meetings hosted by women's communities in many locations. Catt praised the wisdom and competence of Chinese women and suggested that they avoid extreme measures to gain political rights for women. Instead, she suggested that they found women's schools, improve the social climate, and expand publicity on the issue to prepare the way for women's political participation. Her suggestions were warmly received by the moderates. After leaving China, Catt kept in contact with the Chinese women's organizations.[15]

In November 1912, the legislature again deliberated the issue of the petition presented by Tang Qunying and others. Only six votes were cast in favor of the petition, so it was defeated. Although ten women served as legislators in the interim provincial legislature of Guangdong, their presence did not have a wide-ranging social impact. The first campaign for women's participation in politics finally ended in defeat. One of the reasons for this outcome was that, as bourgeois political parties, the United League and the populist Guomindang valued the strength shown by women during the revolution when they were opposing the parties' political enemies, but when women demanded a share of political rights, these political parties protected the interests of men. Another reason was that the women's movement was weak and lacked effective organization and mature leadership and strategies.

FROM "THE DISCOVERY OF MAN" TO "THE DISCOVERY OF WOMAN"— THE MAY FOURTH MOVEMENT AND WOMEN'S LIBERATION

Yuan Shikai's establishment of the Northern Warlords regime meant taking a step backward to earlier times. To counter this backsliding trend, beginning in 1916 intellectual circles developed a new intellectual movement—the New Culture movement, which criticized old ways of thinking, old morals, and the old culture. Women's issues became a focus of concern.

During the Reform Movement of 1898 and the 1911 Revolution, people were concerned about women's duty and their rights. During the period of the New Culture movement the emphasis was on the independent personality of women. Some people pointed out: "a woman should have personality, because she is a 'person' among the masses!" Throughout history, "the cause of women's misfortune has been that women's personality is incomplete—or nonexistent."[16] The issue of women's chastity became an early focus of discussion. In May 1918, Zhou Zuoren translated and published *Zhencao lun* (The Doctrine of

The Women's Movement in the Early 20th Century

Chastity) by the Japanese female scholar Yosano Akiko. Hu Shi published articles titled "Zhencao wenti" (The Question of Chastity) and "Lun zhencao
wenti" (Discussion on the Question of Chastity), which severely criticized the
old feudal concept of chastity. Discussions of women's issues during the New
Culture movement touched on nearly every problem related to women's liberation. Li Dazhao, Chen Duxiu, Lu Xun, Hu Shi, Wu Yu, and other famous
scholars repeatedly voiced their opinions in *Xin qingnian* (New Youth) and
other magazines. During this period, everyone who aligned him- or herself
with the New Culture movement was in favor of equality of the sexes, and progressive views on women were widely disseminated.

The May Fourth movement, which shook both China and the world,
erupted in China on 4 May 1919. The movement was initially prompted by
anger over the refusal of European nations at the Paris peace talks following
World War I to allow China to recover Shandong province (seized by Japan in
1914) and indignation that the corrupt Northern Warlord regime was prepared
to sign the treaty. Long-simmering public discontent finally erupted. On 4
May, thousands of Beijing students gathered in Tiananmen Square to demonstrate. They also burned the Zhao building, the residence of the traitors who
had sold out the country. Female students were kept away from the demonstrations by school authorities.

The first women to respond to the May Fourth movement were students in
Beijing. When the students at the Beijing Women's Senior Normal School
heard about the burning of the Zhao building, they were encouraged to join
with other girls' schools to form the Beijing Women Students Alliance. They
broke free of the repression by the schools and their families and joined in a
series of strikes organized by the citywide league. On 4 June, fifteen girls'
schools conducted their own demonstration march and petition drive to protest
the unreasonable arrest of students by the authorities. Ignoring threats and
attempts to prevent them from participating, the students of the Women's
Senior Normal School knocked down the wall surrounding the school, chanted
slogans, and gave speeches as they marched. Once the students from all the
schools had gathered in Tiananmen Square, they proceeded to the presidential
office building, where they presented their petitions. There was a terrible sand-
storm that day, and heavily armed police forces followed the demonstrators
closely, but the students were not intimidated. The students at the Women's
Senior Normal School also successfully drove out the school's president, who
had been very repressive to the students, and forced the Ministry of Education
to relieve him of his post.

The female students in Tianjin and Shanghai quickly rallied to support the
students in Beijing. The students in Tianjin staged gatherings and marches and
went to the capital to present petitions. On 10 October, people from all walks

of life gathered at the Nankai Middle School in Tianjin, and the female students and their comrades from the women's community formed the outermost circle of the crowd, taking the lead as the march got under way. Two female students were injured when the demonstrators encountered military police armed with guns. The courageous initiative shown by the female students was widely praised by the public. In Shanghai, twenty-four girls' schools joined the Shanghai Student Alliance and joined with the boys' schools to organize a general strike of classes. Beginning on 3 June, female students also participated in the famous triple strike struggle (a workers' strike, a students' strike, and a strike by businesspeople). By mid-June, nineteen provinces across the nation were conducting activities in response to the student movement in Beijing. A telegram from the women's community in Hunan read, "Better to be a shattered piece of jade than an intact piece of clay. Although we are women, we pledge to fight to the death as the shield that protects the nation's people."[17] Some of the female students even cut their fingers to write messages in blood to show their patriotic resolve. Female students everywhere were active in the boycott of Japanese products. Many of them took to the streets or went deep into the countryside to spread the message. Some established "patriotic shops" that sold products for daily use that the female students had made themselves. In the May Fourth movement Chinese women relied on the strength they had gained by organizing to mobilize a broad range of people at all levels of society. In addition to establishing female student alliances, this general mobilization also established a variety of influential women's groups. Female students were the main force and backbone of the women's community, and many outstanding women emerged from their ranks. These women were not only influential within the women's community but also became quite well known by the general public. Groups of women workers were a newly emerging force, and although they did not yet have independent organizations and activities, they actively participated in the triple strike struggle. This was the first time women workers had fought for a political objective, showing that the political consciousness of women workers had been awakened. The waves of patriotism also shattered the isolation of traditional households, and many housewives joined in the boycott of Japanese products. Even prostitutes, who were at the lowest level of society, responded positively to the movement. In Shanghai, Suzhou, and other places, prostitutes "went on strike" (refused to service their patrons). They also formed "bordello associations to save the nation," raising funds and expressing sympathy for the patriotic students. In religious circles, the YWCA (Young Women's Christian Association) and other groups clearly stated their support for the patriotic movement. The women's lofty patriotic fervor and outstanding accomplishments in organizing and conducting activities showed society that, as a group, women had broken away from the auxiliary role they had played during the Reform Movement of 1898 and the 1911 Revolution and had become one of the main forces in the movement.

The May Fourth movement had two clear themes: anti-imperialist patriotism, and democracy and science. The patriotic democracy movement spurred the women's movement to new heights and presented a comprehensive challenge to traditional unequal gender relationships.

The first struggle was for equal educational rights for men and women. The New Culture movement had exposed and attacked the inequities in education for men and women. Prior to the May Fourth movement, primary and secondary schools accepted female students, and primary schools were coeducational. However, except for universities founded by missionaries, the Chinese-run universities did not implement coeducation.[18] In the spring of 1919, some of the faculty and students of Peking University began to discuss the question of coeducation through newspaper articles. On 19 May, a twenty-three-year-old primary school teacher named Deng Chunlan wrote a letter to Peking University president Cai Yuanpei, calling on the university to lift the ban on women. In her letter, she stated that equality in all things should be based on equality in education. With the support of the university, in the spring of 1920 Peking University allowed Deng Chunlan, Wang Lan, and nine other female students to audit classes. This action shook the world of education. After the summer term, Peking University and other universities began formally admitting female students. Many universities subsequently lifted the ban on female students. By 1922 there were 887 female university students, which was 2.6 percent of the national total.[19] The lifting of the ban on female students by universities was a major milestone in the development of women's education.

"Open social interactions" was another urgent demand of the May Fourth youth, in direct opposition to "Men and women are different," a basic principle of traditional Chinese morality. The Confucian ethical code not only kept women and men separate from each other; it also kept women isolated from society. The May Fourth youth courageously broke down traditional concepts and outmoded customs. The patriotic movement promoted liberalized social relationships. Prior to the May Fourth movement, the Xinmin xuehui (New People's Study Group) of Changsha, Hunan, admitted only male students, but after the movement began, it admitted nineteen female members. The association also amended its bylaws, establishing a women's section within the executive department. Female students served as vice committee chairs and evaluators as well as in other positions.

Similarly, the Tianjin Enlightenment Society, founded during the May Fourth movement, established a model for eradicating the "Confucian ethical code" for the entire society. They implemented principles of equal numbers of male and female members and equal rights. Members of the society were issued numbers to use instead of their names to show that the distinction between male and female had been abolished. Among others, Zhou Enlai and Deng Yingchao, who later went on to become leaders in China's political arena, were members of the society. Young men and women members discussed current events openly, participated in activities together, and even "shared offices." Although these actions were criticized and opposed by some, they marked the irreversible collapse of the Confucian ethical code. Across the nation the patriotic struggle to save the nation promoted alliances between young men and women in organizations and actions, creating the greatest driving force behind the liberalization of social relationships.

"Autonomy in marriage" was one of the most resounding slogans of the May Fourth period. Progressive youth of the time were no longer satisfied with condemning the old system of marriage with speeches and in writing; they wanted to take action. Some of them demanded that marriages arranged by their parents be dissolved, while others argued for divorce to end loveless marriages. Some resisted marriage, ran away from home, or even took the extreme step of suicide. The play *A Doll's House* by Henrik Ibsen was translated into Chinese, and Nora's bravery in leaving home encouraged many young men and women. In November 1919, Zhao Wuzhen, a bride in Changsha, protested her arranged marriage by committing suicide in her bridal sedan, an act that stunned the nation and resulted in discussions about altering the unreasonable marriage system. The *Dagong bao* (Dagong Daily) printed many pieces on the subject. The young Mao Zedong published nine articles on the incident, in which he claimed that the death of Zhao "is a result of a corrupt marriage system, a dark social system, a will that cannot be independent, and love that cannot be free."[20] In August of that year Li Chao, a student at the Beijing Women's Senior Normal School, was persecuted so mercilessly by her traditional family that she ended up in the hospital and died. This incident brought about a new round of criticism of the old family system and even resulted in discussions of the issues of women's education and the right of women to inherit property.

By the early twentieth century women had achieved much progress in employment and participation in politics. Most pronouncements on these issues considered economic independence and equal opportunities for employment to be important conditions for women's development. Continuing to heed the rise of female workers as well as a small number of female physicians and teachers, Guangdong was the first place in which women worked as train conductors, telephone operators, and bank tellers. The movement for women's participation in politics also flourished after the May Fourth movement as campaigns for provincial autonomy grew stronger. As a result of the unrelenting struggle by women, the city of Guangzhou and the province of Hunan elected a number of women legislators. Female students in Beijing and Nanjing established women's rights leagues to lobby for the inclusion in the constitution of women's rights to political participation.

The latter part of the May Fourth movement was a time of flourishing development for various branches of socialism, and "reforming society" became the new goal of some progressive youths.[21] In early 1920, some young women in Beijing and Tianjin left home and founded a work-study mutual aid group. Studying and working part time, they attempted to create a new kind of lifestyle through collective labor and living together. Their experiment lasted only a few months, and although it was heavily laden with unrealistic socialist fantasies, it showed a valuable pioneering spirit. From 1919 to 1920, when such programs were at their height of popularity, another group of young women went to France on a work-study program. The Charter of the Work-Study Program in France Association clearly stated its goals: "to reform society and emphasize education. If we want to bring world culture to China, it is necessary to study abroad in Europe."[22] A total of twenty young women went to France. Two of these women, Xiang Jingyu and Cai Chang, learned Marxism there and became well-known women's activists.

As the intellectual community explored the reform of China, beginning in the latter half of 1920, some progressive intellectuals turned to scientific socialism, contributing to the rapid spread of Marxism. Intellectuals attempted to study the problems of Chinese women from that perspective. During this time, many influential articles such as "Funü jiefang yu Democracy" (Women's Emancipation and Democracy) and "Nüzi wenti yu shehuizhuyi" (Women's Issues and Socialism) were written, and new ideas concerning women's emancipation were proposed. One new idea was that women would be truly emancipated only if the existing social system was overthrown. Another idea held that the women's movement had to be divided into "a movement of third-class women" (a movement of bourgeois women) and "a movement of fourth-class women" (a movement of working-class women), and that the center of the women's rights movement should be shifted to the working class.[23] These ideas formed the important theoretical basis for the policies on women eventually adopted by the Chinese Communist Party.

The May Fourth movement influenced an entire era. Its thoroughgoing and uncompromising spirit of resistance against feudalism was the lifelong spiritual pursuit of many women of the time and created the internal momentum of the women's movement of the 1920s and 1930s. At the same time, as the most profound movement of intellectual liberation in contemporary Chinese history, the May Fourth movement disseminated new concepts about women, marriage, and the family, and created a climate of public opinion and social atmosphere conducive to women's emancipation. That era also spawned a generation of women heroes who were both influential and appealing and who became the leaders of the women's movement of the 1920s and 1930s. From the perspective of women's emancipation, the significance of the May Fourth movement lies not only in its immediate impact but also in its laying a foundation for the development of later women's movements.

NOTES

1. In 1877, there were 2,101 female students enrolled in Catholic schools. In 1879, there were 2,791 female students enrolled in Protestant schools. By the early twentieth century at least this many girls were enrolled in missionary schools. In 1909, there were 14,054 students enrolled in girls' schools founded by Chinese. The cumulative total of graduates puts the number of women intellectuals in the tens of thousands.

2. Xu Yucheng, "First Address by Xu Yucheng of Jinkui to the World of Women," *Zhongguo xinnüjie zazhi* (New Chinese Women's Magazine), Vol. 5, 1907.

3. Lü Bicheng (1883–1943) was from Jingde, Anhui. Due to their skill at writing poetry, calligraphy, and painting, she and her two sisters were known as the "three Lüs of western Anhui." In 1903 Lü went to Tianjin to edit *Dagong bao* (Dagong Daily) and participated in the founding of the Beiyang Public Girls' School. She was also a member of the revolutionary literary group Southern Society. In her later years she converted to Buddhism.

4. Shan Shili (1856–1943) was from Xiaoshan, Zhejiang. Beginning in 1899 she accompanied her diplomat husband on trips to Japan, Russia, Italy, and other countries, becoming one of the first women in contemporary Chinese history to travel abroad. Her works *Guimao lüyou ji* (Voyage of 1903) and *Guiqian ji* (Notes on the Quiet Return to Home) reflect her observations and thoughts about the world, as well as her consciousness of women's emancipation.

5. There are different opinions on when the women's movement in China began. Chen Dongyuan argues that it began with the May Fourth movement, but Li Youning and others believe it began with the 1911 Revolution. In recent years, scholars both on the mainland and in Taiwan have suggested that it began during the Reform Movement of 1898. They base this on the antifootbinding campaigns and the development of education for girls that occurred at the time and the appearance of the first women's groups and periodicals. A small number of progressive women were at the early stages of awakening and participated in these events.

6. "Nüzi yi ji jie tuanti lun" (On the Urgent Need for Women to Form Groups), *Zhongguo funübao* (Chinese Women's Gazette), Vol. 2, 1907.

7. In 1875, missionaries in Xiamen organized China's first "Natural Feet Society."

8. "Tianzuhui xingsheng shuwen" (An Account of the Rise of the Natural Feet Society), *Wanguo gongbao* (Chinese Globe Magazine), April 1905.

9. "Quanxing nüxue qi" (Encouraging Women's Education), *Nüxue bao* (Chinese Girl's Progress), Vol. 4, 1898.

10. *Nüzi shijie* (Women's World), Vol. 4, 1904; *Jiangsu*, Vol. 2, 1903.

11. *Minlibao* (People's Gazette), 12 January 1912; *Sun Zhongshan quanji* (Complete Writings of Sun Yat-sen), Vol. 2 (Shanghai: Zhonghua shuju, 1982), 52–53.

12. "Fu nüjie gonghe xiejihui han" (Letter in Response to the Women's Republican Society), *Sun Zhongshan quanji*, Vol. 2, 52–53.

13. Tang Qunying (1871–1937) was from Hengshan, Hunan. Beginning in 1904 she made three trips to Japan to study at her own expense. In 1905 she joined the United League and was a major leader in the movement for women's participation in politics during the period of the 1911 Revolution. She founded several women's publications and was one of the first female members of the Southern Society, a progressive literary society founded in 1909, well-known for its opposition to the Qing government. After the 1920s she devoted herself to women's education.

14. *Sun Zhongshan quanji*, Vol. 2, 438.

15. "Wanguo nüzi canzhenghui xunbao" (Report on the International Woman Suffrage Association), *People's Gazette*, Vol. 1, 5 September 1912; *Shenzhou nübao* (Shenzhou Women's Gazette), Vols. 5 and 7, 1912.

16. "Nüzi renge wenti" (The Question of Women's Personality), *Xin chao* (New Currents), Vol. 1, no. 2, 1919.

17. *Wusi aiguo yundong* (The May Fourth Patriotic Movement), Vol. 1 (Beijing: Zhongquo shehui kexue chubanshe, 1979), 229, 235.

18. In 1905, Protestant missionary groups in China jointly founded the Northern China Women's Allied University, providing the first opportunity for higher education to Chinese women. In 1918, Lingnan University, which was also founded by missionaries, started to admit female students, beginning coeducation at the university level.

19. Yu Qingtang, *Sanshiwu nianlai Zhongguo zhi nüzi jiaoyu* (The Last Thirty-five Years of Women's Education in China). Quoted from Luo Suwen, *Women and Contemporary Chinese Society* (Shanghai: Shanghai renmin chubanshe, 1996).

20. Mao Zedong, "Dui Zhao nüshi zishadi piping" (Critique of the Suicide of Miss Zhao), *Dagong bao* (Dagong Daily) (Changsha), 16 November 1919.

21. The main branches of socialism popular at the time included anarchism, new estate-ism, cooperativism, pan-laborism, and work-studyism.

22. *Liufa qingongjianxue yundong* (The Work-Study in France Movement), Vol. 1 (Shanghai: Shanghai renmin chubanshe, 1980), 11–12.

23. Jian Hong, "Nüquan yundongdi zhongxin ying yidao disi jieji" (The Center of the Women's Rights Movement Should Be Shifted to the Fourth Class), in *Wusi shiqi funü wenti wenxuan* (Writings on Women's Issues During the May Fourth Period) (Beijing: Sanlian shudian, 1981), 94.

REFERENCES

All-China Women's Federation Institute of the History of the Women's Movement. *Zhongguo jindai funü yundong shi ziliao (1840–1918)* (Historical Materials from the Contemporary Women's Movement in China [1840–1918]). Beijing: Zhongguo funü chubanshe, 1991.

Chen Dongyuan. *Zhongguo funü shenghuo shi* (History of the Lives of Chinese Women). Shangwu yinshuguan, 1928.

Chen Sanjing. *Jindai Zhongguo funü yundong shi* (History of the Women's Movement in Contemporary China). Tapei: Jindai Zhongguo chubanshe, 2000.

Chen Yilin. *Zuijin sanshi nian Zhongguo jiaoyushi* (A History of Chinese Education in the Last Thirty Years). Shanghai: Shanghai Pacific Bookstore, 1930.

Cheng Zhefan. *Xiandai nüzi jiaoyu shi* (History of Modern Education for Girls). Shanghai: Zhonghua shuju, 1936.

Fang Hanqi. *Zhongguo jindai baokan shi* (History of Contemporary Chinese Periodicals). Shanxi: Renmin chubanshe, 1981.

Guo Yanli. *Qiu Jin nianpu* (Chronology of Qiu Jin). Shandong: Qilu shushe, 1983.

Li Youning and Zhang Yufa. *Jindai Zhongguo funü yundong shiliao (1842–1911)* (Materials on the History of the Women's Movement in Contemporary China [1842–1911]). Taipei: Zhuanji wenxue chubanshe, 1975.

Liu Jucai. *Zhongguo jindai funü yundong shi* (History of the Contemporary Chinese Women's Movement). Beijing: Zhongguo funü chubanshe, 1989.

Lü Meiyi and Zheng Yongfu. *Zhongguo funü yundong (1840–1921)* (The Chinese Women's Movement [1840–1921]). Zhengzhon: Henan renmin chubanshe, 1990.

Min Jiayin. *Yanggang yu yinroudi bianzou—liangxing guanxi he shehui moshi* (Variations on Men's Strength and Women's Softness—Gender Relations and Social Models). Beijing: Zhongguo shehui kexue chubanshe, 1995.

Tan Sheying. *Zhongguo funü yundong tongshi* (General History of the Chinese Women's Movement). Beijing: Funü gongmingshe, 1936.

Wusi shiqi funü wenti wenxuan (Collected Writings on Women's Issues from the May Fourth Period). Beijing: Sanlian shudian, 1981.

Yao Lingxi. "Cai Fei lu" (Record of Cai Fei). In *Zhongguo funü chanzu shiliao* (Historical Materials on Women's Foot-binding in China). Tianjin: Shidai gongsi, 1934.

Yao Shunsheng. *Zhongguo funü dashiji* (Record of the Great Deeds of Chinese Women). Shanghai: Nüzi shudian, 1932.

Zhang Yufa. *Qingjidi geming tuanti* (Revolutionary Groups in Qing Times). Taipei: Academia Sinica Institute of Contemporary Chinese History, 1975.

THE CHINESE WOMEN'S MOVEMENT BEFORE AND AFTER THE LONG MARCH

Lily Xiao Hong Lee

In October 1934 thirty women began the monumental journey from Ruijin, Jiangxi province, that eventually came to be known as the Long March. Many women from Hubei and Sichuan later joined as well, and although there is no accurate figure on the total number of women who took part in its different stages, there is no doubt it would exceed a thousand.[1] Why did all these women embark on such an arduous odyssey, one that so tested the endurance of men? There must have been as many reasons as there were women. Linking all of them was a consciousness of the poverty of women's lives. Something better was being offered to women in the name of Marxism. This hope for a better life motivated them to become involved with the Chinese Communist Party (CCP) in the first place and, once deeply involved, to follow it on the Long March. At the other end of the equation, because the women on the Long March had shown firm loyalty to the Party and had been effective in political work, after the Long March ended in northern Shaanxi they were the ones entrusted with carrying on "women's work," meaning the organizing of women. They continued this work when the CCP took over the whole of China in 1949. This essay aims to clarify the links between the Long March and the Chinese women's movement by tracing the lives and work of these women and the circumstances under which they joined the Long March. It also attempts to assess what this close relationship meant for both the women and the movement.

THE WOMEN'S MOVEMENT BEFORE THE LONG MARCH

As the nineteenth century drew to a close, Western ideas of gender equality were becoming known in China, often through Japan, as more and more men and women sought educational opportunities in that country. Women members of the Tongmenghui (United League, or Revolutionary Alliance), led by Sun Yat-sen, were important early activists of the women's movement. They wrote articles and published magazines and newspapers calling for the liberation of women and encouraging women to fight for their freedom and become self-reliant.[2] Warlord rule in the early Republican period all but extinguished the fire of the new women's movement, but after the May Fourth movement of 1919 it burned more brightly, with many young female students swelling the ranks. A group of women students in Tianjin was especially important in the fight against imperialism as well as for gender equality. In Hunan, young people gathered together in study groups and were vocal on women's issues. Some women in this group also devoted attention to women's education.

The CCP was formally established in 1921, but in its early years did not fully support the women's movement. Christina Gilmartin points out that the text of the second congress of the CCP clearly indicates that the decision to establish a women's bureau came from the Comintern (Communist International) and had little support among male Chinese communists.[3] Not until the pioneer feminist Xiang Jingyu took up the cause of women was there evidence of interest in this direction. Meanwhile, in the Guomindang (Nationalist Party) camp, women such as He Xiangning and Song Qingling were strong advocates for the women's movement. Hence, during the first coalition of the CCP and the Guomindang in the early 1920s, the women's movement underwent a quantum leap in the province of Guangdong because of the cooperation between women leaders of both parties. They gained support and inspiration from each other. When these two political groups ended their coalition in bloodshed in the late 1920s, the women's movement also suffered. It had depended on the men's movement and had reflected the political alliances and struggles of the men's parties. The leaders of the women's movement dispersed, attempting to work in their own individual areas.

In the 1920s and 1930s, under the leadership of Xiang Jingyu and Cai Chang, the CCP continued its women's program, especially successfully with women students and factory workers of Shanghai. After the establishment of the Jiangxi Soviet and the destruction of the CCP headquarters in Shanghai, the CCP's power center shifted to Jiangxi. By 1934, the CCP had built a base area in the southwest of that province, requiring a sizable staff to run the soviet administration. Mobilizing women to take part in the various organizations and government departments, as well as trying to convince women to work the land while their men were away fighting, were important developments of the Jiangxi Soviet.

HUNAN—CAI CHANG AND XIANG JINGYU

The Xinmin xuehui (New People's Study Group), a progressive study group formed in 1918 by Mao Zedong, Cai Hesen, and others, often held its meetings at the home of Cai Hesen. Two of the first women to become aware of gender issues in this period were associated with this study group. Cai's younger sister Cai Chang often attended these meetings as an informal member because she was so young, and she too supported the group's activities.[4]

The Cai family is said to have made a small fortune from chili sauce, and Cai Chang's father inherited one-third of that fortune. He dissipated it, however, on opium smoking and acquiring a concubine, so the family finances suffered a gradual decline. Cai Chang's mother, a woman of independent thought, grew to despise her husband and finally left him, bringing up her children alone. She even started a school for girls in her home county; Cai and many other girls in the county attended school there for the first time. In 1915, when Cai was fifteen, her father arranged a marriage for her. With the help of her mother, however, she ran away to the provincial capital, Changsha. Her family background and her childhood experiences opened Cai's eyes to how precarious it was to be a woman in traditional Chinese society. She realized that, for women to be able to take control of their own lives, something better had to be put in place—though at that stage she may not have had a clear idea of what that would be. Xiang Jingyu, Cai's school friend and later sister-in-law, was one of the first women to join the Xinmin xuehui. She was an activist in her own right: She had started a girls' school in her native Xupu, a remote county in Hunan, and had passed it into the care of others while she sought further self-development in Changsha and later in France.[5]

The Xinmin xuehui concerned itself with the liberation of and equality for women, among other issues. When a girl student from Hunan, Zhao Wuzhen, killed herself in protest against an arranged marriage, Mao Zedong wrote nine articles in the national newspaper *Dagong bao* (Dagong Daily) to publicize the event and criticize the social institutions that had forced her to follow that path. He enlisted the help of Xiang Jingyu and organized a protest meeting among the female students. In China, as in other parts of the world, organizing women is seen solely as women's responsibility, especially since the sexes are mainly segregated. In response to the May Fourth movement, in Beijing Mao Zedong organized protests and Cai Chang organized the teachers and students of the school in which she was teaching to join the protest march and to put on plays full of patriotic sentiment.

Later in 1919, Xiang and Cai organized the Hunan Women's Association for the Work-Study Scheme to promote a program for women studying abroad.[6] This was in response to Cai Hesen and Mao Zedong's founding the Work-Study Scheme whereby young people with limited means could go to study in France. Both Xiang Jingyu and Cai Chang went to France under that scheme. While in France, they deepened their understanding of gender issues, and they joined a European branch of the CCP. Cai was then sent to Moscow to study women's and children's work in the Soviet Union. On her return the following year, after the CCP sent her to Guangzhou to organize women during the first United Front, she was concurrently invited by He Xiangning to work as a secretary of the Women's Department of the Guomindang Central Committee.

In short, Xiang and Cai realized early in their lives that it was necessary for women to stand up and be counted. The conviction they developed in Hunan made them pioneers of the Chinese women's movement.

TIANJIN—DENG YINGCHAO

The May Fourth movement that exploded in Beijing in 1919 spread naturally to the nearby city of Tianjin. Young men around Nankai University, including the high school attached to it, as well as young women centered at the First Women's Normal School of Zhili, formed a union of Tianjin students. The women established the Tianjin nüjie aiguo tongzhihui (Tianjin Women's Patriotic League) and went out into the streets to tell the people how the warlord government had sold out China's rights at the Paris Peace Conference. They called on all patriotic Chinese to raise their voices in protest. These young women also aired issues that were closer to their hearts. They dealt with the topics of equality for women, the freedom to choose one's marriage partner and the importance of women's self-reliance. A number of women, among them Deng Yingchao, Guo Longzhen, and Liu Qingyang, emerged as leaders of this student movement. Fifteen-year-old Deng Yingchao was first elected as leader of the Yanjiang tuan (Speech-making Troop). There was no corner of Tianjian that she and her comrades did not visit to open people's eyes to young women publicly making radical speeches.

In the years that followed, Deng came to lead all Tianjin students, female and male, in their struggle against the warlord government in their city. Because many of their colleagues were in prison or had left to study in France, Deng remained at the helm of the student movement and the women's movement in Tianjin. She coordinated and presided over rallies of over a hundred thousand people. In the 1920s, Deng worked through the Tianjin branch of the Nüquan yundong tongmenghui (League of Women's Rights Movement) and the Nüxing she (Women's Star Society) to promote women's rights. Not only did she continue to speak publicly and write articles for newspapers and magazines; she also began adult classes for illiterate women and organized assistance for victimized women.

Deng was arguably the youngest leader of the women's movement in China. She knew from personal experience how badly women were treated. Her mother had been one of her father's several wives. Having often suffered abuse herself, Deng's mother was not willing to allow her newborn daughter to be given away and defended the infant with her life.[7] Soon after Deng's birth, her father was exiled to Xinjiang, where he died. Deng's mother brought up her daughter by herself. Although gentle by nature, she proved to be a resilient and resourceful woman who undoubtedly served as a model for her daughter of a self-reliant woman. The training and experience Deng gained in Tianjin were only the beginning of her long and distinguished career in the women's movement.

GUANGDONG—HE XIANGNING, CAI CHANG, AND DENG YINGCHAO

When Sun Yat-sen formed his provisional government in Guangzhou in 1917, He Xiangning, his long-standing comrade-in-arms and the wife of his old friend Liao Zhongkai, held a leading position among the women of Guangdong. As head of the Women's Department of the Guomindang Central Committee, she initiated a number of activities, including what would be the first celebration in China of International Women's Day on March 8, 1924. He and her department were responsible for establishing an obstetrics hospital, trade schools to give women the skills to earn a living, and night classes for women workers. Women in Guangdong were encouraged to participate in political activities. In support of Sun Yat-sen, He headed a women's association that advocated the re-opening of the parliament closed down by the warlords and supported a strike in Guangzhou and Hong Kong in 1925. He and Cai Chang helped to feed and house the striking women and provided temporary work and night classes.[8] Some of the women workers involved in the strike were absorbed into the movement, among them Chen Huiqing, who joined the CCP the following year.

With the help of Deng Yingchao, women's work in Guangdong was extended beyond the provincial capital of Guangzhou to include cities and counties such as Chaozhou and Shantou.[9] Cai and Deng also tried to consolidate the various women's groups in Guangdong into the United Women's Organization of Guangdong, which encompassed more than fifty associations of women ranging from workers, students, and peasants to businesswomen. He and Cai saw the importance of training women and began in 1926 to run training courses for the women's movement.[10]

SHANGHAI—XIANG JINGYU, ZHANG QINQIU, LIU QUNXIAN, AND JIN WEIYING

The foreign concessions of the 1920s and 1930s made Shanghai an international city, where the CCP decided to locate its Central Committee. In 1922, after the second congress of the CCP held in Shanghai, Xiang Jingyu became the first head of the Women's Department of the CCP Central Committee. She was responsible for giving the Chinese women's movement some theoretical guidance as well as establishing some direction for its work. One of the practical suggestions she made was for intellectuals to use "sisterhood" to win the confidence of women factory workers concentrated in Shanghai.

Even more important was Xiang's decision to send women students to organize factory workers. In 1923, Shanghai University was established under the auspices of the CCP. Many of the lecturers were Party leaders or were close to the Party. A number of women students came from the provinces to study here. Xiang lived in a house near by and often visited the students, lecturing on Marxist ideology. She argued that, in class awareness and fighting spirit, working women were superior to intellectual women, and she urged the women students to learn from workers and to spread Marxist and feminist ideologies.[11] Through her influence Zhang Qinqiu and other women students established a night school that attracted two to three hundred women workers. They taught the women to read and write and visited them in their homes, befriending them in order to understand their problems. In 1924, under Xiang's leadership, women students such as Zhang Qinqiu and Yang Zhihua helped to organize a strike of silk workers, providing communication among different factories and between the Party and the workers. In the combined strike of men and women workers in the cotton textile industry, Zhang formed women workers' *jiuchadui* (security teams) to ensure the safety of the strikers. She also visited workers' clubs to speak to them, handing out leaflets and teaching them anti-imperialist songs such as the *Internationale*. Her close relationship with women workers allowed her to recruit some of them into the CCP.[12]

Unlike Cai Chang and Deng Yingchao, Zhang came from a reasonably happy family. She was given the opportunity to study first in a primary school, then in Hangzhou Provincial Normal School in Zhejiang. There she took part in protest marches, advocating the cutting of women's hair as a gesture of liberation. She was one of the first to cut her hair. Her idealism and intellect took her to Shanghai, where she entered the left-wing Shanghai University. The experience she gained in organizing women workers in Shanghai proved useful in her later career as vice minister of textile industry of the People's Republic of China (PRC). She married Shen Zemin, and she and her husband were sent by the Party to Moscow for further studies.

In 1925, Xiang Jingyu also left Shanghai for a period of study in Moscow. She did not return to Shanghai but was sent to Wuhan, where, not long after, she was arrested by the Guomindang and executed. In the same year (1928), Cai Chang returned to Shanghai and was named one of the eight members of the women's committee of the CCP Central Committee. In that capacity, she helped organize strikes of women workers in the textile factories in west Shanghai and the silk factories of Zhabei.[13]

Another woman who was active in the Shanghai area was Jin Weiying. Jin began in her native Dinghai, Zhejiang province, where she helped to organize labor unions and foment strikes among the salt workers of Ningbo. At the same time, she agitated for the equality of women and fought against arranged marriages and selling women as wives, concubines, and slaves. She was later sent to Shanghai, where she worked in the labor movement. Whether under the leadership of Xiang Jingyu or on her own, she devoted herself to the strikes of the silk and textile workers in the 1920s.

Liu Qunxian was yet another labor union leader from this area. A native of Wuxi, Jiangsu province, she was a textile worker by the age of fourteen. At that time, radical Shanghai women workers were going to Wuxi to promote Marxist ideas. Influenced by them, Liu joined the CCP and worked among the textile workers of Wuxi. When it became dangerous for her to stay in Wuxi, she went to Shanghai, from where she was sent to Moscow. At the end of 1927, she addressed the World Labor Congress held in Moscow as a member of the Chinese delegation. When she returned to Shanghai, she headed the women workers' department of the General Labor Union, a position she held until she went to Jiangxi.

JIANGXI SOVIET

The situation for the CCP Central Committee and its members in Shanghai suddenly became dangerous in 1931, when the Guomindang began tightening its net around the CCP. The defection of some high-level members placed all underground organizations in Shanghai in immediate danger. Some had high prices on their heads. The leaders of the Party therefore had to move to the base that Zhu De and Mao Zedong had already established in Jiangxi.

In 1926, the Northern Expedition had left Guangdong to try to reclaim areas to the north for the Guomindang. Members of the CCP went as part of the Guomindang, but when the army reached Shanghai, Chiang Kai-shek initiated a purge of the Party and had a large number of CCP members killed. Those CCP members who escaped the purge either went underground or started an open revolt against the Guomindang. Two of these groups, led by Zhu De and Mao Zedong, found their way to a mountain stronghold called Jinggangshan, in southwestern Jiangxi. The remoteness of the area and the natural strategic advantages of Jinggangshan allowed the defeated CCP at first a respite and later an environment in which they could develop the surrounding region into a base area from which to expand and launch attacks. At the peak of its influence, the base occupied several counties and controlled a total population of three million. It was formally known as the Soviet Republic of China, although it is commonly known in English as the Jiangxi Soviet. It had a central government, provincial governments, and various levels of local government.[14] A large number of men and women were needed to staff these governments. In addition to the CCP members who came from cities where it was no longer safe for them to stay, the Jiangxi Soviet needed to recruit and train many local cadres.

Since one of the goals of the CCP had always been to mobilize women, women's organizing began soon after they had arrived in Jiangxi. The responsibility for breaking women's submission to tradition and leading them to new ideas fell on the women who had come from the cities. Cai Chang, as head of the provincial women's department, organized the work and trained hundreds of women leaders to take up positions. Sensitive to local traditions and practices, Cai learned how to work in the fields as an example to local women who needed to harvest rice. Some local women who accepted the challenge wanted to escape an arranged marriage or domestic mistreatment. Others simply saw the CCP as a shining new life that they might not quite comprehend but that nevertheless seemed to offer more hope and glamour than they could ever have dreamed of. The stories of some of the women recruits bear out these assumptions.

Deng Liujin was born into an impoverished family and was given away at birth to an itinerant barber and his wife as a child bride for their boy.[15] Her adoptive family was just as poor as her biological family, so when the Red Army came to her village she joined them wholeheartedly from the time she was old enough to be part of the children's corps. She progressed from inspector with the county women's department to the provincial women's department of Fujian. She proved to be an outstanding worker who recruited soldiers for the Red Army and was a living example of a peasant woman who became a responsible woman cadre.

In military work women also achieved some success. Kang Keqing was a child bride, but after her intended husband died, her in-laws adopted her as their foster daughter so that she might be a cheap domestic for their family. She narrowly escaped having her feet bound, and when she realized that her foster father was marrying her off, she ran away to join the Red Army. She was a member, then head, of the women's volunteers and was later sent to receive military and political training at a cadres' school. At one time, she was in command of a small group of Red Army soldiers who beat back a local enemy militia. She was one of a handful of women in the Jiangxi Soviet who had formal, albeit limited, military training.[16]

Unlike Deng Liujin and Kang Keqing, who were given away as child brides but never endured the suffering of being one, Wei Xiuying, who was given away as a child bride at the age of six, worked from dawn to dusk, continually cursed and beaten, sometimes without food. She joined the Red Army as soon as she heard it was in her area.[17] Two years later, she became a member of the government of her county and head of the women's department while concurrently serving as a member of the provincial women's department of Jiangxi. Still illiterate, she was taught to read and write simple reports by Cai Chang. Just before the start of the Long March, Wei was given the mission of recruiting thirty soldiers for the Red Army. Although many recruitment campaigns had preceded hers, Wei succeeded in recruiting four hundred men by working through the women of the community.

In the Jiangxi Soviet many women first heard of such concepts as equality and the right of women to work and participate in politics. For the first time, many women experienced freedom.

As was to be expected, Chiang Kai-shek launched five expeditions to try to crush the Jiangxi Soviet. Four of these "encirclement and extermination" campaigns ended in failure, although they weakened the Red Army considerably. In anticipation of the fifth campaign, in which Chiang Kai-shek had invested an unprecedented amount of personnel and arms, the Red Army decided to carry out what it called a "strategic retreat" from Jiangxi with no clear destination in mind. The army wound its way through many provinces and covered thousands of kilometers: hence the expedition's name, the Long March.

THE WOMEN WHO WENT ON THE LONG MARCH: FIRST THIRTY

A retrospective look at the planning of CCP leaders makes it apparent that they did not intend to return soon to Jiangxi. All the leaders took their wives, even those who were sick or pregnant. It is also apparent that they were planning a long journey because they selected only men and women in the best physical condition. Literature on the women of the Long March mentions a physical examination they had to pass to qualify for the march.[18] It is not clear whether this physical examination was also required of men who were selected. Guo Chen maintains that senior women in the central government and the army were exempt from this examination, which would have included most of the wives of the leaders.[19] However, some sources also say that twelve young women were selected in this manner.[20]

Speculation on the reason women were included in the Long March at all and a rough classification of the thirty women who marched from Jiangxi can be found in Lily Xiao Hong Lee and Sue Wiles's recent book on the women of the Long March.[21] For the purposes of this essay, however, I have adopted a different analysis. According to Guo Chen, three conditions controlled the selection of women: They had to be well trained in political ideology; able to work independently, especially with the masses; and physically fit, able to endure hardship and carry heavy loads.[22] When one applies these conditions to the women who were allowed to go on the Long March, we find that they fall into two main groups. The first was composed of long-standing members of the CCP who came to Jiangxi from other centers, having built up credible records of accomplishment in revolutionary work and women's organizing. Many of these women were also wives of the CCP leaders. The second group was young, healthy, and strong women recruited in Jiangxi, who had proved themselves at various levels of local government, often holding positions as heads of women's departments. They also shared the honor of having been successful recruitment officers for the Red Army.

The first group of women included veterans of the women's movement such as Cai Chang and Deng Yingchao. From Hunan came Liu Ying, who headed the Hunan women's bureau but later worked in Shanghai and also studied in Moscow.[23] It likewise included Chen Huiqing, mentioned earlier, who joined the Party in Guangdong, where she did women's work, and Liao Siguang, another Cantonese who began her work with youth in Guangdong and Shanghai and continued it in Jiangxi.[24] It also included Li Jianzhen, who began her revolutionary life in the Dongjiang area of Guangdong and was sent to work in Fujian, eventually heading the central women's bureau in Ruijin, the capital of the Jiangxi Soviet.[25] Xiao Yuehua, another political worker from Guangdong, became the wife of Otto Braun (Li De), the military adviser sent by the Comintern to the CCP in Jiangxi. From the Shanghai area came Jin Weiying, Liu Qunxian, Qian Xijun, and Li Bozhao. Women from other centers than those mentioned above included He Zizhen, Qiu Yihan, Wei Gongzhi, Han Siying, Xie Fei, and Xie Xiaomei.

The second group, the women recruited and trained in Jiangxi, consisted of Deng Liujin, Kang Keqing, Li Guiying, Li Jianhua, Liu Caixiang, Wang Quanyuan, Wei Xiuying, Wu Fulian, Wu Zhonglian, Yang Houzhen, Zeng Yu, Zhong Yuelin, and Zhou Yuehua. Of these, Zeng Yu joined the Long March illegally, having been rejected because she was pregnant. She tagged along with great persistence, however, living on the rations of other women who were willing to share with her out of compassion.[26]

We find some inconsistencies, of course, in the selection of the women. Zeng Yu and Yang Houzhen, for example, were neither senior women cadres nor strong and healthy young women; their only previous experience had been running cooperatives and the like in the Jiangxi Soviet. Yang had bound feet, and Zeng was pregnant. If Zeng was rejected because of her pregnancy, then the other pregnant women—He Zizhen, Chen Huiqing, and Liao Siguang—should have been rejected as well. It was not feasible to reject He, however, because she was Mao Zedong's wife, and once she was allowed to go, then all the others had to be allowed, even if illegally, as in Zeng's case. The missing factor is perhaps that both Yang and Zeng were married to Red Army commanders.[27]

The Women's Army

Of course, not all of those who participated in the Long March started off from Jiangxi. About two months before the mainstream Red Army marched out of Jiangxi, a regiment had been sent to test the waters for the main group.

This was the Red Sixth Regiment headed by Ren Bishi and Xiao Ke. Five women marched with this regiment, including Li Zhen and Ren Bishi's wife, Chen Congying.[28] When this Sixth Regiment joined the Red Second Regiment led by He Long in Guizhou, they formed the Second Front Army. More than twenty women marched with the Second Army.[29]

Li Zhen, a child bride who became a leader of the women in her area in the 1920s, was from Hunan. Later she joined the guerrillas at Liuyang before being sent in 1933 to study in Ruijin. She was one of the women in the Second Front Army who had combat experience.[30] Chen Congying had been engaged to Ren Bishi when they were both very young. Ren went first to Changsha and afterward to the Soviet Union to study, and he asked Chen to keep up her studies so that they could build a life together on the same intellectual footing. When Ren returned to China and began underground Party work in Shanghai, he employed Chen as his trusted messenger. After two Shanghai members defected, she was arrested and went to jail with her three-month-old baby. She was rescued from the Guomindang prison and finally joined her husband in Jiangxi. In Jiangxi and afterward during the Long March, Chen was responsible for Ren's confidential documents no matter what position he occupied. During the Long March, she was head of the confidential documents bureau and hid on her person the secret code used to communicate with other Red Army outfits. The Jian sisters, Xianren and Xianfo, were students who joined the CCP in the 1920s and 1930s respectively. They taught and did clerical work in the army. Before the Long March, Jian Xianren married He Long and Jian Xianfo married Xiao Ke, both Red Army commanders of the Second Front Army. Each of the sisters gave birth to a child during the Long March and was able to keep her baby.

Before the Long March, the Fourth Front Army was stationed in the Hubei-Henan-Anhui (E-Yu-Wan) base area and, like the First Front Army, was forced to move because of pressure from the Guomindang attack. It went initially to the border of Sichuan and Shaanxi, where it established a base. This army, headed by Zhang Guotao, recruited by far the largest number of women to perform a variety of functions. There were political and military leaders such as Zhang Qinqiu, but also combat women who were formed into the Women's Independent Battalion, which grew into a regiment and later an army. This group underwent a long and complicated metamorphosis, which will be discussed below. There were women working in hospitals; in a factory attached to a hospital whose duty it was to "spin and weave, make shoes and caps"; and in the drama troupe.[31] At the time the Fourth Front Army began its own Long March (1935), it had approximately 2,500 women. To list the well-known women in this long march would take too much space, but their names can be found in a book compiled by Xi Jun.[32]

Zhang Qinqiu, a leader in the Fourth Front Army, was partly responsible for the recruitment of women. She became the head of the general political department, a position on par with the commander, Zhang Guotao. In this position she established a drama group and trained large numbers of young women in propaganda work. A disagreement with Zhang Guotao led to her being transferred to head the political department of the General Hospital, where large numbers of women worked. When the Fourth Front Army was planning its Long March in 1935, Zhang Guotao gathered all women cadres and workers into the Women's Independent Regiment. This increased its numbers such that the regiment had to be upgraded to an army of two regiments. Zhang Qinqiu was for a time given command of the Women's Independent Army and its first regiment. However, after about three months, Zhang Guotao changed his mind and transferred her to head the women's department of the Sichuan-Shaanxi provincial committee. This was clearly a move intended to reduce her power.

The Women's Independent Army fought its way from Sichuan to Xikang, twice crossing the inhospitable grasslands as well as the snowy mountains. By the time it reached north of Xikang, a reassessment of the Fourth Front Army found that its numbers had been reduced by half. With a restructure in April 1936, the Women's Independent Army reverted to a regiment of 1,800 fighters whose responsibilities were redefined: They were now to provide security for headquarters, replacing the men who had carried out those duties before. In October 1936, when the First, Second, and Fourth Front Armies met in Huining, the leaders decided that the First and Fourth armies should each take some of the others' personnel for the sake of better understanding and cooperation. The Women's Anti-Japanese Vanguard Regiment was created from the independent women's regiment, with Wang Quanyuan and Wu Fulian of the First Front Army as commander and political commissar respectively. This regiment crossed the Yellow River in late 1936 and became isolated from the main Red Army before being virtually annihilated by the cavalry of the Muslim warlords, the Ma brothers. The women fought desperately, first in Linze, later in Nijia Yingzi, and lastly near Shiwo beside Qilian Mountain, until their ammunition ran out. Then they fought with sticks, stones, and finally with their bare hands. Ultimately, all of them were wounded, killed, or captured. Many of the captured women were raped and horrifically killed. One source wrote, "The cold and steep peaks of Qilian Mountain stood in the stiff wind like iron men. They witnessed the cruelest and most poignant scene in the history of the Workers and Peasants Red Army. The battle song written in blood by the Women's Independent Regiment will forever echo in the mountains of the Qilian Range."[33] For most members of the First Front Army, the Long March officially ended in the north of Shaanxi in October 1935, almost exactly a year after it began in October 1934.

THE WOMEN'S MOVEMENT AFTER THE LONG MARCH

Yan'an in northern Shaanxi soon became the "capital" of the CCP territory. A base area was built around it that encompassed parts of northern Shaanxi, Gansu, and Ningxia (Shaan-Gan-Ning Base Area), and the CCP established a central government as well as a provincial-level government for the base area. As in Jiangxi, cadres of every kind had to be recruited and trained. Those who had made the Long March formed the core of this network of cadres, usually holding responsible positions. The women who completed the Long March were also assigned different levels of responsibilities. The seemingly miraculous feat of the Long March had greatly impressed the Chinese people, while the CCP's anti-Japanese stance won the approval of most of the nation's intellectuals. Reports of foreign correspondents Agnes Smedley, Helen Foster Snow (Nym Wales), and Edgar Snow painted such favorable pictures of Mao Zedong, Zhu De, and Zhou Enlai that they approached hero status. The destiny of the CCP was permanently changed by the "Xi'an Incident" of 1936, which forced Chiang Kai-shek to cooperate with the Red Army in resisting the invading Japanese.[34] This second United Front allowed the CCP to work freely as long as it kept within the parameters of fighting the Japanese. Its army was renamed the Eighth Route Army as it fought side by side with the Guomindang armies.

As the prestige of the CCP rose, more and more people wanted to join the cause. With the help of underground workers in the big cities, male and female intellectuals, especially students, followed their hearts and made pilgrimages to Yan'an. This influx of large numbers of intelligent, attractive young women to Yan'an had important social implications. Many of the Long March women separated from their partners in Yan'an, often for no stated reason. An examination of the timing of these separations and the women married by the men subsequently is revealing. The best-known case is the divorce of Mao Zedong and He Zizhen. The Central Committee formally approved their divorce in 1939, after He had been sent away to Moscow, but it was no secret that Jiang Qing had already moved to Mao's cave before the divorce was finalized.[35] Other women who had similar experiences were Jin Weiying, Liu Qunxian, Qian Xijun, Jian Xianren, Xie Fei, and Xiao Yuehua.[36] By no means complete, this list includes some of the well-known women of the March whose partners married young women who came from the big cities.

Almost all the women who completed the Long March and reached Yan'an were given opportunities to further their studies. Since many of them had received only limited education, this was indeed a precious gift from the Party. Most of them went to Yan'an kang-Ri junzheng daxue (Yan'an Anti-Japanese Military and Political University) and Zhongyang dangxiao (Central Party School) and its branches.[37] Some scholars have speculated that, as a result of these opportunities for education, none of the Long March women remained illiterate.[38] The period of study varied, with some women being sent to the front again before even completing the usual six months. Others went on to further schooling. The more senior of the Long March women, such as Jin Weiying, Jian Xianren, and Zhang Qinqiu, became leaders of women students in these schools and academies. Zhang headed the Women's University from 1939 to 1941. These women were in charge not only of students who were also women of the March, but also of better-educated young women who had come from various urban centers. Other Long March women did organizing in the central government and Party central as well as at the various local levels.

In 1936, Cai Chang was appointed to the Shaan-Gan-Ning provincial committee and was made head of the provincial women's department. The next year, she took up the responsibility of women's organizing in the Party central. She devoted her attention to all three groups of women in Yan'an: the women of the Long March; the women underground workers from the "white areas," or those dominated by the Guomindang; and young students from urban centers. In the same year, she helped to formulate the "Outline of Women's Organizing," which focused on women of the poorer classes—workers, peasants, and the urban poor. In practical terms, Cai saw that, unless women cadres could be freed from child care, they could not go to work. Therefore, she made sure that a nursery was established so that mothers could continue to devote themselves to their work. She also opened a school for Red Army spouses who had little or no education and therefore could not find work.

After four more areas were taken from the Japanese, each of these established its own women's department. After the Women's University merged with Yan'an University in 1941, Zhang Qinqiu was transferred to the women's committee of the Central Committee and made general secretary of the Women's Federation of the Liberated Areas.

Oddly enough, from 1938 to 1941, a man held the CCP's top job dealing with women. In October 1938, Wang Ming became secretary of the Central Women's Committee, with Cai Chang and five other women as members. This period seems to have coincided with Cai's sojourn in Moscow, where she went to study and rest. She took over the secretaryship from Wang in 1941, when Deng Yingchao was also appointed vice secretary.

After she took over women's organizing from Wang, Cai criticized his line of forcing gender equality and marital choice on a population without understanding its local conditions.[39] She advocated improving women's lives through increased economic production and improving their status in the family by teaching them skills that would enable them to help the family achieve a better life. This was also a response to the extreme material hardship in the base areas. The Party was encouraging the masses to produce more. To solve the problem of a lack of textiles for clothing, Cai wanted women to spin and weave, but she understood that the women of western China had no tradition of spinning and weaving. Hence, as she had in Jiangxi, where she had learned to harvest rice in order to mobilize the local women, she learned to spin and weave and then taught these skills to the peasant women of the northwest. Moreover, she expected her cadres to do the same. Luo Qiong, the editor of the magazine *Zhongguo funü* (Chinese Women), taught women to spin and weave even as she continued to edit the magazine.[40] Cai brought a new direction to women's work during this period. The cadres for organizing often doubled as primary school teachers, village clerks, and instructors for spinning and weaving.[41] One scholar has described this phase of women's political work as a "forum for education and propaganda discussion as well as coordinating of child care and production."[42]

In 1947, Cai left Yan'an for Harbin to take up the position of secretary of the women's committee of the Northeast Bureau. Her work in Yan'an was taken over by Deng Yingchao, who basically continued Cai's policies, specifically the emphasis on women's production and seeking to raise women's status through raising their achievements in the economic area.[43]

Other women from the Long March supported Cai and Deng in their work with women in the post–Long March period. Deng Liujin worked as an inspector in the central women's department in 1937.[44] After Li Guiying was released from the Guomindang political prison, she was sent to do women's work with the New Fourth Army in southern Anhui.[45] Wang Dinguo and Quan Weihua worked with the women's federation in Yan'an. Wei Xiuying, one of Cai's protégées, continued her work. She was secretary of the northern Shaanxi provincial women's committee in the early 1940s and rose to secretary of the Jilin provincial women's committee.[46] Han Siying was in charge of women's work in Sichuan and Shijiazhuang in Hebei, while Xie Fei directed the women's federation in eastern China from the early 1940s until 1949. Li Jianzhen was one of the highest-ranking leaders in the women's movement during the post–Long March period. She held the positions of both head of the northern Shaanxi provincial women's committee and head of the central women's department. In 1938, Li and her husband were sent back to Jiangxi to help integrate guerrilla fighters into the New Fourth Army, and she was responsible for women's organizing in Jiangxi and later for the whole of southeastern China.[47]

We have seen that the Long March women usually were sent to newly liberated and guerrilla areas after spending some time in Yan'an. Perhaps their services were valued more in these new areas because of their loyalty and experience, which equipped them to face the more challenging areas in addition to the more stable Shaan-Gan-Ning border area. Important women's organizing took place not only in the CCP-controlled areas, but also in the areas under Guomindang, or "white," rule. After their joint declaration of war against Japan, the two political groups were meant to pool their resources and offer unified resistance to the invading army of Japan under the umbrella of the Republican government. As the Japanese penetrated more deeply into inland China, Chiang Kai-shek moved his capital first to Wuhan then to Chongqing (Chungking). The CCP had offices in both cities and as long as their activities were not seen as undermining the Guomindang's authority and promoting communism, they were able to operate openly. However, their political ideology and their success in the Long March and in expanding their territory behind enemy lines generated a great deal of interest. CCP operatives in the "white" areas walked a tight rope between arousing the suspicions of the Guomindang and promoting their cause among those who showed interest.

Deng Yingchao, who accompanied her husband, Zhou Enlai, to Wuhan and Chongqing, led the work of reaching out to nonaligned yet progressive women in the "white" areas. She used anti-Japanese sentiment to unite women around her, while quietly winning them over to the communist cause. With the help of underground Party members who held legitimate positions, she met such distinguished women as Shi Liang, Li Dequan, Shen Zijiu, and Luo Qiong. Shen and Luo were both connected to the influential women's magazine *Funü shenghuo* (Women's Life) and later joined the CCP. Deng even cooperated with Song Meiling, first lady of Republican China (and sister of Song Qingling), and the YWCA. When Song organized a meeting at Lushan to discuss the cooperation of women of all political parties and from all social classes to fight the Japanese, Deng attended and made a speech describing the life of women in the Shaan-Gan-Ning border area. She also expressed her willingness to cooperate with Song, agreeing to become part of her Women's Guidance Committee of the New Life movement so long as member organizations were not required to give up their own identities. Leadership of the new organization expanded to include representatives of different elements. Several communist and leftist women eventually became committee members of this organization.

Another Long March woman was assigned to work with Deng Yingchao in the "white" areas. This was Liao Siguang, who assisted Deng to form the delegation representing the women's federation of the Shaan-Gan-Ning border area in Wuhan and Chongqing, and helped with the work of uniting progressive women in those cities around the CCP.[48]

Examining the women's movement after the Long March, we find that women from the March who held positions on the various women's committees and departments dominated it. Cai Chang and Deng Yingchao were the highest office holders in the field of women's work, and their philosophy left an indelible imprint on this period. Both favored economic means for improving the standing of women and both criticized the confrontational methods Wang Ming used to enforce feminist policies. They preferred not to force communist ideas on peasants who still held conservative views of women. Their policies were also more appropriate for the Party's needs of the moment.

THE WOMEN'S MOVEMENT AFTER 1949

By January 1949, when it was clear that the CCP would take over the whole of China, the communists began to organize people of various sectors under its banner. A preparatory committee started to plan a women's association that would encompass all factions under the All-China Democratic Women's Federation. In addition to the Women's Federation of Liberated Areas, women from "white" areas were also included in this new federation, which later became the All-China Women's Federation (ACWF), the flagship of the CCP women's movement. Delegates to the meeting to form the ACWF included Long March veterans Cai Chang, Deng Yingchao, Zhang Qinqiu, Kang Keqing, Li Jianzhen, and Liu Ying. Cai was elected president, while Deng and Li Dequan became vice presidents. Most of the surviving women of the Long March worked in the ACWF, whether at the central, provincial, or local level, although it does indeed seem to have been a waste of talent to put two such high caliber women leaders as Cai and Deng together there.[49] Some women who specifically expressed their aversion to organizing women were nevertheless required to undertake that work.[50]

The aspirations and the activities of the women of the Long March and the ACWF were closely intertwined. Not only were those women assigned to the central, provincial, and local levels of the ACWF, but three of them occupied the top positions of the federation during its first four decades, apart from the 1960s, when the work of the ACWF was disrupted by the Cultural Revolution. Cai Chang was the first chair, from its inception in 1949 until Kang Keqing succeeded her in 1978 at the first meeting of the ACWF after the end of the Cultural Revolution. During Cai's years as chair, Deng Yingchao was vice chair, exerting a great deal of influence. When Chen Muhua was elected chair of the ACWF in 1989, she was the first woman to hold the position who had not taken part in the Long March. The fact is, however, that by the 1990s most women of the Long March had died or were very old.[51]

CONCLUSION

In this essay, I have reviewed the close relationship between the Long March women and the women's movement in China during the greater part of the twentieth century, arguing that those women who were allowed to go on the Long March had been gender conscious early in their lives. The earliest group of women to be influenced by feminist thought—the more privileged intellectuals—may have been aware of Western ideas. These women may not have suffered maltreatment and discrimination, but witnessing the misfortune of women around them aroused their social conscience. At the same time, many of them were also strongly attracted to socialist ideology. This influential group began the work of awakening their sisters to end social institutions oppressive to women. Peasant women, on the other hand, joined the revolution for the most part because they were victims of oppression. They, too, had the courage to break free of prescribed destiny and search for alternatives in the communists' promise of equality and liberation. They fought loyally under that banner. These women were responsible for mobilizing other women in their own localities as well as in the soviet bases in the 1920s and early 1930s, when the CCP consolidated its power there. Some of these women became the Long March women. The selection process was much tighter for the First Front Army than, for example, for the Fourth Front Army, probably because the former was expecting a much longer journey, with survival at the end uncertain. The Fourth Front Army accepted the largest number of women, about 2,500.

As the territory of the CCP expanded, the Long March women were given more and more responsibility for organizing women, culminating in the formation of the ACWF in 1949. For four decades from its foundation, the ACWF was headed by Long March women. Discounting the ten disruptive years of the Cultural Revolution, the impact of those women on the women's movement is still monumental. The women of the Long March gave the women's movement a solid foundation upon which later generations have continued to build a multifaceted, multivoiced women's movement.

NOTES
1. Lily Xiao Hong Lee, "Where Are the Heroines of the Long March Now? A Survey of Their Lives and Work After 1949," in Lee 1994, 68.
2. Beahan, 1975, 379–416.
3. Gilmartin 1995, 6.
4. Dong et al., 1992, 259–260.
5. Dai, 1991, 28–29.
6. Su, 1990, 28.
7. Jin, 1993, 8.
8. Li, 1993, 48–55; Su, 1990, 51–52.

9. Jin, 1993, 107–113.

10. Dong et al., 1992, 265; Su, 1990, 53.

11. Dai, 1991, 88–101.

12. Lü, 1984, 231–233.

13. Dong et al., 1992, 268.

14. At various times the territory of the soviet extended from Jiangxi to parts of Hunan and Fujian.

15. This was a cheap way to acquire a daughter-in-law and provided an extra pair of hands in the house for the mere keep of an extra mouth.

16. Liaowang bianjibu, 1986, 31–35.

17. Ibid., 165.

18. Ibid., 122, 192.

19. Guo 1986, 4.

20. Liaowang bianjibu, 1986, 192. Those mentioned by name as having undergone the same physical examination as Wang Quanyuan are Li Bozhao, Deng Liujin, Zhong Yuelin, and Wei Xiuying.

21. Lee and Wiles, 1999, 25–26.

22. Guo, 1986, 3.

23. Liaowang bianjibu, 1986, 43–44.

24. Guo, 1986, 48–52; Liaowang bianjibu, 1986, 129–140.

25. Guo, 1986, 23–26; Liaowang bianjibu, 1986, 53–65.

26. Guo, 1986, 79–81.

27. Yang Houzhen was married to Luo Binghui; Zeng Yu was married to Zhou Zikun.

28. Xi, 1995, 108.

29. Ibid., 111.

30. Liaowang bianjibu, 1986, 209–211.

31. Xi, 1995, 177.

32. Ibid., 173.

33. Ibid., 235.

34. In 1936, two of Chiang Kai-shek's generals kidnapped him in Xi'an and forced him to sign an agreement to ally with the Chinese communists to fight the Japanese.

35. Terrill, 1992, 152–154.

36. Lee, 74. Jian Xianren's experience was perhaps a little different from the others. See Terrill, 1994, 151.

37. Lee, 1994, 73.

38. Ibid.

39. Su, 1990, 119.

40. She summarized her experience in an article, "The Three Forms of Development of the Textile Industry in the Border Area of Shan-Gan-Ning," which was published in the magazine. Ibid., 123.

41. Ibid.

42. Stranahan, 1983, 44.

43. Jin, 1993, 389–390.

44. Zeng, 1987, Vol. 2, 72.

45. Liaowang bianjibu, 1986, 161.
46. *Huaxia funü mingren cidian*, 1988, 242; Lee and Wiles, 1999, 266.
47. Liaowang bianjibu, 1986, 63; Lee and Wiles, 1999, 258.
48. Liaowang bianjibu, 1986, 134–136; Lee and Wiles, 1999, 259–260.
49. Lee, 2000, 30.
50. Kang Keqing expressed great reluctance to do women's work. See Kang, 1993, 374.
51. After the establishment of the ACWF, women of the Long March were active at all levels of the organization. Involved at the national level were Cai Chang, Deng Yingchao, Kang Keqing, Lin Yueqin, Wei Xiuying, Zhang Qinqiu, Li Zhen, and Li Jianzhen; at the regional level were Qiu Yihan and Han Siying; at the provincial level were Wei Xiuying, Chen Huiqing, and Wu Zhonglian; at the county level was Yang Wenju; and at the trade union level was Wu Shunying.

REFERENCES

Beahan, Charlotte. "Feminism and Nationalism in the Chinese Women's Press, 1902–1911," *Modern China* , 1975, 379–416.
"Chen Muhua: Yanjing gaosu ni yiqie" (Chen Muhua: Eyes Tell You Everything), *Zhonghua yingcai*, no. 120, June 1995, 4–9.
Dai Xugong. *Xiang Jingyu zhuan* (A Biography of Xiang Jingyu). Beijing: Renmin chubanshe, 1991.
Davin, Delia. *Women-work: Women and the Party in Revolutionary China.* Oxford: Clarendon Press, 1976.
Dong Bian, Cai Asong, and Tan Deshan, eds. "Cai Chang shengping jishi" (A Chronology of Cai Chang's Life). In *Women de hao dajie Cai Chang* (Our Wonderful Big Sister Cai Chang). Beijing: Zhongyang wenxian chubanshe, 1992.
Gilmartin, Christina. *Engendering the Chinese Revolution: Radical Women, Communist Politics and Mass Movements in the 1920s.* Berkeley: University of California Press, 1995.
Guo Chen. *Jinguo liezhuan: Hong yifangmianjun sanshi wei changzheng nühongjun shengping shiji* (Biographies of Brave Women: Thirty Women Soldiers of the First Front Red Army). Beijing: Nongcun duwu chubanshe, 1986.
Huaxia funü mingren cidian (Huaxia Dictionary of Famous Women). Beijing: Huaxia chubanshe, 1988.
Jin Feng. *Deng Yingchao zhuan* (A Biography of Deng Yingchao). Beijing: Renmin chubanshe, 1993.
Kang Keqing. *Kang Keqing huiyilu* (Reminiscences of Kang Keqing). Beijing: Jiefangjun chubanshe, 1993.
Lee, Lily Xiao Hong. "Poised Between Breakthrough and Constraint: The Political Career of Deng Yingchao." Paper presented at the Women, Modernity, and Opportunity in Twentieth-Century China Workshop, University of Sydney, 2000.
———. *Virtue of Yin: Studies on Chinese Women.* Sydney: Wild Peony, 1994.
Lee, Lily Xiao Hong, and Sue Wiles. *Women of the Long March.* Sydney: Allen and Unwin, 1999.
Li Yong, Wen Lequn, and Wang Yunsheng. *He Xiangning zhuan* (A Biography of He Xiangning). Beijing: Huaqiao chubanshe, 1993.

Liaowang bianjibu, ed. *Hongjun nüyingxiong zhuan* (Heroines of the Red Army). Beijing: Xinhua chubanshe, 1986.

Liu Ningyuan. *Zhongguo nüxingshi leibian* (A Classified Compilation of Women's History). Beijing: Beijing shifan daxue chubanshe, 1990.

Lü Ying. "Zhang Qinqiu." In *Zhonggong dangshi renwu zhuan* (A History of the Chinese Communist Party: Biographies). Vol. 17. Xi'an: Shaanxi renmin chubanshe, 1984, 229–261.

Ropp, Paul S. "The Seeds of Change: References on the Conditions of Women in the Early and Mid-Ch'ing," *Signs*, no. 2, 1976, 5–23.

Snow, Edgar. *Red Star over China*. London: Victor Gollanz, 1968.

Snow, Helen Foster. *Inside Red China*. New York: Da Capo Press, 1939; reprint 1977.

Stranahan, Patricia. *Yan'an Women and the Communist Party*. Berkeley: Institute of Asian Studies, University of California, 1983.

Su Ping. *Cai Chang zhuan* (A Biography of Cai Chang). Beijing: Zhongguo funü chubanshe, 1990.

Terrill, Ross. *Madame Mao, The White-Boned Demon: A Biography of Madame Mao Zedong*. New York: Simon and Schuster, 1992.

Wiles, Sue. "Red Army Heroines: Real Soldiers or Women Warriors?" Paper presented at the Women, Modernity, and Opportunity in Twentieth-Century China Workshop, University of Sydney, 2000.

Xi Jun. *Jinguo beige: Nühongjun chanzheng quanjing baodao* (An Elegy for Women Warriors: A Comprehensive Report on Red Army Women During the Long March). Chengdu: Sichuan renmin chubanshe, 1995.

Zeng Zhi, ed. *Changzheng nüzhanshi* (Women Fighters of the Long March), 2 vols. Changchun: Beifang funü ertong chubanshe, 1987.

THE HISTORY AND CURRENT STATUS OF CHINESE WOMEN'S PARTICIPATION IN POLITICS

Wang Qingshu

Women's participation in politics is an important component in building democratic politics and an important measure of women's status and social advancement. As citizens, women have a right, as well as a duty and responsibility, to participate in politics on an equal basis with men. Social development cannot be divorced from women's development: Women's participation in politics allows them to become a positive force for social development, while also giving women the opportunity to improve themselves as they participate in this development. During the latter half of the twentieth century, Chinese women made great strides in political participation and effectively promoted the development of every aspect of Chinese society. By participating in politics, women have made historic progress.

WOMEN'S PARTICIPATION IN POLITICS THROUGHOUT CHINESE HISTORY

After the decline of the matriarchal culture of ancient China, women's status gave them no rights to intervene in public affairs. In the slaveholding society of the Xia (2205–1766 BCE) and Shang (1766–1122 BCE) dynasties, some women served as mystic mediums, influencing political policies under the guise of speaking for the gods. Others wielded political influence by participating in military activities. Lady Fu Hao, the first female military strategist in Chinese history and the wife of the Shang dynasty king Wu Ding, can perhaps be seen as a reminder of the matriarchy. After the Shang dynasty, however, women's involvement in politics met with vigorous suppression. Approximately 3,100 years ago, King Wu of Zhou made a punitive expedition against King Zhou of Shang. As he is reported to have said, "Hens do not crow at daybreak. If the hens crow at daybreak, the household may be in decline. I fear that the king of Shang is now taking counsel from a woman."

After the Eastern Zhou (770–256 BCE) dynasty, Confucian thinking gradually became the mainstream ideology of feudal society. Confucianism propounded the viewpoint that "women should not participate in politics, and if they do, it is a disaster for the state." A passage in the *Shi jing* (Classic of Poetry) reads, "Wise men build cities, but wise women destroy cities. When disasters come down from heaven, it is the doing of women." The *Yi jing* (Book of Changes) states that "a woman's place is in the home, a man's place is outside." The *Li ji* (Book of Rites) states, "A woman has no rank of nobility. Her rank comes from her husband." In *Baihu tong* (Discussion of Chinese Classics), the Han dynasty (202 BCE–220 CE) Confucian thinkers proposed that "Women have no duty to become involved in politics, no obligation to govern the masses, and no need to learn how to deal with people tactfully." Both in the dominant ideology and in the social system, women were prohibited from participating in politics for thousands of years, but a few outstanding women broke free of these prohibitions in order to cope with specific social demands. Their participation in politics took several forms.

First, as wives of rulers, they might assist emperor-husbands in managing the state. Women with excellent reputations for administration include Empress Lu of the Han dynasty, Empress Zhangsun of the Tang (618–907 CE), Empress Dugu of the Sui (581–618), Empress Ma of the Ming (1368–1644), and Empress Xiao Zhuangwen, who made great contributions to three courts in the early Qing (1644–1911). Sometimes, when an aging emperor became weak or impotent, or when the emperor was very young because the father emperor died early, the empress would "hold court from behind a screen" or take charge of governance openly. The Empress Wu (Zetian) of the Tang dynasty ruled for a total of fifty years, first behind the scenes in the capacity of empress and then at court as the empress dowager. Finally, she changed the name of the dynasty to Zhou and ruled as the official emperor for fifteen years. She was the only female emperor and was also a talented strategist and consummate politician, while Cixi of the late Qing dynasty, who also ruled at court as empress dowager, was a representative of the weak and impotent rule of feudalism at its downfall.

Second, as daughters of the imperial family or the nobility, young women might link the court with other clans through marriage. As "peaceful envoys," these princesses were sent to faraway places and served to promote friendly alliances of ethnic groups and to foster progress in other clans. Among them were the Princess Jieyou of a Western Han dynasty and Princess Wencheng of the Tang dynasty.

Third, as leaders of peasant uprisings against the imperial court, many women "made themselves kings." They led armies of rebellious peasants numbering in the tens of thousands, opposing the rule of corrupt courts under slogans such as "doing Heaven's will." Most of the women who resisted the government suffered harsh repression and had little chance to establish political authority. Only Chen Shuozhen of the Tang dynasty, who styled herself

"Emperor Wen Jia," set up an official bureaucracy and established an embryonic form of peasant government. Although it lasted only two months before collapsing, it had a far-reaching impact on later peasant rebellions.

In addition, individual women displayed courage and political skill on important occasions. Lady Xian, for example, a woman of the Yue people who lived during the Southern and Northern dynasties (420–589), worked tirelessly to "bring the Yue people and the Han people together in peace" and to develop the Lingnan region (modern-day Guangdong and Guangxi). Another woman, "dressed as a man," Huang Chonggu, who lived during the early Tang, passed the imperial examinations to become an official. In office, she was just, selfless, and competent, but when officials discovered her gender, she was forced out of office.

The Taiping Rebellion (1850–1864) was a peasant revolutionary movement at the end of the Qing dynasty. Many women participated in the uprising, going bravely into battle and making significant contributions to the movement. The Taiping revolutionaries claimed that all men and women in the world were equal brothers and sisters, and their sociopolitical ideas contained the seeds of the contemporary concept of equality of the sexes. Taiping armies included women's battalions and women soldiers. They also set up schools for women. The rebellion produced such women leaders as Hong Xuanjiao and Su Sanniang. After establishing a capital in Nanjing, the revolutionary government practiced a number of policies that promoted equality of the sexes and, to a certain extent, supported women's participation in politics. These policies proceeded from the belief that "all land should be divided on the basis of population, regardless of gender" and included the appointment of female officials, whose numbers and duties were the same as male officials. These unprecedented policies clearly raised the political status of women. For the first time, the government established a women's department and set up an exam system to select and promote talented women to fill the ranks of female officials. Female officials were equal in rank with male officials. The highest-ranking female officials were military advisors.

In spite of all this, as a peasant movement, the Taiping rebellion could not break free of feudal ideology. The kings and generals of the Taiping Kingdom practiced polygamy. The movement openly advocated *nandao*, a code of behavior for men, and *nüdao*, *fudao*, and *qidao*, codes of behavior for women in general and for various groups of women, such as wives. It resurrected Ban Zhao's *Admonitions for Women* and placed heavy restrictions on high-ranking women. Influenced by Western ideas of "God-given rights," equality, and liberty, the participants in the Reform Movement of 1898 at the end of the Qing advocated "equality and independence of the sexes." Their rallying cry awakened a small number of intellectual women to strive for liberation. The reformers, however, wanted to improve the system, not to strike at the root of the patriarchal clan system, and they did not initiate or support women's participation in politics. In 1911, after the bourgeois revolutionaries had won, female members of the Tongmenghui (United League, or Revolutionary Alliance) such as Tang Qunying, Lin Zongsu, and Wu Mulan were encouraged by the victorious revolution. Influenced by the suffrage movement in the West, they represented a group of Chinese women in initiating China's first movement for women's participation in politics.

These were advanced women with democratic ideas, and in the democratic revolution led by Sun Yat-sen, they had worked alongside men in political struggles and military actions. Now they demanded a share of the victory: equal rights in the management of the state. To this end, they organized women's groups for political participation, the most influential of which was the Women's League for Political Participation. The League demanded that the legislature revise the provisional constitution of the Republic of China to grant women the right to political participation. Second, the League opposed the "revolutionaries'" abandonment of equality of the sexes as part of its platform when the United League was reorganized into the Guomindang (Nationalist Party). Tang Qunying and others led groups to "cause a scene at the legislature" as they got into heated debates with the president of the legislature. Regrettably, these struggles ended in failure, and the women's groups for political participation were ordered disbanded.

The Nationalist and Communist Parties entered into their first period of cooperation in 1927. He Xiangning, a female representative at the Nationalists' first national people's congress proposed "confirming equality of the sexes." After the congress passed her proposal, it wrote an announcement forcing the subsequent revision of the constitution to grant women equal voting rights with men. When the cooperation between the Nationalists and communists collapsed, the Nationalists abandoned the principle of equality, dealing a serious blow to the women's movement in the areas they controlled. During the period of Nationalist rule, although a few upper-class women joined political participation organizations, these groups lacked a popular base and became little more than a type of democratic embellishment on a crumbling regime. They did not wield any actual influence over women's participation in politics nor did they truly represent the rights, interests, and demands of the masses of women.

PROGRESS IN WOMEN'S POLITICAL PARTICIPATION IN THE REVOLUTIONARY BASE AREAS AND AFTER THE FOUNDING OF NEW CHINA

The People's Republic of China was founded under the leadership of the Chinese Communist Party (CCP), which mobilized the masses on a broad scale, established revolutionary base areas, pursued a path of armed revolution, and, after more than twenty years, overthrew the Nationalist regime to found the new republic. Based on the nature, principles, and goals of the CCP, the Party incorporated the women's liberation movement as part of its political program to liberate the people. Beginning with the second Party congress in 1922, which made the resolution to promote the formation of a women's movement, the Party consistently affirmed the realization of equality of the sexes as one of its basic principles. Women who had been severely repressed in the old society recognized through actual struggle that, as long as they connected their fates closely to the fates of the people and of the working class, they could strive for their own liberation while working to liberate all the people. Based on this realization, tens of thousands of women decided to devote themselves to the people's revolution.

The situation of women's participation in politics in the revolutionary base areas was very different from that in the Nationalist-controlled areas. During the establishment of democratic politics in the base areas during the 1930s, the regime gave women equal rights with men to vote and hold office and also began searching for ways to ensure women's political participation through codified quotas. In 1933 the central agency of the communist regime ruled that, in elections for basic-level representatives, at least 25 percent of the representatives had to be women. The base areas not only made masses of women active members of legislatures at all levels; they also made special use of women worker's assemblies, peasant women's assemblies, and women's congresses to give women organized training in political participation. These assemblies provided women with opportunities to express their opinions and demands and to draft proposals for submission to administrative and legislative agencies. The CCP also attached great importance to the cultivation of female cadres. In the revolutionary base areas, all levels and types of cadre schools recruited female students. The Yan'an Women's University and women's departments of Party schools at all levels were bases for cultivating female cadres.

In September 1949, on the eve of the establishment of the central people's government, the Chinese People's Political Consultative Conference held its first plenary session in Beijing. Present at this watershed political moment were sixty-nine female representatives, who made up 10.4 percent of the representatives and who discussed plans for the establishment of the republic. The outstanding female revolutionary Song Qingling was elected vice chairman of the central people's government. A number of well-known female activists and cadres from the CCP and other democratic parties took on positions of leadership within the government. The conference passed the "Common Principles," which served as a provisional constitution, and made the solemn announcement to the entire nation that the government was discarding the feudal system of oppressing women. Women were to enjoy equal rights with men in every aspect of politics, economics, culture, and social life. From this point on, women were to enter a new period as equals to men.

During the early period of the People's Republic, women's political participation grew both qualitatively and quantitatively. In addition to positions of leadership already held by veteran women revolutionaries, many women intellectuals, outstanding female workers, and peasant women from the newly liberated areas joined the ranks of cadres. In 1951, there were 366,000 female cadres nationwide, accounting for 13.5 percent of all cadres. During this time, a large number of outstanding female workers, peasant women, and women intellectuals were elected as people's representatives and members of political consultative conferences at different levels to represent women by participating in and debating politics. The Election Law of the People's Republic of China, passed in 1953, clearly states that women have equal rights with men to vote and hold office. That same year, China held its first nationwide basic-level general elections, and over 90 percent of eligible female voters cast votes. Of the basic-level people's representatives elected, 17.31 percent were women. In 1956, for the second round of nationwide general elections, the number of women elected as basic-level people's representatives rose to 20.3 percent of all elected representatives. A total of 147 women were elected as national people's representatives, accounting for 12 percent of the representatives. For a nation that had just moved away from being a semifeudal, semicolonial country with a feudal patriarchal ideology and thousands of years of Confucian traditions, this was an earth-shaking change.

During this period, another important accomplishment of the women's movement was the establishment and development of a national women's organization—the All-China Democratic Women's Federation. This organization united all types of women's groups across the nation and established local women's groups all the way down to the grass-roots level. As the CCP's main entity for the masses of women and China's largest popular group, the federation was responsible not only for representing and expressing the special rights, interests, and demands of women, but also for monitoring government actions. The federation promoted all types of women's groups, helping them to work as self-education or special interest groups in the participation in and discussion of politics.

From the second part of the 1950s to the mid-1970s, China implemented a planned economy based on public ownership. During this period, "highlighting politics" was taken to excess, relations between the classes were tense, and management was highly centralized. This was especially true during the Cultural Revolution (1966–1976), when class background determined the selection and promotion of cadres. A large contingent of female workers and peasant women representatives entered politics and were given management duties, while in some places, women intellectuals were overlooked. With respect to the relationship between "equality and efficiency," too much emphasis was placed on "equality." Some places of employment even practiced the radical egalitarianism of paying everyone exactly equal wages, without regard to performance, and ignored special labor protections for women. While such policies rapidly increased women's participation in politics and employment in a formal sense, by diverging from the actual needs and possibilities for social development and women's development, they caused the situation to degenerate, speeding up the process at a high cost. For a while, this not only hindered efficiency but also affected the healthy development of democratic politics. After the mid-1970s, the mistakes of the Cultural Revolution were corrected, and order returned, bringing women's participation in politics back in line with social development.

CHINESE WOMEN'S PARTICIPATION IN POLITICS SINCE THE REFORMS AND OPENING TO THE OUTSIDE

In the late 1970s, China entered a period of development characterized by reform and opening to the outside world. During this period, the constitution and other laws further codified women's equal legal status with men to protect women's political rights. Following the promulgation of the first constitution in 1954, a revised constitution was passed in 1982. This, along with other relevant laws and statutes, especially the Law on the Protection of Women's Rights and Interests, which passed in 1995, comprehensively strengthened the legal status of women and the protection of women's rights and interests.

The right to political democracy was the most crucial of these rights. The Chinese constitution and the Law on Elections, which were revised in the 1980s, both made it the law that women enjoy equal rights with men to vote and be elected to office. The constitution also states that women as well as men enjoy the political right to participate democratically in managing the affairs of the state and enjoy freedom of speech, press, assembly, association, and demonstration. The constitution provides special rules on the state's cultivation and promotion of female cadres.

In 1990, the State Council established a commission on women and children. In 1995, the state solemnly announced that "equality of the sexes" is a basic national policy. Beginning in that same year, the State Council announced the Program for Chinese Women's Development (1995–2000). In 1997, an agency was established to investigate the implementation of this program. This agency began monitoring indices of women's development, including indicators of women's participation in politics. All of these laws and political measures have promoted women's active participation in political activities.

During this period, women made some measurable progress. In March 1998, out of a total of 2,979 representatives elected to the ninth National People's Congress, 650, or 21.82 percent, were women. This was a 1 percent increase over the prior session and a 10 percent increase over the first National People's Congress, in 1954. At the ninth Chinese People's Political Consultative Conference, held at the same time, 341 of the 2,196 delegates (19.52 percent) were women. This represented a 6 percent increase over the prior conference and a 13 percent increase over the first Political Consultative Conference, held in 1949.

At the end of 2000, a total of nearly 15 million Chinese women cadres held public management positions at all levels, accounting for 36.2 percent of all cadres. This was a 3.1 percent increase over 1995 and a 23 percent increase over 1951. Women cadres in Party and government agencies at the county level, division level, and higher numbered 77,300, making up 15.1 percent of the total number of cadres at those levels.

At the same time, there were four women at the highest levels of Party and state leadership. In the twenty-nine ministries and commissions under the State Council, there were eighteen female ministers or deputy ministers. Each Party and government leadership group in the thirty-one provinces, autonomous regions, and municipalities directly administered by the central government included at least one woman, and fifteen of these Party and government leadership groups had more than two women. Nationwide, there were eight women provincial governors or deputy governors. (For comparison, in the period immediately following the founding of the People's Republic, there were only two women at the highest level of Party and state leadership, seven ministers and deputy ministers in the State Council, and two provincial governors and deputy governors.) In the nation's 668 cities, 463 women were elected as mayor or deputy mayor.

Also at the end of 2000, there were 21,000 female judges in the nation's judicial system, accounting for 19 percent of judges. One president of the Supreme People's Court was female, and there were sixteen female court presidents and vice presidents in the superior people's courts at the provincial level.

As China's largest women's group, the All-China Women's Federation (previously the All-China Democratic Women's Federation) has its own representatives at all levels of the people's congress and political consultative conference. The organization continues to expand as it locates and teaches female cadres to promote women's political participation. The All-China Women's Federation now links 68,355 women's groups of all types and at all levels, 2,074 agencies for theoretical research on women, and 859,880 urban

and rural women's organizations. Its staff consists of 98,589 full-time professional women cadres, who were very active in political activities.

Although the participation of Chinese women in politics has made historic
progress, the overall level of women's political participation is not high. From
region to region, development has been unbalanced. As China has engaged in
the process of establishing and perfecting a socialist market economy, new
obstacles have arisen that block women's political participation.

In terms of the gender proportions among cadres, Chinese female cadres are
underrepresented both at the highest decision-making levels and at the basic
level in rural villages. At the highest levels, the percentage of female representatives in the National People's Congress has held at around 21 percent during
the twenty years from the sixth to the ninth congress. In the international
community, China's ranking fell from twelfth place in 1994 to twenty-fourth
place in 2000 in the ranking of countries for their inclusion of women in government. At the ninth Chinese People's Political Consultative Conference,
women delegates made up 15.5 percent of the total. Nationwide, female cadres
make up only 8 percent of the leadership groups at the provincial and ministe-
rial level, a very low showing. Growth in the number of leading female cadres
has been sluggish over the past five years. Female representation at the vast,
basic level of rural villages is also low. For example, according to the requirements of the Program for Chinese Women's Development, there must be at
least one female cadre in the Party and government leadership groups at the
township level. The nationwide average for compliance with this goal is 77.16
percent, but in some western provinces and regions it is only 15.5 percent. At
the village level, 24.1 percent of basic-level village committees have no women.

In terms of female cadres and the hierarchical structure, leading women
cadres in decision-making departments at various levels tend to be concentrated
in education, science and technology, culture, public health, and other government departments. Fewer women are present in major Party and government
agencies and comprehensive economic departments. Leading female cadres tend
to fill positions as deputy heads of departments but not heads of departments.
Female cadres at the intermediate and high levels of government tend to be
older, and the number of younger cadres behind them is too small, making the
supply of new cadres insufficient. In sectors and industries where women are
more concentrated, the gap between the numbers of women in management
levels and numbers of women workers is relatively large.

In terms of the management mechanism of women's participation in politics, state policy requires retirement at age fifty-five, shrinking the time women
can spend participating in the management of public affairs. Moreover, there
are no compensatory rules to offset this situation. Cultivation and recommendation of female cadres at the basic levels lacks vigor, and insufficient attention

is given to the overall rights and interests of women in public office, causing these women to feel powerless and without support.

A lack of comprehensive statistical data on women's participation in the management of state and social affairs and their influence on decision-making leads to the absence of indices and statistical support for the situation of women's participation in leadership both at large- and medium-sized state-run enterprises, as well as non-state-run, large-scale enterprises. Hence, it is difficult to reach objective and comprehensive conclusions. In addition, other obstacles to women's participation include a lack of uniformity in standards and procedures for selection and promotion, blocked channels of advancement, and conservative thinking.

In terms of the climate for women's political participation, public opinion has had a detrimental effect. Surveys of public attitudes indicate that the media is key in limiting women's political participation. The media's ignoring or underreporting news of leading women cadres weakens their status in the public's eye, and results in stereotypes of leading female cadres as embellishment or in supporting positions. Sometimes they are described as jargon-spouting bureaucrats. Furthermore, in addition to the old requirements that women be gentle, kind, and display "traditional virtues," the mass media now require that women be fashionable and beautiful. This puts female cadres in a double bind. The image the mass media have created of strong women as political sacrificial lambs makes young women regard political participation as a perilous endeavor.

CAUSES OF CURRENT PROBLEMS FOR WOMEN'S POLITICAL PARTICIPATION

Many causes contribute to the problems women face in achieving full political participation. First, since opening to the outside world, the focus of China's development strategy has shifted to the economy. The nation is in a period of historical transition from a planned to a market economy, under which the state now implements the principle of "efficiency as the priority, with consideration given to fairness." The mechanisms of competition have led to a philosophy based on the "survival of the fittest," in which women begin at an historical disadvantage, still holding a weaker share of social resources. Moreover, women are now seeing restrictions on the special protections once granted them to ensure their political participation. The old system of setting gender quotas for leadership groups is under challenge. "Competition for posts" makes the appointment and dismissal of cadres more and more dependent on popular opinion and the personal qualities and competitiveness of the candidates. This places higher demands on the development of female cadres.

China's economy is still underdeveloped, and development from region to region is unbalanced, making it impossible to provide sufficient material conditions for women's development. The legacy of the traditional division of labor thousands of years old still exerts an influence in this time of transition and high growth for the industrial sector. The young, energetic rural workforce is shifting to secondary and tertiary industries in the cities and towns, with men outnumbering women. After the 1990s, women made up more than 65 percent of the agricultural workforce and in some areas as much as 80 percent. The dual burdens of farm and domestic work are huge obstacles to rural women's participation in politics. In many villages, this has led to the phenomenon of "male generals and female foot soldiers."

In cities and towns, the adjustments and upgrading of the industrial structure have allowed secondary and tertiary industries to absorb a large labor force, but China's huge population means that the existence of a labor supply greater than demand will remain a prominent problem for a long time to come. In recent years, the deepening of reforms in enterprises, personnel reductions, and increases in efficiency have lowered the employment rate for urban women, who have a harder time than men finding new jobs. According to surveys, the employment rate for urban women age eighteen to forty-nine is 72 percent, a decrease of 16.2 percent from 1990. The re-employment rate for women who have been laid off is only 39 percent, which is 24.9 percent lower than the rate for men. The realities of women's employment have a direct impact on women's activities and development in the political arena.

How women are employed also affects their participation in politics. Gender discrimination exists in formal employment versus informal employment, making it difficult for women to move up from informal employment (the second tier of the labor market) to formal employment (the first tier of the labor market). Women make up the majority of the second tier of the labor market.

A second major cause of these problems, the bias that sees males as superior to females, cannot be underestimated. The influence of China's three thousand-year-old legacy of feudal patriarchy still persists in vast rural areas. In many places, clan power clearly dominates political life, especially elections. Men usually serve as representatives for their clan and kinsmen and receive their support in management. It is rare for married women to receive this kind of support. Unmarried women are considered to be "flying pigeons" who sooner or later will "become part of their husband's family." For this reason, even if they are capable managers, they are not taken seriously. At the same time, fixed concepts about gender roles block women's entrance into the mainstream of political life.

The third cause has to do with the age-old problem of women's education. A woman's level of education is generally directly proportional to her level of political activism, controlling her enthusiasm and her self-confidence for political participation. For historical reasons, Chinese women's levels of education are on the whole lower than men's. According to statistics, 58.8 percent of Chinese women have less than an elementary-school education, and the illiteracy rate is 13.6 percent (as much as 18.8 percent in western areas). These rates are higher than those for men by 21.9 and 9.5 percent respectively. The great majority of women with little education live in rural villages, where women have fewer opportunities for schooling than men. Opportunities for women are particularly scarce in underdeveloped regions. In contrast, urban women, who constitute only a small portion of Chinese women, are much more enthusiastic about politics, have a high opinion of their own political participation and management abilities, and are better able to cope with reforms to the election and cadre systems.

The fourth cause lies within the policies and mechanisms of the selection system. Some surveys and studies have shown that, although China formed rudimentary policies on the cultivation, selection, and promotion of female cadres, factors that negatively affect women's political participation still exist in the implementation of these policies, chiefly because some of these policies were not sufficiently detailed. The ideas are present, but the infrastructure for implementation is lacking, and the policies do not provide enough procedures. Some policies that seem not to discriminate against women have a negative impact on women when they are actually implemented. For example, mandatory retirement ages were formulated in the 1950s, when the rigors of physical labor were much more intense. The idea behind the policy was to take into account the physiological features of women. With progress in science and technology, this factor is now much less important, but this rule, which was originally intended to apply to workers, has been expanded to apply to women professionals and cadres. The policy has become a limiting factor to women's employment and political participation.

The fifth cause has to do with women's burdens of childbearing and housework. Surveys have found that before they have children, female cadres are promoted at nearly the same rate as men. But when women reach the peak of their childbearing years around age thirty, the rate at which they are promoted falls far behind that of equally qualified men. This illustrates the effect of childbearing on women's political participation.

POSSIBLE SOLUTIONS UNDER DISCUSSION

These challenges to women's participation in politics have aroused responses, especially from the All-China Women's Federation. The federation, in cooperation with the Department of Government Personnel and women's research organizations, has convened theoretical and policy seminars on women's participation in politics. The discussion has centered on four main issues: quotas, increasing enthusiasm for female participation, the function of the mass media, and re-evaluating past policies regarding the selection of female cadres.

The argument in favor of quotas for selecting and promoting cadres is that they are not special treatment but "equal conditions, with women as a priority," and an evaluative indicator of the level of political democracy. Under social conditions where gender discrimination is present, in order to represent fully the rights and interests of women so that they may fulfill their legal rights, the government must adopt protective policy measures. Quotas are an important strategy for guaranteeing gains for women of equal power and resources, and an important measure for raising the level of political democracy for the nation. Experience has proved such policies effective, although implementation must be monitored. Some people have pointed out that there should be rules for the systematic increase of current gender quotas. For example, from 2005 to 2010, the percentage of female candidates should reach 30 to 40 percent.

Second, the discussion has also focused on raising women's enthusiasm for and abilities in political participation. The means proposed are encouraging women to take part in activities organized by the Communist Party and other democratic parties, fostering women activists, and promoting compulsory education, developing continuing education, and encouraging especially rural women to study science and technology, politics, and management. Education that strengthens women's self-respect, self-confidence, self-support, and independence is especially important.

Third, serious attention must be given to the role the mass media could play in promoting women's political participation. The media should be encouraged to publicize the basic national policy of equality of the sexes and to raise the public's awareness of equality before the law. The media can also foster a climate of public opinion that overcomes gender bias in all areas. It is necessary to oppose the use of media images that harm women and the use of the media to conduct propaganda that is detrimental to women's participation in politics.

Fourth, in accordance with the basic national policy of equality of the sexes, the government should evaluate past policies and methods relating to the training, selection, and promotion of female cadres, and propose ideas and suggestions for new policy measures to promote women's participation in politics. Existing policies that are not beneficial to women's participation in politics should be revised. Training in gender equality awareness should be strengthened for the entire society, including leading cadres, regular cadres, university students, and mass media workers. Members from all segments of society should come forward to monitor the fulfillment of indicators of women's political participation, which should be used as a basis for evaluating cadres. The mass media should increase positive reporting on images of women who participate in politics. The political achievements of women must be broadly publicized. At the same time, care should be taken to avoid falling into stereotypes when publicizing women's participation in politics.

In general, the development of women's political participation is a historical process that depends on the development of society, of social democratic politics, and of women themselves. History has created a starting point for women's participation in politics that is far behind that of men, and achieving gender equality in this arena will require a relatively long period to eliminate that gap and overcome bias. Solutions to the problems of women's participation in politics require starting from the actual situation, struggling to make progress, to gradually improve conditions and avoid either letting matters take their own course or trying to accelerate the process by excessive enthusiasm. Only by simultaneously promoting the development of China's economy, culture, and the building of democratic politics can we improve the status of women. Only with the support of effective politics and organization and through the efforts of the entire society and women themselves can we overcome gender bias and create better conditions for women's political participation.

BIBLIOGRAPHY

All-China Women's Federation, State Statistics Bureau. *Dierqi Zhongguo funü shehui diwei chouyang diaocha zhuyao shuju baogao* (Report on Major Statistics from the Second Sampling Survey of the Social Status of Chinese Women). Beijing: Zhongguo funü chubanshe, 2001.

All-China Women's Federation Women's Institute, Shaanxi Province Women's Federation Institute. *Zhongguo funü tongji ziliao (1949–1989)* (Statistics for Chinese Women [1949–1989]). Zhongguo tongji chubanshe, 1991.

CCP Central Department of Organization Bureau of Cadre Deployment, All-China Women's Federation, eds. *Peiyang xuanba nüganbu gongzuo* (The Work of Cultivating, Selecting, and Promoting Female Cadres).

Guo Li. "Shixi geji lingdao banzidi xingbie bili peizhi" (Testing and Analysis of Gender Quota Configurations in Leadership Groups at Various Levels). In *Funü yanjiu luncong* (Collected Essays on Women's Studies). 2001.

Liu Zhongyi. "Dui yici minzhu xuanjudi kaocha" (An Investigation of a Democratic Election). In *Funü yanjiu luncong* (Collected Essays on Women's Studies). 2001.

People's Republic of China State Council Information Office. *Zhongguo funü zhuangkuang* (The Situation of Chinese Women). 1994.

Rong Weiyi. "Guanyu canzheng funü xuqiudi yanjiu baogao" (Research Report on the Demand for Women who Participate in Politics). In *Funü yanjiu luncong* (Collected Essays on Women's Studies). 2001.

Seminar on Chinese Women's Political Participation (paper abstracts). *Funü yanjiu luncong* (Collected Essays on Women's Studies). 2001.

Shandong Provincial Committee Department of Organization, Shandong Province Women's Federation Project Team. "'Nülingdao ganbu chengzhang guilü' yanjiu baogao" (Study Report on "Growth Patterns of Leading Female Cadres"). In *Funü yanjiu luncong* (Collected Essays on Women's Studies). 2001.

State Council Commission on Women and Children. "Zhongguo funü fazhan gangyao (1995–2000) zhongqi jiance pinggu baogao" (Interim Monitoring Evaluation Report on the "Program for Chinese Women's Development [1995–2000]"). 2001.

State Statistics Bureau Office of Social and Scientific Statistics. *Zhongguo shehuizhongdi nüren he nanren—shishi he shuju* (Women and Men in Chinese Society—Facts and Data). Beijing: Zhongguo tongji chubanshe, 1995.

"Wo kan funü canzheng—qianming duzhe wenjuan diaocha" (My View of Women's Political Participation—Questionnaire Survey of One Thousand Readers). *Zhongguo funü* (Women of China), April 2001.

Ye Zhonghai, ed. *Zhongguo nülingdao rencai chengzhang he kaifai yanjiu* (Study on the Growth and Development of Chinese Women Leaders). Shanghai: Keji wenxian chubanshe, 1997.

Part III

Women
and
Education

THE READJUSTMENT OF CHINA'S HIGHER EDUCATION STRUCTURE AND WOMEN'S HIGHER EDUCATION

Ma Wanhua

The quality and the amount of education received are basic factors determining women's development and social participation. They are also important indicators of social and economic status. For this reason, in both developed and developing nations, the issue of women's higher education is now receiving more attention. In 1998, the United Nations Educational, Scientific, and Cultural Organization (UNESCO) conference on higher education focused on five major issues facing humankind: empowerment, cooperation, equity, sustainability, and security. The conference emphasized that creating a gender-inclusive culture through education, including higher education, was an important factor in promoting sustainable development and world peace.[1] However, creating a gender-inclusive culture through the development of women's higher education poses a serious challenge for China, because of problems in China's higher education that lead to women's weak position in the broader society. Although China has recently provided opportunities for more women to enter higher education, for a variety of reasons there are still many problems. This essay provides a brief overview of the history, current situation, and problems in women's higher education in China.

THE DEVELOPMENT OF CHINA'S HIGHER EDUCATION AND WOMEN'S HIGHER EDUCATION

China established modern higher education based on the Western model in 1862. In that year, the Qing government established the Capital School for Teachers and Language in Beijing, the purpose of which was to train experts in foreign languages and Western studies. Yet the Capital School was only a junior college and did not accept women. Forty-three years later, in 1905, Protestant missionary groups in China came together to establish the North China Women's University in Beijing. Subsequently, women's universities founded by missionary groups were established in areas with relatively high levels of economic development. For example, the South China Women's

University was founded in Fuzhou in 1907 and the Jinling Women's University was founded in Nanjing in 1917.[2] In 1919, the Beijing National Women's Normal School became the Beijing Women's Senior Normal School, the first institution of higher education for women established by the government. In 1920, Peking University enrolled its first three female students, beginning coeducation in China's institutions of higher education.[3]

In the decades that followed, the lack of economic development coupled with the effects of political turmoil and traditional culture made the progress of China's higher education and women's higher education extremely slow. For example, in 1931, enrollment in China's institutions of higher education in all categories totaled 44,130, of which 5,180, or 12.3 percent, were women. "Based on China's population of 450 million at that time, this meant there was only one university student per ten thousand people, and only one female university student per one hundred thousand."[4] By 1947, the total number of students enrolled in all categories of institutions of higher education had grown to only 155,000, of which 22,700 or 17.8 percent were women.[5] For this reason, when scholars study the development of Chinese higher education on a large scale and the growth of women's higher education, they generally start from the founding of the People's Republic in 1949.

The process of economic recovery and development in the 1950s, the economic reforms that began in the late 1970s, and the policy of revitalizing the nation through science and education during the 1990s all promoted the expansion of China's higher education system as a whole. According to statistics from the *Zhongguo jiaoyushiye tongji nianjian 2000* (Yearbook of Statistics for China's Education Sector 2000), the number of regular institutions of higher education grew from 201 in 1952 to 1,041 in 2000.[6] In 1952, regular institutions of higher education had 79,000 students enrolled. This number increased to 2,206,100 in 2000. The continued expansion of the number of regular institutions of higher education in China and the number of students enrolled had a positive effect on promoting the entrance of Chinese women into higher education. We can observe this effect by looking at the changes in the numbers of female students enrolled in China's regular institutions of higher education as percentages of the total numbers of students enrolled (see Table 1).

Table 1

THE NUMBER OF FEMALE STUDENTS ENROLLED IN REGULAR HIGHER EDUCATION
INSTITUTIONS AS A PERCENTAGE OF THE TOTAL NUMBER OF STUDENTS
(1947–2000)

Year	1947	1955	1960	1965	1975	1980	1985	1990	1995	2000
Percent	17.8	25.9	24.5	26.9	32.6	23.4	30.0	33.7	38.5	41

Sources: Zhao Yezhu, "Studies on Higher Education for Girls in China since the Founding of the
People's Republic," *Studies in Higher Normal Education*, Vol. 5 (1993); Ma Wanhua and Chen
Dingfang, "Great Progress, Serious Challenges—An Overview of Women's Higher Education in
China at the Turn of the Century," *Qinghua University Studies in Education*, Vol. 4 (1998); and
Zhongguo jiaoyushiye tongji nianjian 2000 (Yearbook of Statistics for China's Education Sector
2000) (Beijing: Renmin jiaoyu chubanshe, 2001).

From the percentages of female students shown in Table 1, we can see that
the development of women's higher education has not been smooth. Between the
founding of the People's Republic in 1949 and 1955, the percentage of female
students increased greatly. The anti-Rightist campaign of 1957, the Great Leap
Forward beginning in 1958, natural disasters in 1960, and other factors caused
the percentage of female students in higher education to decline in the early
1960s. During the Cultural Revolution (1966–1976), due to the special historical circumstances of that era, the system for recruiting students and the goals of
education changed dramatically in comparison to previous periods. Between
1970 and 1975 the method of recruiting students depended on recommendations, which not only required students to be political hard-liners but also stipulated a balance between the number of male and female students. Some local
governments even set quotas requiring that one-third of students be female, and
hence female students made up a larger proportion of the student body than ever
before. In 1975, 32.6 percent of enrolled students were female.

The situation changed in the late 1970s when the system of testing for admis-
sion to higher education institutions was restored. By 1980, the percentage of
female university students had fallen markedly. This phenomenon was due in part
to the large number of young women of eligible age who had missed educational
opportunities during the Cultural Revolution. Another reason was a new cycle of
thinking about higher education that considered it useless. For example, in the
early 1980s the generally low salaries for intellectuals contrasted sharply with
salaries in other sectors of the rapidly growing economy. A vendor selling boiled
tea eggs on the street could earn 20 to 30 yuan per day, while a professor or scientist in a level-one government job made no more than 300 yuan per month.
The popular phrase "You're better off selling tea eggs than making atom bombs"
reflected the economic difficulties faced by Chinese intellectuals at the time.

By the mid-1980s, the government had begun to pay some attention to
Chinese intellectuals. For example, the policy on couples who lived in different

locations for work was relaxed, making it easier for couples who had to live apart for employment reasons to transfer to locations where they could be together. Still, the economic difficulties faced by intellectuals remained fundamentally unchanged. The film *Ren dao zhongnian* (At Middle Age), in a moving way, depicts a middle-aged intellectual couple of this time (the husband is an extremely accomplished engineer, the wife a famous ophthalmologist) and their young child, showing how the family lives and works. They live in a nine-square-meter room, all sharing one desk. Despite the hardships, they make sacrifices to give the husband more space and time to pursue his research. The wife decides to let her husband live at the research institute where he works, and she takes on all the housekeeping duties and often stays up late at night researching ophthalmology cases. Even so, she must still endure the disdain of some "ultraleftists." After bringing vision and happiness to countless patients, she is physically and emotionally exhausted and ends up needing an operation. The film vividly depicts the attitudes and living circumstances of Chinese intellectuals during the early 1980s, particularly the sincerity with which Chinese women intellectuals approached family, their work, and society. For this reason, the film gave people a lot to think about.

In order to meet the needs created by economic reforms, beginning in the mid-1980s the Chinese government adopted a series of positive measures to accelerate the reform of higher education. These included changing the old policies on intellectuals, raising their social status, and improving their living conditions. These measures gradually improved people's attitudes about pursuing higher education and, to a certain extent, encouraged women to enter higher education. By 1990, women made up 33.7 percent of all students enrolled in regular higher education institutions, paving the way for the development of women's higher education in the 1990s.

THE EFFECTS OF STRUCTURAL ADJUSTMENTS IN CHINA'S HIGHER EDUCATION ON WOMEN'S HIGHER EDUCATION

As economic reforms have progressed, China's system of higher education has experienced massive changes. Simply citing the increase in the number of regular higher education institutions and the rise in the number of female students gives a very incomplete picture of the current status of women's higher education in China. This is because the structure of China's higher education system, which was reorganized into a unified state-run system in 1952, has developed into the present combination system under which the government is the primary provider of education, and the private sector plays only an auxiliary role. This combination model of higher education includes four main types of educational institutions: (1) regular higher education institutions, (2) adult higher education institutions, (3) informal schooling at non-state-run higher education institutions, and (4) self-study for undergraduate or professional certifications administered by the state. Currently, the number of women studying in the latter three types of institutions continues to rise, and women make up much larger percentages of the student bodies at these institutions than in regular higher education institutions.

China's adult higher education institutions are part of the public system of higher education. They include on-air radio and television universities, vocational schools, agricultural schools, management colleges, learning centers, correspondence schools, and adult schools within regular higher education institutions. China currently has 772 adult higher education institutions. These schools are government-sponsored and thus have a certain level of educational resources, such as guaranteed faculty credentials and quality assurances. As a part of the public system of higher education, the tuition, curriculum, and academic programs at these schools must all adhere to unified national standards. Students wishing to enroll in this category of educational institution must first pass the national adult education examination. Generally, adult education schools offer three-year programs of study with a junior college diploma. Students who have completed a three-year junior college program and wish to obtain a bachelor's degree must study an additional two years. As the name implies, the aim of this type of educational institution is to provide working adults with professional training either on the job or during a leave of absence from a job. Currently, however, there is a sizable contingent of eighteen- to twenty-five-year-old college-age students enrolled in these schools. The number of students enrolled in adult higher education institutions in 2000 was 1,117,700, of which 561,573, or 50.24 percent, were women.

Informal educational programs at higher education institutions sponsored by the private sector are a new development in the history of China's higher education system. These programs differ from the missionary and private universities established prior to 1949 and are distinct from the traditional Chinese concept of private educational institutions. Strictly speaking, these programs are a product of China's policies of reform and opening to the outside world. These non-state-run programs are sponsored by democratic political parties, social groups, and individuals. In situations where state funding of higher education has been inadequate to meet the public's ever-increasing demand, the government has adopted a policy of encouraging the private sector to start schools in order to meet these needs. According to *Zhongguo jiaoyushiye tongji nianjian 2000* (Yearbook of Statistics for China's Education Sector 2000), China has a total of 1,282 institutions in this category.[7] The government exercises quality monitoring and macroscopic control over them but provides little or no funding. Thus, some people have termed this form of education China's version of private higher education. Among these 1,282 educational institutions, only 22 are nationally accredited and may grant undergraduate degrees. The remaining schools are currently not nationally accredited and can only offer students "graduation with diploma" and are thus referred to as informal (nondegree) higher education institutions. In 2000, the total number of students registered in this category of schools was 981,672, of which 477,036, or 48.6 percent, were women.

Most students registered in this category of higher education institution are high school graduates who missed the opportunity to enroll in regular higher education institutions, and young graduates of professional training schools who have not yet found work. Programs at this type of school are geared toward the job market, and students who enroll are mainly interested in obtaining professional skills closely related to a particular job, such as accounting, secretarial skills, English, or word processing. People enrolled in this type of school are considered students, but they do not enjoy the benefits provided to university students required by government regulations, such as discounted fares for train tickets during the holidays, medical insurance, scholarships, and student loans. Due to the high cost of tuition, some students drop out because they cannot afford to continue their studies. In addition, with the exception of a small number of schools, the facilities and quality of teaching at the majority of this type of school is inferior to that of regular higher education institutions. For these reasons, students enrolled at these schools may be unable to earn diplomas. Out of 489,871 students who completed their studies at this type of school in 2000, only 43,971 received a diploma. This translates to a passing rate of 9 percent. Of the total number of students who did receive diplomas, 23,600, or 53.6 percent, were women. The passing rate for women was higher than that for men. This shows that, although problems still exist in this type of educational institution, for women who fail the entrance examinations for regular higher education institutions or adult higher education institutions, these schools offer opportunities for higher education or postsecondary professional training.

China's system of self-study examinations was established in 1981. This is an open and socialized form of higher education in which students study a curriculum on their own and take an examination administered by the government in order to earn an undergraduate or junior college diploma. State-run self-study testing centers administer uniform national examinations in the spring and fall of each year. Students learn the material through correspondence courses, by attending night school, listening to radio broadcasts, watching educational television programs, or participating in online education. Students determine which courses and examinations to take and how many years they will need to complete a program based on the amount of time they have available and their personal academic situations. After registering for the examinations required for a particular major, the student can apply for an undergraduate or junior college equivalent degree. The aim of the self-study examination system is to encourage working people who have not had the opportunity to attend university to improve their knowledge and business skills through self-study. When the higher education self-study examination system was first started, it did not attract a lot of attention. But with the changes brought about by economic reforms and changes in the hiring system, people began to attach more importance to improving their levels of knowledge. In particular, many young working women, confronted with the social reality of the large numbers of laid-off women workers, believed that improving themselves was very important and became active participants in self-study programs. According to *Quanguo gaodeng jiaoyu zixuekaoshi tongjiziliao huibian (1994–1999)* (Collected Statistics for the National Higher Education Self-Study Examination Program [1994–1999]), in 1995 there were only 6,995,784 registrations for undergraduate and junior college examinations, of which 3,349,226, or 47.87 percent, were by women. By 1999, the number of such registrations rose to 13,044,591, of which 7,173,457, or 55 percent, were by women.[8] The composition of the body of women students who register for the national self-study examinations and obtain a degree is relatively complex. According to additional data from the same source, in 1999, the largest group of women who obtained undergraduate and junior college degrees through this system were civil servants, followed by laborers, teachers, the military, farmers, and the unemployed. The age span of these women can be divided into three segments: eighteen to twenty-five-year-olds, who make up the largest segment; twenty-six to thirty-five-year-olds, who are the next largest; and finally those thirty-six years old and higher. The geographical distribution of the students is also relatively uneven. Of the thirty-two provinces, municipalities, and autonomous regions where women participated in the self-study examinations, the greatest numbers were concentrated in the economically and educationally more developed areas on the coast and in east central China, such as Hunan, Guangdong, Henan, and Hebei. Border provinces and regions such as Qinghai province, the Ningxia Hui Autonomous Region, and the Guangxi Zhuang Autonomous Region had fewer participants. This shows that regions with a higher level of economic development have higher educational demands for women workers. An analysis of the age span shows that women who did not have the opportunity to attend university use the self-study examination system as a way to improve their level of education.

Currently, China's regular higher education institutions form the backbone of undergraduate and professional higher education and shoulder the responsibility for training high-level experts. After students are accepted into these institutions and have completed the four-year course of studies, they earn a bachelor's degree as a matter of course. In comparison to the students in the three nontraditional forms of education, students in regular higher education institutions have more opportunities to pursue graduate training or to apply to study abroad. They also face more favorable employment situations, and their prospects for career development are better. In addition to undergraduate or junior college training, many regular higher education institutions also offer education at the master's and doctoral levels.

In China, two types of educational institutions provide graduate training at the master's and doctoral levels. One type is graduate education in regular higher education institutions. Their goal is to train university professors, senior research personnel, and administrative management personnel. The other type of graduate training is through research institutes, such as the Chinese Academy of Sciences, the Academy of Agricultural Science, and the Academy of Social Science. The primary aim of these institutions is to train senior experts, research personnel, and management personnel in various fields of the natural and social sciences. Graduate education in China developed on a large scale after the promulgation of the "Regulations of the People's Republic of China on Academic Degrees" in 1980, which designated the master's and doctoral levels. Thus, conventional graduate education has a history of only twenty years in China and is relatively small in scale. The number of master's students recruited in 2000 was 102,923, of which 37,373, or 36.3 percent, were women. The number of doctoral students recruited was even smaller, at 25,142. Of these, 6,689, or 26.6 percent, were women. Female graduate students specialize in natural sciences, engineering, agriculture, medicine, and the humanities and social sciences, but the greatest numbers are concentrated in the fields of medicine and the humanities and social sciences. Liang Guizhi has studied graduate education for women in China and discovered that, in the top ten disciplines in which academic degrees are awarded, the discipline with the highest representation of women is medicine, at 25 to 40 percent. This is followed by the humanities, social sciences, and natural sciences, where women make up 20 to 35 percent of the total. Women make up 30 percent of the graduate students in agriculture sciences and approximately 13 percent in engineering and technology.[9]

PROBLEMS FACING WOMEN'S HIGHER EDUCATION IN CHINA

A basic analysis summarizing the current situation of women's participation in the various types of higher education institutions shows that, with the development and structural adjustment of China's higher education, the ways in which women access higher education have become more diverse. Passing the highly competitive entrance exams for regular higher education institutions is no longer the only avenue to higher education. Diversification in the forms of higher education meets women's educational needs. For example, self-study examinations provide extremely flexible continuing education opportunities for working and married women. Higher education institutions sponsored by the private sector provide women who are unable to enroll in regular higher education institutions with opportunities for higher education. However, at the same time that we applaud the diversification and development of women's higher education, we cannot overlook some remaining problems.

First, higher education for Chinese women still operates at a fairly rudimentary level and does not necessarily provide a means of social advancement. The self-study examination program offers great flexibility and autonomy, and in 2000, women accounted for more than 50 percent of all test registrations. In terms of time and cost, this program is very beneficial to professional women who have not received conventional higher education. However, it is difficult for students who obtain academic credentials and diplomas through this form of education to enter the high-income sectors of the job market.

According to a survey by the Guangdong Research Topic Group, the top ten areas of study chosen by women who take the self-study examinations were secretarial skills, elementary education, education studies, nursing, finance, tour guiding, hotel management, file management, public relations, and English. Women make up 53.6 percent of the students in informal programs at non-state-run higher education institutions and 50.24 percent of the students in adult higher education schools, and the range of disciplines they study is somewhat broader (than in the self-study group).[10] Nevertheless, these two types of education are mainly three-year junior college programs with the goal of training people for the job market. They mainly provide professional training in skills that are in high demand in the market. Most women in these programs of study concentrate on secretarial skills, nursing, public relations, finance, business English, tour guiding, office automation, and computer applications. Due to the general difficulty of finding a job at the present time, many women are pursuing an education in order to make a livelihood in the intensely competitive labor market. Thus, although women account for more than 50 percent of the students in these three types of educational programs, this does not translate into a notable rise in women's overall social status.

Second, in regular higher education institutions, not only is women's level of participation low, but there is also a severe gender imbalance in some disciplines. According to the *2000 Beijing daxue gexike benkesheng zhaosheng fen xingbie tongji shuju* (2000 Beijing University Statistical Data on the Breakdown of Students Within Various Departments on the Basis of Gender), in the fields of linguistics, history, legal studies, foreign languages, and economics, women far outnumbered men, making up 72, 61, 61, 60, and 57 percent of the total number of students in these departments respectively. By contrast, in physics, mechanics and engineering, computer science, chemistry, and molecular engineering, men far outnumbered women, accounting for 85.6, 85.5, 78.3, 73.1, 65.4, and 65.3 percent respectively.[11] Among the ranks of China's scientific and technical specialists, female scientists account for only one-third of the total. Women account for only 4.8 percent of the academicians at the Chinese Academy of Sciences and the Chinese Academy of Engineering, and that figure may be even lower now.[12] In light of these phenomena, Xiao Jie called for more attention to be paid to the training of women scientists.[13]

Third, there are noticeably fewer women than men at the highest levels of higher education in China. This is particularly obvious in China's regular higher education institutions and graduate education. At the undergraduate and junior college level, women accounted for 41 percent of all students enrolled in 2000. Yet at higher levels of education women make up far smaller percentages of the student body. Out of all graduate students recruited nationally in 2000, women at the master's candidate level accounted for 36.3 percent of the total. Women doctoral students accounted for 26.6 percent of all doctoral students recruited. The underrepresentation of women in the highest levels of higher education severely limits women's entrance into higher-paying jobs and higher positions in society. We can further explain this issue by tying it to the patterns of women's participation in higher education. The conventional wisdom holds that education has always been a field where women's participation is strong, and higher education is no exception. In reality, women's level of participation is strongest at the lowest levels of academe and declines dramatically at the higher levels. According to statistics from 1999 on the number of female professors in higher education, 47.9 percent of teaching assistants were women, 41.8 percent of lecturers were women, 30 percent of associate professors were women, and only 15.07 percent of full professors were women. This shows that, although national laws require gender equity, women are at a disadvantage in the mechanism of social competition.

AN EXPLORATION OF THE CAUSES BEHIND THE CURRENT PROBLEMS

One of the chief causes behind the problems described above is the lack of adequate resources for women's education. Lu Li has found that "during the nearly forty years from 1952 to 1990, 40 percent of the national annual investment in primary education was used for women. At the secondary level 35 percent of education investment was used for women, and in higher education 27 percent of annual investment was used for women."[14] Women receive less financial support for education from their families, who devote far greater resources to the education of sons than daughters. In situations where resources are limited, parents are usually unwilling to invest in their daughter's education, because sooner or later their daughter will marry and join her husband's family. The more time a family spends investing in a daughter's education, the less time it has to reap the benefits of their investment. This is what leads girls in impoverished areas to drop out of school. Even in the economically more developed areas, girls enjoy far fewer educational resources from the family than boys. According to Lu Li, "sons get 55 percent, daughters 45 percent." Due to the lack of educational resources, some girls, particularly those who live in poorer border areas, basically do not have the opportunity to receive higher education. What is even more unfair is that, even though girls receive a smaller portion of educational resources, they pay a high price for these meager resources, either missing out on educational opportunities or paying the high cost of tuition to attend informal schooling at higher education institutions.

The problem of the gender imbalance in some disciplines in regular higher education institutions may be due to physiological and psychological differences between men and women; the division of labor between the sexes in society also hinders women from entering the fields of science and engineering. There is also the influence of sociocultural stereotypes. Sayings like "Girls are good at thinking in images and language; boys are good at logic and abstract thinking" are frequently heard in daily life. Based on these ideas, teachers at the primary and secondary levels often consciously or unconsciously guide boys and girls to develop in opposite directions. These cultural stereotypes in schools can be manifested in many ways throughout a student's academic career. Recently, in a survey of junior high school vocational training programs in impoverished areas, we discovered that, in order to attract more female students, some junior high schools in the area had instituted professional training courses that included classes on fashion and embroidery just for girls. There is nothing inherently wrong with setting up such classes, but in terms of gender consciousness it appears that girls can only learn fashion and embroidery, not modern scientific technology.[15]

Another problem stems from the fact that the pedagogy and management in higher education today do not take into account the increased number of women among university students; the unique characteristics of women as they undergo the learning process are "ignored." The Guangdong Research Topic Group explains that to say they are "ignored" means that: "In practice, educators focus on boys because there are more of them and they are more active. Educators usually concentrate their efforts on the male students."[16] This model of education centered on boys affects the physical and psychological growth of female university students and their establishment of self-confidence. In their studies of the psychology of female university students, Yi Liguo and Feng Mei discovered that female university students tend to have a sense of inferiority and to underestimate themselves. Faced with academic pressures, female university students are forced to display abilities that go against the traditional ideal of women as compliant and quiet; "but these abilities are limited to what is considered acceptable. If a woman gets too 'pushy,' she may very well be considered 'unfeminine.' Thus, female university students are caught between a rock and a hard place, and unconsciously underestimate themselves and give up on competing." Yi and Feng recommend that more attention be paid to female university students academically and in other areas of their lives, based on their psychological characteristics, and that the physical and psychological cultivation of female university students be strengthened.[17]

Another issue closely related to female university students' underestimating themselves is the problem of women's employment. The economic reforms have introduced the element of competition in the workplace, and economic benefit is now the primary goal of businesses. Employers often consider women to be a burden because of reproductive issues, physiological issues, and differences in physical strength. Some people recognize that, in comparison to men, women have some psychological features that are more beneficial to the development of a business, but they are still unwilling to hire women. The difficulty women experience in finding employment has become a serious social problem. This problem affects not only laid-off women workers with relatively low levels of education but also highly educated women. Job advertisements often include language that excludes women. When hiring university graduates, many employers place no additional conditions on men, but they place strict limitations on women. Some employers even say, "We'd hire C- men rather than A+ women"; or they simply post ads that read, "Only hiring men." This phenomenon forces some women who have earned master's degrees or doctorates to lower their standards when it comes to finding employment. It is not uncommon for women who hold master's degrees and doctorates from premier institutions such as Peking University and Qinghua University to face this sort of problem.[18]

The difficulty women experience in finding employment greatly reduces women's incentive to pursue higher education. Our studies found that some female university students were unwilling to pursue a master's degree or doctorate. They fear that, if they become too specialized, the range of jobs open to them will become even narrower. Notably, a recent research project sponsored by the Ford Foundation entitled "Why Girls in Impoverished Areas Drop out of School Early" found similar attitudes.[19] Girls who had not yet graduated from junior high school told us in no uncertain terms that, if you could not get a job after going to university, what was the point of wasting all that time? If the worries these girls express over their futures become tomorrow's reality, it will affect not only the development of the girls themselves but will also seriously hamper the development of the entire society.

The problems encountered by girls in the course of their education and development come from all aspects of society and are comprehensive in nature. Solving this problem, in a situation where nearly one hundred million women are illiterate or semiliterate, will require a very long time if we rely solely on women's self-awareness and awakening of their consciousness. For this reason, the "Outline for the Development of Chinese Women (2001–2010)" proposes responsibility for the government.[20] The government should incorporate the major goals of women's education into its development plans for national education. The government should also enact and perfect laws, statutes, and policies that benefit equal educational opportunities for women and men and guarantee women's rights to education. In addition, the government should adopt specific, proactive policies and measures, such as increasing funding for women's education and reducing tuition fees for girls in impoverished areas. By doing so, the government can ensure that girls in impoverished areas not only will complete the nine years of compulsory education but will also have the opportunity to attend university and pursue higher education. In order to encourage more women to enter the fields of science and engineering, the government should monitor university admissions processes to ensure that male and female candidates receive equal consideration. Higher education institutions should establish scholarships for women in the fields of science and engineering to encourage women to enter these fields and to ensure that they complete their studies. In order to improve employment prospects for women, especially in the high-tech sector, the government should use a variety of methods to improve the employment environment.

NOTES

1. "Thematic Debate: Women and Higher Education: Issues and Perspective in Higher Education in the Twenty-first Century: Vision and Action," UNESCO, Paris, 5–9 October 1998.

2. Wu Jing, "Lun Zhongguo jiaohui nüzi gaodeng jiaoyudi zaoqi fazhan" (On the Early Development of Women's Education by Missionaries in China), *Gaodeng jiaoyu yanjiu* (Studies in Higher Education), Vol. 4, 1997.

3. Mao Zhongying, ed., *Yu Qingtang jiaoyulun zhuxuan* (Educational Writings of Yu Qingtang) (Beijing: Renmin jiaoyu chubanshe, 1993).

4. Ma Wanhua and Chen Dingfang, "Judadi jinbu, yanjundi tiaozhan—Zhongguo funü gaodeng jiaoyu shizi zhi jiao di huigu" (Great Progress, Serious Challenges—An Overview of Women's Higher Education in China at the Turn of the Century), *Qinghua daxue jiaoyu yanjiu* (Qinghua University Studies in Education), Vol. 4, 1998.

5. Zhao Yezhu, "Jianguohou woguo nüxing jieshou gaodeng jiaoyou yanjiu" (Studies

on Higher Education for Girls in China Since the Founding of the People's Republic), *Gaodeng shifan jiaoyu yanjiu* (Studies in Higher Normal Education), Vol. 5, 1993.

6. *Zhongguo jiaoyu nianjian 1949–1981* (Yearbook of Chinese Education 1949–1981) (Beijing: Renmin jiaoyu chubanshe, 1983).

7. *Zhongguo jiaoyushiye tongji nianjian 2000* (Yearbook of Statistics for China's Education Sector 2000) (Beijing: Renmin jiaoyu chubanshe, 2001).

8. *Quanguo gaodeng jiaoyu zixuekaoshi tongjiziliao huibian (1994–1999)* (Collected Statistics for the National Higher Education Self-Study Examination Program [1994–1999]) (Beijing: Gaodeng jiaoyu chubanshe, 2001).

9. Liang Guizhi, "Woguo yanjiusheng jiaoyuzhongdi nüxing jiaoyu" (Women's Education in Chinese Graduate Student Education), *Yanjiusheng jiaoyu* (Graduate Student Education), Vol. 2, 1995, 23–29.

10. Guangdong Research Topic Group, "Zhongguo nüxing gaodeng jiaoyudi kuashiji sikao" (Thoughts on Higher Education for Chinese Women at the Turn of the Century), *Zhonghua nüzixueyuan xuebao* (Bulletin of the Chinese Women's College), Vol. 1, 2001.

11. *2000 Beijing daxue gexike benkesheng zhaosheng fen xingbie tongji shuju* (2000 Peking University Statistical Data on the Breakdown of Students Within Various Departments on the Basis of Gender).

12. Zhu Lilan, "Zhongguo nükeji renyuan yeji dingtianlidi" (The Tremendous Accomplishments of Women Chinese Scientific and Technical Personnel), *Keji ribao* (Sci-Tech Daily), 12 July 1995.

13. Xiao Jie, "Woguo nüwulixuejia weihe yuelai yueshao" (Why China Has Fewer and Fewer Female Physicists), *Kexue shibao* (Science Times), 21 September 2001.

14. Lu Li, "Funü jingjidiwei yu funü renliziben guanxide shizhengyanjiu" (A Study on the Relationship Between Women's Economic Status and Labor Capital), *Renkou yanjiu* (Population Studies), Vol. 2, 1997.

15. Ma Wanhua, "Pinkun diqu shentou zhiye jishu jiaoyu xiangmu" (Vocational Skills Educational Projects in Impoverished Areas), Assessment Report, 2000.

16. Guangdong Research Topic Group, "Thoughts on Higher Education."

17. Yi Liguo and Feng Mei, "Gaige kaifangzhongdi nüdaxuesheng xintai ji guanli" (The Psychology and Management of Female University Students in the Context of the Reforms and Opening to the Outside), *Hunan shifandaxue shehuikexue xuebao* (Hunan Normal University Bulletin of Social Science), Vol. 1, 1993.

18. Yang Siqin, "Nüyanjiusheng xianzhuang fenxi ji zhanwang" (Analysis of the Current Situation and Prospects for Female Graduate Students), *Yanjiusheng jiaoyu* (Graduate Student Education), Vol. 2, 1995.

19. Ma Wanhua and Zheng Zhenzhen, "Pinkundiqu nütong chuoxue wenti yanjiu" (Why Girls in Impoverished Areas Drop out of School Early), *Bejing daxue jiaoyu pinglun* (Peking University Review of Education), Vol. 3., 2003.

20. "Zhongguo funü fazhan gangyao (2001–2010)" (Outline for the Development of Chinese Women [2001–2010]), State Council, May 2001.

GENDER INEQUALITY IN EDUCATION IN RURAL CHINA

Danke Li

Historically in China females had less access to schooling than males. After the Chinese Communist Party took power in 1949, the government launched large-scale campaigns to improve literacy rates as part of the socialist revolution to liberate the people from oppression and ignorance (Edwards and Roces, 2000, 77). Since women constituted the majority of the illiterate population, literacy campaigns benefited Chinese females, even though these campaigns were intended to be gender-neutral. From the 1950s to 1980, some improvement was also made in providing access to schooling for Chinese females. However, when the economic reform movement began in the early 1980s and deepened in the 1990s, females' relatively limited access to schooling was still a major problem in Chinese education.

During the past twenty years, modernization reform has significantly changed the Chinese economy. To meet the demand of a skilled labor force for a fast-developing national economy, the Chinese government launched an educational reform movement in 1985 to achieve nine-year compulsory education and to reform secondary and higher education. The establishment of the Compulsory Education Law in China in 1986 formally laid the legal and structural bases for gender equality in schooling. But in the implementation of the reform policies, one of the challenging issues concerns females' unequal treatment in education and its relationship to gender inequality in the larger society.

A resurgence of substantial educational disparities between urban and rural areas, coastal and inland regions, and males and females has accompanied rapid economic development over the past two decades. Increasingly, both policy-makers and educators alike regard these disparities as significant problems because of their negative implications for socioeconomic inequality and inequity.

Gender inequality in access to schooling is visible in statistics provided in Table 1. The information reveals three important facts about the enrollment of women in education during the period 1980 to 1999. First, it shows that, at all three levels of schooling, the percentage of female enrollment was smaller than that for males. Second, the higher the schooling level, the lower the percentage

Table 1
PERCENTAGE OF DISTRIBUTION OF TOTAL ENROLLMENT BY SEX AT DIFFERENT
LEVELS OF SCHOOLING, 1980–1999

% Distribution of Enrollment by Gender	1980	1985	1990	1995	1998	1999
Institutions of Higher Education						
Female	23.4	30.0	33.7	35.4	38.3	39.2
Male	76.6	70.0	66.3	64.6	61.7	60.8
Regular Secondary Schools						
Female	39.6	40.2	41.9	44.8	45.7	45.9
Male	60.4	59.8	58.1	55.2	54.3	54.1
Primary Schools						
Female	44.6	44.8	46.2	47.3	47.6	47.6
Male	55.4	55.2	53.8	52.7	52.4	52.4

Source: National Bureau of Statistics, 657.

of female students present. Third, female enrollments increased over time at all three levels of schooling.

Large disparities in females' access to schooling exist between mostly urban areas, like Shanghai and Beijing, and rural regions like Qinghai and Tibet. In 1999, Shanghai, a relatively more developed municipality, had the highest enrollment rate of 99.99 percent for female school-age children. In the same year Beijing, the capital, achieved a 99.94 percent enrollment rate. However, in Tibet, a relatively less developed minority region, only 77.9 percent of school-age female children were enrolled in school. In Qinghai the rate was 92.39 percent. Given China's huge population, even a small percentage of female children who are not in school translates into a large number of people. For example, in Sichuan province female school-age children numbered 3,852,044, 95.3 percent of whom were enrolled in school in 1999. The 4.7 percent not enrolled amounted to 181,046 children (Ministry of Education, 1999, 277).

The dropout rate of school-age children is another indicator of gender inequality. During the past two decades, the nonattendance rate was higher among females than males. In the early 1990s, among the total of 2.61 million school-age children not enrolled in school, two-thirds were girls and the majority of them lived in poor rural areas (Wang and Zhou, 1995, 82). In addition, the substantial majority of the dropouts were females (Ministry of Education 2000, 803). Gansu province, one of the mostly rural poor provinces, had a dropout rate of 3 percent for elementary school and 4.6 percent for junior high school in 1999, among which 2.75 and 4.27 percent were female students respectively.

Gender inequality in access to schooling is reflected in China's illiteracy and semiliteracy rates as well. According to scholars' estimates, in 1997, over 71 percent of China's 164 million illiterates were women (Edwards and Roces,

2000, 77). In 1999, while 8.81 percent of the male population over the age of fifteen was classified as illiterate or semiliterate, the percentage of females in the same age group and categories was 21.56 percent (National Bureau of Statistics, 2000, 103).

A large gap in the female illiterate and semiliterate rate can be found also between mostly urban and mostly poor rural regions. In 1999, for example, in Beijing only 10 percent of women were illiterate or semiliterate, but in Tibet and Qinghai, the figures were 74.60 and 41.53 percent respectively (Ibid., 103).

Gender inequality in access to schooling was most severe in poor rural areas during the past two decades. In 1980, 80.6 percent of China's population lived in the countryside. As a result of the economic reforms, by 1999 rural population had decreased to 69.1 percent of China's population (Ibid., 95). In general urban residents are better educated and the one-child family policy is more successful in these areas. Most urban families are willing to pay for their daughters' education. Thus, most urban girls face relatively less discrimination in access to schooling. However, the majority of Chinese still live in the countryside and in general are less educated and have less economic security than their urban counterparts. School-age girls in poor rural areas face much greater difficulties in access to schooling (Edwards and Roces, 2000, 78–79). Hence this essay focuses on gender inequality in access to schooling in poor, rural areas in China, particularly through a study of family decisions about the education of girls.

RURAL FAMILIES AND GIRLS' EDUCATION

During the past twenty years, China's economic reforms have renewed the function of the household as an economic unit, especially in rural areas. Along with the deepening of China's educational reforms, the household has also become an important unit for financing education. China's economic reforms have significantly altered economic life in the rural areas. While some households have increased their income, the vast majority remain relatively poor. The shifting of financing for education from the government to households has created substantial economic burdens on rural households, which could have profound effects on access to compulsory and postcompulsory education for children in China, especially for girls in poor areas.

A study conducted in the mid-1990s of four hundred poor rural households in four counties in Gansu and Hebei provinces sheds light on gender inequality in access to schooling in poor rural areas. First, the study shows that household educational decisions in rural China were sex-differentiated. In general, parents had different educational expectations for boys and girls in rural China. Most rural parents had higher educational expectations for their sons than for their daughters and were more likely to be supportive of boys than girls in decisions regarding access to schooling. Second, a variety of social, economic, and cultural institutions and practices influenced these decisions. Some of them are traditional forces, like attitudes discriminating against women; some of them are new problems associated with China's economic reforms (Li and Tsang, 2003).

In rural China, traditional attitudes regarding women in society and gender relationships in households disadvantage rural girls, especially with regard to education. Traditionally sons are expected to continue the family line and support aging parents. Daughters are considered nonpermanent members of households. They are expected to marry into other people's households; hence their well-being is dependent on whether they make a good marriage. Thus, parents are less likely to spend scarce resources on a daughter's education.

Some households not only are reluctant to spend money on a daughter's education, but are also eager to seek a quick return of the money already spent on a daughter. Parents may pull their daughters out of schools to push them into jobs with good temporary earnings but without long-term career prospects.

During the past two decades, the decollectivization of the rural economy, the reform of state-owned enterprises, and the transition to a market-oriented economy have allowed many privately owned enterprises to hire large numbers of young female workers with limited education in the manufacturing and service sectors, especially in the booming coastal cities. In addition, many rural village and township enterprises also have developed small-scale factories and enterprises that hire young women with limited education. However, this type of employment is temporary and perceived by both young women themselves and the employers as transitional work for young women before their marriage, without career potential for young women with only elementary and lower secondary education. Nevertheless, it is an important household economic strategy for rural families regardless of whether young rural women take these temporary jobs of their own free will to seek freedom and personal identity or whether they are forced to contribute in this way to their families' financial well-being. In most cases, the young women either send money back to their families or save their hard-earned money for their own weddings. Either way, the employment helps rural households realize monetary returns from their daughters. But after marriage, with no long-term career prospects and less education than their husbands, rural women will have to remain in the countryside doing farming work while their better-educated husbands may seek nonfarming and cash-earning jobs, thus perpetuating the inequality of gender relationships in rural households.

The additional costs of schooling may also influence households' decisions regarding education. Under the 1986 Compulsory Education Law, school-age children should receive nine years of tuition-free education. But this does not include supplementary expenses for school fees, textbooks, supplies, clothing, food, and other boarding costs, which the family must pay.

The Gansu and Hebei study reveals that, in the rural areas, household educational spending was quite high, averaging about 10 percent of total household spending. At the national level, statistics show that household education and cultural spending as a proportion of total household spending in rural areas has been increasing over time, for example, from 7.8 percent in 1995 to 10.7 percent in 1999. In 1999 the proportion was 11.1 percent in Gansu and 10.2 percent in Hebei (National Bureau of Statistics, 2000, 334–335). Household education spending was especially heavy among the poorest rural households. The Gansu and Hebei study reveals that, for the bottom 20 percent of the poorest households, education spending amounted to between one-fifth and one-third of total household spending (Li and Tsang, 2003). When the economic burden of education is heavy for rural families, parents will likely spend the scarce resources on their sons rather than their daughters.

Economic burdens on household education spending could also affect rural female children's dropout rates. The Gansu and Hebei study shows that, when household budgets became so tight that households had to make decisions about who would stay in school, parents favored boys over girls, leading to a higher dropout rate for rural girls.

In addition to the economic burden of education on households, school availability and quality also affect rural girls' access to schooling. Historically, rural regions in especially poor areas have less-developed transportation, communication, and education systems. In many scattered villages, the availability and quality of schools for rural children have always been problems. In some remote areas, elementary school children have to walk miles to go to school, and this situation is especially severe in minority areas. Because villagers are dispersed throughout isolated areas, many villagers do not have their own elementary schools. When children have to walk long distances, rain or shine, to go to school with poor academic and material resources, parents are less likely to send their daughters. With few lower and upper secondary schools in rural regions, fewer parents still would consider sending their daughters to those schools (Xiao and Ma, 1993, 13–14).

Another problem that hinders females' access to schooling in poor rural areas is a lack of qualified teachers, especially qualified female teachers. The poor rural districts usually do not have the financial strength and material resources to recruit and retain qualified teachers, especially female ones, who are crucial to recruiting female students, particularly in post-elementary schools. Normally in rural areas one junior high school has to serve students who live so far away from the school that they must become residents. The lack of female teachers often contributes to parents' reluctance to allow their daughter to reside at such schools (Yang, 1995, 43).

The quality of schools and the usefulness of schooling for rural children, especially for rural girls, also are factors determining education for girls in these communities. In China, the ultimate aspiration for many students is to get into postsecondary schools. Only then can they get desirable nonfarming jobs. In most of the schools in poor rural regions, the quality of teaching is poorer than that of relatively more affluent and urban areas, hence, the proportion of students able to enter postsecondary institutions is relatively low. With a diminished chance for postsecondary education even for rural boys and the abolition in 1992 of the policy of government-guaranteed jobs for college students, parents are less likely to consider sending their daughters to school. Furthermore, researchers in China have pointed out that, because of the use of standardized teaching materials and textbooks, the education of rural students has very little to do with their lives (Wang, 1994, 10; He, 1993, 14).

In the late 1990s, researchers in China concluded that, in addition to family and the mass media, education is important for students' development, including their understanding of gender. In general, however, instead of providing active guidance on gender issues, school education often reinforces gender stereotyping. Such stereotyping exists in standard textbooks and in the differential treatment of male and female students by teachers.

A study of ten volumes of Chinese language and literature textbooks used in Chinese elementary education revealed that gender bias exists in at least four ways. First, there are more male characters in the stories and illustrations chosen. For example, 132 texts feature male characters as compared to only 21 texts that feature females. Second, males always appear to be smarter than females in the texts. In most stories, the smart kids who actively use their brains are always boys. Third, males always have higher status and better and more meaningful jobs than females. Doctors and engineers are mostly males, while females are primarily nurses and teachers. In many texts and illustrations females are jobless and do household chores only. Last, in many texts females are portrayed in a negative manner. For instance, in the story of "The Fisherman and the Goldfish," the wife is evil and greedy. In general such textbooks view females as ignorant and shortsighted or weak and in need of protection and compassion.

In addition, the same study also shows that teachers often treat boys and girls differently in school. Boys and girls are often assigned to sex-differentiated activities and in general boys are regarded as smarter than girls (Qiang, 2000, 151–153). The gender stereotyping and gender role socialization in school contributes to the existing belief in rural society that it is useless for females to go to school.

In the early 1990s, the Women's Studies Center of Peking University, together with researchers from education and research institutes in three poor northwestern provinces (Ningxia, Gansu, and Qinghai), organized a large-scale project to study girls' education in poor rural regions. The result was the publication of an oral history on female education in the three northwestern provinces that recorded the personal stories of poor rural girls, teachers, and parents. These stories corroborate the general findings we have summarized. The following story comes from this project.

THE STORY OF GAO CAIQIN

"If I have the opportunity, I want to go back to school," said Gao Caiqing when the Beijing researchers met the seventeen-year-old girl.

"My name is Gao Caiqin and I am seventeen. My family is in Gao Village in Xiangnan township, Tongwei county of Gansu province. There are four children in our family, and I am the third one. Both my brother and an older sister have graduated from junior high school. My younger brother is in the fifth grade in elementary school. I am the only one who dropped out of school before my graduation from middle school. Our family condition is relatively better than that of many in our village. We have a hand-operating tractor for transportation business. Farming is not heavy for us, for we only cultivate a little over ten mu [a mu equals 0.165 acre] of land. Due to the scarce rainfall, what we produce is just enough for our own food consumption.

"When I was seven, the age of going to school, I did not go to school because my younger brother was small and I had to take care of him. I did not go to school until I was nine and I was older than my classmates. My school was called Gaodian Elementary School, about five minutes away from my house. There were about thirty students in my class. When I was in the first, second, and third grades, there were not many female students in my classes. However, when I got into the fourth grade, the number of female students increased. The main reason was that many girls had to repeat the fourth grade. There were more than ten repeating fourth graders in my class, and most of them were girls. After knowing them better, I learned that the main reason for them to repeat the fourth grade was that most of them lived far away from the school. They had to walk on mountain trails everyday. If it rained or snowed, it became very dangerous and they could not go to school. After they missed many classes, they could not move up with the rest of the class and had to repeat the fourth grade. I liked school very much, and in elementary and junior high I was one of the top students in my classes and I never had to repeat a grade.

"Our curriculum included Chinese language and literature, mathematics, and science. After the fourth grade, it also included history and geography. After-school curriculum included horizontal bars and parallel bars, basketball, and soccer. I liked playing badminton best. In terms of academic studies, I liked history and Chinese language and literature best.

"Even today I cannot forget my life at the elementary school. Every morning and evening I spent time on the school field studying and playing with my classmates. My teacher told us to study and to play in the school field, because the air was fresh there. On that beautiful campus I finished my elementary education.

"In the fall of 1992, I entered Haishituo Middle School. The school was more than ten li [a li equals 0.311 mile] away from my home, and I had to walk over an hour every day to get there. School started at 9:00 A.M. After breakfast we walked to school and stayed there until evening and had our supper at home. At the beginning, we had fifty-four students in the class with only fifteen girls. After a year, most of the fifteen girls stopped coming to school and only four girls remained.

"In the middle school we learned Chinese language and literature, algebra, and English. Although everyone said that English was the most difficult subject, I liked it. In the first year of the middle school, we often made into ministage shows and stories what we learned in English classes and performed them in English to our class. But in the second year, our English teacher was sick and an algebra teacher taught us English. However, nobody could understand this teacher and we lost interest in learning English.

"I dropped out of school when I was in the second year of middle school. I will never forget what happened in the few days after the Chinese New Year in 1994.

"In the afternoon of the sixth day of the Chinese New Year, I finished my winter break homework and began to make homework exercise books for the coming term. My father walked toward me and asked: 'What are you doing?'

"'Making homework books for next term,' I said.

"My father then said: 'Who said that you are going to school? I don't have money to send you to school any more.'

"At first I thought that my father was joking with me and paid no attention to him. After supper I was writing my last winter break diary. When my father saw me, he angrily threw all my books and notebooks away from the desk. I was dumbstruck. My mother got very upset and quarreled with my father and then left for her brother's house. With only my brother and me left at the house, my father scolded us angrily. He gave my brother the registration money and paid no attention to me. Only then did I realize that it was true, that my father would not let me go to school any more. Tears started to flow from my eyes.

"I remembered that my mother paid my brother's and sister's elementary school fees and mine, too, from the money she earned selling eggs. She did this for years. Every term, after she paid the fees, she immediately started to save the egg money for the next term. However, in 1994 my father took a loan to purchase the tractor, and all our household income was used to pay back the money. That year my mother was ill and did not raise hens for eggs and therefore had no money for my school fees. The school fee was 60 yuan. However, since I could use my older brother's books, I needed only 48 yuan. My mother managed to borrow 40 yuan from other people and tried to persuade my father to pay the 8 yuan difference, but my father refused. He said that if all of us went to school, no one would be left to do the household chores. The common wisdom in my village is that it is useless to educate girls. Instead of education, girls should learn how to do farming and household chores early. As a result, families with good situations would provide their daughters with some education and poor families would not even consider doing that.

"On the seventh day of the Chinese New Year local schools started. In the morning I stood on the side of the road watching local kids happily walking to school. I felt extremely sad and anxious. With tears in my eyes, I returned to my house and begged my father for the money. He took out 10 yuan and said to me: 'If you can get yourself in with the 10 yuan, you can go to school.' I knew that I couldn't and that there was nothing I could do to change his mind.

"Ten days later, while I was getting water for our family from the village stream, I met a schoolmate who had dropped out a year before me. She told me how much she regretted that she had done so. Our conversation reopened my wound. When I got into our house, I told my mother that I still wanted to go to school. My father heard me and said to me: 'The school door is still open and if you are able, get yourself in.'

"Feeling wronged and acting rashly, I went to see the middle school principal and talked to a geography teacher who lived in my village. I was told that that year the school had financial difficulties and the principal was leaving; therefore they could not help me. The new principal was my former algebra teacher, who knew my situation. He came to our house to try to persuade my father to let me go to school. However, my father still insisted that he did not have money to send me to school. My homeroom teacher, Ms Bai, was in her fifties and had a kind heart. She came to our house to tell my father that she was willing to pay my fees to have me in school. My father refused her offer, saying that I was needed in the fields to do farming work. I know that the lack of money was only one reason that my father did not let me go to school. The other reason was that my father wanted me to be like the rest of girls in our community working in the fields.

"I tried many ways to get myself back to school. I tried to persuade my father to go out of town to work so that my mother would be in charge of our household, thinking that she would let me return to school. I also mobilized my grandmother and other relatives to persuade my father to let me return to school. However, all my efforts failed. Last June, when I was talking about going back to school, my father said to me: 'Sitting idly in classrooms—I can get used to that, too.' On the matter of wanting to go to school, I felt that I was wronged and that I did not have enough education.

"When my mother saw how sad I was, she tried to make me feel better and said: 'It is your unlucky fate, poor child. When your older sister was in school, the school fees were low. Nowadays the school fees are very high even though children have to go to school.' While she was saying this to me, she was crying. My mother has heart problems and is in poor health. I knew that our family indeed had financial difficulties, and I had to restrain myself and give up my desire to go back to school. After that, during the day I worked with my mother in the field and in the house, and in the evening I helped my younger brother with his homework.

"Seven or eight of my female classmates dropped out school at the same time I did. Their situation was almost the same as mine. One of them was very good in school academically. Like me, her father did not want her to continue her education.

"When I was in school, I liked classical Chinese. After dropping out of school, some times when I met my classmates and engaged in conversation with them, I still could use some of the language. This is because I kept reading my books, and my teacher told me that it was self-learning.

"I received a total of six and a half years of education. I feel that the six and a half years of education were useful to me. Reading skills enabled me to read books and engage in self-learning in order to enrich myself. The moral education I received in school from my teachers enabled me to examine myself critically when I did something wrong.

"I feel that some of the subjects I learned in school have been useful afterward. The most useful ones are Chinese, mathematics, biology, and science. For example, I tried what I learned about grafting in my biology class on our own fruit trees and was successful. I was very pleased by my success. However, subjects like art, music, and English are not useful in my life after school.

"In my village, women over age forty have hardly any education. In many households, when a family's financial condition is poor, parents always take their daughters out of school. I continue to ask why we girls cannot be like boys, who go to school and study. If you ask me what I want to do in the future, I can tell you that a person with some education always has her own ideas. I don't want to spend my life only doing farming work. I want to learn some practical skills and do some professional work. Of course, I have a big wish—if opportunity allows, I want to go back to school" (Yang, 1995, 231–235).

Gender Inequality in Education in Rural China

MEASURES TAKEN

In the past decade, gender inequality in access to schooling has caught the attention of both government officials and researchers. Since 1990 the government has taken some measures to improve rural females' access to schooling. Chinese central, provincial, and local governments; international organizations; foreign foundations; academic institutions; and private establishments all have made efforts in the implementation of these measures.

In the mid-1990s, the Chinese central government launched the nine-year Compulsory Education Project, with financial assistance targeting poor rural areas. Central funding for this project during 1996–2000 amounted to 3.9 billion yuan. Although the project was designed to be gender-neutral, this program has benefited rural females particularly, since the denial of education to girls had been the major obstacle that prevented the realization of nine-year compulsory education. However, the effectiveness of the program in the improvement of rural females' access to schooling remains to be studied.

With China's joining the World Trade Organization, the reduction of education inequality in rural areas becomes an urgent issue. To compete in a global economy, China needs to make sure that its education system can produce skilled labor. On 27 December 2001, the central government passed a resolution in a meeting of top government officials and education policy-makers stating that China will mobilize resources from society and periodically provide financial assistance to needy students in poor rural areas (*Renmin ribao haiwaiban* [People's Daily, Overseas Edition]). The policy will contribute to the improvement of females' access to schooling in rural areas.

Since the 1990s many Chinese provincial and local governments have also made efforts to improve rural females' access to schooling in order to accomplish the nine-year compulsory education required by the central government. They have achieved notable improvements over time, for example, in Tibet, Gansu, Qinghai, Ningxia, and Guizhou, the poor provinces of western China with significant problems in rural females' access to schooling. In 1990, in these provinces female school-age children's enrollment rate in elementary school was 63.1, 89.9, 77.15, 88.1, and 81.6 percent respectively. However, in 1995 the enrollment rates increased to 64.2, 94.9, 83.7, 92.75, and 94.1 percent respectively. By 1999, the rate had increased to 78, 98.1, 92.4, 95.7, and 97.8 percent respectively (Ministry of Education 1990, 272–273; 1995, 270–271; 1999, 274–275). In Gansu province in the 1990s some local governments included the improvement of the realization of the nine-year compulsory education as one of the criteria in evaluating and promoting local cadres. In addition, since the 1990s, the Chinese government has allowed international and foreign institutions to participate in efforts to improve rural females' access to schooling.

During the past decade, the World Bank has funded four large basic education projects in poor rural areas with a component featuring improved access to schools for females. A fifth such project is now under discussion with the Chinese government. In 1995, China's State Education Commission and the World Bank joined forces and organized a seminar on girls' education in rural and minority areas. The seminar invited foreign experts, Chinese government officials, educators, and researchers to discuss the problems and search for solutions. Some specific measures, such as the establishment of special funds for female students, were identified and subsequently implemented. One result has been an improvement in the proportion of female children in schools.

In addition to international organizations and their projects, some foreign foundations have provided funding to foreign and Chinese institutes and scholars to conduct studies. For example, one of the Ford Foundation's projects focuses on female education in poor rural and minority areas in China. Nongovernmental organizations (NGOs) and private efforts in China also contribute to the improvement of female education in rural areas. Since the creation of the first nongovernmental women's studies center in the mid-1980s by Li Xiaojiang, many such centers have been established in China, and some of them have participated in numerous programs. In general the projects and programs carried out by foundations, NGOs, and the women's studies centers in China are academic as well as activist in nature. They focus on gender inequality in access to schooling and on efforts to achieve gender equality in China.

Established in 1989, the "Hope Project" aims to mobilize resources to provide financial assistance to needy students in poor rural areas so that they can go to and remain in school. The program employs the innovative model of connecting the donor and the beneficiary; it encourages the two parties to participate in a long-term relationship. Because of its practical methods, goals, and personal touches, as well as its excellent propaganda, by the mid-1990s this program had attracted more than 300 million yuan in donations from abroad and home. With that money it has been able to support 860,000 children in poor rural areas who go to school, and it has also established 400 new elementary schools in poor areas. Although this program was not targeted especially at females in rural areas, since most of the school-age children who needed financial assistance were females, it benefited girls in general (Liao, 1995, 317–318).

In 1995, taking advantage of the United Nations' Fourth World Conference on Women in Beijing, a "Spring Buds Project" was established, also aiming at improving access to schooling for girls in poor rural areas. This project utilized the fund-raising and program implementation model of the Hope Project. In the same year, a "Happiness Project" was launched to provide financial, educational, health, family planning, and career assistance to needy mothers in poor rural areas. This project was established based on the belief that gender inequality in poor rural areas is a vicious cycle passing from generation to generation among the female population. Assisting needy mothers will help improve educational opportunities for the younger generation in rural China. All three projects are currently going strong in China and contributing to the improvement of education for females in rural areas.

CHALLENGES FOR THE FUTURE

Despite improvements in female access to schooling during the past decade, gender inequality in education in rural areas remains a significant problem. More attention should be focused on several issues. First, studies are needed about gender inequality in the access to knowledge in secondary schools and its relationship to gender inequality in the larger society. Access to schooling and access to knowledge are two different concepts. Access to schooling concerns females' opportunity to attend school, while access to knowledge considers what females actually learn in school. There is no dispute about the importance of access to schooling. However, differential access to knowledge in secondary schools could adversely affect women's access to higher education, desirable job opportunities, and other important choices.

Second, the continuation of nine-year compulsory education is still a necessary and challenging task for many poor rural areas. Although the Chinese government has participated in efforts to improve female education in these areas, it does not regard educational inequality as a gender issue. Very often the official line attributes the problems of inequality to traditional attitudes regarding Chinese women. While such attitudes do exist, they are not the only factors responsible for the problems. Other factors, especially officially adopted gender-blind policies, are as important. Recognizing gender inequality as a problem in China will help the government make gendered efforts and establish policies to improve female education in poor rural areas as part of the larger effort of reducing poverty there. Sex-differentiated policies are necessary. There is a special need to provide more targeted funding for girls like Gao Caiqing so that they can stay in school.

Third, gender inequality in education is a contributor to and a reflection of gender inequality in the larger society. Persistent interventions promoting gender equality outside schooling, in the workplace, and throughout the legal, political, and cultural institutions are all indispensable. Such interventions must involve the participation and support of decision-makers and ordinary people in all walks of life.

REFERENCES

Edwards, Louise, and Mina Roces, eds. *Women in Asia: Tradition, Modernity, and*

Globalization. Ann Arbor: University of Michigan Press, 2000.

"Guojia keji jiaoyu lingdao xiaozu di shici huiyi zhaokai" (The Leading Group of National Science, Technology, and Education Hold Its Tenth Meeting), *Renmin ribao haiwaiban* (People's Daily, Overseas Edition), 29 December 2001, 1.

He, Buqing. "Dushu hu? Jinqian hu? Dangqian zhong xiao xuesheng liushi xianxiang toushi yu sikao" (Schooling? Money? Probing into and Concern about Current Primary and Middle School Students' Dropout Phenomenon), *Gansu jianyu* (Gansu Education), Vol. 6, 1993, 14.

Li, Danke, and Mun Tsang. "Household Decisions on Education Spending and Implications on Gender Inequality in Rural China," *China: An International Journal*, Vol.1, no.2, September 2003, 224–248.

Liao, Xiaoguang. *Zhongguo pinkun yu fan pinkun lilun* (Poverty and Anti-Poverty Theories in China). Nanling: Guangxi renmin chubanshe, 1995.

Ministry of Education. *Educational Statistics Yearbook of China*. Beijing: Renmin jiaoyu chubanshe, 1990.

———. *Educational Statistics Yearbook of China*. Beijing: Renmin jiaoyu chubanshe, 1995.

———. *Educational Statistics Yearbook of China*. Beijing: Renmin jiaoyu chubanshe, 2000.

———. *Education Yearbook of China*. Beijing: Renmin jiaoyu chubanshe, 1999.

National Bureau of Statistics. *China Statistical Yearbook*. Beijing: Tongji chubanshe, 2000.

Qiang, Haiyan. "Gender Difference in Schooling and Its Challenges to Teacher Education in China," *Asia-Pacific Journal of Teacher Education and Development*, Vol. 3, no. 1, 2000, 143–163.

Wang, Letian. "Shichang jinji tizhi xia nongcun jicu jiaoyu gaige wenti zhi guangjian" (My View on Rural Basic Education Reform Under the Market Economy), *Hebei jiaoyu* (Hebei Education), Vol. 11, 1994, 10–11.

Wang, Xiaoping, and Zhou Jian, eds. *Reports from the Frontline of Girls' Education, Gansu*. Beijing: Ministry of Education, 1995.

Xiao, Cunyi, and Ma Jinhua. "Cong nusheng shou jiaoyu zhuangkuang tantao minzu jiaoyu de gaige yu fazhang" (From Female Education Probing into Education Reform and Development for Minorities), *Gansu jiaoyu* (Gansu Education), Vol. 7, 1993, 13–14.

Yang, Liwen, ed. *Chuangzhao pingdeng: Zhongguo xibei nutong jiaoyu koushushi* (Creating Equality: An Oral History of Girls' Education in Northwestern China). Beijing: Minzu chubanshe, 1995.

THE CENTER FOR GENDER STUDIES AT DALIAN UNIVERSITY: A NEW PLAN FOR THE MUTUAL DEVELOPMENT OF WOMEN'S/GENDER STUDIES AND HIGHER EDUCATION

Li Xiaojiang

Beginning in the mid-1980s, many scholars made efforts to build women's education and women's studies, but the question of whether to establish an independent discipline has long remained one on which scholars waver. On the basis of experience and lessons learned over many years, the Center for Gender Studies (CGS) at Dalian University is exploring a new method of mutual development that combines women's/gender studies with the reform of higher education. The ideas behind this new center are "permeation" and "interaction," bringing the fruits of women's studies directly to the campus and applying the novel approach of gender analysis in all aspects of educational reform. This allows women's/gender studies to become part of academic activities and campus life in an interdisciplinary, comprehensive manner. It also establishes the prospect of "sustainability" in training personnel, the establishment of curriculum, and the mutual development of campus and community.

Dalian University is a regular, comprehensive, local university that was formed from the merger of three colleges in 1987. In 1995, the university moved to a new site in the Dalian Economic and Technological Development Zone. It is spacious and fully equipped. In addition to agricultural studies, the university has many other departments, including education, literature, history, natural sciences, engineering, medicine, arts, physical education, industrial and commercial management, and so on. The faculty is young and energetic, but the university is weak in research. After the difficult process of establishing the university, the president, faculty, and students all had high expectations for its development, hoping to make the university stand out among all the other local colleges in China and become something unique. "Development" is the common aspiration of women's/gender studies and Dalian University, and serves as both the precondition and goal of our cooperation.

My selection of Dalian University and Dalian University's selection of me to direct its Center for Gender Studies occurred simultaneously. The university leaders' pioneering vision and strong sense of responsibility saw the urgent need for Dalian University to develop new disciplines. I was attracted by the room for growth within a newly established university, which would provide the possibility for women's/gender studies to participate directly in all aspects of campus life and in educational reform. Prior to my joining the faculty, Dalian University had established a Women's College (1996) and a Women's Studies Institute (1997), and although these had always received the support and encouragement of university leaders, their development had only come with great difficulty. It was precisely these difficulties in development that formed the basis for our mutual support to create something new.

While the recognition and support of the school's leaders were necessary conditions for the effective development of the center, they were not the only conditions.[1] The administration's intervention (or urging) during the early stages of creating the center, although important, could not take the place of effective, willing participation by faculty and students, as well as the sustained development of academic activities. Two questions touch directly on the long-term problems plaguing scholars in women's studies. First, how can we mobilize faculty and students throughout the entire campus to recognize and participate in women's/gender studies? Second, how can we sustain the participation of faculty and students who have been mobilized, so that they consciously become the backbone of the discipline? These questions are really more theoretical than pragmatic, since any errors in awareness can lead to failures in the actual work. People engaged in the work of education know that a campus affords little room to maneuver, and one failure can have persistent negative consequences. This caused us to investigate the campus environment before taking any action, to move carefully to see the task through to its end, and to watch for the pitfall of exhausting ourselves through repeated efforts with little success.

The Dalian University Center for Gender Studies (abbreviated as the Center) was formally established in July 2000. It is the first academic institution in mainland Chinese higher education to affirm "gender" as its direction of research. The Center sponsors and implements international cooperative projects in educational development, "with the university campus as the foundation to establish an interdisciplinary, sustainable, comprehensive development base of education for women's/gender studies." The Center integrates education, pedagogy, and research, cooperating closely with current women's/social development projects in China. It also introduces the fruits of women's studies and methods of gender analysis to the current system of higher education so that they permeate related curricula and campus activities in the hope that this will effectively promote the integration of women's/ gender studies into the mainstream of China's educational/academic fields.

In the year since the Center was established, more than seventy members of the faculty and administrative staff have participated in teaching and research activities in gender studies. Faculty have offered more than ten courses with curricula related to gender studies and undertaken more than twenty research projects on various topics. The Center has its own library resource room, "Women's Oral History" archive, and its own website (www.genwo.ac.cn). The Center has also begun a variety of cooperative development projects in the local community. When school is in session, the Center holds regular meetings every Wednesday to conduct interdisciplinary academic exchanges and to host seminars, forums, and related student activities. The fact that this has all taken place so quickly is in itself a miracle, one that the entire faculty and student body at Dalian University have witnessed. How this "miracle" came to be is the main focus of this chapter.

How It All Started (Raising Questions)

The selection of Dalian University for the "gender studies" center was an experiment based on efforts in the past to make "women's studies" an independent discipline. In 1987, I founded the first women's studies center at an institution of higher education in mainland China, at Zhengzhou University.[2] My colleagues and I explored many avenues in establishing the discipline, making a lot of progress in women's social development but gaining relatively little in terms of academic activities and the establishment of the discipline because our efforts to research women's social development were scattered and not cohesive. Furthermore the problem of "double marginalization" undermined these academic activities and the attempted establishment of the discipline.[3]

"Double marginalization" refers to the marginal position held by the field of women's studies in the academic world. Beginning in the 1990s, most Chinese scholars in women's studies left academia and entered the public and international arenas. By participating in development projects, these scholars originally intended to develop, improve, and strengthen themselves and to remedy their positions on the margins but, instead, ended up going farther down the path of marginalization. The researchers and their research projects strayed ever farther away from the logical track of self-development and from their chosen discipline. Caught up in development issues defined by the women's community and secluded within women's circles, these scholars could not improve the current educational system or the structure of knowledge, nor were they able to provide current students with the benefits of their experience.[4] For a long time, these scholars languished at the margins, "speaking their own language to each other."

In the mid-1990s, thanks to the influence of the United Nations' Fourth

World Conference on Women in Beijing in 1995, many universities and research institutions established women's studies centers. At the beginning, these institutions provided a good organizational basis for the development of the discipline, but after the conference ended, the lack of social resources and support within academia caused the newly founded women's studies centers to wither and die.[5] In June 1998, as part of its centennial celebration, Peking University hosted an international seminar titled "Women's Studies and Development in the Twenty-First Century," which once again put the establishment of women's studies as a discipline on the agenda. The seminar resulted in renewed efforts at some women's studies centers in higher education institutions.[6] The women's studies community reached a consensus that, instead of the arduous process of creating an entirely native discipline, as attempted during the 1980s, the way to promote the establishment of women's/gender studies as a self-regulating system on university campuses was through writing teaching materials, organizing training courses, and offering courses at universities. This idea quickly came to have widespread influence, and although it did not lack for moral or financial support, programs still stumbled along and faced difficulties of every sort.[7]

The greatest difficulty to overcome was finding the legitimate position of women's studies within mainstream academia. This was essentially the question of whether women's/gender studies needed to be an independent discipline and, if so, what sort of position it should occupy. This question concerned not only the traditional value system of the academic world and traditional academic models but also touched on the fundamental principles of women's/gender studies. According to current feminist doctrines, the discipline's marginal status was in itself a kind of position, one that served as a vanguard and innovative force challenging tradition and remodeling academic structures. Would entering the mainstream and becoming part of "the system" erode this position?

A second question concerned the educational community. Establishing women's/gender studies as a discipline requires offering courses in universities, which would mean a complete and intimate relationship with the current educational system. The constraints of the current system could hinder the development of the discipline, while the reform of the educational system would pose new challenges to the systems constructed by the discipline (including teaching materials, pedagogy, and faculty development). The problems of how to avoid as much as possible the flaws of the old system while establishing the new discipline, and how to integrate organically the discipline into the new educational system, were unavoidable issues.

A third question, and the most important one, was how to go about establishing the discipline. What kinds of theoretical frameworks, methods, and discourse should be used? Indeed, there were ready-made models, almost all of which came from Western feminism. Since Western feminism already had thirty years of experience as a discipline within academia, could we simply use an "off-the-shelf" approach? In some ways, we were already doing this. That approach was a convenient shortcut, but it also created the kinds of problems that happen when an exotic tropical plant is transplanted to a colder climate—conflicts and contradictions between what we are used to and the new model. Making the imported models work in the native educational system presented tremendous difficulties. For many years we went along in this manner, having the vast and familiar body of Western feminist scholarship at our disposal but no way to use it. For us, the problem of "indigenization" was not only a theoretical issue but a practical one as well. Until we could get over this initial hurdle, we could not begin to talk about establishing the discipline.

NEW THINKING, NEW METHODS, NEW EXPLORATIONS

What special conditions were required for the smooth development of the Center? Certain conditions were indeed required, but there was nothing special about them; they could be provided at any higher education institution. The first was the full support of the university president. This support did not have to permeate every aspect of the work, nor did it require direct administrative intervention or large amounts of financial support over a long period of time. It did, however, have to be timely and practical. Especially at the initial stages, the president's ability to provide the necessary support and assistance with organization, departmental coordination, and community activities had a great deal to do with his understanding of women's/gender studies and the importance he attached to it. In May 2001, deputy secretary of Northeast Normal University and director of its Women's Studies Center, Professor Zhang Mingyun, paid us a visit to see for herself how the Center was progressing and what changes had taken place on campus. When she spoke with the president, she asked him, "Why do you support this?"

The president, a male Ph.D. with a degree in computer science, gave a very insightful answer. He provided three reasons: First, gender issues are human issues. They are universal, and, as such, they can have widespread influence in the humanities and pull the humanities out of their long slump. Second, women's/gender studies provide a new perspective and new methods. They can become a bright spot in a young institution such as Dalian University, making it stand out from all the other institutions of higher education. Third, women make up the majority of students in many specializations at Dalian University. The university can combine women's studies and women's education, thus providing a more sophisticated education for women, benefiting female students and facilitating the cultivation of female instructors.

"Why not?" he said.

Li Xiaojiang

INTERDISCIPLINARY PERMEATION AND WIDESPREAD MOBILIZATION

Traditional ideas constrain the promotion of gender studies on most university campuses. Chinese higher education has never known any academic institution with the word "gender" in its name. Bias and dismissive attitudes toward "women" and "women's studies," coupled with ambivalent attitudes toward the taboo topic of "sex," affect people's perception of "gender" as a subject and lead to misunderstandings of "gender studies." This type of situation had occurred at large metropolitan universities such as Peking University and was even more likely to be present at the newly founded, local Dalian University.[8] Doubt and resentment that "gender" and "center" were being brought together were prevalent attitudes among the faculty and students at Dalian.

To mobilize the campus and help the faculty and students perceive gender studies correctly, I began with the faculty. For the first two months of the first semester I did not involve the students at all, hoping first to create a core group within the faculty to facilitate the broad inclusion of students later. To accomplish this task, I presented scholarly reports in a series of lectures based on the faculty's changes in perception and need to know more. The first lecture was presented on my second day at the university. Entitled "Gender Studies and Dalian University," it linked the establishment of the Center and its direction of research closely to the development of Dalian University. More than two hundred people attended the lecture, and afterward eighty-nine of them signed up for voluntary training and to participate in the Center's activities.

The second lecture was aimed at faculty who had volunteered for the training mentioned above and was presented before I began inviting scholars from outside the university. Entitled "Gender Studies and Higher Education," the lecture emphasized the motivation for having relevant research serve pedagogy and invited the faculty to bring questions from their own fields of research to the lecture. After the training session, faculty could sign up to offer curriculum suggestions.

The third lecture took place before the faculty submitted research topics. This lecture, titled "Women's Studies and Gender Studies," examined the standpoints, methods, historical evolution, keywords, and important problems of the disciplines, providing a theoretical analysis of the relationship between women's studies and gender studies and how they differ. The lecture helped the faculty to apply methods of gender analysis to various disciplines, opening up a new direction in the traditional academic framework. Here, the idea of "permeation" or permeating the curriculum began to take shape and continue as a lasting theme.

In order to find space for women's/gender studies to exist within the field of academia/education, it was necessary to recognize clearly how much potential room for development existed there. On campus, room for development was extremely limited due to the practical pressures facing the faculty and students and also due to the direction of development. Ideas and methodologies of the past emphasized the necessity of "women's studies" and the need for "women's development." This frequently led to one-sided calls for "attention" to be paid to "women" and "women's studies" and demands for a "position." This method received a very poor response on campuses. In order to get faculty and students interested in women's/gender studies, the new methods and perspectives afforded by the discipline had to be in tune with the faculty's academic growth and with student life. Academic concerns had to be bidirectional and specifically pragmatic, not unidirectional and esoteric. A "needs survey" was thus very important.

Early in the project we conducted two major surveys and obtained two unexpected results. One survey was given to faculty who had signed up for training and consisted of a questionnaire on "gender knowledge." We did not expect that the act of filling out the questionnaire would become for the faculty an exercise in self-examination, reflection, and questioning on their awareness of gender. The faculty was startled by their general level of "ignorance." The second survey was conducted in cooperation with student groups. We conducted "gender needs" surveys separately for men and women, using on-site (classroom and dorm room) interviews, discussions, questionnaires, and other formats. For the first time, "sex" and "gender" were presented in a positive manner as part of campus activities and student life. This allowed the surveys to become a process of widespread mobilization among the students. The surveys became very important in subsequent student participation.

From the perspective of "needs," the survey results were surprising, for although faculty recognized their "ignorance," they did not believe there was a clear need for "gender knowledge" on campus. Furthermore, they did not believe that the issue had anything to do with their personal academic development, and thus they did not advocate the establishment of an independent department on campus. A similar problem arose in the student surveys. Despite our repeated attempts and even personal visits with students, we were unable to elicit much demand for awareness and knowledge about gender. Many students, including women, openly opposed the establishment of courses especially for female students and were not willing to add a gender curriculum to their already heavy course loads. If we had merely acted based on the "needs" and suggestions of the faculty and students, the first thing we should have done was to shut down the Center, which would have run counter to the development needs of women and society in general.

These problems—similar to those described in the establishment of the Center—prompted us to conduct a reverse analysis of our needs survey and to question it. The results of the campus surveys led us to consider the following questions: Was it appropriate to extrapolate local needs from generalized developmental needs? Would blindly catering to "needs" create still larger errors in real life? Should activating new "needs" be an important part of development studies? Finally, since our faculty and students recognized their ignorance, why did they at the same time fail to have "a need for knowledge"? Was it because the developmental needs of the faculty and students were generally lagging, or was it because the developmental needs of the present society as a whole lacked room for the growth of gender knowledge?

FACULTY TRAINING

Based on these questions, we believed that the training process was one not only of transmitting knowledge but also of continually raising and answering questions. During the 2000–2001 academic year, we spent the entire time on faculty training. Under the condition of increasing the faculty's workload as little as possible, we scheduled routine meeting days on Wednesdays, when all the faculty would be on campus. The meetings consisted of training or discussions. We announced the training topics in advance, and all faculty could choose the sessions they wanted to attend. Anyone (including students) could at any time participate in Center activities they found interesting.

The gradual progression of the training topics was closely matched to the faculty's level of understanding and participation, and to campus activities. Instead of the older style of lectures that emphasized "women's issues" in society, we took "campus life" as our point of departure, focusing on two main aspects. One was basic theory and methodology; the second was information on the progress of the discipline and related teaching activities.

The lecturers for the training came from two sources. The first source was outside experts. During the first semester we mainly invited outsiders, including influential Chinese scholars in relevant fields.[9] Drawing on current research results and "standing on the shoulders of giants" were ways that allowed us to develop quickly. The second source was within our own faculty. When we discovered that a faculty member who participated in Center activities was working on a related topic, we would ask him or her to give a report.[10] Practice proved that this was an extremely important exploration in making the training "interactive." Not only was it a test of the training results; it also served to invigorate the sustainability of the training. The Center thus became an academic clearinghouse for faculty to share interdisciplinary knowledge.

One of the primary goals of the faculty training was to encourage faculty members to offer related courses in their own disciplines. To this end, we repeatedly emphasized the importance of establishing a curriculum and encouraged the combination of research and teaching so that the results of current women's/gender studies research could be rapidly implemented in the class-room. This transformed the entire training process into one of developing course curricula. At the end of a year of training, faculty research topics and plans for courses had begun to take shape. The concept of "permeation" became one of our most frequently repeated keywords when discussing the establishment of curricula.

CURRICULUM ESTABLISHMENT

Curriculum establishment is in fact also a process of research. Due to the lack of prior native experience in this field and the absence of relevant teaching materials, the faculty had no choice but to experiment with course content and new teaching methods. They had to accomplish three tasks before they could offer a course. First, the instructor had to become familiar with current research in the field, both domestic and foreign, and had to form a new perspective and integrate new concepts. Second, instructors had to diligently re-evaluate teaching materials and pedagogical methods in light of a gender perspective. Third, on the basis of this "critique," the instructor had to attempt to "reconstruct" the curriculum.

Unlike discussions at the theoretical level, the critique and reconstruction of a curriculum can take place simultaneously. Due to the large volume of research available in women's/gender studies from both domestic and foreign sources, this simultaneous approach was not only feasible but necessary. This approach made it possible to avoid becoming bogged down in conceptual problems and paying mere lip service to "indigenization." Theory was translated into action and tested in the practice of actual teaching. Moreover, innovations were made.

Establishing a curriculum appears to be a simple task done solely by instructors, but this is not the case. In China, the establishment of curriculum is closely connected to the educational system, the instructor's position, the establishment of a major, and the employment intentions of students. The problem we faced was that, in order to achieve practical participation in women's/gender studies and the reconstruction of knowledge, we needed to offer courses at institutions of higher education. However, for these courses to hold on to their places within the curricula of higher education, relying merely on a few enthusiastic individuals or influential professors (or officials) to promote or even "endow" these courses would be ineffective. These courses had to find their place within the current educational system. In addition, they had to keep pace with and participate actively in educational reform, finding the native resources necessary for "sustainable" development on campus. Here, the word "native" refers not only to China but also to "local" and "school" resources.

At Dalian University, we set up four types of courses to target the qualities and pedagogical methods of different curricula:

1. Open electives (open to the entire school, general in nature). Examples include Fundamentals of Sexuality, Fundamentals of Women's/Gender Studies, Marriage and the Family in Ancient China, Psychology of Marriage and Love among University Students.

2. Specialized courses (electives open to upper-class students from any department, containing a certain level of academic content). Examples include Gender Analysis (Introductory and Intermediate), English Language Teaching Materials and Pedagogical Methods (College of Foreign Languages), Appreciation of Great Works by Female Authors of British and American Literature (English Multimedia, College of Foreign Languages), Women's Literature in Ancient China, and Creation and Critique of Contemporary Chinese Women's Literature (College of Humanities).

3. "Permeation" courses (offered within specialized mainstream curricula). These are experimental courses offered by the Center. Development here is proceeding in two directions: first, to bring gender awareness and analytical methods to "pedagogical methods" curricula. Instructors working on this are from seven disciplines, including Chinese, history, English, physics, mathematics, physical education, and the arts. The second brings women's history and methods of gender analysis to the "historiography" curriculum. Eight instructors have agreed to work here in the areas of ancient Chinese history, the history of the Chinese republic, ancient world history, contemporary world history, and the theory of historiography.

4. Women's education courses (targeted specifically at women). Examples include Women's Self-Awareness, a required course for students in the Women's College, a one-semester, sixty-four-hour, four-credit course that began in September 2001 to be taught by student workers (counselors) and two teams totaling ten instructors from educational psychology. The Center takes charge of the developing of the course content and has emphasized heuristic, participatory pedagogical methods.

In a way, the process of establishing a curriculum is one of educational reform, providing the women's/gender studies curriculum with room for potential growth within higher education. To meet the current developmental needs of higher education, to participate actively in the reformulation of teaching materials and the renovation of the system, to serve as a good model for pedagogical reform, and to address weaknesses in the area of research, two priorities are essential.

First, in situations where one's individual resources are inadequate, collective wisdom and pooled interdisciplinary strengths must be used to create "teams" in certain areas of specialization. These teams work together to review and reformulate current curricula, teaching materials, and pedagogical methods (for courses on topics such as pedagogical methods or history), or they develop new courses (such as women's literature and women's self-awareness). Each course is carefully developed through actual teaching practice, interdepartmental and interdisciplinary cooperation, collective discussions, independent preparation of lectures, classroom (student) participation, tracking records (audio and video recordings), observing classes, after-class discussions, and repeated deliberations. The features of each discipline must be fully respected when offering courses, such as in the selection of course titles. We avoid a mentality that assumes "one size fits all." This is particularly true for the "permeation" courses, where battles over changing course titles, increasing the number of course hours, and changes in format are avoided, and the work focuses instead on pedagogical methods and teaching materials.

Second, instructors must be cultivated from among the younger faculty. When inviting an instructor to participate, we first consider the direction of his or her own academic development. The instructor should be encouraged to "get involved in" (not specialize in) women's/gender studies without straying from his or her original mainstream discipline. Instructors are encouraged to "introduce" (but not switch to exclusively) a gender perspective and the methods of gender analysis into the practice of his or her discipline. In the past year, the Center has sent more than twenty faculty members in the fields of education, literature, history, legal studies, development studies, and medicine for further study (to places such as Hong Kong and the Netherlands) or for training (at places like Beijing Normal University). This not only cultivates specialized talent for the school but also builds the strength of women's/gender studies.

NEW EXPLORATIONS: COOPERATION AND INTERACTION ON AND OFF CAMPUS

Accomplishing the tasks outlined above could not be done by relying solely on the Center or on individuals—cooperation was an essential and fundamental feature. Cooperation was the key link connecting theory and practice. In July 2001, twenty faculty members from the Yanbian University Women's Studies Center attended the international forum titled "Women's/Gender Studies and the Practice of Higher Education," where they experienced firsthand the level of faculty participation and institutional support at Dalian University. Their question was: "What strategy was needed to achieve this?" Our answer was: "Cooperation, understanding, and catering to the developmental needs of the school, the faculty, and the students, and by working to open up room for the growth of women's/gender studies in every project and every person we developed together."

Responses and cooperation from the international community are indispensable in the development of today's society (including the humanities and social sciences). This was especially true in our case, where one of our project's goals was to be "an international cooperative educational development project." The entire operation of the project was not merely "native" but also "nativized." We wanted not only to respond to the question of establishing the discipline domestically but also to contribute to the development of women and society on a world scale and to relevant theoretical questions. Our advantages lay not only in the experience and training I brought with me when I joined the faculty, as well as abundant domestic resources, but also the unconditional support from the international community in the form of timely financial sponsorship and the responses of scholars abroad.[11] All of these factors constituted the basic conditions for the early period of the Center's establishment.

When we established the Center, we chose a "virtual" form (without permanent staffing or our own faculty and students) in order to avoid the problem of women's/gender studies' tendency toward isolation and to prevent scholars (especially young female scholars) from leaving their mainstream disciplines and winding up on a sidetrack (which could very possibly be the sidetrack of feminism). This also allowed the Center to avoid becoming bogged down in the detailed problems of "entity" management and, instead, to focus on building the discipline. The difficulty of being "virtual" is that, since there is no entity, nothing can be accomplished without cooperating with others. The advantage of this approach is that the process of cooperation can embody the vigor and tensions of the research while affording a degree of flexibility. Our mission is not that the Center will continue to survive indefinitely but, rather, to allow the academic ideas and methods championed by the Center to "enter" the campus effectively, finding legitimate, reasonable, and permanent room to grow within the educational system.

Over the past year, we have cooperated with faculty in many departments for both research and pedagogical activities. Cooperation has been particularly strong with the Colleges of Humanities, Foreign Languages, and Medicine, and the Women's College, with most of the core membership coming from these places. We cooperate with administrative departments when planning projects. Timely communication with the Office of Academic Affairs and the Office of Research is especially important in order to provide the background support for curriculum development and the initiation of research projects. In the area of campus/community activities we cooperate with cadres who work with students (the Youth League Committee), counselors, and the Office of Dormitory Management. We cooperate directly with student groups and youth volunteers in order to open channels for women's/gender studies to gain access to student "territory" (in the past this was always the greatest source of difficulty).

The next questions are: What are the preconditions for cooperation? What need or interest do people have in taking time out of their busy schedules to cooperate with you and help you establish this new discipline that seemingly has no relation to mainstream disciplines?

There are no preconditions other than "development"—the need for not merely one's own personal development but mutual development. By "mutual development" I do not mean the type of project in which we go out to the countryside to help the impoverished peasants in some condescending manner. This is not an enterprise in which we come down from the ivory tower and "take care of you." It also differs from the "woman-centered" approach championed by feminism and the "you help me" demands we once made in the women's liberation movement. The aim and strategy of this approach is to combine the needs of both sides and to take the path of mutual development.

BRINGING "DEVELOPMENT" TO THE CAMPUS

Development is the major feature of all developing countries, manifested not only in impoverished areas and among the weakest groups in society, but also prominently reflected in the faculty and students at institutions of higher education by such phenomena as insufficient academic exchanges and inadequate faculty resources. These factors strategically affect the self-confidence of faculty and students, limiting the amount of concern students have for their society and the cultivation of their awareness as citizens. How to make full use of the resources available on campus and locally, how to bring into play the faculty's and students' awareness and abilities to help themselves and each other, and how to develop fully under the present conditions are prominent problems for faculty and students at all local, regular higher education institutions. These problems are also universal among those engaged in women's studies in China and are manifested in the academic track of every scholar in the field.

To address these problems, to integrate the character-building education advocated by the Ministry of Education, the Center formally initiated "Campus Self-Help Action" to meet the development needs of the school and its students, with the support of the president of the university. This action brings the concept of "development" to the building of campus culture at institutions of higher education. Our most frequently repeated keywords in this action are "self-help" and "interaction."

SELF-HELP ACTION

"Self-help" actually refers to helping one another on campus and in the community. For the school, this means fully utilizing the resources currently available on campus, including the knowledge of faculty and upper-division students in different majors. For the students, this means setting up "self-help action teams" with student groups as the core and youth volunteers as the main workforce to strengthen the students' spirit of helping each other and create a sense of autonomy. For the community, this means bringing personnel and resources into situations where outside help is lacking. The sustainability of such resources is based on students' participation. For students, the process of helping the weaker groups in society becomes a process of self-cultivation. This action has become a model for the thousands of regular higher education institutions across mainland China. The weak help each other and develop mutually. Relying on our own strength, we establish autonomy and a healthy community (campus) of citizens. The primary mission of the Center is to permeate the entire process of project planning and implementation with contemporary gender consciousness and to apply this directly to student actions. To this end, we proposed "mental and physical health" as the goal of this action. At Dalian University and at many regular higher education institutions in China, seizing on the need for mental and physical health, which relates to every student, is an important avenue for bringing gender and the results of gender studies directly into student's lives.

The self-help action generated tremendous support among the students in under two months. The students formed a group on their own, and with the help of the Center, set up a "women students division," project teams, and a "caring" hotline. At the encouragement of the Center, the students organized their own "gender forums" (male and female students separately).[12] These activities quickly reached the "helping each other" stage, and many students participated actively in planning at the Center and in service actions to assist the weaker groups in the community. Students participated directly in social/community development. It was in the process of this student participation that we began to consider issues of the "price of development" and "bidirectional development" and introduced the concept of "interaction," making it a fundamental principle of self-help actions.

THE PRINCIPLE OF INTERACTION

Introducing the principle of "interaction" was in itself a lesson. For the past few years, many women scholars (including the author) have left campuses and participated directly in or led women's development projects, spending long periods of time in the field in rural and mountainous areas, making contributions toward "women's development" in impoverished areas. In doing so, we set the development of our own academic careers aside, which was not the result we had intended. For this reason, "bidirectional development" must be seen as the precondition for cooperation. All participants in "development projects" must grow through their involvement in the project, and projects cannot be a simple combination of "donors" and "recipients."

Based on the principle of interaction, we organized five projects in the areas of community development and scholastic and international cooperation.

First, we provided faculty resources for "Weekend Classroom," a project for the women worker cadres of the general municipal trade union. To address the development needs of women workers, the project offered classes such as Women and the Internet, Investment and Financial Management for Women, Women and the Law, Women's Physiology and Health Care, and Women and the World Trade Organization. The union chose the titles for all the courses, and all the instructors received training at the Center before they began teaching. The classes were highly focused in nature and very well received by the women workers, which boosted the university's reputation. The university supported the project by confirming that it was a cooperative effort between the school and the community, and by acknowledging the time spent teaching. Our instructors not only became core members of the Center but also opened up new space in the community. It is a model of a win-win, or even a win-win-win, situation.

Second, we cooperated with the Department of Women Workers to provide volunteer assistance to the weakest group in the city of Dalian, the children of "single parents, the deeply impoverished, and laid-off women workers." Activities such as "Big Hands Hold Little Hands, and Little Hands Go to Campus" were held on weekends. These activities were cooperative efforts of the Center, the Youth League Committee, and the Student Union. Here, students were in the forefront. The students initiated the project and organized activities on their own. The university recognized and supported this project, providing facilities and school vehicles free of charge. Using this program as a springboard, the students organized a "Caring Summer Camp" during the summer, which presented a series of activities centered on the theme of "How Far Am I from the University?" This program generated a sustained effect among the women workers and the children of single-parent households and led to many follow-up actions (such as volunteers providing tutoring and participation by students and parents). This led to the cultivation of a sense of citizenship among the students and also improved their capabilities for social service.

Third, we trained instructors for the "Women Workers Night Schools" at foreign-owned enterprises in Dalian's economic development zone. We encouraged and trained students to become instructors. Dalian's economic development zone is dominated by foreign-owned enterprises, and the workers there consist almost entirely of people from the surrounding mountainous and impoverished areas. More than 80 percent of the workers are women. Of the hundreds of foreign-owned enterprises currently operating, eighteen of them have night schools for the women workers but lack sufficient faculty. Labor unions from the development zone contacted the Center, hoping to invite some "influential" instructors. The Center had to consider the "cost of development" and decided that our faculty resources should be used primarily for training and not to meet the long-term need for teachers on the frontlines of education for women workers. We persuaded the unions and factories to use local resources as much as possible and recommended that students teach the women workers. In this way we explored a new sustainable, bidirectional road to development. Once this project was put in motion, the students participated actively. The Center organized training sessions and provided students with guidance from faculty members in different specializations. This project is still ongoing, and more than forty students from the Colleges of Medicine, Industrial and Commercial Management, and Humanities have participated and taught in it.

The fourth project involved cooperation between schools. At the invitation of the Dalian Yuwen School (a nine-year school), we attempted to introduce modern gender awareness and methods of gender analysis directly into basic education. The Center designed and initiated the project, "The Influence of Adolescent Sexual Physiology (Psychology) on the Selection of a Major (Career) and Interventionist Pedagogy." The project explored balanced development paths that would benefit students (especially girls) in their physical and mental health and in their academic careers. Currently, five faculty members (from mathematics, physics, Chinese, English, and politics) and three faculty members in educational psychology are working on this project. They work with the appropriate grades and class leaders at the Yuwen School to improve the capacity for independent research on the part of young teachers by forming pairs to help each other.

The fifth project was a cooperative one with the "Women/Gender and Development" curriculum group at the Institute of Social Studies (ISS) in the Netherlands. We invited scholars from the ISS to lecture for us and sent young teachers to the Netherlands for advanced studies. The Center agreed to participate in the "Gender Studies Institute Network in Asia" project initiated by the ISS at higher education institutions in a number of Asian countries.[13] We contributed our own research topics and suggestions during the planning of this project.

Finally, in order to strengthen academic exchanges within the university and with other institutions, we took full advantage of the cultural advantages of the campus environment. Based on the principle of sharing resources, and with the support of the university's president, the Center established the visiting scholars house. In June and July 2001, we hosted two groups of ten scholars from

China and abroad. In April 2002, we began the visiting scholars exchange program officially. We established these projects on the principles of interaction and mutual benefit. Visiting scholars can pursue their own research topics and participate in our activities on a volunteer basis. While providing amenities for the visiting scholars, we also share in the resources they bring with them, arranging seminars, discussions, training sessions, and equal exchanges based on the scholar's area of specialization, so that we grow together.[14]

CONCLUSION

During the past year, the woman's/gender perspective has effectively been introduced into campus activities, and subtle changes have definitely begun to take place on the campus. Sex and gender issues have become topics both faculty and students can discuss openly. Methods of gender analysis have become ways of approaching interdisciplinary academic exchanges. The series of activities presented by the Center has attracted the students, and the Center has become a base from which faculty and students can help themselves and each other. At present, more than thirty faculty members are engaged in research projects relating in various degrees to women's/gender studies, and many students have written papers connected to these topics. All of these faculty and students can use the library at the Center to look for materials and to exchange information on an equal basis.

In conclusion, we offer some preliminary thoughts on "needs," the price of development, the relationship between women's studies and gender studies, and the issue of sustainability. Can "spoken" needs be handled in a simplified way? Should we cater to or meet immediate needs? Is a survey of the singular needs of a particular group reasonable? The unquestioning and facile belief in "needs" that characterized our development of the Center in the past left us no choice but to analyze their necessity. To improve our survey techniques and establish theoretical assumptions, we had to consider the relationship between the parts and the whole and to make assessments and distinctions among "needs."

Development requires cooperation, but can we stop at the level of unilateral "giving" or "providing"? How should we adopt the appropriate stance when cooperating with different interest groups and levels of society? Do development problems similarly exist in higher education institutions? How can we make sure that both sides participating in cooperative projects benefit? The concept of "bidirectional development" is one response to these questions. The effective implementation of the principle of interaction allows us to take a pragmatic step forward in the direction of development.

What position can women's studies occupy on campus and how much room is there for it to develop? Is it appropriate or feasible to establish an independent department and discipline in China at this time? Is "woman-centered" the appropriate wording on campus? Does it promote or hinder women's development? Our reasons for ultimately choosing "gender" and not "women" for the name of the Center are in fact a response to this question. Practice has proved that in some areas (such as family planning and women's literature) and at some stages, it is necessary to highlight "women" or "women-centeredness," but it is not appropriate to do this universally. In academe in particular, people suspect that this type of wording runs counter to educational goals and academic ideals. In actual practice, it may create negative effects.

The issue of sustainable development in women's/gender studies projects two possible futures. The discipline may fade away due to a lack of response from the academic community and even from women. This is the case in many higher education institutions in China today, where women's studies centers exist in name only. The alternative is for the women's/gender studies perspective and methods to be integrated organically into the current educational system and structure of knowledge, blending into the mainstream, much as the methods of class struggle and class analysis did in the past. We tend to favor the second fate. For this reason we have set two important goals in designing this project, curriculum revision and personnel re-education. We see these goals as necessary conditions for the "sustainable" development of women's/gender studies. These are the areas of our accomplishments to date and also the directions in which we need to work in the future.

In our field, curriculum revision and educational reform have needed to proceed simultaneously. Teaching and edifying people are bidirectional tasks. "Establishing the discipline" and "mainstreaming" women's/gender studies may be quite different from the struggle for social rights. They are not accomplished through advocacy or by voting or by merely striving for a place within mainstream academe. In order to enter the mainstream disciplines and become an organic part of the educational process, one must have respect for the system even as you "criticize" it, and one must adhere to basic academic standards. When "reconstructing," one must examine one's own academic perspective and share a common concern for the humanities and academic ideals of your colleagues.

NOTES

1. In many higher education institutions in China, leaders in the school serve directly as the directors of women's studies centers or play major roles in organizing center activities, such as at the China Party Central School (1994), Northeast Normal University (1993), Hangzhou University (1989), and Peking University (2000).

2. For a detailed account of the process, see Li Xiaojiang, "Gonggong kongjiande chuangzao" (The Creation of Public Space), in *Zhongguo gean: funü yanjiu yundong* (China Case Study: The Women's Studies Movement) (Hong Kong: Oxford University

The Center for Gender Studies at Dalian University

Press, 1996); in English, *Asia Journal of Women's Studies*, Vol. 2, 1996; in Japanese, *Chugoku kenkyu* (China Studies), spring 1996.

3. See Li Xiaojiang, "Funü/xingbie yanjiude kunjing ji tukun" (Difficulties and Breakthroughs in Women's/Gender Studies), in *Zhongguo nüxing wenhua* (Chinese Women's Culture) (Beijing: Zhongguo wenlian chubangongsi, 2000), Vol. 1; Christine Hunefeldt and Jennifer Troutner, eds., *Building New Societies: Women in Asia and Latin America* (Berkeley: University of California Press, 2001).

4. Some scholars promptly pointed out this issue, stating that "the higher the argument, the smaller the circle becomes." See *Funü yanjiulun cong* (Collection of Women's Studies Theory), Vol. 1, 1998.

5. See Du Fangqin, "'Yunming' yu 'shiming': Gaoxiao funü yanjiu zhongxindi licheng he qianjing" ("Fate" and "Mission": The History and Prospects of Women's Studies Centers in Higher Education), *Zhejiang xuekan* (Zhejiang Bulletin), Vol. 3, 2000.

6. For example, Zhengzhou University (1996) sponsored the "Women's Studies Lecture Series." The Beijing Normal University Department of Education (beginning in 1997) offered "gender education" as part of the undergraduate curriculum. Shaanxi Normal University joined with other normal colleges in 1998 in a joint project between China and Canada titled "The Development and Education of Female University Students" and wrote teaching materials for gender studies. The China Women's College and Ewha University of South Korea (1999) jointly sponsored the seminar "Establishing a Discipline."

7. When the All-China Women's Studies Association was founded in 1999, professors at the meeting urged the minister of education to promote the offering of women's studies courses. In 2000, an educational project of the Ford Foundation provided financial assistance to establish gender studies as a discipline and actively supported the translation of Western feminist theories. In 2001, the chair of the All-China Women's Federation, Peng Peiyun, called on the Chinese Academy of Social Sciences to establish relevant academic research units.

8. See Zheng Bijun, "The Establishment and Consideration of the Women's Studies Department at Peking University," remarks given at the "Women's/Gender Studies and the Practice of Higher Education" international forum held at Dalian University in July 2001.

9. See the relevant pages on the Center's "True Me" website: www.genwo.ac.cn.

10. Examples include "The Biological Basis for Gender" (College of Medicine), "A Gender Analysis of English Vocabulary" (College of Foreign Languages), "Women and the Internet" and "Investment and Financial Management for Women" (College of Industrial and Commercial Management), and "Chinese Feminist Literary Criticism" (College of Humanities).

11. Early in its inception, the Center received timely financial assistance from the Ford Foundation and the Asia Foundation.

12. See the relevant pages on the Center's "True Me" website: www.genwo.ac.cn.

13. The Gender Studies Institute Network in Asia has received the support of the Ministry of Foreign Affairs of the Netherlands and began operations in 2002.

14. I presented academic reports related to these issues during the routine meetings at the Center: "Women's/Gender Studies: Standpoints and Methods," which can be found on the "True Me" website.

Part IV

Marriage and Family

THE MARRIAGE LAW AND THE RIGHTS OF CHINESE WOMEN IN MARRIAGE AND THE FAMILY

Chen Mingxia

In 1950, the People's Republic of China drew up its first Marriage and Family Law (abbreviated as the "1950 Marriage Law").[1] In 1980 this law was revised for the first time (abbreviated as the "1980 Marriage Law").[2] In 2001, the 1980 Marriage Law was revised again, reaffirming the principles of the 1950 and 1980 laws, including the freedom to marry the person of one's choosing, monogamy, equality between men and women, and the protection of the legal rights of women, children, and the elderly.[3] The 2001 revision also added language prohibiting domestic violence, created a system of compensation for losses due to divorce, and strengthened and improved the joint marital property system. The new revision also established a system for voiding marriage.[4] Thus, through the continual revision of the Marriage Law, women now enjoy equal rights with men in the family.

Equality under the law, however, does not always equate to equality in practice. Chinese women today still face challenges in translating law into practice. These challenges require the constant improvement and strengthening of the national legal system, but, more important, they also require radical changes in the concept of gender by every person in society.

Article 48 of the Chinese constitution states, "Women of the People's Republic of China enjoy equal rights with men in all spheres of life, including political, economic, cultural, social, family life, and in all other respects." Article 49 states, "Marriage, the family, mothers, and children are protected by the state. Infringement on freedom of marriage and the abuse of the elderly, women, and children are prohibited." Based on the principles of the constitution, the Marriage Law makes the following clear provisions for women's enjoyment of equal rights with men in marriage and the family, which consist mainly of women's personal rights and property rights. For personal rights, women have the following seven rights:

1. The right of freedom in marriage: Articles 2, 3, 31, and 32 of the Marriage Law provide for freedom of marriage and freedom to divorce.

2. The right to equal status: Articles 1, 9, and 13 provide for the equal status of husband and wife in the family.

3. The right to keep one's name: Article 14 states that both husband and wife have the right to use their own names.

4. The right of personal freedom: Article 15 states that both husband and wife have the freedom to participate in production, work, study, and social activities and that the other party may not interfere or limit this participation.

5. Parental rights over children (custody rights): Articles 21, 22, 36, 37, and 38 state that fathers and mothers have equal rights and duties in raising and educating children. After a divorce, both husband and wife have equal visitation rights.

6. Adoption rights: Article 26 states that both husband and wife have equal adoption rights.

7. The right to life and health: Articles 3 and 43–46 prohibit domestic violence and provide legal remedies.

Women also have six property rights within marriage and in the event of divorce. First, community property rights: Article 17 states that any property obtained over the duration of a conjugal relationship falls within the scope of community property. Both husband and wife have equal rights to dispose of such property. Article 39 states that, in the event of a divorce, the disposal of community property is to be agreed upon through negotiation by both parties. In the event that both sides cannot reach an agreement, the people's court will make a determination based on the property and in consideration of the rights and interests of the children and the woman. The law further states that the woman's rights and interests in any contractual management enterprise conducted on family property are legally protected.

Second, the protection of a woman's personal property rights: Article 18 states that, in a conjugal relationship, any property that falls within the scope of the property belonging to one party to the marriage, including property owned prior to marriage, is personal property.

Third, property inheritance rights: Article 24 states that parents and children and husband and wife have the right to inherit estates from each other.

Fourth, the right of support: Articles 20, 21, and 44 state that husband and wife and parents and children are obligated to support each other. Parties who do not fulfill this obligation are held legally liable.

Fifth, the right to economic compensation and economic assistance in the event of a divorce: Articles 40 and 41 state that, in the event of a divorce, under the common-law property system, the party who contributes more to the family (usually the woman) and the party who is economically distressed (usually the woman) is entitled to appropriate assistance. A judicial interpretation of this portion of the law in December 2001 made the clarification that, in the event of a divorce, not having a place to live qualifies as distress, and the other party should provide assistance.

Sixth, the right to seek compensation for damages in the event of a divorce: Articles 46 and 47 state that, in the event of a divorce resulting from domestic violence, bigamy, or other wrongdoing, the injured party (usually the woman) has the right to seek compensation for damages. The law also provides legal remedies for cases in which the other party has transferred or sold off property.

In China, in addition to the constitution and the Marriage Law, the marriage and family rights of women are also legally protected by the Criminal Code, the General Principles of Civil Law, the Law on the Protection of the Rights and Interests of Women, the Inheritance Law, the Adoption Law, the Law on the Health Protection of Mothers and Infants, and by procedural law. These laws contain provisions for the protection of women's rights to freedom of marriage and personal freedoms, including sexual rights, portraiture rights, reputation rights, privacy rights, the right to life and health, reproductive rights, family community property rights, property inheritance rights, and other rights concerning marriage and the family. In addition, a series of ordinances, regulations, and judicial interpretations complete these laws. All levels of government, from the central government to local governments, have drawn up "Programs for Women's Development" based on the "Platform for Action" from the 1995 United Nations' Fourth World Conference on Women and have drafted concrete goals and measures. In the area of women's rights in marriage and the family, in terms of systematic regulations and legal provisions, China has basically created a set of legal relationships in which men and women are equal. It is an incontrovertible fact that, under the law, women have gained equal rights with men in marriage and the family.

TRANSLATING EQUALITY UNDER THE LAW TO EQUALITY IN PRACTICE

The process of translating equality under the law into equality in practice is a long and difficult one, which I will explain by looking at six specific areas. We begin by looking at a woman's right to freedom in marriage, which is one of the most important principles of the Marriage Law. After the implementation of the 1950 Marriage Law, a woman's right to marry the person of her choosing represented a fundamental change from the old system in which all marriages were arranged by parents. Generally speaking, the practices of arranged marriages and marriages by sale have gradually diminished.

But even forty years later, according to statistics from the first survey on the status of Chinese women in 1990, the marriages of 20.1 percent of urban women were still arranged by the woman's parents. In rural villages the percentage was

Chen Mingxia

36.5.[5] According to a 1994 survey on the status of women in contemporary China, the marriages of 4.98 percent of urban women were arranged by the woman's parents, while in rural villages the rate was 28.98 percent.[6] Statistics from a sampling survey conducted as part of the second survey on the status of Chinese women in 2001 by the All-China Women's Federation State Statistics Bureau showed that, as of 2000, 6.8 percent of urban women and 16.1 percent of rural women still suffered from marriages arranged by their parents. An item of particular concern is that, in 2000, the percentage of urban women whose marriages were arranged by the woman's parents actually exceeded the percentage from the mid-1990s.[7]

Second, women now have a greater right to participate in major family decisions. Statistics from the second national survey on the status of women show that, for 67.4 percent of couples, the decision on "what kind of production to engage in" is reached by the husband and wife together or primarily by the wife. This is 17.3 percent higher than ten years earlier. Regarding decisions on "family investments or loans" and "the sale or construction of a home," the rates of women's participation in the decision-making are 60.7 and 70.7 percent, which are 10.2 and 15.1 percent higher than ten years earlier, respectively.[8] However, in 30 to 40 percent of families, wives still do not have the right to participate in decision-making processes. This shows clearly that the woman's status in the family needs improvement.

Third, under the circumstances of China's low level of economic development and generally low wages, in the great majority of families, both in the cities and in rural villages, both husband and wife work outside the home. Thus, according to the principle of equal status in the family under the Marriage Law, husbands and wives should share housework equally. Although a perfect fifty-fifty division of housework is not required, the work should be shared based on the actual family situation. However, surveys show that, compared to 1990, in 2000, although the amount of time spent by both sexes on housework had declined both in the cities and rural areas, the pattern of women's being responsible for the majority of the housework had not changed. In more than 85 percent of families, wives primarily did the daily tasks of cooking, washing dishes, laundry, housecleaning, and other chores. Women spend an average of 4.01 hours per day on housework, which is 2.71 more hours than the time spent by men. The gap between the amount of time spent by men and women on housework has shrunk only six minutes compared to 1990.[9] The greatly reduced amount of time women spend studying and participating in social activities and society's refusal to acknowledge the social value of housework put women at a disadvantage in the family. How can women's equal rights in the family be realized?

Fourth, the reforms and opening to the outside world have brought tremendous social and economic changes, some of which are also changing people's thinking. People are reconsidering the quality of their marriages, and divorce rates have begun to show a gradual upward trend. When a couple is incompatible, it is now normal for them to divorce, but problems remain. How can the side that suffers from the divorce (often women) and children be protected? This is a challenge confronting China and its laws. An example is the problem of housing following a divorce. According to surveys, from August 1998 to August 1999, the Beijing First Intermediate People's Court adjudicated 277 divorce cases involving disputes over housing, which represented 48.3 percent of all divorce cases.[10] In many of these cases, the woman had no place to go following the divorce. The problem of housing is often a thorny one in divorce cases handled by the courts. In one northeastern province, for example, a woman who had no place to live following her divorce was spending the night on the street in −30°C weather when the police found her and took her in. The housing problem for divorced women has become a serious obstacle to women's exercising their freedom to divorce and remarry.

Fifth, according to surveys, the problem of female suicide in the rural areas of China is quite widespread. Those who commit suicide generally are between ages fifteen and thirty-nine. According to calculations based on the 1990 and 1994 survey statistics, the number of Chinese rural women who died as a result of suicide was 173,230, and the death rate was 38.77 per 100,000. The death rate from suicide among China's rural women is much higher than that of urban women and much higher than the rates for urban or rural males. It is also higher than the national average death rate from suicide. There are many reasons for this phenomenon, but, based on a survey of 260 cases of suicide by rural women, the most direct causes in 86.29 percent of the cases were problems in the marriage or family.[11]

Sixth, the problem of domestic violence remains prevalent. In Chinese history there have always been popular folk sayings such as, "If you don't beat your wife, she will get on the roof and within three days break down the house," and "The wife I marry is like the horse I buy. They are mine to ride and mine to beat." Beating one's wife is considered a private family matter, one in which judges find it difficult to intervene. For this reason, when our "rural village subproject" went to the outskirts of Beijing to conduct surveys with officials and local residents and asked them about domestic violence, the immediate response was: "We have no domestic violence!"[12] But when we asked whether people beat their wives, the answer was: "Of course some people beat their wives. Couples everywhere get into arguments, and men beat their wives!" Wife-beating was such an everyday occurrence that people did not consider it violence. How can women who live in homes where there is domestic violence enjoy an equal status and equal rights with men? Although current Chinese law clearly provides equal status and equal rights for men and women in marriage and the family, the achievement of true equality will require much greater and more strenuous efforts.

OBSTACLES TO ACHIEVING EQUAL RIGHTS: TRADITIONAL NOTIONS OF MALE SUPERIORITY

Although there are several obstacles to the achievement of equal rights, the most significant is the stubborn, traditional idea of male superiority and the bias against women that follows from it. Perceptions about women's work in and outside the home are key here. Alone, women's work in the home is not considered important. Yet women who work outside the home must still manage household affairs or else they will not be acknowledged or esteemed by society. A common Chinese expression claims that "Women hold up half the sky," but given traditional expectations, women actually bear responsibility for "more than half the sky." For a woman to do otherwise invites doubts about whether she is a "good woman." The media also promote this message. If a woman achieves some outstanding success, her qualities as a "good wife" and "good mother," her tenderness, gentleness, and skill at managing the household and educating the children must also be touted at the same time, making it seem as though this is the only way she can be a "good woman." If a man achieves success, even if he completely ignores his family and abandons his wife and children, he will still be praised as a great man, one who has sacrificed his personal needs for the greater good. Alternatively, it may be said that he has a "good helpmate," but no requirements are placed on the man to be a good husband and father. In this way, a man who devotes himself solely to his career is a "good man," but a woman who devotes herself entirely to her career is a "bad woman," a "flawed woman," a "woman you can't get close to," a "frightful woman," an "unfeminine woman," an "incomplete woman," or, the most euphemistic of all, a "strong woman."

These perceptions are supported by statistics from the second survey on the social status of Chinese women. When the survey asked women questions about women's abilities, 82.4 percent responded that they "had confidence in their own abilities," and 80 percent answered that they "are not content to accomplish nothing." In response to the statement "Men are naturally more capable than women," which blatantly embodies the traditional gender concept of "strong men, weak women," 66 percent of respondents disagreed, of which 66.7 percent were women, a rate 1.5 percent higher than for male respondents. When asked about their attitudes toward traditional gender roles and the division of labor, most respondents disagreed with the statement "A woman should avoid at all costs attaining a higher social position than her husband," and only 18.5 percent of women agreed with the statement (for men the rate was 21.4

percent), a decrease of 3 percent from the 1990 figure. An even lower proportion, 14.4 percent, of urban women agreed with the statement.

However, when the survey asked more specific questions about the division of labor between the sexes in the new market economy, the results showed that traditional gender concepts still influence people to a high degree. In response to the statement "Men's lives center on society, and women's lives center on the family," which reflects the traditional division of labor between the sexes, 53.9 percent of men and 50.4 percent of women agreed. The percentage of men agreeing with this statement was 2.1 percent higher than it was in 1990. In response to the idea that "It is better to marry well than to be competent," which has become prevalent in Chinese society in recent years, 34.1 percent of respondents agreed. Note particularly that the rate of women agreeing with this concept was 37.3 percent, or 7.1 percent higher than the percentage of men.[13] This is simply another version of the traditional saying, "Get married and you'll have clothes to wear and food to eat!" The return to this way of thinking must be considered a type of "reaction" by society to the demands for women to accept their traditional place. It is a negative phenomenon and manifestation of the internalization of patriarchal culture in women's minds.

In summary, as Chinese women have gained equality with men under the law, and economic pressures have limited the quality of life, more women are working outside the home. In the meantime, society has not changed its expectations of women in terms of their traditional position in the family but has actually placed even more expectations on women. Society now demands that women be not only good housewives but also good workers. Within the family, especially in rural families, due to the influence of traditional concepts, men and women receive unequal resources, including access to education. Facing a fiercely competitive market situation, women who are still living under these traditional concepts are forced to carry an even heavier burden.

In this period of social transformation, the demands placed on people by intense economic competition intersects with the traditional bias against women. Traditional gender concepts, gender roles, and the division of labor, coupled with traditional attitudes of male superiority and discrimination against women, fill the family lives of contemporary Chinese women with contradictions and conflicts. These traditional ideas heavily influence enforcement of the laws that spell out equality between men and women.

A second obstacle is ineffectual law enforcement that prevents women who are victims from obtaining the protection they deserve. Enforcement of the legal right of equality of the sexes in the family requires not only the efforts of law enforcement personnel, but also a high level of professionalism, professional ethics, and an awareness of the contradictions between elements in the law and the biases against women from those personnel. Complete statistics are not available, but our surveys conducted as part of an anti–domestic violence project show that a considerable portion of judicial personnel do not have the proper awareness of domestic violence.[14] Many believe that domestic violence is a private matter and that it is difficult for judicial officials to make judgments on family matters. They are reluctant to get involved and even believe that domestic violence is usually provoked by women. How can this type of person administer the law impartially and protect the legal rights and interests of women?

A woman named Li, for example, endured years of severe abuse at home. After getting a divorce, she was raped, beaten, and locked up by her ex-husband, who threatened to kill the entire family. The woman found someone to murder her ex-husband and dump his body in a ditch. The woman was tried and sentenced to death with a two-year reprieve. After repeated efforts by the woman's attorneys, her sentence was commuted to fifteen years in prison. While the case stirred up controversy in judicial and legal circles, it also provoked some profound reflection on how our law enforcement personnel handle cases of domestic violence. As far as we know, currently, except for the gender training for law enforcement personnel conducted as part of our project and the training sessions that have been conducted in some provinces and municipalities that have joined our anti–domestic violence network, law enforcement personnel receive training in professional ethics without incorporating gender training into the curriculum. Gender awareness is actually an important precondition for the fulfillment of the legal protection of the rights and interests of vulnerable groups, the protection of the rights and interests of women, fair law enforcement, and the promotion of equality of the sexes.

The third obstacle may lie in certain legislation that lacks a gender perspective. In the Beijing Declaration passed at the Fourth World Conference on Women, the governments of many nations explicitly promised to "prevent and eliminate all forms of discrimination against women and girls" (Article 29). "We hereby adopt and commit ourselves as Governments to implement the following Platform for Action, ensuring that a gender perspective is reflected in all our policies and programmes" (Article 38). The Platform for Action clearly states, "Equality between women and men is a matter of human rights and a condition for social justice and is also a necessary and fundamental prerequisite for equality, development, and peace. A transformed partnership based on equality between women and men is a condition for people-centered sustainable development" (Article 1). "The success of policies and measures aimed at supporting or strengthening the promotion of gender equality and the improvement of the status of women should be based on the integration of the gender perspective in general policies relating to all spheres of society as well as the implementation of positive measures with adequate institutional and financial support at all levels" (Article 57). Clearly, according to the United Nations, a gender perspective in legislation is essential to guaranteeing the rights of women.

If we use the provisions of the Beijing Declaration and the Platform for Action to evaluate China's Marriage Law, especially the 2001 revision of the law, we find two problems. One is the abstract way in which the law is written. The other is that inequitable results arise from a law that was intended to be neutral. The chapter on divorce in the revised version of the Marriage Law states that, in the event of a divorce, the disposal of a couple's community property is to be agreed upon through negotiations by both parties. When the parties cannot reach an agreement, the people's court is to make a judgment based on the actual situation of the property and in consideration of the rights and interests of the children and wife. The law states further that, in the event of a divorce, if one party is experiencing difficulties with living expenses, the other party should provide assistance by drawing on his residence and other personal property. Other language in the law makes similar provisions.

The basic intent of the law is benign, to take care of the rights and interests of women and children. But how is "care" defined? How is such care to be realized? What are the standards of such care? With regard to the "difficulties experienced by one party," what constitutes a difficulty? What amount of assistance is appropriate? None of this is defined in the law (even in principle), and thus, in situations where the divorcing parties cannot agree upon a settlement, they must rely on a judge to make the determination. A judicial interpretation from 2001 explains "difficulty with living expenses" as "the inability to maintain a basic level of living in the local area by relying on one's own property and the property obtained as a result of the divorce settlement."[15] This does not consider in any way how one's rights and interests as a married person change after a divorce. The ability to maintain only the most basic level of existence after a divorce is not considered being in "difficulty." In light of the fact that, in general, women tend to be in a weaker position, this part of the law and the specific ruling are both unfair to women. They were not written by people sensitive to gender.

The revised Marriage Law appears to treat men and women equally in matters concerning the rights and interests enjoyed by a husband or wife who undertake a contractual management enterprise on the family property. The same is true for compensation to the injured party in the event of a divorce, when an agreement cannot be reached in the event of a void marriage or a revoked marriage. The provisions in the law appear to ensure equal rights for men and women, but the legislators seem to have overlooked the fact that in Chinese marriages, 95 to 98 percent of women move into the man's home. Legislators apparently did not consider the extent to which "marrying out" affects a woman's land-use rights over her lifetime. A similar issue is the problem of a woman's right to a place to live, in particular, the problem of where she lives following a divorce. Legislation that appears to be neutral leads directly to the loss of land-use rights for women who marry and the loss of the right to a place to live for divorced women. This affects the enjoyment and guarantee of women's other rights, such as the right to freedom in marriage, economic rights, and the right to exist.

With regard to the system of compensation for the injured party in the event of a divorce and the principle of caring for the party not at fault used by the courts when determining the division of joint property obtained during the period of cohabitation in the event of a void marriage or a revoked marriage, the intent of the legislation appears to provide for the rights and interests of women, who are in a weaker position. But how many of these women have the money and ability to gather the evidence to prove that the other party is at fault and to obtain "compensation" or "allowances"?

Hence we conclude that the abstract nature of the law and its seemingly neutral provisions lead to inequitable decisions. Clearly, the government has been blind to issues of gender when drafting legislation on marriage and the family. The intentions of the legislators may have been good, but their blindness about gender has caused them to ignore the current social situation and the practical circumstances and needs of women, particularly during this period of social transformation. The legislation lacks a deeper level of cultural reflection and consciousness about gender. Drawing up laws on the basis of the traditional notion of "equality" makes it difficult to achieve the basic intent of the law, especially since it relies wholly on the good will of judges. For these reasons, the provisions for women's marriage and family rights are difficult to enforce.

CONCLUSION

We expect that China's legal system will continually improve and become more democratic, thereby creating more beneficial conditions for the perfection and advancement of marriage and family law. According to recent reports, China's civil code has recently entered the draft stages, and laws on marriage and the family will be incorporated into that code. This means that further improvements in and revisions to the Marriage Law will soon appear. This is an opportune moment to integrate a gender perspective into legislation. In China today, scholars in the field of legal studies have begun to introduce feminist legal studies from abroad to China, combining them with the practical aspects of China's situation and using the perspective of gender to analyze China's legislation and legal practice.[16] A new group of young, female scholars of marriage and family law is emerging. Scholars and activists in legal studies, sociology, psychology, medicine, and social work are now working to combat domestic violence against women—one of the most critical issues affecting the status and rights enjoyed by women in the family. These experts are studying and testing policies to counter domestic violence and drafting recommendations for "An Act Prohibiting Domestic Violence" to be submitted to the government together with the revisions to the marriage and family laws. This will guarantee women's rights and give them homes free of violence, where they can truly enjoy equal rights with men. But, of course, the challenges are many, the tasks are difficult, and the road is long.

NOTES

1.   China's Marriage Law has its roots in the period of revolutionary struggle and is the successor to the "Marriage Ordinances" and "Provisional Marriage Ordinances" that governed marriage and the family in the base areas and liberated areas prior to the establishment of the People's Republic of China in 1949. The 1950 Marriage Law, the first law on marriage and the family after the establishment of New China on 1 October 1949 consists of eight chapters and twenty-seven articles and is a tremendous work of social revolution that thoroughly eliminated the feudalistic marriage and family system in mainland China. Its "legislative spirit is to overturn male-centered" domination of the husband and to protect the legitimate rights and interests of women and children (*Renmin ribao* [People's Daily], editorial, 16 April 1950). The law was one of the fruits of women's continual participation in the struggle against feudalism beginning with the May Fourth movement in 1919. The feudal system of marriage and the family was an important component of China's social system, which had persisted for thousands of years. Chinese men were oppressed by the power of the government, the clan, and theocracy. In addition to these three forms of oppression, Chinese women were also under the "power of the husband." Women in old China were required to follow the "three obediences and four virtues" (obedience to one's father [prior to marriage], obedience to one's husband in marriage, and obedience to one's sons following the death of one's husband). Women did not have their own personalities or ideas. For the masses of women, the elimination of the feudal marriage and family system amounted to the abolition of a "family slavery system." For this reason, the 1950 Marriage Law was warmly welcomed by women and youth and made a deep impression on people. The situation of 90 percent of marriages have been arranged or for sale's quickly changed.

2.   The 1980 Marriage Law was passed on 10 September 1980 and formally implemented on 1 January 1981. During the Cultural Revolution (1966–1976), China's marriage and family law, like the rest of the legal system, was destroyed. During that period there were many problems in the area of marriage and the family, such as political marriages, loveless marriages, arranged marriages and marriages for sale, and the betrothal of little boys and girls by their parents. The enactment of the 1980 Marriage Law restored the rule of law to the sphere of marriage and the family. The law consists of five chapters and thirty-seven articles and confirms the principle of the freedom to divorce, which states, "when there is incompatibility that cannot be remedied, divorce

should be permitted." This concluded a thirty-year debate that began in the 1950s on whether divorce was justified by "grounds" or by "incompatibility." Based on the legal system that provided the freedom to divorce, people came to accept this concept. This was a major step forward on the path to realizing women's rights.

3. The 2001 Marriage Law was revised per the "Resolution on the (1980) Marriage Law of the People's Republic of China" issued by the twenty-first session of the Standing Committee of the Ninth National People's Congress on 28 April 2001.

4. The revised version made thirty-three major and minor changes to the 1980 Marriage Law, including the addition of a chapter on relief measures and legal liability. One of the basic intents of the revised law was to protect the legal rights and interests of women (see Hu Kangsheng, *Zhonghua renmin gongheguo hunyinfa shiyi* [Commentary on the Marriage Law of the People's Republic of China] [Falü chubanshe, 2001]). The law consists of six chapters and fifty-one articles. The major systematic changes include (1) the establishment of a void marriage system; (2) revision of the rules concerning community property and the addition of specific rules on a husband's and wife's personal property; and (3) the establishment of a compensation system in the event of a divorce. Articles such as the one on "prohibiting domestic violence" were also added.

5. Figures published in All-China Women's Federation, State Statistics Bureau, *Dierqi Zhongguo funü shehui diwei chouyang diaocha zhuyao shuju baogao* (Report on Major Statistics from the Second Sampling Survey of the Social Status of Chinese Women) (Beijing, September 2001).

6. Sha Jicai, ed., *Dangdai Zhongguo funü diwei* (The Status of Women in Contemporary China) (Beijing: Beijing daxue chubanshe, 1995), p. 79.

7. See All-China Women's Federation, *Dierqi.*

8. Ibid.

9. Ibid.

10. Tian Lan, *Beijingshi funü faxue yanjiuhui tongbao* (Bulletin of the Beijing Women's Legal Studies Council), Vol. 2, 2000.

11. See Special Topic Team, Xie Lihua, ed., "Zhongguo nongcun funü zisha baogao" (Report on Suicide among China's Rural Women) in *Nongjianü baishitong* (The Rural Woman's Almanac) (Guizhou: Guizhou renmin chubanshe, 1999), 6, 7, 33.

12. The project "Domestic Violence in China: Research, Intervention, and Prevention" (China Law Society) was initiated in mid-June 2000 and was to run for three years. The project includes fifteen subprojects. The rural village subproject works to test intervention. Project participants include experts from the fields of law, sociology, social work, philosophy, medicine, psychology, and other specializations; scholars; women activists; law enforcement personnel from prosecutorial offices; and legislators from the National People's Congress. The project has established grassroots networks to oppose domestic violence within and outside Beijing. The project has also launched a website: www.stopdv.org.cn.

13. See All-China Women's Federation, *Dierqi.*

14. "Domestic Violence in China" project. Judicial personnel refers to police, prosecutors, judges, officials in judicial bureaus, and any civil servant engaged in the actual work of executing and publicizing the law.

15. See *Zuigao renmin fayuan guanyu shiyong 'Zhongguo renmin gongheguo hunyinfa' ruogan wentidi jieshi (yi)* (The Supreme People's Court Explanation on Several Issues Relating to the Application of the Marriage Law of the People's Republic of China [I]), passed by the 1,202nd session of the Supreme People's Court Adjudicatory Committee, 24 December 2001, Legal Interpretations, No. 30, Articles 27, 29.

16. See, for instance, Chen Mingxia, "Shehui xingbie yishi: hunyinfa xiugai xin zhidian" (Social Gender Consciousness: A New Fulcrum for the Revision of the Marriage Law), *Zhongguo funü bao* (Chinese Women's Gazette), 24 June 2000.

THE STATUS OF CHINESE WOMEN IN MARRIAGE AND THE FAMILY

Xiong Yu

Chinese women's rights in marriage and the family at present are still bound by the inequitable status of women and men. A woman's status is primarily granted to her by her family and her husband as a dependent. She may also gain status from accomplishments achieved through their own efforts. We see four ways in which women gain status through the family. First, they can bear sons. In a patrilineal social structure, sons are valuable to the mother because they provide her with "insurance": a share in the family's resources, assurance that she will not be abandoned by her husband, and economic support after her husband dies and when she reaches her old age. In rural villages, where this traditional viewpoint is still quite prevalent, some women do not stop having children until they bear a son. However, studies also indicate that bearing a son is growing less important, since women can gain status through other ways and means, especially now that the costs of having more children have begun to outweigh the benefits. Second, a woman can pass the status of a powerful father on to a husband. Her family's social status or wealth may benefit her husband's career and thereby enhance her own position. Third, a husband's love for his wife may grant her many rights, including participation in decision-making on family matters. Fourth, a woman may marry a powerful or wealthy man and thus raise her own social status.

The status a woman gains through her own efforts—her knowledge, profession, and income—is entirely different. Most Chinese urban women today can attain economic independence and an improved social status through employment, which may also allow women to share household responsibilities on an equal footing with men. Work outside the home also alters the status of rural women. When a rural woman leaves home to find work and sends the money she earns back home to build a house or to help her brothers with the expenses of getting married, she goes from being an economic liability to a respected member of the family and is admired by the other villagers.

Many indicators can be used to measure the current status of Chinese women in marriage and in the family. In terms of rights, we can monitor women's autonomy in marriage, reproductive rights, the right to manage and allocate income, the right to decide on spending, and the right to choose to improve oneself. In terms of status within marriage and in the family, we can compare the status of women against that of men within the family, in urban and rural areas, and in different geographic regions.

The selection of a spouse is a precondition for marriage and is the primary requirement for autonomy in marriage. The right to decide on a first marriage is a direct indicator of women's autonomy. Statistics from the 1991 "Survey of the Status of Women in Contemporary China" conducted by the Institute of Population Studies of the Chinese Academy of Social Sciences (CASS) indicate that most Chinese men and women in both urban and rural areas have achieved the right of autonomy to decide on a first marriage. In urban areas 94.64 percent of women "make their own decision" on a first marriage, while in rural villages the rate is 70.88 percent. The "Sampling Survey of the Social Status of Chinese Women" conducted by the All-China Women's Federation and the State Statistics Bureau provides further proof of this. By 2000, the percentage of marriages "decided upon by parents" had declined from that of ten years earlier for both urban and rural areas, and for both men and women. However, there is still an imbalance between the urban and the rural areas. Rural women do not enjoy as much the right of autonomy to decide on a first marriage as urban women. And they enjoy much less than rural men.

The freedom to divorce is another important manifestation of autonomy in marriage. While stability is a feature of Chinese marriages, the rate of divorce has accelerated since the 1980s from 4.7 percent in 1979 to 8.9 percent in 1992 to 19 percent in 2000. All told, the divorce rate has grown nearly fourfold in the last twenty years.[1] Since 1949, divorce in China has peaked three times, and each peak has been intimately connected to social transformations. The first occurred in the 1950s, after the promulgation of the Marriage Law, which allowed women to dissolve arranged marriages. The second peak happened in the early 1980s, following the end of the Cultural Revolution in 1976, and was mainly a result of the previous ten years of tumult during which marriages for sale, arranged marriages, and other distortions in marital relationships had become widespread. The third peak occurred when the policies of reform and opening to the outside world expanded working and living space and changed people's ideas about many things, including divorce. Women today are ending marriages that exist in name only, and this is now the leading cause of divorce. Great changes have also occurred in concepts about divorce and remarriage for divorced women. The notion that "a woman must remain faithful to one man until the end of her life" has been challenged.

On the other hand, the tradition of male superiority over females that formed several thousand years ago in China runs deep in the Chinese psyche. Compounding this is an overemphasis on the importance of money, which affects relationships, leading to hasty marriages, casual divorces, an obsession with new trends at the expense of tradition, meddling by third parties, and other phenomena. After a man attains a certain social standing and a bit of wealth, he may look for a mistress or date someone new on the side, and he may find his wife, who was originally a good match for him, of little interest. There are women who believe that the husband is the whole world and that their job is to help the man to go up the social ladder. Sometimes when women devote themselves completely to the task of helping their husbands get promoted or do business, they end up losing everything, husband, family, and career.

In married life, both men and women should have the right to make decisions about their own bodies and minds. Traditional values, however, still regard sexual relations for any purpose other than procreation as evil and sinful. The sole purpose of sex remains creating children and producing a male heir to continue the family line. In this context, women's personal needs and desires are not acknowledged or respected, even by women themselves. During the 1980s, however, people's ideas about sex began to change. For example, when the Survey on the Status of Women in Contemporary China asked, "May a wife refuse the sexual demands of her husband?" or "May a wife initiate sex?" not only were the men's responses forthright, but the women also expressed their views openly. Although men and women, and urban and rural dwellers, expressed different opinions, respondents recognized a woman's right to autonomy in sexual relations. Of course, gaps exist between recognition and practice. In real married life, the man's dominant status to a large extent controls the couple's sexual relations. Potential conflicts arising from differences in sexual needs are usually resolved by the wife's passivity and submissiveness. In this regard, two sets of statistics are worth noting: First, 78 percent more urban women than men reported that they frequently or always "satisfy their partner's sexual demands," while the percentage of rural women responding this way was nearly double that of men. Second, the percentage of men responding that they "take the initiative in expressing sexual demands to their partner" was several times higher than that for women both in cities and rural villages.[2] Women fear taking the initiative because they fear provoking a negative reaction from their husbands or damaging the marital relationship. This is a reflection of gender inequity on an even deeper level.

Thus, one may conclude that in marital relationships, men and women are moving toward equality. Both enjoy a certain amount of autonomy. At the same time, we also see that marriage is by nature a social activity, and that the norms governing social behavior still constrain it. Different social systems and economic and cultural contexts all affect marital status and imbalances in rights.

Bearing children is one of the basic functions of the family. The percentage of urban wives who make their own decisions regarding procreation is more than double the percentage in rural villages. Democratic consultation is now the mainstream method used by families when making decisions about procreation. An average of more than 80 percent of couples, both in urban and rural areas, decide together whether to have children and when to have them. Urban couples show little preference for girls or boys. In rural villages, whether it is the first child or the last, couples show a much greater preference for boy babies than for girls.

According to surveys, approximately 44 percent of urban women have access to opportunities for self-improvement, and 92 percent of these women can decide on their own whether to pursue further training without permission from someone else. Urban women enjoy a relatively high level of autonomy in making decisions regarding self-improvement, and the gap between men and women is small. In rural villages, both men and women have fewer opportunities to receive adult education than do city dwellers. Women have few opportunities for self-improvement, and their level of autonomy is low.

In addition to the opportunities for learning mentioned above, another important aspect of self-improvement includes the time allocated to the effort. In the family, the amount of leisure time women have available for their own use is an important condition for their development. According to a survey by the All-China Women's Federation in 2000, the amount of leisure time women had for their own personal use increased during the past ten years, and 5 percent of urban women and 0.5 percent of rural women had access to online technology as a source of information. However, in addition to the eight-hour fixed work day, women are also responsible for the household. This responsibility severely limits women's opportunities for self-improvement. Except for those rural women who have found jobs outside the home, most rural women are involved in the agricultural production that the family undertakes on a contractual basis, and they have a heavy burden of housework, which is currently not acknowledged by society as having social value. All in all, few rural women have the time for self-improvement.

Generally speaking, both in urban and rural areas in China today, husbands and wives manage the family's income together. In cities, 76.25 percent of couples manage family finances together, while in rural villages the rate is 81 percent. Comparisons between the amount of authority men and women have over the management of family incomes show that, in cities, women generally have more control than men. Using the municipality of Shanghai and the provinces of Shaanxi, Guangdong, and Shandong as examples, the rates of women in urban areas in charge of managing the family income are higher than for men by 18.4, 17.2, 11.6, and 6 percent respectively. In rural villages, with the exception of Shanghai where the percentage of women is higher than the percentage of men, the percentages for women are all lower than for men (see Table 1).

Xiong Yu

Table 1

COMPARISON OF THE PERCENTAGES OF HUSBANDS' AND WIVES' INCOME
MANAGEMENT RIGHTS IN URBAN AND RURAL AREAS (%)

Region	Shanghai			Shandong		
	Wife	Husband	Difference	Wife	Husband	Difference
Urban	93.7	75.3	18.4	95.4	89.4	6.0
Rural	95.7	93.7	2.0	92.2	94.4	−2.2

Region	Shaanxi			Guangdong		
	Wife	Husband	Difference	Wife	Husband	Difference
Urban	93.9	76.7	17.2	95.7	84.0	11.6
Rural	84.8	91.4	−6.6	89.2	95.3	−6.1

Source: Institute of Population Studies of the Chinese Academy of Social Sciences, "Dangdai Zhongguo funü diwei chouyang diaocha" (Sampling Survey of the Status of Contemporary Chinese Women) Database.

Income management includes allocation for personal consumption and consumption for the entire family. The right to spend money on personal consumption refers to the range of money that may be spent at one's discretion. In China, patterns of spending rights in urban and rural areas show that, in cities, the rights of husbands and wives differ only slightly and are basically equal. In rural areas, the difference is more pronounced, and husbands have greater rights than wives (see Table 2). In addition, differences in the rights to personal consumption are also reflected in the actual amounts spent by husbands and wives. Survey data shows that the percentage of wives making expenditures in small amounts is greater than the percentage of husbands. As the amount allocated for an expenditure increases (including nonmonetary upper limits), at the level of 200 yuan and above in cities and 100 yuan and above in rural villages, husbands clearly have more rights than wives. The good news is that, even in rural villages, 12 percent of women can now spend freely on personal consumption without monetary limits.

Table 2

COMPARISON OF RIGHTS TO PERSONAL CONSUMPTION BETWEEN HUSBANDS AND
WIVES IN URBAN AND RURAL AREAS (%)

Region	Shanghai			Shandong		
	Wife	Husband	Difference	Wife	Husband	Difference
Urban	55.5	57.9	−2.4	44.0	44.2	−0.2
Rural	52.5	63.0	−10.5	14.5	28.4	−14.3

Region	Shaanxi			Guangdong		
	Wife	Husband	Difference	Wife	Husband	Difference
Urban	44.3	43.9	0.4	83.2	85.7	−2.5
Rural	17.5	44.8	−27.3	73.8	85.1	−11.3

Source: See Table 1.

Family consumption expenditures generally include the purchase of durable consumer goods, the purchase or construction of a home, and production materials. Data from the Chinese Academy of Social Sciences, Institute of Population's "Survey on the Status of Contemporary Chinese Women" show that in decision-making in this category, men and women in both cities and rural areas are moving toward equality. However, if decision-making percentages for men and women are compared separately, data from Shanghai, Shandong, Shaanxi, and Guangdong show that both in urban and rural areas, husbands have more decision-making rights than wives (see Table 3).

Table 3
COMPARISON BETWEEN HUSBANDS AND WIVES ON THE RIGHT TO MAKE
DECISIONS ON FAMILY CONSUMPTION IN URBAN AND RURAL AREAS (%)

Region	Shanghai			Shandong		
	Wife	Husband	Difference	Wife	Husband	Difference
Urban	70.2	82.8	12.6	66.6	78.1	11.5
Rural	88.8	91.5	2.7	88.0	90.5	2.5

Region	Shaanxi			Guangdong		
	Wife	Husband	Difference	Wife	Husband	Difference
Urban	56.7	72.2	15.5	62.1	77.0	14.9
Rural	76.2	86.5	10.3	82.1	84.5	2.4

Source: See Table 1.

An analysis of the indicators presented above shows that the status of Chinese women in marriage and the family has clearly risen, but that development is not balanced. This is due not only to the differences among women as individuals but also to the level of development and diverse social characteristics of the locations. If we look at women in isolation, generally speaking, the status of Chinese women in marriage and the family is higher in the economically developed regions than in economically less-developed regions. If we compare the rights of men and women in marriage and the family, generally speaking, men have a higher status than women, and the gap between men and women is greater in rural villages than in cities. The status of Chinese women in marriage and the family is largely connected to the level of economic development and the openness of a particular area. In the cities and rural areas of developed coastal regions such as Shanghai and Guangdong, indicators of women's status are higher than those for Shandong, Jilin, Shaanxi, and Ningxia, and the status of women declines as one moves farther west. Differences in the indicators that reflect the status of women in marriage and the family show that, in the home, women have more responsibilities than rights. Many indicators reveal this pattern, and it is most apparent where women have as much or more right to manage family income, but they do not have the corresponding right to make decisions on allocations for family consumption.

NOTES

1. The divorce rates here are a comparison of the logarithms of divorces for that year and marriages for that year.

2. The "Survey on the Social Status of Contemporary Chinese Women" was conducted by the Institute of Population of the Chinese Academy of Social Sciences and sponsored by the United Nations Population Fund, project number CPR/90/P06.

REFERENCES

All-China Women's Federation, State Statistics Bureau. *Dierqi Zhongguo funü shehui diwei chouyang diaocha zhuyao shuju baogao* (Report on Major Statistics from the Second Sampling Survey of the Social Status of Chinese Women). September 2001.

Deng Weizhi. *Jiatingdi mingtian* (The Future of the Family). Guizhou: Guizhou renmin chubanshe, 1986.

Project on Rural Women Who Leave Home to Work, Institute of Sociology, Chinese Academy of Social Sciences. *Nongmin liudong yu xingbie* (Peasant Migration and Gender). Henan: Zhongyuan nongmin chubanshe, 2000.

Sha Jicai and Xiong Yu, eds. *Dangdai Zhongguo funü diwei chouyang diaocha baogao* (Report on the Sampling Survey of the Status of Contemporary Chinese Women). Beijing: Wanguo xueshu chubanshe, 1994.

Sha Jicai, Xiong Yu, et al., eds. *Dangdai Zhongguo funü jiating diwei yanjiu* (Study of the Status of Contemporary Chinese Women in the Family). Tianjin: Tianjin renmin chubanshe, 1994.

Tao Chunfang and Jiang Yongping, eds. *Zhongguo funü shehui diwei gaiguan* (Overview of the Social Status of Chinese Women). Beijing: Zhonguo funü chubanshe, 1993.

Xiong Yu, ed. *Mianxiang 21 shijidi xuanze—Dangdai funü yanjiu zuixin lilun gailan* (Choices in Facing the 21st Century—Overview of the Newest Theories in Contemporary Women's Studies). Tianjin: Tianjin renmin chubanshe, 1993.

Xiong Yu and N. E. Riley. *Zhongguo funü jiating quanli tanxi* (An Exploration and Analysis of the Rights of Chinese Women in the Family). Beijing: Beijing daxue chubanshe, 1995.

Xu Dixin et al., eds. *Dangdai Zhongguo die renkou* (The Population of Contemporary China). Beijing: Zhongguo shehui kexue chubanshe, 1988.

DOMESTIC VIOLENCE IN CHINA

Wang Xingjuan

Since China entered the era of reform and opening to the outside world, the media has occasionally published shocking stories of domestic abuse that create a public uproar. Unfortunately, government agencies, judicial departments, and women as a group tend to see these incidents as isolated events. Under pressure from public criticism, the perpetrator is punished, the victim taken care of, and the controversy dies down. The cycle begins again when another instance of domestic abuse appears. In 1994, a foreign visitor asked one of China's leading women about domestic violence in China. The woman pointed to isolated incidents but denied that domestic violence is a problem for Chinese women.

Statistics, however, would dispute that view. The most authoritative data come from the "Social Survey of Chinese Women" conducted jointly in 1990 by the All-China Women's Federation and the State Statistics Bureau, a sampling conducted in twenty-three provinces, municipalities, and autonomous regions across the nation. More than forty thousand questionnaires were collected. The results of the survey show that 0.9 percent of women are beaten frequently, 8.2 percent of women are beaten sometimes, and 20.1 percent of women are beaten occasionally.[1] This means that 71 percent of women throughout the country do not suffer from domestic violence, and that 29 percent of women suffer to varying degrees. The percentage who suffer is not an insignificant number.

Surveys conducted in Beijing and Shanghai support the reliability of these figures.[2] In 1994, the Beijing Council on Marriage and the Family collected 2,400 valid questionnaires, 88 percent of the number distributed, in 8 districts of the city to conduct a survey about the quality of marriages. Shanghai conducted an analysis based on the data obtained from surveys conducted in 1987 and 1990. The data from these two cities are presented in Table 1:

Table 1

DOMESTIC VIOLENCE IN BEIJING AND SHANGHAI

Husband beats his wife	1994 Beijing (%)	1994 Shanghai (%)	
		Urban districts	Suburban counties
Frequently	1.0	0.80	0.20
Sometimes	4.4	0.6	5.20
Rarely	15.9	6.20	11.0
Never	78.7	92.4	83.6
No. of samples (persons)	2,029	268	268

The survey results from Beijing are basically consistent with those from the national survey; the percentages in Shanghai are somewhat lower. Both of these surveys reflect the fact that, like women in countries around the world, a significant number of Chinese women are beaten by their husbands. Richer, high-status women are not spared from violence at the hands of their husbands. On the contrary, some data show that, as the reforms and policies of opening to the outside world have progressed, the restraining power of traditional ethics has weakened, social monitoring and control have become lax, the gap between rich and poor has widened, and domestic violence has risen. Mo Hongxian points out, that according to statistics from the Beijing Women's Federation, the number of court cases filed for domestic violence was 25 percent higher in the first half of 1998 than for the same period in 1997.[3] According to statistics from the Xi'an Women's Federation, domestic violence cases accounted for 35.2 percent of all the court cases filed in 1995. In 1996, this rate rose 3 percent, and the first quarter of 1997 saw a 22.54 percent increase over the same period in 1996. The issue of sexual violence has also begun to attract attention. In one city in Shanxi province, in over one-quarter of the 3,300 divorce cases adjudicated, the wife had brought charges against the husband for rape.

Domestic violence not only injures, disables, and kills women; it also leads wives to murder their husbands. Some statistics show that domestic violence is the leading cause of women's committing murder or serious injury to another person. Statistics from Liaoning province show that domestic violence was a factor in more than 50 percent of the crimes committed by women, and the cause of 80 percent of serious injury or murder committed by women.[4] More than one hundred of the one thousand–plus inmates at the Liaoning Provincial Women's Prison were convicted of killing their husbands. In one county-level court in western Liaoning, thirty-three of the ninety-six criminal injury cases involved domestic violence. Tieling county saw seven cases in three years of wives' killing their husbands because they could no longer endure the abuse.

The Jiangsu Women's Federation conducted a survey in 2000 at the Women's Division of the Nantong Prison and discovered that 46.2 percent of the female inmates had been victims of domestic violence. For 52.74 percent of the female inmates, their crime was directly linked to domestic violence. These women were beaten at home nearly every day, and the abuse continued for ten or more years or even for decades.[5]

GOVERNMENT ACTION

Combating domestic violence requires government action, since governments should protect the personal safety of their own citizens. The first reference to domestic violence in official documents from the Chinese government appears in the "Program for Women's Development, 1995–2000," submitted by the Chinese government in 1995 to the United Nations' Fourth World Conference on Women. The program named eleven major goals for the development of Chinese women by the end of the century, the eleventh of which proposed the legal protection of the equal status of women in the home. This was the first time the Chinese government had clearly asserted its opposition to domestic violence.

In 1995, the UN World Conference on Women held in Beijing passed the "Platform for Action," listing twelve major areas of concern, the fourth of which was violence against women. The Chinese government voted in favor of the platform, expressing its commitment to combating domestic violence. In May 2001, the State Council issued another "Program for Women's Development" for the years 2001 to 2010. In the new program, the Chinese government reiterated the goals of protecting women's rights:

> Establish and perfect laws and statues that promote the equality of men and women; develop educational propaganda on the laws and statutes that protect women's rights and interests; protect the personal rights of women and prohibit all forms of violence towards women; protect equal property rights between men and women; protect women's rights to press charges and file suits and their interests in litigation; provide legal assistance to women.

Drawing up laws to curb domestic violence began at the local level. The first local statute was enacted in the city of Changsha in Hunan province, where in 1995, a particularly flagrant case stunned the nation. A man had thrown his wife out the window of a tall building, killing her. The leaders of Changsha unveiled on 10 January 1996 "Regulations on Preventing and Curbing Domestic Violence," becoming the nation's first city government to enact such local statutes. In February 2000, government departments in Liaoning province jointly issued "Resolutions Concerning Preventing and Curbing Domestic Violence." By the end of 2000, thirteen provinces and municipalities across the nation, including Shaanxi province, Hunan province, Tianjin municipality, Sichuan province, Hebei province, and Ningxia Hui Autonomous Region, had drawn up local statutes and regulations on curbing domestic violence.

On 30 April 2001, the Standing Committee of the National People's Congress passed the revised Marriage Law. The new law includes language concerning domestic violence and clearly defines the legal responsibilities of public security agencies in curbing domestic violence. The revised law also provides the legal basis for punishing domestic violence. On 26 December 2001, the Supreme People's Court issued a judicial interpretation of the new Marriage Law that provides a legal definition of domestic violence: behavior toward a member of the family that results in injurious consequences physically, emotionally, or in other ways by "beating, tying up, injuring, forcibly restricting one's personal freedom, or by other means." This definition has been helpful in carrying out activities to combat domestic violence.

The outpost tribunal Shanxi Datong Rights Protection Court was established in April 1995. By September 1998 there were eighty-seven "Courts to Protect the Legal Rights and Interests of Women and Children" in Shanxi, eighty of which are courts of first instance, and seven of which are courts of second instance. The work of these courts includes pretrial investigations, legal guidance, follow-up visits, education on the law, and case handling. Lower-level courts in Shanxi, Hebei, Heilongjiang, Jilin, Liaoning, Henan, Jiangsu, Tianjin, and other provinces and municipalities have joined with the All-China Women's Federation to establish a corps of jurors for cases involving the rights and interests of women. Some lower-level courts have established courts for the protection of women's rights and interests, collegial bench systems, and circuit courts, increasing the protection of women's rights and interests.

Providing legal assistance to women who have been abused is one important measure adopted by judicial agencies. Currently, judicial departments in twenty-eight provinces, municipalities, and autonomous regions have established legal aid agencies to provide legal representation for women free of charge or at reduced rates. Legal consultation agencies to protect women have been established in 85 to 90 percent of relevant departments above the county level. These agencies provide legal information to women and help them to proceed with litigation.

Beijing now offers the "148" legal assistance telephone hotline. In December 2001, the Beijing municipal court system for the first time provided detailed regulations on judicial assistance. The regulations list twelve categories of persons, including personal injury victims, whose legal rights have been violated and who are in financial difficulty and who could receive financial assistance, reduced fees, or litigation fee waivers.

Public security agencies are now actively participating in efforts to combat domestic violence. The best example of this is the Liaoning Provincial Bureau of Public Security. They have implemented community policing to increase the sense of responsibility on the part of local police for preventing and curbing domestic violence. Targeting the misconceptions held by some people that "even honest officials cannot intervene in family affairs," the government has proposed the principles of "priority policing, priority assistance, priority handling." Shenyang, Jinzhou, and ten other cities in the province have now established "110" domestic violence reporting centers and domestic violence forensic expertise centers to facilitate prompt intervention by public security agencies and prompt gathering of evidence. Government agencies in many cities, such as Shaoxing in Zhejiang province and Huaibei in Jiangsu province, have brought together public security, prosecutorial, legal, and judicial agencies to cooperate with women's federations and other departments and to bring curbing domestic violence into the sphere of social administration.

The establishment of the first National Coordinating Group for the Protection of the Rights and Interests of Women and Children connected these agencies throughout the nation in November 2001. Led by the All-China Women's Federation, the group comprises fourteen agencies, including the Central Department of Propaganda, the Central Commission on Political Science and Law, the Supreme People's Court, the Supreme People's Procuratorate, the Ministry of State Security, the Ministry of Justice, the Ministry of Civil Affairs, the Ministry of Labor and Social Guarantees, the Ministry of Agriculture, the Ministry of Culture, the Ministry of Health, the State Family Planning Commission, and the State Administration for Industry and Commerce. The missions of the coordinating group are multiple: to communicate the status of efforts to protect the rights and interests of women and children; to coordinate difficult key issues in the protection of these rights and interests; to investigate typical cases in which these rights and interests have been violated; and to promote the establishment and perfection of laws and statutes to protect these rights and interests.

Nongovernmental organizations (NGOs) are one of the most active forces combating domestic violence. The participation of experts in the fields of law, sociology, philosophy, psychology, medicine, and women activists have played an important role in deepening and broadening the scope of anti–domestic violence activities. Among China's NGOs, the largest women's organization is the Women's Federation, branches of which stretch from the national level to the provincial and municipal, as well as to cities and villages. The organization forms a tight network as the main force combating domestic violence. In addition, other grass-roots women's organizations have also become involved in anti–domestic violence activities and are at the forefront of these efforts. The enactment of many local anti–domestic violence statutes and regulations at the provincial and municipal level has occurred because of vigorous lobbying by women's organizations. The draft of the revised Marriage Law passed by the Standing Committee of the National People's Congress includes language against domestic violence, formulated first by members of nongovernmental women's organizations.

At the Fourth World Conference on Women in 1995, three grass-roots organizations held NGO forums on domestic violence. The China Association of Women Judges held a forum on the topic of combating and eliminating violence against women. The China Council on Marriage and the Family held a forum on Chinese marriage and family and women's roles. The Women's Institute of the China College of Management Science (which later changed its name to the Beijing Red Maple Center for Women's Psychological Counseling) held a forum on women's groups and social assistance. These forums used incontrovertible facts to expose the damage done to women from domestic violence and expressed the resolve of women's organizations to curb domestic violence.

Women's groups have also been innovative in monitoring enforcement of the laws. They have provided suggestions for the establishment of local rights protection courts and the setting up of the jury system and joint conferences on rights protection. Women's organizations, studying the experiences of foreign countries and Hong Kong, organized a social gender training corps that trains female cadres, government officials, judicial personnel, public security personnel, and community workers in gender awareness, including awareness about domestic violence.

More and more grass-roots organizations are recognizing that preventing and curbing domestic violence is a job for the entire society and that united collective efforts are necessary. For this reason, at the same time that they promote the coordination of government activities, women's organizations are joining together on their own projects. In June 1999 three grass-roots organizations in Beijing—the Center for Women's Law Studies and Legal Services of the Law School of Peking University, the Beijing Red Maple Center for Women's Psychological Counseling, and the Women's Counseling and Development Center of China Women's College—joined forces with the Shaanxi Institute on Women's Theory and Marriage and the Family to organize a task force to combat domestic violence. They sponsored "Beijing Plus Five" activities to review and evaluate the efforts made by the government and grass-roots organizations in combating domestic violence since the Fourth World Conference on Women. This was the first time anyone in China had collected materials on government and grass-roots organizations' anti–domestic violence activities. It provided a valuable reference for assessing the progress and status of China's efforts.

In June 2000, grass-roots organizations in the Beijing area voluntarily organized and launched a project called "Domestic Violence in China: Research, Intervention, and Prevention," conducted through the China Law Society. Since its inception, the project has developed more than ten subprojects, such as conducting surveys on domestic violence and judicial intervention in cities and villages and setting up pilot communities for domestic violence intervention in Beijing and its suburbs.

EMPOWERING WOMEN

The efforts of China's grass-roots organizations against domestic violence are guided by feminist concepts about gender. The concept of empowerment includes awareness about legislation and law enforcement, interpersonal relations, and personal rights to security. The first task in empowering women is to educate them about the law. They need to know that the laws enacted by the state are tools for combating domestic violence. In 1998, a five-year Sino-Canadian project headed by the All-China Women's Federation began to inform women throughout the nation about the law. Recently, with the support of the United Nations' Women's Development Fund, the All-China Women's Federation Rights and Interests Department has implemented another project called "Sharing the Strategies in Test Provinces to Eliminate Violence Against Women." The project mainly involves developing observation and questionnaire surveys and organizing training to develop male and community gender awareness, publicize the laws against domestic violence, and establish mechanisms for comprehensive cooperation in the provinces of Liaoning, Jiangxi, and Shaanxi, and the city of Wuhan.

The second task in empowering women is to provide abused women with direct legal assistance and services. Many grass-roots women's legal assistance agencies have been established since 1995, the best of which is the Center for Women's Law Studies and Legal Services of the Law School of Peking University. In 2001, this center handled litigation for twelve cases of abused women. The Tianjin Hongshun Community Legal Services Station, established in 2001, handled five cases of domestic violence in the first half-year of its existence. The station has provided 458 face-to-face and telephone legal counseling sessions and legal support for battered women.

The third task in empowering women is to provide battered women with psychological support by offering women's hotlines and developing psychological counseling services. These give women the opportunities to express their feelings and help to relieve them of their psychological pressures. These are themselves a way to empower women. Hotline counselors help battered women to improve their self-awareness, find resources outside themselves, discover their potential, and improve their self-confidence and independence. Psychological counseling can also provide relevant information about possible interventions. Currently, in addition to the domestic violence hotline that has been set up in Shaanxi province, women's federations in more than twenty provinces, municipalities, and autonomous regions throughout the nation have established nearly one hundred rights-protection hotlines. Women's hotlines that offer psychological counseling have been set up in the cities of Beijing, Shenyang, Shijiazhuang, Shanghai, and Chengdu, and the provinces of Shaanxi, Guangxi, and Shandong.

Anti–domestic violence activities feature tight interconnections between practice and theoretical research, particularly in the area of sexual violence.

Sexual violence touches the most private aspects of a couple's relationship. In foreign countries such violence is referred to as marital rape, but even in some developed countries, the establishment of marital rape as a legal concept is still controversial. The question of whether rape can exist within marriage has caused heated discussions in women's circles and the legal community in China since the 1990s. The thread of this discussion can be traced in the magazine *Women's Life*, published in Henan province, which ran a yearlong series of articles devoted to the topic from 1990 to 1991. The stream of cases handled by the courts in different places of women accusing their husbands of rape during marriage gave these discussions a practical significance.

In summary, the twenty or so cases of marital rape brought before the courts fall into three categories. First, in an arranged marriage of coercion, the man overpowers a woman and rapes her. Second, a rape occurs during the course of divorce proceedings or after a divorce has been approved but the procedures have yet to be completed. In this case, a man forces a woman to have sexual relations with him before the divorce settlement goes into effect. Third, rape occurs prior to the normal consummation of a marriage that has been officially registered. Before the couple has begun living together, the woman requests that the marriage be dissolved. In order to make the marriage a *fait accompli*, the man enlists the help of others to carry out forcible sexual relations with the woman. In all cases of alleged marital rape, the courts' responses varied greatly. Sometimes the court found the husband guilty, sometimes not guilty, and sometimes simply agreed to allow the couple to divorce.

China's Criminal Code provides punishment for the rape of a woman. The key part of this legal text is that rape must occur against a woman's will and that sexual intercourse must occur using coercive measures. The text of the law does not indicate its applicability inside or outside marriage, although judicial practice applies the law only to cases of rape outside marriage.

There are three opinions on this issue, the first of which holds that rape does not exist within a marriage. Yang Lixin believes that spousal rights include the obligation to cohabit.[6] This duty is a fundamental one for husband and wife and a basic condition for sustaining a marital relationship. The first and foremost obligation of cohabitation is the duty to have sexual relations. Sexual relations between husband and wife are the foundation of the couple's life together, and both parties are obligated to have sexual intercourse with each other. Refusing to engage in sexual intercourse without a legitimate reason violates a legal obligation.

Li Shun, who vigorously advocates the existence of the crime of marital rape, has written many articles questioning this opinion. He believes that the mainstream legal community's treatment of sexual relations between husband and wife as both a right and a duty is wrong.[7] A right admits the possibility of a behavior chosen voluntarily, while a duty is required behavior or behavior that is not voluntary. Considering a particular behavior to be both a right and a duty is not only illogical but in practice also tends to undermine the "possibility of choice" that the basic principles of modern law have established. The law thus interpreted will yield the following result: Chinese law establishes that Chinese women have the right to decide about their own sexual behavior. However, marriage cancels the right of a spouse "to choose" and obligates the spouses to have sexual intercourse with each other, so that "refusing to engage in sexual intercourse without a legitimate reason violates a legal obligation." Therefore, a woman has the right to determine her own sexual behavior but acquiescing to the sexual demands of her husband is her "duty" as a wife. When the great majority of Chinese women become wives, in practice, then, their rights are canceled or severely limited.

A third opinion lies between these first two. Fu Liqing believes that, in China's current criminal code, the regulations against rape are written in the form of a general stipulation.[8] The law does not explicitly state that husbands can be the perpetrators of rape, nor does it explicitly state that husbands are excluded. The doctrine that "rape does not exist within marriage" is basically the doctrine of the obligation to cohabit. The fatal flaw in this doctrine is that the right and duty to cohabit are not a legal right or duty, and the law cannot be used to regulate sexual relations as a duty. Love is the only effective guarantee of maintaining proper cohabitation. The law grants husbands and wives only "the right to request cohabitation" and not "the right to fulfill cohabitation."

Nevertheless, Fu believes that when legislators stipulate that a particular behavior is a crime, they must take into consideration other factors, such as social mores, national politics, the economy, culture, and the history of past struggles against this particular crime. In other words, it is necessary to consider fully China's situation as a nation. When a husband forces his wife to have sexual relations with him, the wife has been injured in an objective sense. But this fact must be viewed in the context of balancing ideas about social order and individual justice. Ultimately, the resolution of this issue will depend on the further development of the market economy, further reforms in the political system, gradual changes in traditional culture, and many other factors. Chinese society today is still one in which the social group is preeminent, and individuals are to a certain extent subordinate to the collective and to the society. Independent individuality is lacking. In the current context, not treating marital rape as a crime may be the only alternative. It may be the rational choice.

Nevertheless, some grass-roots women's organizations are conducting surveys to study sexual violence and to demonstrate that it harms women's lives. These groups are also striving for legislation to support their perspectives.

"Indigenization" in Chinese Research and Theory

Research on domestic violence by China's theorists and the women's community is in its initial stages, whereas theorists and researchers abroad have been studying the subject for more than thirty years. Using foreign research as a reference, China's theoretical researchers are attacking the problem by beginning from China's culture and family system and conducting native research on domestic violence.

Many papers on the problem of domestic violence in China have pointed to the traditional culture and the preeminence of the patriarchal family as the primary historical and social roots of domestic violence against women. Luo Ping believes domestic violence is a product of male-dominated culture and that today's culture is basically one of the male-centered family.[9] As the early Marxist Li Da pointed out in *Theory of Women's Emancipation*, "All of society's morals, customs, habits, laws, politics, and economics are centered on men."[10] In such a society, men and women are not equal in the family or the social structure. Men control economic and political power. Both in the family and in society, men make decisions and women obey them.

Li Shun also points to women's subordinate status in the family.[11] He notes that contemporary China is in some obvious ways very similar to ancient China, especially in terms of social structure and law. In traditional society women were subordinate to the family, but modernization seemingly liberated the individual from the family. Within the family, individuals were the parts and the family was the "whole." After 1949, within the scope of the state, families were the parts and the state was the whole. From the Chinese perspective, the interests of the whole take precedence over everything else. Individuals and families are components of the whole, and as such, their interests are completely subsumed by those of the whole. Individuals do not have independent interests and choices separable from the whole.

In May 2001, the Beijing Red Maple Center for Women's Psychological Counseling completed a research project titled "Case Studies of Domestic Violence from the Women's Hotline."[12] Using the methods of gender analysis, researchers aware of the preeminence of the family under feudalism studied one hundred cases of domestic violence that had been handled by the hotline and asked why most of these complaining women stayed in their abusive situations. The study concluded that the family was still the basic unit of society. Moreover, the concept of preserving the integrity of the family had far-reaching effects in battered women and in social networks.

First, domestic violence itself is obscured. The concept of the patriarchal family unit prevents social support systems from recognizing domestic violence. The attitudes of social support networks toward domestic violence are reflected in the advice to women to "reconcile and not leave," the notions that "a harmonious family prospers" and that "even just officials have difficulty intervening in family matters." The first consideration of all involved is for the family and the integrity of the family, not the violence. This desire or practice to obscure domestic violence makes it difficult for women who want to get out of abusive situations to be heard, and they may be victimized again.

Second, the researchers point to the glorification of women who remain in abusive situations. Society teaches women that "maintaining a family situation is a woman's responsibility." Women are reminded in particular of their responsibility as mothers to "keep the family together for the sake of the children." The good mother is an important standard of female virtue in patriarchal culture. "A woman who divorces is a delinquent mother" and "it is better to sacrifice yourself to preserve the family" are both articles of faith for women. Women who make sacrifices for their children win sympathy and praise from society.

Third, many view domestic violence apathetically and fatalistically. A culture of domestic violence, the examples of women in the older generation who endured years of abuse, and the adages passed down through society that women must be beaten all produce a cultural legacy that sees "husbands as the guiding force for their wives," a view that has evolved into grounds for husbands to beat their wives. These ideas have been passed down generation after generation. When a battered woman seeks help, such ideas, often in her own head as well as in others, make her "put up with it and accept it because, after all, this is a woman's lot in life." Thus, the family-centered patriarchy continues to keep abused women locked into situations of domestic violence.

THE DIRECTION OF FUTURE DEVELOPMENT

In only a few short years, China's efforts to combat domestic violence have begun to achieve results, but much work still remains to be done. The government of China is well aware of this. In June 2000, the Chinese government's report to the UN Beijing Plus Five Special Session, entitled "Report from the People's Republic of China on the Results of Implementing the Beijing Declaration and Platform for Action from Fourth World Conference on Women," noted the following obstacles to combating domestic violence.

> Violence against women has not been effectively curbed, especially trafficking in women and domestic violence. An effective mechanism to protect women from violence has not yet fully formed. Further improvement is needed in the areas of punishing perpetrators of violence, and in assisting and providing remedies for victims. Laws against domestic violence have not yet been drawn up. The public has

little awareness of the law and little gender consciousness, and lacks sensitivity to the issue of violence against women.

The Chinese government also proposed measures to improve the work.

Further perfection of legislation and better law enforcement and monitoring. Vigorous development of education on the law for the entire society in order to strengthen people's concept of the law. Expand publicity efforts with regard to the Law on the Protection of the Rights and Interests of Women, the Marriage Law, the Criminal Code, and other relevant laws and develop education on marriage ethics. Strengthen cooperation among public security, prosecutorial, and legislative agencies to protect women from violence. Improve mechanisms for social assistance, so that abused women can receive prompt assistance. The Marriage Law currently being revised by the National People's Congress will include more detailed regulations on the rights, responsibilities, and duties of family members.

Further, the "Platform for Women's Development" for the next ten years, passed by the State Council in May 2001, includes specific measures for implementing these strategies. First, legislators were to accomplish the following.

- Fully embody social gender consciousness in national legislation and provide norms for social behavior that affects women's development.
- Using the Constitution of the People's Republic of China and the Law on the Protection of the Rights and Interests of Women of the People's Republic of China as a basis, further strengthen and improve specialized legislation to protect the legal rights and interests of women.
- Pay attention to women's issues in the process of establishing and improving relevant laws and statutes to guarantee women's enjoyment of equal rights with men in politics, economics, culture, society and family life.

Second, as for justice and law enforcement, officials were to "strengthen judicial protection and legal monitoring and to improve law enforcement." Third, publicity and education about the law are to be strengthened. Fourth, support from legal and judicial departments will allow grass-roots organizations to develop more activities to combat domestic violence. We may believe that through the cooperation of the government and grass-roots organizations, efforts to prevent domestic violence will increase in the next few years and that these efforts will yield even better results.

Domestic Violence in China

Notes

1. Chinese Women's Social Status Survey Project Group, *Zhongguo funü shehui diwei gaiguan* (Overview of the Social Status of Chinese Women) (Beijing: Zhongguo funü chubanshe, 1993), 237.

2. Li Yinhe, "Beijingshi hunyin zhiliangdi diaocha yu fenxi" (Survey and Analysis of the Quality of Marriage in Beijing), *Zhongguo shehuikexue jikan* (China Sociology Quarterly), Vol. 15, 1996, 60–66; Xu Anqi, "Jiating baolidi faduan: Fuqi gongji xingweidi xianzhuang ji tezheng" (The Beginnings of Domestic Violence: The Current Status and Characteristics of Assaults Between Husband and Wife), *Shehuixue* (Sociology), Vol. 1, 1994, 86.

3. Mo Hongxian, "Lun nüxing xingshi beihairen quanyi jiuji" (Discussion on the Rights and Interests of Victims of Female Crime), *'95 shijie funü dahui 5 zhounian yantaohui lunwenji* (Proceedings of the Fifth Anniversary Seminar of the 1995 World Conference on Women) (2000), 320.

4. "Tamen heyi sha fu" (Why They Kill Their Husbands), *Zhongguo funü bao* (Chinese Women's Gazette), 12 January 1996, 3.

5. "Jiating baoli yu nüxing fanzui" (Domestic Violence and Female Crime), *Zhongguo funü bao* (Chinese Women's Gazette), 28 November 2000, 3.

6. Yang Lixin, *Renshen quan falun* (The Legal Doctrine of Personal Rights) (Zhongguo jiancha chubanshe, 1996). Taken from Li Shun, "Hunnei qiangjian zai Zhongguo: Dui geti quanli yu zhengti liyi guanxidi falu shehuixue fenxi" (Marital Rape in China: A Legal and Sociological Analysis of the Relationship Between Individual Rights and the Interests of the Whole), Proceedings of the "Combating Violence Against Women in the Home, Specialist Seminar on Social Ethics and Legal Issues," Beijing, November 1997, 21.

7. Ibid.

8. Fu Liqing, "Hunnei qiangjian zenma kan" (How to Look at Marital Rape), *Zhongguo qingnian bao* (China Youth Daily), 8 January 2001.

9. Luo Ping, "Zhongguo jiating baolidi xianzhuang, yuanyin ji falu cuoshi qianyi" (A Look at the Current Status, Causes, and Legal Measures Against Domestic Violence in China), *Xinjiang University Bulletin*, April 1997, 48.

10. Li Da, *Theory of Women's Emancipation* (Changsha: New Youth).

11. Li Shun, "Hunnei qiangjian zai Zhongguo", 19.

12. Wang Xingjuan, Wang Fengxian, and Wang Kairong, "Funü rexian jiating baoli gean yanjiu" (Case Studies of Domestic Violence from the Women's Hotline), unpublished paper. Part of this paper is included in *On Domestic Violence Against Women* (Beijing: Social Science Press, 2002), 31–41.

Bibliography

"Beijing 12 lei ke mianfe dagongsi" (Twelve Categories of Suits That May Be Filed Free of Charge), *Beijing ribao* (Beijing Daily), 14 December 2001.

China's Task Force to Combat Domestic Violence. "Zhongguo zhengfu fandui jiating baoli xingdong huigu" (Overview of Actions Taken by the Chinese Government to Combat Domestic Violence), unpublished paper.

"Falu xiang jiating baoli kaidao" (The Law Operates on Domestic Violence), *Beijing qingnian bao* (Beijing Youth Daily), 31 October 2000, 17.

"Goujian fan jiating baolidi Zhongguo moshi" (Establishing a Chinese Model for Combating Domestic Violence), *Zhongguo funü bao* (Chinese Women's Gazette), 26 November 2001, 3.

"Hunyinfa sifa jieshi chutai" (Judicial Interpretation Issued on the Marriage Law), *Zhongguo qingnian bao* (China Youth Daily), 27 December 2001, 2.

Liaoning Provincial Office of Public Security. "Qianghua gongan zhineng luoshi gongzuo cuoshi quanli zuohao yufang he zhizhi jiating baoli gongzuo" (Strengthening the Function of Public Security Agencies to Put More Effort into Preventing and Curbing Domestic Violence), United Nations "Eliminate Violence Against Women Day," second anniversary, 26 November 2001.

Liu Hairong, remarks, United Nations "Eliminate Violence Against Women Day," second anniversary, 26 November 2001.

"Youguan hunnei qiangjiandi shiwuge anli" (Concerning Fifteen Cases of Marital Rape), Proceedings of "Combating Violence Against Women in the Home, Specialist Seminar on Social Ethics and Legal Issues," Beijing, background materials, October 1997.

"Zonghe zhili chujian chengxiao" (Initial Results of Comprehensive Control), *Zhongguo funü bao* (Chinese Women's Gazette), 26 November 2001, 3.

THE LIVES AND NEEDS OF ELDERLY WOMEN IN URBAN CHINA

Liu Ying

As the twenty-first century began, China was becoming a society with an aging population. The effects of this trend on social and economic development and on people's lives have attracted the attention of the government and society. The state has enacted a series of laws, regulations, and policy measures in an attempt to solve the problems of the elderly. As a developing nation in a period of social transformation, however, China faces the phenomenon of an aging population as one characterized by an intense rate of change at a pace that is out of step with economic development.

Elderly women constitute a special group—poorer and weaker—among the elderly. They face discrimination not only because of age but also because of gender. They tend to live a long time, their economic status is low, and their living situation has for a long time been overlooked. In 1953, the population of women over age sixty in China was 22.86 million, accounting for 8.3 percent of the total female population. In 1999, this proportion reached 65.78 million or 11 percent of the female population, according to a survey conducted by the Beijing Center on the Problems of Ageing. Moreover, the number of elderly women now increases incrementally at a rate of 3 percent annually. Reports project that, within the next twenty to thirty years, elderly women will make up approximately 25 percent of the female population. For this reason, the problems of elderly women are very important and require special attention.

A survey carried out in Beijing found that, among women sixty to seventy-four years old, 44.16 percent were illiterate or semiliterate, and for women over the age of seventy-five the rate was 62.33 percent. Among sixty to seventy-four-year-olds, 32.36 percent had completed elementary school; the rate for women over seventy-five was 23.72 percent. The rates of those who had completed middle school were 17.76 percent for the first group and 8.37 percent for the latter; high school, 5.72 percent for the former and 5.58 percent for the latter; and the rates of those who had attended university or more were 5.69 percent for the former and zero percent for the latter. A lack of education puts severe limitations on the quality of life for elderly women and causes them many inconveniences in their later years.

Liu Ying

In China, people are deeply attached to their home areas and tend to stay put. In addition, restrictions on the population's movement, the "one-child policy," and imbalances in economic development across a vast national territory mean that China's urban population is aging earlier and faster than the population in rural areas. Shanghai, Beijing, and Tianjin already contain large elderly communities, with 10 percent of the population in those cities over age sixty. Since 1999, I have participated in social surveys conducted by the Chinese Academy of Social Sciences, the All-China Women's Federation, the Beijing Women's Federation, and other organizations to study the social participation, living conditions, and needs of elderly urban women. A number of seminars and interviews were also arranged.[1]

Chinese people have an outstanding tradition of honoring, respecting, and caring for the elderly. At present, there are two major ways of caring for the elderly in China, family care and social (or public) care. Family care is the traditional method; socialist care has emerged with the development of the socialist economy. Under current economic conditions, however, China relies primarily on families to care for the elderly, while social care remains an auxiliary method.

Urban elderly women have seen great improvements in their economic lives and attained a certain level of economic independence. Currently, the vast majority of urban elderly women over age sixty at one time worked outside the home. According to one Beijing survey, 56.34 percent of elderly women rely on their pensions as their primary source of income; 27.15 percent rely on their children; 7.93 percent rely on a spouse; 2.61 percent rely on wages; 0.84 percent rely on death benefits; and 0.93 percent rely on social assistance. Elderly women's levels of satisfaction with their current economic conditions are relatively high: 55.04 percent reported that they were satisfied; 57.20 percent reported that they have enough money each month; and 21.83 percent believed they have more than enough money. These figures suggest that urban elderly women have now achieved a certain level of economic independence. They have solved the problems of paying for food and shelter, gained the right to spend money, and are now seeking a better quality of life.

In comparison to middle-aged and young women, urban elderly women in China have relatively stable marital relations, and the proportion of unmarried and divorced women is extremely low. One Beijing survey found that the rate for unmarried and divorced women combined was only 0.65 percent, with the great majority of urban elderly women still married to their original spouses. Moreover, the relationships between husbands and wives tend to be good, and the women report relatively high levels of satisfaction with their marriages. According to the survey, 73.4 percent of respondents believed that their marital relationships have always been good, and 79 percent believed that their marital relationships at the present time were good or very good.

The current generation of elderly women did not experience "family planning" and often have many children. According to statistics from the 1999 survey in Beijing, most elderly women had living children, with childless women representing only 0.8 percent of the population. On average, each woman had 2.14 sons and 2.09 daughters; 56.37 percent of elderly women with children live with their children, while 17.55 percent live in the same neighborhood, and in 98.92 percent of cases both mother and children live in Beijing. Only 1.08 percent had children living in other places. In terms of care for the elderly, the presence of their children allows elderly women ample sources of financial support. When children live together with their parents or in close proximity, the short distances make it more convenient for the children to care for elderly parents promptly.

According to several surveys, most elderly people in urban China today fall into the lower age bracket of sixty to seventy-four years old. The 1999 Beijing survey found that 79.9 percent of all elderly women were below age seventy-five. Only 9.6 percent were in the high age bracket of eighty and above. In 1989 the average life span in Beijing was 77.5 years for women and 73.8 years for men, a difference of 3.7 years.

Urban elderly women are active socially in many ways. Some return to work after retirement, taking on new jobs, working on research projects, and writing. Most people in these categories are elderly intellectuals with specialized skills who were formerly engaged in research at colleges, schools, and scientific research units. Others participate in public service projects, working as volunteers, providing services to the community. Many are active in nongovernmental organizations (NGOs), do psychological counseling, provide medical care, or offer community services. The Beijing Red Maple Center for Women's Psychological Counseling, for example, is an NGO set up by elderly retired women that engages in public service activities. Their "Elderly Women's Hotline" has twenty-six counselors, thirteen of whom are women volunteers over the age of sixty. According to statistics from the Beijing Women's Federation, over ten thousand "Three-Eight Service Organizations" have been established in neighborhoods ("Three-Eight" refers to March 8, International Women's Day), and over half of the participants are elderly women. These organizations assist the elderly with the needs of daily life by providing low-pay household services . Many elderly women participate in community organizations like the Heroines Volunteer Service Corps. Many more retired women also serve on neighborhood committees. These women contribute to the neighborhood's public security, healthcare, public hygiene, and environmental protection. They also care for the elderly and for children. Most elderly women, however, combine activities with leisure pursuits, hobbies, and physical exercse.

One of the greatest effects of modernization has been a dramatic increase in the amount of leisure time, in part because of such household appliances as rice cookers, washing machines, refrigerators, coal or natural gas stoves, microwave ovens, and vacuum cleaners. In addition, China's falling birthrate means that urban couples usually have only one child, and hence elderly women no longer need to spend their time looking after grandchildren. Thus urban elderly women today have leisure time and can use it to step into the public sphere and to seek space for personal development. During the past few years, elderly women have come to realize the connection between exercise and longevity and are now spending more time outdoors, conscientiously participating in such physical activities as aerobics and folk dancing. In the past two years, more and more people have begun traveling.

Both diversionary and developmental leisure activities are popular. The Beijing survey concluded that watching television was the favorite pastime of elderly women (80 percent), followed by walking (59.6 percent), listening to the radio (48.9 percent), gardening and caring for pets (25.6 percent), strolling in the park (22.1 percent), and reading books, newspapers, and magazines (21.2 percent). Some had other interests, such as physical training (16.7 percent); playing mahjong, cards, or chess (16.3 percent); and watching films or listening to opera (12.7 percent). Since 1983, the issue of aging in China has been on the government's agenda, and universities for seniors have sprung up all over the country. The elderly are very enthusiastic about studying at these universities, and most of the students are elderly women.

While the lives of elderly women in China today are vastly different from those of earlier generations, and while most say that they are content, there are problems. Serious differences between the sexes still exist. Moreover, although urban elderly women now have pensions, they often leave their jobs at a time when social guarantees are not fully in place. Because Chinese women retire at an earlier age than men, and because their educational levels are lower, their total incomes are also lower. The 1999 Beijing survey found that the average total monthly income of elderly women in the Beijing suburbs was 448.61 yuan, while the average total monthly income of elderly men was 679.59 yuan. The rate of elderly men with monthly incomes below 500 yuan was 24.88 percent, while for women the rate was 39.55 percent. The percent of men with incomes ranging from 500 yuan to 999 yuan was 50.85 percent, while for women the rate was 52.61 percent. The rate of men with incomes over 1,000 yuan per month was 24.28 percent, but for women the rate was only 7.8 percent. The rate of elderly women falling into the low-income group with average monthly incomes of less than 200 yuan was 17.44 percent, while only 8.84 percent of elderly men were in this group. In addition, fewer women have old-age insurance, and most rely on their families for support. Although some urban elderly women in China enjoy old-age insurance, the rate is lower than it is for men. Statistics from the 1999 Beijing survey showed that 52.15 percent of elderly women had pensions, whereas 72.95 percent of men did, some twenty percentage points higher. Similarly, 37.59 percent of elderly women do not enjoy pensions, while for men the rate was only 19.61 percent. Spending levels were also higher for elderly men than for women. Elderly women spent an average of 447.44 yuan per month while men spent an average of 532.33 yuan per month.

The income levels of the elderly directly affect the quality of their economic security in old age and have an even greater impact on their status in the society and in the home. Hence fewer elderly women are in the position of being the spenders, and they are more reliant on their families to care for them. The 1999 Beijing survey found that 55.04 percent of elderly women were satisfied with their current economic situation compared to 62.28 percent for elderly men, a difference of seven percentage points. Of the elderly women surveyed, 20.63 percent believed they were in difficulty, while for elderly men this rate was only 13.04 percent. The rate of elderly women who believed they had enough money to spend on a monthly basis was 57.20 percent, while for men the rate was 55.50 percent, or nearly the same as for women. The rate of elderly women who considered themselves to be well-off was 21.83 percent, but for men this figure was nearly ten percentage points higher, at 30.82 percent. In terms of economic autonomy, elderly women are not on par either with young women or with elderly men. For this reason, raising the economic status of elderly women, expanding the coverage provided by social guarantees, improving the quality of life for elderly women, and allowing elderly women to enjoy full rights to old-age insurance have become basic needs for urban elderly women.

The marital status of elderly women is relatively stable but they receive little care from their spouses and it is difficult for elderly women to remarry. Elderly men still do relatively little housework or household management. In empty-nest families, elderly women must look after their husbands, do housework, and manage the household's affairs. In families where parents and children live together, elderly women do most of the housework. Thus, urban elderly women in China bear heavy burdens of responsibility for family life. Women spend their entire lives taking care of their children and spouses, but in their later years they receive little care from their spouses. Statistics from Beijing show that 49.5 percent of elderly men have spouses looking after them, but for women the rate is only 12.2 percent.

On average, elderly women can expect to live longer and the rate of widowhood is high. Remarrying, however, is difficult. The Beijing survey showed that 47.20 percent of women had lost their spouses, while 20.80 percent of men had. The rate of elderly men with living spouses was 76.83 percent, but only 51.86 percent of elderly women still had living spouses. The high rate of widowhood means that women are widows for long periods of time. Surveys show that as women's ages increase, the rate of widowhood climbs. As the number of older women increases, the rate of widowhood will also increase. Most of these widows are elderly and in poor health with numerous economic and healthcare problems.

The high rate of widowhood among elderly women means that many women are living alone and facing the issue of remarrying at an advanced age. China's marriage laws clearly state that marriage is an act of free choice, and that no one, under any pretext, may interfere in the legal marriage of a couple. As the economy develops, and the ideas of male-female equality and freedom of choice in marriage take hold, the society is now supporting the remarriage of elderly people. The media promotes remarriage, and in large cities some matchmaking services work specifically for the elderly. Many elderly people who have lost their spouses through death or divorce are moving toward remarriage to live happier and more fulfilled lives in their later years. However, due to the combined influences of traditional ideas and practical concerns, elderly women today still face many difficulties in remarrying, and the success rate for remarriage is relatively low.

Family structures are shrinking and becoming more nuclear. Many families do not have children living at home, and the role of the family in caring for the elderly is weakening. This is particularly true in cities: While most elderly women are willing to be cared for by their families, caring for the elderly at home raises new problems and new needs. According to surveys, 29.36 percent of elderly women in Beijing live in empty-nest households. Among these, 10.51 percent live alone and 18.84 percent live with a spouse. For elderly men, the rate living in empty-nest households is 42.56 percent, with 6.62 percent living alone and 35.94 percent living with a spouse. The percentages of elderly men living in empty-nest households and with a spouse are both higher than the percentages for elderly women, mainly because of the high rate of widowhood among elderly women. Another survey of 493 elderly intellectual women in Beijing showed that 9.5 percent lived in one-person households and 42.5 percent lived in two-person households, for a total of 52 percent. In summary, more than one-third of elderly women live in empty-nest households, and 96.36 percent of elderly women living alone have lost their spouses. The shrinking structure and nuclearization of families have led to a weakening in the function of families and less help from relatives. Elderly women living in empty-nest households receive little help from their families.

Although economic support from their children is still very important to elderly women, it is no longer the primary source and has fallen to second or even third place.[2] In fact, some elderly women provide financial assistance to their children. According to statistics, 22.8 percent of elderly women in Beijing with a monthly income of more than 280 yuan frequently or occasionally give their children financial help. The economic relationship between today's elderly women and their children is therefore bidirectional. Many elderly women are frugal in order to give their extra money to their children and grandchildren. In a survey of what women intended to do with extra money, 14.83 percent stated that they intended to give their extra money to their children. Most of the current generation of elderly women have children who are married with children, and 56.37 percent of elderly women live with their children. Living together makes it easier to take care of each other, but the small size of housing units means it is usually the elderly women who are squeezed into cramped quarters. According to surveys, elderly couples living together are generally able to have a room of their own, but some share a room with a grandchild. If an elderly women is alone, she typically shares a room with a grandchild, and the grandchild is usually considered the primary occupant of the room.

We interviewed elderly women on Chongwai Street in Beijing. This street has many dangerously dilapidated buildings that are targeted for demolition and reconstruction, and preparations are currently under way to move the residents. When we asked about what the women wanted in their new homes, they all agreed that they wanted rooms for themselves and their husbands, or for themselves alone. In other words, they wanted personal living space. This desire has led some seniors to express an unwillingness to live with their children. One Beijing survey found that 28.17 percent of elderly women were unwilling to live with their children. For men the rate was 31.47 percent.

Most elderly women (77.98 percent) reported that they discussed matters in their lives with their children. By contrast, only 46.15 percent of their children sought out their parents to discuss matters in their lives. With regard to intergenerational relations, the majority of elderly women, 82.65 percent, believed that their children showed filial piety toward them; only 3.17 percent believed that their children did not show them filial respect. While it is relatively common for elderly women to interact with their children in the course of daily life, obstacles prevent some communication between the generations. According to surveys, only 29.11 percent of respondents wanted to hear the elderly or the older generation talking about events of the past; 21.64 percent found it annoying and 42.91 percent were indifferent.

While elderly women may want to be taken care of by their children, their children's busy work schedules or their locations may make this difficult. According to surveys, elderly women expect more help from their children and grandchildren with such daily activities as cooking, going up and down stairs, walking, managing finances, and shopping than they do from their spouses. They believe that their children will do what they ask, but that it is difficult to get their husbands to do anything. When asked about who was taking care of them in their later years, 60.67 percent of elderly women said their children were, and 28.08 percent answered that their spouses were. However, the reality of the current situation is that many parents and children do not live together, and although the children and their families still maintain close relationships with their parents, it is difficult to care for parents on a daily basis. The children tend to check in on their parents occasionally.

For children who do live with their parents, the intensity of busy work lives and numerous social commitments not only leave them no time for looking after their parents, but usually lead them to ask the elders, especially mothers, to help take care of the children and do the housework. Most elderly women who live with their children cook, take care of the children, and do housework. Today's elderly women are still young enough to handle some household chores, but they always feel tired. Some younger elderly women are still caring for older relatives. One seventy-year-old woman, who was caring for her ninety-three-year-old mother-in-law, said that since her marriage, she had been taking care of her mother- and father-in-law. She also had two children of her own and a job, so she was busy all day long and never had a life of her own. Now that she is older and retired, she would really like to take some time off, but she still has to take care of her elderly in-law. Today's urban elderly women are mostly satisfied with their family lives, but China is experiencing a period of social transformation. The women would like to spend their later years enjoying their grandchildren and families; however, the changing concept of the family, weakening relationships between parents and children, and even a family's economic situation all make this difficult. These women continue to hope to improve their family's standards of living and to live relaxed, happy, and healthy lives in their later years.

Finally, the government and relevant agencies have made great efforts in the area of protecting and promoting the health of the elderly. In recent years the mortality rate among the elderly has decreased noticeably, and the average expected life span for people in China has increased considerably. The Elderly Rights and Guarantees Law of the People's Republic of China clearly specifies the regulations concerning healthcare guarantees for the elderly. But because China is in a period of transformation with a changing economy, all people's healthcare needs cannot be met. As a weak group, elderly women in particular tend to encounter more problems. According to surveys, urban elderly women today do not believe they are in good health. Beijing surveys found that 39.8 percent of elderly women considered themselves to be in good health or very good health, and 29.01 percent believed themselves to be in poor or very poor health. The proportion of men who considered themselves to be healthy or very healthy was 48.28 percent, nearly ten percentage points higher than for women. Only 22.63 percent of men believed themselves to be in poor or very poor health. The great majority of elderly women, 75.46 percent, considered their physical condition to be extremely important or very important. Due to the elderly women's low appraisal of their health, their level of satisfaction with their health is lower than that of men. The major problems elderly women encounter in healthcare are summarized below.

The system of healthcare guarantees is incomplete; medical costs are rising fast, severely affecting elderly women's access to healthcare. Beginning in the 1950s, China implemented a system of workers' healthcare guarantees, including government funded healthcare and labor insurance healthcare systems. Retirees enjoy the same medical care as those still on the job. This solved the basic problem of medical care for retired elderly women. However, over the past two years prescription drug costs have risen dramatically, while reforms in medical care and an economic downturn in some industries have increased the cost of healthcare for individuals. The resulting situation is one in which, even though retired elderly women have access to public healthcare, their claims submitted for medical expenses are not processed for such a long time that they often do not seek treatment when ill. Moreover, only some elderly women enjoy government-funded healthcare. The Beijing survey found that 31.52 percent of elderly women had access to government-funded healthcare, and 13.25 percent were on major medical plans, meaning that less than half are covered by a plan. The rates of coverage for men are higher than for women: 52.80 percent of men have access to public healthcare and 15.41 percent are covered under major medical plans. Women make up 48.41 percent of the elderly population, but most of them must pay medical costs out of pocket. Furthermore, the percentage of women with access to public healthcare drops as their age increases, and older women often do not have pensions. These older women rely on their spouses or children for financial support and lack economic power, so paying medical costs is even more difficult for them. The physiological deterioration women experience in old age and the lowered resistance to disease result in higher rates of illness. According to a survey from 1992, 80 percent of urban elderly women suffer from chronic diseases. Because they do not have formal education, many elderly women lack information on hygiene and health. They do not understand menopause and the physiological changes that occur with old age. They lack knowledge on the prevention of osteoporosis, breast cancer, cervical cancer, and other diseases. Without an awareness of their own health, they often "go running to all kinds of doctors when they get sick."

In the 1980s, before the reform movement, little attention was paid to people's psychological and spiritual well-being. Now, as people enter old age, they are having difficulty coping with changes in their interpersonal relationships. In addition, anxiety about age-related illnesses negatively affects their emotional states. One Beijing survey found that 67.91 percent of elderly women considered their disposition to be good or very good, 23.4 percent believed it was average, and 7.28 percent reported that their disposition was not very good or not good. Some elderly women today experience difficulties and pressures due to the lack of an independent source of income, the loss of a spouse, too much housework, monotony or the lack of leisure time, and a lack of medical care or medicine. These factors cause elderly women to be more likely than elderly men to experience emotional difficulties. Surveys show that 77.7 percent of elderly women do not feel lonely, while the rate for elderly men is 81.1 percent. This is merely a self-assessment; many women do not know about psychological health. Psychological care is poorly developed in Chinese society, and many people have no concept of loneliness, anxiety, depression, self-isolation, or other psychological problems. Some elderly women mistakenly believe that mental illness means insanity. For many years, the author of this paper has provided counseling services at the Beijing Red Maple Center Women's Hotline (Elderly Women's Hotline). Elderly women rarely take the initiative to phone in for psychological counseling or seek psychological treatment. Unless they have a physical manifestation, they rarely seek help.

Psychological health is increasingly becoming an important component of elderly women's health. As standards of living rise, the demands of urban elderly women for emotional support are increasing, and the modern elderly, especially elderly women, now place intense demands for emotional support on their children. However, many young people still hold the traditional belief that all their parents need is enough to eat, clothes to wear, and a place to live. They commonly overlook their parents' needs for emotional support. Among the cases of elderly women seeking emotional support in Beijing, more than 25 percent sought support from their children.

From a healthcare perspective, China's implementation of a system that guarantees the elderly access to medical care means that as health insurance coverage expands, healthcare and treatment issues for urban elderly women will gradually improve. However, because China's current system of healthcare services is still incomplete, many elderly women suffer from chronic diseases and the funding for their medical care is insufficient. This has a tremendous impact on the lives of elderly women. For these reasons, in addition to elderly women's further strengthening their own awareness of health issues and establishing healthy lifestyles, the system of medical care guarantees must be further improved.

NOTES
1. The data on the living conditions of elderly women in this article come from surveys I have participated in since 1999 conducted by the Chinese Academy of Social Sciences, the National Women's Federation, and the Beijing Municipal Women's Federation and from the "1999 Survey of the Basic Needs of Elderly People" conducted by the Beijing Center on the Problems of Aging. This 1999 survey selected 1,200 valid samples from eight districts in the Beijing municipality. Computer processing was performed on the data collected from all the surveys, and a "Survey of the Living Conditions of Urban Elderly Women" database was established. Unless otherwise noted, the figures cited in this paper are from Beijing and come from this database.
2. In Beijing, 27.53 percent of elderly women rely on their children as their primary means of financial support; for 65.64 percent of women their children rank second as a means of financial support; for 42.37 percent their children rank third.

REFERENCES
Du Peng and Wu Chao. "Zhongguo laonianren zhuyao jingji laiyuan fenxi" (Analysis of the Main Sources of Income for China's Elderly), *Zhongguo shehui gongzuo* (China Social Work), 1998.
Liu Ying and Yuan Liming. "Laonian funü shehui canyu he yanglao wentidi diaocha yu sikao" (Survey and Reflections on the Issues of Elderly Women's Participation in Society and Caring for the Elderly). In *2000 nian Beijing shehui fazhan huigu yu zhanwang* (Overview and Prospects for Beijing's Social Development in 2000). Beijing, 2001.
Wang Shunhua. *Laonianren quanyidi falü baozhang* (Legal Guarantees for the Rights and Interests of the Elderly). Beijing: Jingji guanli chubanshe, 1995.
Xiong Bijun. *Baozhang laoyousuoyangdi lilun yu shiji* (The Theory and Practice of Ensuring Care for the Elderly). Beijing: Jingji guanli chubanshe, 1999.
1995 nian quanguo 1% renkou chouyangdiaocha ziliao (Survey Data from 1995 National Sampling of 1 Percent of the Population). Beijing: Zhongguo tongji chubanshe, 1997.

Part V

Women
and
Work

EMPLOYMENT AND CHINESE URBAN WOMEN UNDER TWO SYSTEMS

✻ ✻ ✻

Jiang Yongping

With the founding of a new people's republic in China in 1949, women gained equal rights under the law—including economic rights. Until 1978 China practiced a centrally planned employment system. Using its legislative and administrative powers, the state guaranteed the right to employment for all urban workers including women. Many women who previously had not worked outside the home now filled positions doing social production and other public jobs, becoming the creators of social prosperity and the founders of the new China.

In the 1950s, however, China's weak industrial base could not satisfy the employment demands of urban women who now had the right to work. Those who were able to find employment were educated and skilled. Thus at the end of 1952 women accounted for only 11.7 percent of the workers in state-owned units, while women accounted for 41.4 percent of the nationwide registrations of requests for employment by unemployed workers.[1] In 1958, against the backdrop of the Great Leap Forward, the vast majority of urban workers and housewives were mobilized, organized, and assigned to state-run units and neighborhood collective enterprises. With this, the long-postponed wish of urban women for employment came true virtually overnight. From that point on, a mechanism for planned assignments to distribute work to women began to take shape, a process that reached its peak during the Cultural Revolution. Urban women who were of legal age and able to work were assigned to positions where the state needed them. They did not need to choose a job, nor were they able to make a choice. Both the scope and quality of women's employment increased during this period. In 1960, the total number of employed women nationwide shot up to 10.087 million, a more than twofold increase over the 3.286 million women employed in 1957. The portion of the total workforce made up of women increased from 13.4 percent in 1957 to 20 percent in 1960.[2] Another peak in urban women's employment occurred during the late 1960s and early 1970s, when a large contingent of young intellectual urban workers answered the call to go to rural villages and border areas. This led to a shortage of labor, and quite a number of urban housewives were organized into "May 7" factories (so named for a crucial directive issued on that day by Mao) or "platoons of housewives" affiliated with state-owned factories. By the end of the 1970s, the employment rate for urban women old enough to work was more than 90 percent.

During the period of the planned economy, gaining and ensuring the right to work had a tremendous impact on the development of Chinese urban women. Women could now freely choose to work outside the home and be compensated for their labor. Since they did not need to seek permission from their fathers or husbands, this signaled the emancipation of urban women from the control of male heads of households.[3] In addition, people came to accept women's employment as a normal part of the social economy, and hence work became a significant indicator of equality. Since women as well as men worked outside the home and both were responsible for the family's finances, women's status inside the family was strengthened. At the same time, under the planned system of employment, women's inability to choose jobs created an obstacle to improving the quality of their employment. In addition, as transitional guarantees and protections liberated women from the confines of the family, these measures also increased the reliance of urban women on the state and the work unit. These factors later proved to be disadvantages to urban women.

Beginning in the 1980s, China began a transition from a planned economic system to a socialist market economic system. As the systems of ownership were restructured and the operational mechanisms of enterprises changed, China's method of allocating labor resources painfully but steadily shifted from a planned to a market mechanism of employment. During the period of transition to a market system of employment, the masses of urban women workers, like their male counterparts, initially experienced unprecedented opportunities for development. This was particularly true for outstanding women, who used their talents and the opportunities for entrepreneurship to find new positions in which they could benefit society, as well as increase their income and gain other material benefits that accompanied the reforms. As the market system became established, however, shrinking employment opportunities were not equally distributed between the sexes. Statistics show that, prior to 1995, as the economy grew, both the proportion and total number of employed urban women increased steadily. Beginning in 1996, these numbers began a gradual decline, and by the end of 1999, the number of women employed in urban units nationwide had fallen by 12.756 million, a relative decrease of 1.5 percentage points (see Table 1). Statistics from the second survey of the social status of Chinese women, conducted by the All-China Women's Federation and the State Statistics Bureau, show that in 2000, the employment rate for urban Chinese women between the ages of eighteen and forty-nine was 72.0 percent, a decrease of 16.2 percentage points from 1990.[4]

Employment Under Two Systems

Table 1

NUMBERS OF URBAN WOMEN WORKERS IN MAJOR YEARS AS A PERCENTAGE
OF THE TOTAL WORKFORCE

Year	1978	1990	1995	1999
Number of women workers (in millions)	31.280	52.941	58.890	46.134
Percentage of total workforce made up of women	32.9	37.7	39.5	38.0

Source: *Zhongguo laodong tongji nianjian* (China Yearbook of Labor Statistics).

The decline in the number of employed women is closely connected to the difficulties of university-educated women in finding work, large lay-offs of and high unemployment for women workers, the difficulties of women in finding re-employment, and other problems of urban women. In particular, the numbers of laid-off and unemployed female workers are disproportionately high, considering the percentage of women in the workforce. According to a survey conducted by the Institute of Labor Sciences of the Ministry of Labor and Social Guarantees in June 2000, women accounted for 57.5 percent of all laid-off workers. The re-employment rate for women was only 38.8 percent, which was 18.8 percentage points lower than the rate for men.[5]

Why have women become the group whose rights and interests are harmed by the market employment system? The market's "economic rationalism" combined with a weakening of state protections deals a double blow to women. With profit as its main objective, the market first eliminates women workers whose skill levels are too low. Under market conditions, the administrative guarantees that functioned effectively within the planned economy have now lost their binding force. Still another important influence comes from a return to traditional patriarchal culture. To many men, "equality of the sexes" as a mainstream ideology has only symbolic political significance. Today, as people take freedom of thought for granted, some have begun to question and criticize the idea of equality of the sexes. Such questioners believe that women's entrance into the workforce is one reason that Chinese society is experiencing "role deviance," and they hope to return to the traditional division of labor in which "men take care of matters outside the home, and women take care of matters within the home."

Since 1978, China has experienced four controversies concerning women's employment. During these debates, some of the "theoretical elite" have proposed "women's returning to the home" and "employment in stages" as panaceas for the country's rising unemployment rates. The last controversy, which occurred early in 2001, shifted the discussion from the theoretical level to the arena of public policy alternatives. Under intense pressure from the All-China Women's Federation and other groups, the "employment in stages" plan, with its clear gender agenda, was not included in the fifteenth five-year plan, but the debate over its inclusion reflects the profound effects of traditional patriarchies on policy-makers at the highest levels of government and on socioeconomic policy researchers.

Of course, the decline in rates of employment for urban Chinese women under the market system is not entirely due to negative factors. The rise in the numbers of women pursuing an education, the prolonged length of time required to get an education, and the diversification of lifestyles all influence the employment rate for women. Many young women want lifestyles different from those of the previous generation and expect to have more options. They are not in a hurry to find jobs upon graduation. These women are willing to spend a period of time as stay-at-home mothers, confident that, when the time comes, they will be able to find work that suits them. For the majority of urban Chinese women, however, freedom of choice is only a dream. Some experts estimate that gender inequalities in employment opportunities have already become a dark cloud hanging over the development of China's market employment system and that they will only be exacerbated with China's entrance to the World Trade Organization (WTO).

CHANGING FROM AN ASSIGNED SYSTEM OF EMPLOYMENT TO ONE OF CHOICE: CAREER DEVELOPMENT AND GENDER ISOLATION

As both a symbol and a way of meeting the nation's needs for development, the employment of Chinese women from the start broke down the old divisions of labor. In mobilizing women to leave their homes for the workplace, the state encouraged women to enter professions formerly held only by men. As women's employment developed, women made inroads into many fields that were once off-limits. The professional and trade options available to women became broader as the first women filled positions in many occupations, such as tractor driver, railroad engineer, and pilot. It is especially worth noting that some jobs now held primarily by women, such as salesperson, ticket vendor, and letter carrier, were only opened to women after a great deal of effort on their part. Historical documentation shows that, in the early days of the People's Republic, the government used administrative measures to promote a policy of replacing male workers with women in the commercial and service sectors.[6] When deciding on the allocations of workers to enterprises, government labor departments used a quota system to ensure that women would make up a certain percentage of workers in every industry. During the period of the planned economy, the employment of China's urban women spanned a broad range of occupations, covering every sector of the national economy, every industry, and every profession, revealing a huge potential labor force that had never before been recognized or understood by the society or by women themselves.

Many women leaders and senior academicians at the Chinese Academy of Science and the Chinese Academy of Engineering Sciences, still active in economic management and policy-making, are women of talent who were cultivated during the period of the planned economy. According to available statistics, during the first thirty years of the People's Republic women maintained a consistent level of representation in many different industries. The system of assigned employment, however, suppressed women's individual potential. In general, the efficiency of the labor system as a whole was low. The influence of leftist thinking, which overemphasized the idea that "men and women are the same," ignored gender differences when making labor allocations and led to high concentrations of women in sectors involving heavy physical labor. This situation became particularly serious during the ten years of turmoil during the Cultural Revolution (1966–1976), when a contingent of young women passionate about "revolution" took jobs involving working at heights, in pits, and in industries involving heavy physical labor and toxic or dangerous conditions in order to demonstrate their break with old traditions. During that time, many "girls" work teams and work brigades were established. In the construction industry, for example, in 1957 women made up only 9.6 percent of the workforce, but by 1982 the proportion had risen to 22.5 percent, a historical high. With the exception of a few model workers, the efficiency of most of the female workers in these work units was clearly quite low. The negative effects of not considering the physiological differences between men and women and striving solely for "equality of the sexes" were not fully recognized until after the reform of the labor system in the late 1980s.

The advent of market reforms in the fields of labor and employment empowered enterprises to make their own decisions regarding the hiring and firing of workers as well as returning the right to workers to choose their occupations. As barriers fell between urban and rural areas and circulation within professions opened up, urban professional women who had previously lived by the standards of "being a cog in the machine of the revolution" and "love what[ever] you do" began to consider pursuing their own career development. In the context of the market employment system, in which selection is a two-way street that hires the best workers, many complex factors have brought about dramatic changes, both positive and negative, in the structure of employment for urban Chinese women over the past twenty years.

First, the ability to choose one's career has provided many women who once labored in obscurity with opportunities for personal development and success in business, whether the women actively seek these opportunities or passively wait for them to appear. Those who actively seek out these opportunities are usually women who changed their career prospects when the reforms first started by changing their jobs, going back to school for higher education after the resumption of the university entrance examination system, or by starting their own businesses. Not content to be stifled by the old system, these women worked their way up into the fields of science, technology, and management by using their own abilities, courage, and insight and became outstanding success stories among women. Others, perhaps more passive, or lacking courage and self-reliance, may have missed opportunities and became laid-off or unemployed during the heartless economic restructuring of the 1990s. Yet many of these women also started their own enterprises, and with a lot of hard work, developed small and medium-sized businesses. What was most valuable to them was that they discovered their real selves and potential in the difficult process of founding their enterprises.

The rising level of professionalism among urban Chinese women was due in part to improvements in education for women and the development of information technology. In the past ten years, the gap between men's and women's education in urban China has shrunk considerably. In 1998, female students made up 51.8 and 38.4 percent of the student bodies at secondary vocational schools and universities respectively.[7] The rise in their levels of education created the conditions for women to enter higher-level professions. Information technology has spurred the development of new industries such as networking, finance, insurance, and telecommunications and has offered women new opportunities for employment. In these new economic sectors, differences in knowledge and skill are more important than gender differences. According to reports, women hold a higher percentage of jobs in network-related industries, both in staff and managerial positions, than in almost any other industry with the exception of textiles.[8]

Data from the second survey on the social status of Chinese women show that, in terms of the employment structure in 2000, 6.1 percent of employed urban women held positions of responsibility, which is 3.2 percent higher than in 1990. Technical specialists make up 22.8 percent of the female workforce, an increase of 5.4 percentage points over 1990. In terms of their distribution in different industries, women outnumber men in wholesale and retail sales, social services, education, culture, health, and other sectors. In the fields of finance and insurance, scientific research and general technical services, party and government agencies, and civic groups, the numbers of women employed are nearly on par with the numbers of men. These changes have resulted in clear improvements to the long-standing problems of women's low positions in the employment hierarchy and the unreasonable employment structure.

Even as this trend toward a more reasonable employment gender structure continues, the phenomenon of gender isolation and the decline of some women's careers remain apparent. Many signs indicate that in the fiercely competitive labor market, women are gradually becoming marginalized. Faced with gender discrimination in employment, some highly educated women are frustrated in their search for jobs and have no choice but to lower their expectations and take positions for which they are overqualified. For laid-off and unemployed women, the trend is toward taking jobs in residential services and other unconventional sectors or taking unconventional jobs in the conventional sectors, such as doing odd jobs or cleaning in government agencies, enterprises, and work units. Short-term and temporary in nature, these jobs pay poorly, provide few benefits, and offer virtually no possibility for career development. In addition, the spread of consumerism and trend of treating sex as a commodity has led to the appearance of "youth careers" and "gender careers." "Youth careers" are jobs only for young people, such as being flight attendants, PR personnel, and service personnel (waiters and waitresses) in big hotels. "Gender careers" are jobs to satisfy the needs of mainly male consumers, including the need for sex. The typical worker is a young woman who accompanies men to meals, social activities, and so on. All of these factors exacerbate the decline in women's employment status.

EQUAL PAY FOR EQUAL WORK AND WAGE DISTRIBUTION ACCORDING TO OCCUPATION: THE GAP BETWEEN MEN'S AND WOMEN'S INCOMES

Under the planned economy, equal pay for equal work was an important method of guaranteeing the labor rights and interests of Chinese women. In the early 1950s, equal pay for equal work was widely implemented in state-run enterprises.[9] State-run units and urban collective enterprises implemented a system of graded wages under which the pay grade for the same position or type of work was mainly determined by the length of time on the job. With this system, the differences between women's incomes and those of their male peers were small. Of course, this system did not exclude the possibility that men had far greater chances for promotions than did women. The doctrine of "male generals and women foot soldiers" summed up the gender structure by which all enterprise units, including those in the textile industry, were organized. In addition, at a time when wages were not widely adjusted (for example, when adjustments were made for only 40 percent of a workforce), prized limited opportunities were usually given to men who had families to support. Due to unwritten rules like these, in many cases married couples who worked in the same unit found that, after a few years, the wife's wages fell behind those of her husband by several grades.

Another factor influencing the disparity between men's and women's incomes was differences in wage standards from industry to industry. Although the eight-grade wage system was used almost universally, the wage standards in heavy industry and state-run enterprises affiliated with the central government were usually higher than those in light industry, local enterprises, and neighborhood collective enterprises. Women tended to be more concentrated in light industry and textiles and in collective enterprises, and, under the principle of equal pay for equal work, it is understandable that women's wage incomes were, on the whole, lower than men's. Nevertheless, over the thirty years of the graded-wage system, the gap between men's and women's incomes in urban China was relatively small. According to a sampling survey of 218 enterprises in Shanghai, Shijiazhuang, and Jinzhou conducted by the Ministry of Labor, in 1978 the average standard monthly wage for men was 53 yuan. For women, the average standard monthly wage was 43.1 yuan, or 83 percent of the wage for men.

Undoubtedly, the breakdown of parity in compensation and the shift to valuing labor based mainly on knowledge, skill, and productivity have encouraged workers to improve efficiency and helped stimulate economic growth. In this time of economic transformation, those adjusting China's mechanism for allocating income began with these goals in mind. However, as the reforms have progressed, widening income gaps under the market system have become more pronounced. According to estimates by experts, in China the Gini coefficient for income distribution is currently between 0.39 and 0.55, and income disparities have already reached a relatively high level.[10] Regrettably, the widening income gap under the market system is very apparent between men and women. What researchers sensed intuitively has now been proved by survey data.

Data from the second survey of the social status of Chinese women show that, in comparison to 1990, the incomes of employed urban women have risen considerably but the gap between men's and women's incomes has also widened. In 1999 the average annual income of employed women, including all types of income, was 7,409.7 yuan, an increase of 4.1 times over the amount ten years earlier. Women's incomes are now 70.1 percent of men's incomes, and the gap between men's and women's incomes is 7.4 percent higher than ten years before. In terms of income distribution, 47.4 percent of employed urban women have an annual income under 5,000 yuan, and only 6.1 percent of them have incomes above 15,000 yuan. The proportion of low-income women is 19.3 percentage points higher than the proportion of low-income men, and the percentage of women with incomes above mid-level is 6.6 percentage points lower than for men.[11]

The data show that the income gap between urban men and women is directly linked to employment situations and occupational levels. Women tend to be concentrated in low-wage occupations, and, within the same occupation, women tend to hold lower-level positions than men. Although the data show an increase in the number of women in management, and women outnumbering men in various technical specialties, due to the lower positions and titles held by women in general, women's incomes in these two categories are only 57.9 and 68.3 percent, respectively, of men's incomes, lower than average levels.

An analysis of the correspondence between income and occupation clearly reveals the historical causes of women's low economic status. Raising women's occupational levels is a long process, and there is no quick fix. Through a comparative analysis of education and income, researchers have found that gender discrimination under the market system has a profound impact on the widening income gap between men and women. First, when levels of education are the same, men have more opportunities than women to obtain employment in high-income occupations. Even when they are doing the same work, women's labor is valued below that of men's; men's work is deemed more significant and indispensable, thus resulting in higher compensation for men. Second, in the fierce competition of the labor market, women's occupational mobility usually forces shifts downward in levels of occupation, such as shifting out of a job in a conventional department to a job in an unconventional department. This kind of occupational trend necessarily results in decreased incomes. In addition, women's incomes are also affected by the pattern of job-seeking strategies employed by families that steer men toward high-risk, high-reward jobs and women toward low-risk, low-reward jobs. The possibility of a man's earning a high income coupled with the difficulties faced by women in finding employment cause some families to put their expectations for large earnings and success in business on men. In the process of the reforms, this "one family, two systems" pattern has taken the form of the husband's going into business ventures while the wife takes a job with secure benefits at a government agency.

DIFFERENTIAL VERSUS EQUAL TREATMENT: LABOR PROTECTION AND OCCUPATIONAL SAFETY FOR URBAN WOMEN

None of the rules governing the legal protection of the labor rights and interests of Chinese women are more practical than the statutes concerning women and childbearing. The special protections of women's employment—regulations guaranteeing protection for menstruation, pregnancy, childbirth, and breastfeeding, as well as maternity leave—were clearly spelled out in the revised Regulations on Labor Insurance of the People's Republic of China in 1953 and in the Regulations on the Protection of Female Workers in 1956. The government enforced these regulations until 1988, when it issued the new Regulations on the Protection of Female Labor.

During the period from 1953 up through the reforms, government agencies and state-run enterprises effectively implemented the mandated protections for women during pregnancy, childbirth, and while nursing. Pregnant women were given lighter duties, and after giving birth they enjoyed maternity leave with full pay. Prior to 1988 this leave was fifty-six days; in 1988 it was increased to ninety days. Female employees in some units enjoy six months to several years of leave to raise children. When nursing, women are given a nursing leave, and the medical expenses for giving birth are completely covered by the work unit. In addition, many work units have showering facilities for female workers, rest rooms for pregnant women, day-care, nursery schools, and other amenities. Female workers are given periodic gynecological check-ups and preventative care. All these measures demonstrate the esteem and affirmation the state has for women's childbearing and work.

Enterprises outside the state-run system are another matter, and special protections for female workers have not been given the attention they deserve at these businesses. Data from a survey I conducted in 1997, looking at female workers at non-state-run enterprises in Guangdong, Zhejiang, and five other provinces and the municipalities of Beijing and Tianjin, showed that gynecological check-ups and healthcare facilities for women were generally poor at these companies, and the other prescribed protections were virtually nonexistent. When drafting labor contracts, most private enterprises use a variety of methods to avoid granting pregnancy and maternity leave for female workers. Some enterprises claim to allow women to give birth during their period of employment, but my survey found almost no record of employees giving birth. Some enterprises go so far as to state plainly in the contract that becoming pregnant and giving birth are prohibited during the term of the contract. Women who do get pregnant are soon fired or quit. As enterprises expand their operational autonomy, long-standing rules concerning the responsibilities of employers toward employees who give birth are facing unprecedented challenges in the state-run and collective enterprises. According to recent reports, it has become increasingly difficult to protect the labor rights of female workers. Some enterprises that were doing a good job of protecting such rights before are now facing financial difficulties, and providing women with benefits during pregnancy, childbirth, and nursing is becoming difficult. Some enterprises have not provided women with gynecological check-ups and breast cancer screenings for several years in a row and can only cover a portion of a female employee's medical costs for prenatal check-ups, delivery, hospitalization, and prescriptions.[12] In addition, the widespread use of the labor contract system has made it possible to evade providing benefits to pregnant employees.

These practical difficulties have led to theoretical reflections, with experts questioning the idea of differential treatment and labor legislation that takes care of women who become mothers. Some experts believe that under the conditions of a market economy, this legislative principle has become a double-edged sword, protecting women's rights and interests while simultaneously creating an obstacle to women's achievement of equal employment rights. Under the impetus of research in this area, at the end of the 1980s cities such as Nantong and Zhuzhou began experimenting with socialized maternity care. Maternity medical care was socialized so that both the husband's and the wife's employers shared the burden of medical costs. On the basis of these trial programs, in 1994 the Ministry of Labor announced the Methods for the Trial Implementation of the Enterprise Employee Maternity Insurance Program. Now more than half of the cities and counties nationwide are using a socialized program for maternity costs. The reforms of the maternity insurance system allow enterprises to share the burden of medical costs evenly and help to reduce obstacles to women's employment. Still, resistance to the implementation of this program continues because some leaders believe that the responsibility of rearing children is a personal matter and that within families this duty naturally falls to the mother. This kind of thinking has led to the exclusion of maternity insurance from the major types of social insurance—elder care, medical, and unemployment. Intensive reform of the social insurance system is now under way, but maternity insurance has not received the attention it deserves.

As the occupational safety system undergoes a process of transformation, urban women workers face a number of labor rights issues. These primarily include extended working hours; toxic and dangerous jobs; a deteriorating work environment; companies that fall behind in paying wages, embezzle from employees' pay, or keep wages low; personal injury; and sexual harassment. Although many of these problems fall under the category of general labor issues and are not exclusively women's issues, women suffer more than men from their detrimental effects. Women tend to be concentrated in labor-intensive industries such as light industry, textiles, and electronics, where occupational safety problems are the most serious. One example is the frequent occurrence of fires in factories. Another problem is benzene poisoning among workers in the footwear industry, a major problem for China, the world's largest manufacturer of footwear. Most of the injured workers are young migrant women. Recent incidents such as mandatory body searches of female employees and the forcing of women into unwanted sexual services seriously damage women workers physically and emotionally. They may suffer anxiety and depression for the rest of their lives.

In recent years, women have begun to accept nonconventional employment where labor rights issues are more serious. To make ends meet, they have taken jobs that provide no insurance, no days off, and extremely low wages, jobs where they "tough it out." All these phenomena indicate that, under the conditions of market employment, women at the lowest occupational levels, who have no bargaining power, have been marginalized. Although they allegedly enjoy the right to equal employment, the current lack of necessary social concern and affirmative policies cause equal treatment to result in unequal consequences.

CONCLUSION

It is very difficult to capture in simple terms the impact that China's two economic systems have had on the employment of Chinese women and on women's development. The political significance of the social mobilization and empowerment of women to work during the period of the planned economy provided the foundation for the development of urban women's employment and the rise in their economic and social status. In particular, the employment of women on a large scale changed women's economic identities and raised women's socioeconomic status, while at the same time creating a subtle shift in the traditional gender division of labor in urban families. Even today many men cling to their sense of superiority, but they no longer wish to support the family alone. Despite the dual pressures of market competition and an oversupply of labor, this view still provides the widest base of cultural and public support for continuing women's employment. For this reason, the political legacy of the vigorous promotion of women's employment and the historical granting of equal treatment to women in employment should not be underestimated.

The problems that have currently curtailed women's rights and interests and caused the marginalization of women workers are due partly to the state of the market and partly to a patriarchal ideology. Other important factors are incomplete and inappropriate government intervention and the lack of a mechanism for guaranteeing women's employment. The government's macroeconomic regulation is the most important force in society, but since the reforms, the ways in which state policies influence social and economic behavior have changed. The old system of guaranteeing women's employment through administrative intervention has gradually weakened, and the new management system, which relies on economic measures, is still in the development stages. As the government and nongovernmental organizations work to promote gender as a mainstream issue, China is now establishing effective methods and operational mechanisms of state intervention in women's employment that fit the market system. There is reason to expect that, although future development involves many variables, prospects for improving the employment of urban women are good.

Employment Under Two Systems

NOTES

1. State Statistics Bureau, Office of Social Statistics, *Zhongguo laodong gongzi tongji ziliao 1949–1985* (China Labor and Wage Statistics Data 1949–1985) (Beijing: Zhongguo tongji chubanshe, 1987), 32; Contemporary Chinese Compendia Editorial Department, ed., *Dangdai Zhongguo funü* (Contemporary Chinese Women) (Beijing: Dangdai Zhongguo chubanshe, 1994), 41.

2. State Statistics Bureau, *Zhongguo.*

3. Lisa Rofel, "Modern Images and 'Other' Modernities," in *Shijizhijiao die Zhongguo funü yu fazhan* (Chinese Women and Development at the Turn of the Century) (Nanjing: Nanjing daxue chubanshe, 1998), 31.

4. Second Survey on the Status of Chinese Women Project Team, "Dierqi zhongguo funü shehui diwei chouyang diaocha zhuyao shuju baogao" (Report on the Major Data from the Second Sampling Survey of the Social Status of Chinese Women), *Funü yanjiu luncong* (Collected Essays on Women's Studies), Vol. 5 (Beijing: All-China Women's Federation, 2001).

5. Mo Rong, "Jiuye: Xin shiji mianlindi tiaozhan yu jueze" (Employment: Challenges and Choices Facing the New Century), in Ru Xin, Lu Xueyi, and Chan Tianlun, eds., *2001 nian: Zhongguo shehui xingshi fenxi yu yuce* (2001: Analysis and Projections for China's Social Situation) (Beijing: Shehui kexue wenxian chubanshe, 2001), 218.

6. Institute of Women's Studies, All-China Women's Federation, ed., *Zhongguo funü wushi nian* (Fifty Years of Chinese Women), in *Renmin ribao xuanbian* (Selected Articles from *People's Daily*, CD-ROM) (Beijing: Zhongguo funü chubanshe, 1999).

7. State Statistics Bureau, Office of Population and Social Science, ed., *Zhongguo shehuidi nüren he nanren* (Women and Men in Chinese Society) (Beijing: Zhongguo tongji chubanshe, 1999).

8. Ding Xiuwei, "IT yedi fazhan dailai jiuye xin jiyu, Shanghai nüxing tingjin xinxing hangye" (Development of the IT Industry Brings New Employment Opportunities, Women in Shanghai Press Forward into the New Industry), *Zhongguo funü bao* (Chinese Women's Gazette), 11 September 2001, 2.

9. Deng Yingchao, "Xin Zhongguo funü qianjin zai qianjin" (New Chinese Women Progress Further and Further), *Renmin ribao* (People's Daily), September 1952.

10. Xiang Ling and Li Shi, "Shouru fenpei gejudi xin bianhua" (New Changes in Patterns of Income Allocation), in Ru, Lu, and Chan, *2001 nian,* 148.

11. Second Survey, "Dierqi."

12. City of Zibo, Shandong General Labor Union Survey, "Nüzhigong baohu nandu jiada" (The Difficulty of Protecting Female Workers Increases), *Zhongguo funü bao* (Chinese Women's Gazette), 7 May 1998, 3.

BIBLIOGRAPHY

Jiang Yongping. "50 nian Zhongguo chengshi funü jiuyedi huigu yu fansi" (Review and Reflections on Fifty Years of Urban Chinese Women's Employment). In Li Qiufang, ed., *Bange shijidi funü fazhan* (Half a Century of Women's Development). Beijing: Dangdai Zhongguo chubanshe, 2001.

Jin Yihong. "Quanqiuhua shiyezhongdi Zhongguo funü" (Chinese Women in View of

Jiang Yongping

Globalization), *Zhongguo funü bao* (Chinese Women's Gazette), 22 July 2001, 3.

Lin Chun. "Guojia yu shichang dui funüdi shuangzhong zuoyong" (The Dual Effect of the State and the Market on Women). In Qiu Renzong, Jin Yihong, and Wang Yanguang, eds., *Zhongguo funü yu nüxingzhuyi sixiang* (Chinese Women and Feminist Thinking). Beijing: Zhongguo shehui kexue chubanshe, 1998.

Tan Shen. "Biangezhong funüdi liangge zhongda wenti" (Two Important Issues for Women During the Time of Reform). In Qiu, Jin, and Wang, *Zhongguo funü yu nüxingzhuyi sixiang.*

RURAL WOMEN AND THEIR ROAD TO PUBLIC PARTICIPATION

Jin Yihong

Since 1980 tremendous changes have occurred in China's rural villages. Deagriculturalization has proceeded at an unprecedented rate: The absolute numbers of laborers engaged in agricultural production have decreased, and a large part of the workforce has shifted from agriculture to nonagricultural industries. By the early 1990s, more than 100 million of the nation's total rural workforce of 450 million had left farming and taken jobs in the manufacturing, service, and other nonagricultural sectors. The reclassification of rural occupations accompanied this shift of the workforce. Rural residents, formerly listed under the single heading of "peasant," are now classified into such occupational groups as agricultural laborers; rural workers; township or village collective enterprise managers; operators of sole-proprietor or corporate businesses; private enterprise owners; hired laborers; village cadres; rural intellectuals engaged in education, science and technology, medicine and public health, or culture; and domestic workers. This differentiation has resulted in huge changes in the social structure of rural villages and altered the fate of peasants.

In the process of this differentiation, two changes are having a far-reaching impact on the development of rural women: First, a large number of women peasants have become village wage-earners. Second, a group of women managers has emerged. The first change allows more rural women to gain an independent professional identity. The second change raises the level of participation by rural women in village public affairs.

How many rural women administrative cadres does China now have? According to statistics from the civil administration, in 1998 there were 834,000 village committees nationwide and 3.58 million elected village committee cadres. Women accounted for 20 percent of village committee members. This means that 716,000 women had entered management at the village level. However, women made up only 1 percent of village committee directors (village heads).[1]

Rural industry has provided rural women with more opportunities to enter management, though in the new social structure of rural villages, women remain concentrated at the bottom of the pyramid.[2] Still, in comparison to the previous period of industrialization, the number of women entering management has increased dramatically. According to a survey conducted in 1992 by the Ministry of Agriculture and the Chinese Communist Party Central Policy Institute of 312 fixed observation points spread over 29 provinces and municipalities nationwide, only 0.2 and 0.3 percent of the female workforce had become village administrative managers and town enterprise managers respectively. In both the areas of administrative management and economic management, men outnumbered women by an average of five to one. In these 312 villages, the basic social structure still centered on the agricultural economy—the proportion of the workforce engaged in agriculture remained over 63 percent.[3] In rural village regions of Jiangsu and Zhejiang provinces, where the level of industrialization is relatively high, women make up a higher percentage of managers.

In 1995, I conducted a survey in three highly industrialized villages in Suzhou, Changzhou, and Yangzhou in Jiangsu province, where the value of production from nonagricultural sectors accounted for more than 90 percent of the gross value of social production for all three of the villages. My survey found that, in these three villages, women held positions in administrative and economic management at the rates of 0.42 and 3.18 percent respectively.[4] The numbers of women entering economic management had increased tenfold! The female to male ratio in overall management had shrunk to around 1:2.4. Because rural industry has only recently begun to develop and has not yet stabilized, no accurate statistics are available on the number of rural entrepreneurs. However, a 1991 sampling survey of town enterprises conducted throughout Jiangsu province showed that women make up 11.15 percent of factory-level cadres in town enterprises, 25.25 percent of middle-level cadres, and 43.41 percent of basic-level team leaders. In addition, among those engaged in private enterprise, 20 percent are women. There is also a growing group of female managers, as well as women who manage business enterprises together with their husbands.[5] Clearly, all of these figures indicate that a cohort of women managers—referred to as female cadres, female entrepreneurs, female bosses, and "bosses' wives"—has formed in rural villages

Female cadres in rural villages are directly involved in the management of rural communities. In particular, women who take on the work of village branch secretary, town head, town Party committee secretary, and town mayor have the power to make decisions about township and village community affairs. Female entrepreneurs and female bosses undoubtedly have the power to make decisions about running their enterprises. An interesting case is that of the "bosses' wives." Their direct involvement in an enterprise usually takes the form of helping their husbands to manage the business, and they tend to hold positions in such key departments as finance, personnel, sales, and quality control. They also have indirect influence over decision-making in areas such as investments, loans, hiring, and changes in operational direction, where consultation between husband and wife is common. The family-based and rudimentary nature of rural industry in China, where bureaucracy is limited, allows women to share more of the management. "Bosses' wives" in smaller family workshop factories often carry out their management duties in conjunction with household tasks, for example, managing production while attending to the daily needs of the hired help.

Although female entrepreneurs, female bosses, and bosses' wives are mainly engaged in economic management, the provincial nature of rural industries means that they also have a large obligation in terms of community development. These women frequently serve in such positions of prestige within the community as town representative to the local people's congress, member of the women's committee, or participant in the labor union's women's committee. These women are often involved in projects to benefit the community: Of the fourteen female entrepreneurs, female bosses, and bosses' wives we surveyed, all of them had donated money to build roads, sponsored schools, helped orphans, or served as "love heart mothers," working with the disadvantaged. As their economic status rises, these women wield more influence over community affairs and can speak their minds more freely.

RURAL WOMEN'S PATHS TO BECOMING MANAGERS

On the whole, the level of rural Chinese women's participation in public affairs is still quite low. Except for the elections held for village committees every four years, women "exist silently." They have few chances to enter public management. In the 312 villages surveyed, the difference between the sexes was greatest in the area of management, with men outnumbering women five to one. In the survey of the three southern villages described previously, although the overall ratio of men to women in management was 2.4:1, at the highest level of enterprise management, the gap grew to 16:1. Of the thirty-four top managers in the survey, only two were women. Nearly all of the women managers held positions as factory work shop directors, inspectors, storekeepers, or other general management personnel, but were not decision-makers. The higher up the pyramid one goes, the fewer women one finds. When interviewed, the rural women in our survey habitually referred to women who had broken away from farming and their fates as women who "stood out." The difficulty of "standing out" can be likened to the struggle of blades of grass pushing their way up through many layers of earth.

Between 1995 and 2001 I recorded individual interviews and seminars with thirty-six basic-level female cadres and fourteen female factory heads, female managers, female bosses, and "bosses wives" from rural Jiangsu province. While selection of these interview subjects was random, the primary criterion was that they were "grass-roots" women, either born in a rural village or sent to work in one. In addition, they all had worked their way up the hierarchy from the lowest level to management. One of the women was a factory head who had been a farmer for eleven years before she started working in the factory and was promoted. Some of the women interviewees still live in their rural villages, serving as village officials or female bosses, while others have become formal cadres of the government, the highest ranking among them being a division-level official. This study analyzed the stages they went through in developing from the grass-roots level to managers.

For the purposes of discussion, I will separate administrative managers from managers of economic entities, since their experiences differ. Administrative managers are cadres at the village and town levels, the most basic rural unit. Village cadres are not officials but, rather, persons responsible for self-government at the most basic village level. They receive fixed stipends, and they are called "township controlled cadres" to distinguish them from other cadres who are not part of official staffing quotas. The number of positions at the village level is fixed, usually at five to seven, depending on the size of the village, and include a secretary and deputy secretary, village committee director and deputy director, director of women's affairs, and a bookkeeper. Organizational reforms in some villages have reduced the number of positions to three. In this study, I considered only village cadres who fell under official staffing quotas. By looking at the process under which these women became managers, we can see that those women who were able to "stand out" successfully among other women and move into positions of power constitute a minority. What paths did these women take to achieve their goals?

Before the 1980s, most basic-level rural cadres were activists and model workers winnowed from various political movements. The thirty-six female cadres I interviewed were no exception. Twenty-one of them came of age before the 1980s, and one of them had been part of a Maoist propaganda team during the Cultural Revolution (1966–1976). Nine of them were involved in the Party or Youth League reorganization of the 1970s. Five of them got their start up the ladder by participating in the socialist line education teams, and four of them led in studying the example of Dazhai Village (a model community praised during the Great Leap Forward for increasing its agricultural production through hard work inspired by revolutionary zeal), by building water conservancy projects, eradicating disease-harboring freshwater snails, and organizing "iron girl" shock teams.

Different eras provide different opportunities. When the Party issued a call, these so-called activists were the first to respond. By becoming an activist, a young rural woman could gain the attention of party leaders, who would treat her as a "sprout," the target of cultivation by the organization. Being an activist was a process by which an individual accumulated political resources, the most important of which was Party membership, a necessary route to becoming a female cadre. One woman village head was very grateful to the Party branch in her family's town for allowing her, an orphan with no one to rely on, to join the Party, thus providing her with the "capital" she later used to "come out and work." All twenty-one women had joined the Party before they left the grass-roots level. For some the path was smooth; for others it was not. When another female cadre was working on the two-line struggle education team, she "kept a polite distance" from the Party secretary, who harbored ill will against her. The secretary blocked her membership in the Party for a long time, thus making it impossible for her to move up.

For rural men, joining the military is an important shortcut to positions of power, and its significance outweighs even being an activist. In almost every village in China former military men have become cadres. The military provides them with important political resources, including the opportunity to join the Party during their service. Serving in the military also gives them the chance to form a much wider network of social relationships than that afforded by the village and clan. Women do not have this avenue to power. Instead, women can use family relationships to enter management levels. It is an open secret that positions of power (such as accountant, bookkeeper, and chief of warehouse management) are often held by the wives, daughters-in-law, and daughters of cadres. If becoming an activist is a woman's path to power through "independent participation," then relying on family relationships to enter management levels is a type of "shared participation," because the women share the resources of their male relatives. This sharing mechanism has a special significance for women as they move into management levels. Men can also move into positions of power by relying on family relationships, but, for them, service in the military is a more important factor.

Today the standards used to measure individuals include an emphasis on ability in addition to politics. For this reason, in addition to taking traditional political paths, women may demonstrate that they are qualified by participating in the new economic activities of rural villages and entering economic management levels. This new path is very important to women, since the openings in administration are few: A village has only one fixed position reserved for women, the director of women's affairs; townships have two, the directors of family planning and of women's affairs. Other positions of real power, such as village head, secretary, and town mayor are not only limited in number but also very difficult for women to attain, unless policies mandate a specified percentage of female cadres. Opportunities for participation in economic management are much broader and have fewer restrictions.

This new path also brings with it a new concept: Ability cannot completely replace "political performance" but it is becoming an important condition for entrance into management levels. A woman selected by the cadres as a "sprout" for promotion is highly dependent on the will of a superior manager. Relying on her own abilities requires a much more active approach. It is easier for capable women to stand out in the area of economic management.

Most of the fourteen female entrepreneurs, female bosses, and bosses' wives I interviewed went from farming to working in village and township enterprises, although their experiences after that differed. Five of them went on to become team leaders, shop directors, and then directors of factory offices, moving up step by step until they were heading the collective enterprise. These women basically achieved the positions they now hold through personal abilities and hard work.

Three of the women interviewed started out working in the same town enterprises as their husbands. After the enterprise was "changed" or "transformed"—usually because their husbands took it over as a "subcontracted enterprise" or "acquisition," and it became a private or stock-issuing corporation—their husbands became the bosses, and the wives automatically became bosses' wives. In this way, these women smoothly gained entrance into management positions.

Five of the women interviewed worked for a period of time in town enterprises and then started their own enterprises or followed their husbands into business, becoming private business owners or bosses' wives. The experience of working in a town enterprise gave them a way to learn about technology and operational management.

Not all of the women running their own private enterprises followed their husbands into business. Some of the women struck out on their own or started businesses mainly on their own. Of the fourteen cases, five of the women run independent corporate entities. Four are actually in charge of enterprises; the other woman runs a corporate entity in name only, since her husband still serves as village Party branch secretary, and it would be awkward for him to be the boss of a private enterprise at this time.

This new path is especially significant for women's gaining access to management positions, because it provides new criteria for advancement, such as personal ability, in addition to political status. Three of these fourteen women "did not have good family backgrounds." Prior to the recent reforms, how well they performed would not have mattered—they would not have been cultivated and promoted. Take the example of Jufang, who was from a rich peasant's family. Although she was extremely competent and everyone called her a "quick study" and a "can-do gal," the best opportunity she ever got was to serve for six years as a work points recorder. After she married into a family also considered to be rich peasants, even that job was taken away. Only after the policies in rural villages were liberalized in the 1980s was she given a chance. She then "stood out" by becoming wealthy through starting a business refining spent mining slag into metallic molybdenum.

The shift from "politics" to "ability" as the criterion for selecting managers has broken down the old gender system for women, although old ideas are still prevalent, even among women themselves. One example was the "can-do gal," Jufang. Jufang was actually a key person at the factory, yet she let her husband serve as the nominal representative of the corporate entity. She says, "I don't want to stand out. I let my husband take center stage, because that's what you have to do in a rural village." In contrast, four other women were in charge of their own business with their husbands as assistants. These women believed that they had the ability, and they did not feel any psychological pressure. Miao Lanchun, head of the Lanchun Yarn-Dyed Fabric Mill in Wujin county says proudly, "In our family we do things differently from everyone else—the woman manages the external affairs, and the man manages the internal affairs. I'm responsible for operations and development, and he does internal management and is learning to do the finances. When it comes to decision-making, I have the final say."

The effect of this era's emphasis on individual abilities not only allows women with managerial abilities to stand out; it also gives other women opportunities to move to administrative management levels. Standards that measure a village cadre's abilities ("political achievements" and prestige among the masses) are beginning to receive more emphasis. The progress of democratization in China's rural basic-level organizations has also given talented women more impetus to "break new ground." Among our interview subjects, the five village branch Party secretaries and village heads were all democratically elected to their posts. However, competent women still face obstacles to ascending to management levels.

One obstacle comes in the form of gender bias and discrimination. For example, Gu Yongfen of Liyang, a village in Changzhou, was nominated by Party members to run for village branch Party secretary in 1999. However, when the report was sent to the next level, the township standing committee did not approve her nomination. The Party committee secretary said, "It's fine for a woman to be the head of a factory, but a woman cannot be a Party branch secretary." The position of Party branch secretary is vested with more real power than any other in the village. Finally, as a result of petitions from the masses and Party members, Gu was allowed to become village Party branch secretary.

Highly competent people usually tend to have strong personalities, and the people favored by the masses are not necessarily liked by the leaders at higher levels. In the complex network of village relationships, ability is usually subordinate to other criteria. Xiufang, for example, was elected in 1990 to the position of deputy town mayor in a multicandidate election. The townspeople voted down the other two of the three candidates originally recommended for the post of deputy mayor, a result entirely outside the plans of town leaders. To deal with this "accident," the leader at the next level held an emergency meeting and organized another election. Again, neither of the two candidates the leader wanted to win was able to get the majority of votes as required by law. The leader had no choice but to allow Xiufang to hold the post of deputy mayor by herself. This incident left the leader with bad feelings toward Xiufang; after a few years, though, he had to admit that "Xiufang has some ability."

The latent pathway to managerial levels through clan connections has always existed in rural villages. This method is considered latent because this is the way cadres "divide the spoils" and exchange public resources by tacit agreement and not through openness. In the private economy, however, the sharing of private resources through family connections does not need to be done surreptitiously. Here it is more appropriate to use the term "family connections" in order to distinguish the process from the traditional clan-based pattern that existed in rural villages. The influence of the clan in modern rural economic activities is much weaker than before, and in the network of social connections, relationships through marriage are as important as kinship ties. The family connection most women rely on is the husband-wife relationship.

Most private rural industries begin as family-run workshops operated from home. In rural villages in south China, husband-wife partnerships are often the pattern for home-based workshops. In 1997, I surveyed three villages, one of which was Zhou village. Out of the 481 households in the village, 35 were engaged in individually or privately operated industrial production enterprises. Twenty-three of these households operated as husband-wife partnerships. Although the husbands and wives went into these home workshops and enterprises together, the husband was usually responsible for making operational decisions while the wife was assistant manager. The local people described the arrangement as: The man is the boss, and the woman is the boss's wife. Except for a few cases, the division of labor in these home-based enterprises followed the traditional pattern. Although the women participated in a passive and subordinate way, this shortcut still gave them unprecedented opportunities to be engaged in management. Take Juying, for example, from the town of Fangqiao near the city of Yixing. Her husband runs a group company consisting of five factories with assets approaching 100 million yuan. On the one hand, she says, "I rely on him for all the important matters pertaining to the business. He's the general manager, and I'm his assistant and staff. I obey him absolutely." On the other hand, "shared" participation does not necessarily mean total subordination to one's husband. Juying was also able to develop herself.

I started out in finance and accounting, and then he let me work on technological development. I put out six new products, and this year we have applied for a national patent. Now he's letting me do sales development. I spent three months in the sales department learning about commercial negotiations and sales. With this firm grounding in business, I then began to develop my special skills unique to women. Negotiating skills are very important. Clients are very impressed with me and admire me. Actually, it's easy to negotiate prices. I can figure out deals of five or six million [yuan] in my head. The technology is not something you can know all about in just a day or two, but if you don't understand the technology, you won't be any good at sales. I understand both, so when clients ask me technical questions about the products, I can answer without hesitation. After meeting with me once, they know how good I am, and they want to offer me a lot of money to hire me away. They don't know that I'm the general manager's wife! I'm not willing to reveal my identity at work. I want to do business by relying on my own efforts. I even went to the Light Industrial University for further study.

To a certain extent, a marital relationship may provide some women with a way to exhibit their talents. Juying was delighted to find this kind of opportunity: "I never expected that a country girl like me born to a family of farmers would now be staying at world-class hotels and doing business deals worth millions. It's like a dream."

OPPORTUNITIES AND CONDITIONS

For women, opportunities to rise to the ranks of management are rare. In China, however, these opportunities often ebb and flow with changes in policy. When policies change, it is possible for opportunities to suddenly "enlarge." For this reason, the path of women's advancement often exhibits a wavelike pattern that follows the ebbs and flows of China's policies. Outstanding women admitted the importance of opportunity in changing a woman's destiny. Some of them said over and over, "There were many women in the village more educated and more competent than I, but I was just fortunate enough to take advantage of an opportunity." By looking at the cases of the thirty-six administrative cadres we interviewed, we can see that their significant progress clustered during several special time periods.

The period of the late Cultural Revolution, 1974–1976, was a time of Party and Youth League reorganization that emphasized the cultivation of female cadres. According to many of the interviewees, Jiang Qing, Mao's wife, was responsible for the interest in women's development. Of the thirty-six women interviewed, nine joined the Party during this period and nineteen received promotions. For example, in 1974, the district where Aili lived suddenly required that each of the ten townships in that district have a female leading cadre. Qualified women were quickly selected from the "reserves," which is how Aili was promoted from an ordinary cadre in the Communist Youth League to deputy head of the township. In a few short days, she jumped to a level that ordinarily would have taken her years to attain. Among the thirty-six cases, there were six township heads and five township directors of women's affairs who, like Aili, gained their positions during the period when policies required a certain percentage of female cadres. All these women became township-level cadres when they were barely twenty years old.

The second period of concentrated opportunities occurred in 1983 and 1984, during the reforms of basic-level organizational structure. The reforms required that leading cadres be younger and better educated, and thus some educated young female cadres were admitted to leadership levels. Within the group of thirty-six interviewees, twelve received promotions during this period. Five of the women became township heads, and one person jumped to deputy county magistrate in a single bound.

The early 1990s provided a third period during which opportunities were more numerous. As another wave of democratization swept the country, basic-level cadres began to be subject to testing and competitive hiring as well as selection through open elections. Many female cadres were promoted at this time due to their abilities and prestige with the people. Xiufang, who was unexpectedly elected to deputy mayor, as mentioned above, said with emotion: "If it had not been for the competitive election with more candidates than positions, I essentially could not have moved up." Likewise, Xiangfeng went home to farm after graduating high school. After farming for three years, she took a test that allowed her to be hired as deputy town mayor. The women who were promoted during this period benefited from political democratization and not from their gender.

The fourth period of expanded opportunities occurred around 1995. Because the United Nations' Fourth World Conference on Women was held in Beijing, the government made cultivating, promoting, and using female cadres a high priority for achieving equality of the sexes. This created unprecedented opportunities for female cadres. Among the thirty-six interview subjects, six of them benefited from this occasion.

Some nonpolicy factors also provided important opportunities. After Chunfeng graduated from junior high school, she returned home to her village to work. Barely sixteen years old, she joined the Party in 1975. About one month later she became the Party branch secretary, and at age nineteen she became a member of the township Party committee. Her advancement was extraordinarily rapid. Her explanation for how she "achieved success at a young age" is that the Party branch in her village was "disorganized and not cohesive." The branch had not developed a Party member in eight years, and the remaining Party members were either very elderly or could not get along with each other. They could not agree on who should lead, and as a result, a power vacuum developed in the village, which Chunfeng filled. Among our group of interviewees, three others gained opportunities from "rifts" that occurred in the process of the transfer of power. One interesting question is: How did a young girl of sixteen manage to lead a group of men much older than she? Chunfeng explained that the village's economy was not doing well, and hence the men were not interested in being leader. Also, when the village's problems had prompted leaders at higher levels to send a work team to the village, the team, seeing what a good job Chunfeng was doing with the Communist Youth League, singled her out as a "sprout" to be developed. Her promotion was actually the work of leaders at higher levels. Finally, despite her young age, she had seniority in the clan. The male-centered clan culture actually helped her because of its doctrine that one should obey one's seniors.

Three of the interviewees who had been chosen as team leader or Party secretary got their positions either because there was no suitable man available or because the men were unwilling to take on situations that were basically a mess. Xiuzhen, for example, who was chosen as production team leader in suburban Nanjing in the 1970s, took over a post that had essentially turned into a revolving door. The seven production team leaders who preceded her had done such poor jobs that the villagers, in desperation, let her "come up and give it a try."

During the late 1990s, democratic elections were being promoted for basic-level positions in rural villages, and in many villages the numbers of female cadres was falling. An exception to this trend was Liyang county in Changzhou, where the number of female village officials increased from five to forty-five. How can we explain the Liyang phenomenon? One reason for it was that, despite Liyang's location in the region of Jiangsu and Zhejiang provinces, its town enterprises were not well developed and agriculture dominated the rural economy of the area. The men of the village generally joined construction crews and left to look for work elsewhere, leaving the women behind. The women were key to developing a variety of agricultural operations. In the absence of men, women gained more of a say in the management of community affairs. Of course, in comparison to other communities where the male labor force is also largely employed elsewhere but women still do not have opportunities to manage community affairs, Liyang's relative lack of gender discrimination cannot be ignored.

FAMILY PLANNING WORK: AN IMPORTANT STEPPING STONE

An analysis of individual cases shows that most rural women cadres rise through the hierarchy following the pattern shown below:

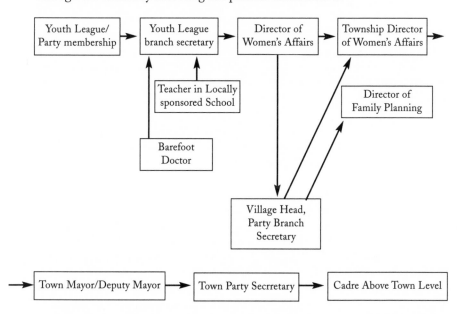

Doing family planning work is an important stepping-stone for female cadres; at the village level the director of women's affairs is also responsible for family planning. Of the thirty-six female cadres we interviewed, eleven had served as directors of women's affairs for villages, eight as directors of women's affairs for towns, and six as directors of family planning for townships. The position of village director of women's affairs is higher than other village positions such as chairman of the public security committee, Youth League branch secretary, or head of a militia battalion, based on the compensation received by village cadres. In the region where I conducted the survey, compensation for village cadres follows a customary pattern: the Party secretary is paid the most, followed by the village head and bookkeeper, who get about 90 to 95 percent of the level of compensation paid to the secretary. The director of women's affairs comes in third, at 70 percent of the secretary's compensation. (This percentage is higher in villages with economic problems, lower in wealthy villages.) Other positions, such as chairman of the public security committee, Youth League branch secretary, and others receive only 33 percent of the amount given to the secretary. Village cadres explain this by saying that if the director of women's affairs were to get as much as the secretary and village head, people would complain, but if she got too little, no one would be willing to take the job.

Clearly, the work of family planning in rural villages is both important and difficult. Whenever there is an opening for a cadre to become formally a cadre of the state, those who work on family planning are often given first priority. Our group of interviewees included four village heads and Party secretaries from Liyang who were directly elected by the village residents in 1999–2000. Prior to being elected village head or secretary, these women had all served as director of women's affairs, the longest holding her post for twelve years. These women believed that, since they had worked in family planning for such a long time and had visited every household in the village and were familiar with all the families and children in the village, they were, unlike male cadres, "close to the masses." Serving as a family planning cadre provided a stepping-stone for many of these women, allowing them to expand their influence and enhance their positions. During the interviews, one cadre named Xiuying summed up the experience by saying,

> There are only two routes open to rural women who want to stand out: the first is to be the director of women's affairs. Being a Youth League branch secretary doesn't work. As the director of women's affairs you're in charge of family planning and you have indices and accomplishments that you can use to demonstrate your performance, so it's easy for leaders at the higher levels to take you seriously. The second route is being the bookkeeper. If you're good at it, then you can "stand out," but this position is usually held by the wives of powerful men and is not available to ordinary people even if they want it. Other than [these routes], you have to start as a worker in a township enterprise and work your way up to group leader, workshop director, and on up until you get to deputy factory director, by which time you're forty or fifty years old.

A new round of reforms of basic-level village organizations since 2000 has resulted in mergers of administrative village and township enterprises and large reductions in the number of village cadres. In some areas, the number of township-controlled cadres has been reduced to two or three, and management levels in townships and villages have shrunk. Nevertheless, the government's commitment to family planning has not changed, and this provides rural women with a legal guarantee that a fixed number of township and village cadre positions will be open to them.

We can analyze the importance of family planning work as a stepping-stone in women's advancement, especially as this issue has shifted from the private sector to the public sector. China's designation of family planning as a "basic national policy" upgraded population control to an important public matter. Leading cadres are judged on the "one vote veto system": If population control targets are not met in one region or sector, the primary leading cadre is given a failing grade. This means that the "number one man"—usually the most powerful local man—must work personally with the director of women's affairs to "get a grip on family planning." Now that the family planning policy has been in place for over twenty years, the once extremely private area of reproduction has gradually become a topic of public discussion in rural villages. In meetings, the media, and daily life, men and women openly discuss birth control, vasectomies and tubal ligations, abortion, and related topics without blushing. Conceptually, people now treat reproduction as a public concern. And once a matter is considered to be part of the public sphere, its value rises.

ANALYSIS OF PERSONAL CHARACTERISTICS OF SUCCESSFUL INDIVIDUALS

In addition to the policy and nonpolicy opportunities described previously, the women managers I have been describing owe their success to their own gifts and personalities. All of these women are outstanding among rural women. They are generally very competitive and self-confident. When describing their own personalities, with the exception of three women who consider themselves "easygoing and not driven to achieve," the others all repeatedly emphasized, "I'm always anxious to be better than others. I cannot lose out to someone else in anything I do!" "I always try my best to win credit for myself." Six of the women particularly emphasized that their strong-willed mothers influenced their own strong personalities. Seven of the women said that, since childhood, their father's high expectations for them had motivated them to be better than other people. In addition to family influences, school environment also shaped these women's strong personalities. Twelve of the women said that in school they had been class officers (class president or secretary of a Youth League branch). The educational system in which the sexes were relatively equal gave them opportunities "to manage people from an early age," refined their management skills, and created a strong sense of self-confidence.

What motivated these women? "To be better than others" and "to change my destiny" were the surprisingly frank answers many of the women gave. The women even expressed contempt for women of the same age who were "content to be mediocre," saying, "The other women my age on the production team started falling in love early on. All they wanted to do was to find a good husband. I had a different idea. I wanted to have ideals and wanted to 'stand out,' to be better than others."

These women's strong desire to "stand out" is often connected to their marginalized social and gender status. Chinese peasants have always been at the bottom of society, and because of the restrictive system of household registration, a girl born into a peasant family is destined to remain one all her life. For this reason, more than one interviewee said that she struggled because she "did not want to quietly till the soil for the rest of her life." The only two shortcuts to changing one's status as a peasant are going to school and becoming a cadre. Women are also a marginalized group within the peasant class. Some of them want to change their destinies because as females they have been treated unfairly. Four of the women resented the preference their fathers or mothers showed for boys over girls. When family finances were tight, they allowed the boys, whose academic performances were not as good their sisters', to continue with their education. No matter how well the woman did at school, she was not allowed to continue. One said, "I'm just not convinced. Why is it that a girl can't be as good as a boy?!" This experience motivated the women to "do their best and be better than others."

Other factors—the humiliations of poverty, being an "outsider" in the village because of marriage, or a "bad" family background—caused the women to feel discrimination, and strongly motivated them to "be better than others." One woman, an orphan, said, "It is my fate to have no one to rely on. The only way I could 'stand out' was through my own efforts." Compensation also motivated these women. Once they became managers, society's mechanism for compensation reinforced these women's desires to keep advancing. Respect is an important part of social compensation. For example, one woman who is now the village director of women's affairs is married to a man who owns a private enterprise. Her husband wanted her to quit her job as a cadre and help him run the business. But she felt that, as a cadre, she was "a key person in the village," and the respect and satisfaction she got from that were things she would not get from being a boss's wife. For this reason, although the compensation she received as a cadre was a pittance to her, she was not willing to give up the job. What is more, the material rewards of being a cadre are very important. Becoming the village director of women's affairs means having to compete fiercely for the post, because the compensation is quite good, compared to that for a peasant. In wealthy villages in southern China, the annual income of a director of women's affairs is around ten thousand yuan.[6] Salaries for major village cadres are even higher. One village head, age forty-eight, was told by her upper-level leader that she was too old to stand for Party election. She was very upset. When the town director of women's affairs tried to console her, the village head said bluntly, "In any case, not serving for another three years means earning one hundred thousand yuan less."

The power to direct other people provides another source of satisfaction and emotional compensation. Four of the interviewees said that, when they are managing a project involving several hundred villagers or enterprise employees or even several thousand workers (on a flood control embankment project), they get a sense of happiness and satisfaction that nothing else can match.

During the interview process, it was interesting to observe how the female managers described the factors contributing to their success. The women frequently mentioned several common characteristics: First, women spoke of dynamism—active participation in public affairs—as an important precondition for "standing out" from the crowd of other village girls and getting attention, and for being cultivated by higher-ranking Party members. Second, women who become cadres must interact with all kinds of people, and women who are not outgoing are considered to be unable to "mount the stage," and are not suited to working in the public arena. Some of the women described in detail how they went from being shy to being outgoing. They had to have the courage to speak in front of several hundred people, and they could not shrink back when men spoke crudely. They needed to be willing to be tough with the people they manage when circumstances required it.

Third, many of the female cadres said that their education, which was often better than that of other girls their age, led organizations to notice them. This was especially true prior to the 1990s, when "few girls graduated from high school, so those who did were very valuable." A large amount of research documentation shows that the degree to which women are discriminated against is inversely proportional to their level of education.[7] On the other hand, although a high school graduate might be considered highly educated among peasants, high school is the lowest level of education among cadres. The increasing emphasis on academic background in China puts tremendous pressure on these women. To avoid being phased out, they all attended schools for female cadres and Communist Party schools, and took correspondence courses to further their education and get higher diplomas. In one typical case, a director of women's affairs continued her studies for ten years, from high school to junior college to an undergraduate education by correspondence course and ultimately to graduate school. Some women work part-time and go to school part-time, while others take a leave of absence from work to pursue their studies. The difficulties of going to school part-time while working do not need elaboration. Taking a leave of absence from work to go to school frequently means leaving one's family, often when a woman's children are still young and need the most care. Three of the women left home to go to school when their children were only one or two years old. These women chose to be separated from their children for a short time in order to secure a better future.

Fourth, virtually all of the female cadres cited their abilities to withstand hardships. They know that as women they have to work harder than men. Fifth, personal competence was another quality the women emphasized, one that gave them self-confidence and pride. One woman repeatedly stressed that she was the youngest woman ever to be town mayor and the youngest member of the Party committee. But, she said with great pride, "I did it by relying entirely on my own abilities. I don't have any special family background. My parents are both peasants and are completely illiterate."

Other outstanding qualities named were fairness, selflessness, and honesty: Many newly elected "village officials" mentioned honesty as an important advantage in defeating their male opponents. Rural villages must have open finances and democratic management, and it is easier for women than men to gain people's trust. Villagers are confident that female cadres will not spend all the collective's money wining and dining: "At the very least, [female cadres] don't drink, and if they have to attend a meeting out of town, they eat very little, and they won't be calling girls who entertain men." Xiuzhen, who had been a senior production team leader, explained why the seven male team leaders who preceded her had failed and she had succeeded, saying, "They are all selfish and clique-driven, and I'm not. The people say that I'm fair in my dealings and very upstanding." Her definition of "just and selfless" was most interesting: "I do more than any man, but I still get a woman's pay. The only way people will let me manage them is if I do a lot but earn a little. Although I'm the team leader, I'm still a woman, and a woman's income can't be more than a man's." When I asked her why a woman cannot surpass a man in income, she replied, "As the saying goes, 'no matter how big the window is, it's still not as big as the door, and no matter how capable a woman is, she's not more capable than a man.'"

Four of the women stressed that their advantage lay in their androgynous qualities: "I've got a man's guts in a woman's body"; "I can work as hard as any man"; "Generous, kind-hearted, resolute, firm—I've got the best qualities of both my father and my mother"; "In dealing with other people I have a woman's soft touch, but in managing and making decisions I'm resolute and strict."

Only one person said that good looks had made a difference for her. She was on the construction site of a water conservancy project when the construction crew leader said in surprise, "This beautiful young girl is so competent." From that point on, she was cultivated as a "barefoot doctor" and did not have to tend the fields anymore. Later, the construction crew leader let her become his daughter-in-law. Although the other women did not talk about the effect their looks had on their careers, the interviewer observed that the least good-looking among the female cadres were "not bad looking," and 80 percent of them could be considered "outstanding" for the local area. Of course, being pretty is not necessarily a good thing. One of the interview subjects was an extremely pretty female cadre about whose promotion the villagers had many misgivings. During the seminars, the women spoke more frankly, because they were citing examples of other people. The women said that a woman's looks were actually very influ-ential, and that leaders at higher levels would "at least have a good impression of you" if you were good-looking. Whereas in the past, just working hard was enough, now the people have very exacting standards for a female cadre's image. If a female cadre is not pretty, then people say, "Can't we choose any prettier women around here?" If she is too pretty, then people think of her as just "eye candy" and assume that she did not get where she is by virtue of her compe-tence and ability. Some good-looking female cadres are harassed by their supe-riors and see their luck go bad if they do not play along. They not only may be denied promotion but also are dogged by rumors and innuendo.

FAMILY FACTORS IN SUCCESS

Parents were important in the lives of these girls. Some parents, themselves cadres, guided their daughters to "mount the stage." Although the female man-agers I interviewed all believed that they got where they are primarily on their own efforts, they did not reject their parents' introductions and arrangements. Even parents without power or advantages may still quietly support their daughters' work. This becomes especially important during times when the demands of a job dramatically conflict with domestic duties. Mothers and mothers-in-law often help to alleviate the pressures of work on the home. For example, some mothers-in-law travel with their daughters-in-law and the chil-dren, so that, no matter where the daughter-in-law has to go for work and meetings, the children can be with her. That way, the daughter-in-law can breast-feed between meetings.

Some families have "insufficient paternal authority" or an "absent father fig-ure" because of a father's political problems or early death. In these cases, the mother, mother-in-law, or sister-in-law may be key. For example, one female village head had a mother-in-law who was herself extremely competent. The mother-in-law could do bookkeeping, write beautiful calligraphy, and pos-sessed a strong personality, but had "never made anything of herself." Everyone looked down on the family because the husband made his living butchering hogs and had had some mental health problems. When the daughter-in-law married into the family, she was already a Party member, and the village lead-ers were grooming her to become a cadre. The daughter-in-law got pregnant and thought it would be difficult to "take the lead" in work with a bulging stomach, so she decided against becoming a cadre. Her mother-in-law, how-ever, wanted very much for her daughter-in-law to be a cadre and supported her in performing public service. As a cadre, the daughter-in-law had to set an example in family planning, so after she gave birth to a daughter, she had no more children, and the mother-in-law accepted this decision. When the daughter-in-law became the village head, the family's status changed and her mother-in-law felt very proud. Before she died, the mother-in-law told her son that he should support his wife in her work outside the home, saying, "If the family's fields go fallow, then let them go fallow!"

Of the thirty-six subjects we interviewed, three of them had similar mothers-in-law. The mothers or mothers-in-law who supported their daughters or daughters-in-law most energetically were those who, despite their personal strengths, never stood out. When their daughters had a chance to stand out, it was as if the accumulated energy of two generations of women burst forth. Their support was wholehearted and unconditional.

Two of the interviewees had fathers who favored boys over girls and did not let their daughters pursue an education. Their mother's insistence allowed the girls opportunities for education, which benefited them for the rest of their lives. One of the mothers said, "I don't want my daughter to be like me, to marry someone and have to rely on him for everything and to be pushed around all the time. My daughter must go to school!"

CONCLUSION: THE HARDSHIPS AND PROSPECTS FOR GRASS-ROOTS PARTICIPATION

For rural women, succeeding on the path to management is a glorious accomplishment in which they can take pride. But this path is covered with the footprints of hardship: When a woman enters a man's world of cadres, she is confronted with the stares of the men and must come out kicking and punching. Steeped in the male-dominated culture captured in sayings like "No matter how big the window is, it's still not as big as the door, and no matter how capable a woman is, she's not more capable than a man," a woman must part ways with traditional rural stereotypes. She must "look after everyone while taking very little for herself"; she must be "public-spirited and selfless." The constant struggle between her work as a good cadre and her work as a good wife and mother is not easy.

Women's path to public management is not only difficult and long; the rate of obsolescence for rural female cadres is also quite high. During the interviews, several of the female cadres who came of age during the 1970s and 1980s said that at least one-third of the women who had worked with them during that time had already faded from view. The women believed that these other women who stood out for a brief time and then disappeared were relieved of their posts because "their level of education was low," "their husbands or families did not support them and were fearful or suspicious," or they had problems with the "three rites of passage"—falling in love, getting married, and having children. In the organizational lingo of cadre education, not handling these challenges well means, for example, not being as enthusiastic or selfless about one's work after having children.

Saying that the road is long means that female cadres must climb a long ladder of advancement. The age standards for the cultivation and use of female cadres differ from those applied to men. A female cadre must be five years younger than her male counterpart in order to be considered for promotion, and the retirement age for women is five years lower than for men, ten years in some villages. To cite one more case, a female cadre began serving as village director of women's affairs at age nineteen. According to the rules, she had to spend three years at each "stage." There are seven stages between village director of women's affairs and secretary of the township Party committee. If she makes it to each stage without delay, by the time she makes it to the township committee she will be forty years old and too old to go any higher. Most of her time will have been spent on the ladder without moving. Among the thirty-six women interviewed, one woman served as village director of women's affairs for twelve consecutive years, and another spent eighteen years as deputy town mayor.

The future of women in rural villages involves many uncertain factors. At the end of the twentieth century, the path for rural women to advance from the basic level was blocked—the new policy for cadres emphasized education and diplomas. Like civil servants, cadres at the township level must take a test for each promotion. This means that, in the future, only university graduates will be eligible to become township cadres. For this reason, many counties now go several years without promoting a female cadre up from the village level. In order to solve the problem of a lack of female cadres at the township level, many localities have reassigned female teachers "down" to the township level. Having participation in village administrative management cut off as a path to advancement is not necessarily a bad thing for rural women: It might force young women either to get more education or to participate in a greater variety of economic activities in rural villages in order to strive for opportunities to develop themselves.

The bosses' wives who participated in management in a shared format are also experiencing some changes. As rural industry becomes more technological, home-based workshops are gradually being replaced by the large factories of nascent modern enterprise. Township enterprises are becoming more scientific, and enterprise managers more specialized. For this reason, some bosses' wives are being sent home to "enjoy a leisurely retired life." Many male bosses are buying out their partners in order to concentrate management power in their own hands. All this will affect how and the extent to which rural women participate in rural village public affairs in the future.

For the present, although the changes in rural China that began during the 1980s have not altered the bifurcation between the public and private spheres, social values, and other issues of social order, to a certain extent they have changed the distribution of men and women in the public and private spheres. The diverse development of rural village economies has given women more opportunities to participate in economic activities and has also increased their influence in the public life of rural villages.

NOTES

1. Fan Yu, "Cunwei xuanju: nongcun funü fazhandi jiyu yu tiaozhan" (Village Committee Elections: Opportunities and Challenges for Rural Women's Development), in '95 shijie funü dahui 5 zhounian yantaohui lunwenji (Proceedings from the Seminar on the Fifth Anniversary of the 1995 World Conference on Women, Beijing) (Beijing, 2000), 273.

2. Jin Yihong, "Changes in Gender Structure During the Process of Deagriculturalization in Rural Areas South of the Changjiang River," Social Sciences in China, 2000, 66–77.

3. Jin Yihong, "Nongcun funü zhiye fenhua yanjiu" (Study of Occupational Differentiation among Rural Women), in Dangdai nongcun funü fazhan yu duice (Development and Policies for Contemporary Rural Women) (Beijing: Zhongguo funü chubanshe, 1995), 15–26.

4. Jin Yihong, "Feinonghua guochengzhongdi nongcun funü" (Rural Women in the Process of Deagriculturalization), Shehui yanjiu (Social Studies), Vol. 5, 1998.

5. According to data announced at the first forum on the private sector economy held in August 2001 in Shenzhen, women are in charge of 10 to 20 percent of the 200,000 privately operated industries nationwide. See Xinhua ribao (Xinhua Daily), September 2001.

6. In 2001, the Women's Federation in the city of Changshu conducted a survey on compensation of all village directors of women's affairs within the city. The basic salary was approximately 10,000 yuan. The lowest annual salary was 6,000 yuan and the highest was 32,000 yuan, for a woman who served concurrently as the bookkeeper, and thus her compensation was the same as that of the Party branch secretary.

7. Xu Anqi, "Fuqi huoban guanxi: Zhongguo chengxiangdi yitong ji qi yuanyin" (Husband and Wife Partnerships: Differences Between Urban and Rural Areas in China and the Causes), Zhongguo renkou kexue (Chinese Population Science), Vol. 4, 1998; Li Shi, "Nongcun funüdi jiuye yu shouru" (Employment and Incomes of Rural Women), Zhongguo shehui kexue (Chinese Social Science), Vol. 3, 2001.

ECONOMIC GROWTH AND WOMEN'S DEVELOPMENT IN CHINA'S WESTERN AREAS: A CASE STUDY

Han Jialing

Implementing the strategy of developing China's western areas and accelerating the economic growth of the central and western regions comprise an important policy as China enters a new stage in its work to build a prosperous society and advance socialist modernization. The development of the west also provides an opportunity for women's development.

Located in southeastern Guizhou province, Leishan county lies in a mountainous region populated mostly by ethnic minorities belonging to the Miao and Dong peoples. Economic production in the area has always been rudimentary, and much of the population lives in poverty. Fiscal resources are very limited. In 1985 the county implemented fiscal reforms, and since then expenditures for education and public health have decreased every year. The county's finances have been especially limited since 1990, and administrative departments such as education and public health have only been able to afford to pay salaries. In 1995 the county had only the 3,760 yuan provided by the central government to spend on public health, which came out to only 0.028 yuan per person for basic healthcare expenditures, far below the nationally regulated minimum standard of 0.15 yuan.[1] Money for education came entirely from limited appropriations provided by the province, the prefecture, and the central government.

In light of this situation, how can impoverished areas develop? Their problems are vastly different from those of the developed regions on the coast. In recent years, some theorists and those engaged in practical work have been hoping that the west could imitate the development patterns of the east, shrinking the gap that divides them. Although industrialization is normally the way to achieve economic development, China's poor areas are rich in natural resources but have been slow to develop processing industries. Over the past decade and more, rural enterprises have not been able to provide the breakthroughs needed to increase wealth in these areas, and this may continue to be the case in the near future.

In their eagerness to break free from poverty, some counties fear that focusing on agriculture requires large financial commitments for many decades before reaping economic rewards. Thus, they tend to squander their financial resources on quick-money projects. These often generate little profit for various reasons, including inexperience, inconvenient transportation, poor information, and failures in the market mechanism. Many impoverished areas lack the basic conditions needed for business, but they charge blindly ahead, only to meet with utter failure. Since the 1980s, Leishan county has seen steel, glass, beverage, and ferro-silicon factories fail, one after the other, costing tens of millions of yuan. The county has been unwilling, however, to invest in low-cost agricultural projects that could alleviate the severe poverty of the residents.

Between 1993 and 1996 the county received a total of 28.30 million yuan in assistance loans from the central government and the province of Guizhou, of which 69.22 percent was spent on industry and township enterprises, while only 28.48 percent went toward agricultural projects and a mere 1.24 percent was spent on loans to farmers that might directly alleviate poverty.[2] The funds that were spent on agriculture were mainly low-interest loans to provide working funds to enterprise units. Hence, in 1996, the Chinese government's antipoverty programs repeatedly stressed that "efforts to alleviate poverty must have clear targets and must assist villages and households."[3]

In order to solve the basic problem of feeding and sheltering people, impoverished regions, especially those in remote areas where natural conditions are poor, must be pragmatic and start with basic projects. These areas must intensively develop agricultural cultivation and the processing of agricultural products. This is an effective route. Currently, women in impoverished mountain areas rely on subsistence farming. The state should greatly increase its expenditures on infrastructure, agricultural technology, and funding for these areas to free impoverished women from the heavy burden of agricultural labor.

Improving the lives of people, especially women, in impoverished areas is not a matter of striving for a certain "level of science and technology" but, rather one of examining the problems from the perspective of the needs of poor people and poor women. The case of Leishan county shows that, if efforts to alleviate poverty do not start with the needs of the poor, then throwing more labor and material resources at the problem is simply wasteful and may even increase the burden on the residents of the impoverished area. First, basic improvements in the delivery of water and electricity can improve the living conditions of rural women and decrease the amount of time they spend on household tasks. However, the effort to be as advanced as the coastal areas does not often benefit the rural women. Unlike the beneficiaries of coastal development, the great majority of rural women are not aided by advanced infrastructure developments. For example, in 1995 preprogrammed, auto-control telephones were installed in Leishan county, making it possible to dial directly to Beijing, Shanghai, and other places. Beginning in 1996, another 1.2 million yuan was spent to expand fiber-optic telephone service, further connecting Leishan county to the rest of the world. But more than 80 percent of rural villages in Leishan county still do not have telephones because they cannot afford the charges, so service was cut off. Affordably priced hand-held telephones have now fallen into disrepair and have been scrapped. With the exception of a scheduled truck that arrives each day, all of the county's connections to the outside world are accomplished on foot or by mail.

The development of the county's use of electricity is similar. At the end of the 1980s, the national power grid was extended to Leishan, replacing the small hydroelectric power plant, which was an unreliable source of energy. However, the cost of bringing the power grid to remote mountainous areas was very high, and the costs were passed on to the rural residents. Electricity fees in rural villages in Leishan are 1 yuan per kilowatt hour, whereas in Beijing electricity fees are only 0.35 yuan per kilowatt hour. As a result, after the power grid was extended, no one could afford to use it. Local residents are now demanding that the abandoned hydroelectric power plant be refurbished, because it costs only 0.3 yuan per kilowatt hour.

Second, since the 1980s, Leishan has continually suffered from a lack of funding for education. In 1991 the county finally secured a loan of 3.1 million yuan from the World Bank. The loan was to be used primarily for repairing and constructing school buildings, but the loan came with three conditions: access to roads, access to electricity, and access to water.[4] Unfortunately, the school buildings in remote mountainous areas in most urgent need of repair, such as the Zhanglei Elementary School, often did not have this access and thus could not get the money for improvement. In addition, the World Bank also required that school buildings be constructed from bricks and concrete. In Leishan county, timber is readily available, and the Miao people are renowned for their skill at constructing stilt houses. Construction costs for a wood school building (200 square meters) are approximately 40,000 yuan, but construction costs for the same size building using brick and concrete are 200,000 yuan, nearly five times as much. The Lianhua Elementary School demolished its perfectly good building to construct a new one. For communities where financial resources are already tight, loans like these do nothing but increase the burden on the local residents. In addition, the residents of the remote areas of Leishan who do not enjoy the benefits of these loans are still forced to share the burden of paying for the World Bank loans in the form of higher fees for education.

Third, an attempt to improve sanitary facilities also failed because an urban model was applied to rural villages. Between 1991 and 1994 the United Nations Children's Fund (UNICEF) installed three sets of flush toilets in model sanitation demonstration villages in Maomaohe and Xiaohe village of Lianhua in Leishan county.[5] At 400–500 yuan apiece, the price for installing the toilets was high. In addition, the toilets were built to urban standards, which meant that the rural residents, particularly the women, had to do more than ten times as much hauling of night soil; as a result, the residents did not use the toilets UNICEF had provided for free. This is a typical example of projects that overlook the needs of rural women and do not start by looking at the actual situation in rural villages.

The examples cited above are not unique to Leishan but are common occurrences in Third World developing countries. In his book *Economic Development in the Third World*, Michael P. Todaro depicts this vividly:

> In developing countries we frequently see physicians who are eager to do research on heart disease, but who consider "the prevention of tropical diseases" to be a second-class specialization, architects who work hard designing national monuments and modern buildings but pay little attention to low-cost homes, schools, and clinics. We see engineers and scientists painstakingly perfect the newest, most modern electronic equipment, but leave the work on simple machine tools, human or animal-powered agricultural tools, basic sanitary equipment and water purification systems, as well as labor intensive manual procedures to the "foreign experts."[6]

Development requires the adoption of a comprehensive plan; otherwise it is difficult to make it work. Single projects do little to solve the basic problems of impoverished areas. Education for girls, technical training, healthcare for women and children, microloans, and other types of schemes all produce important changes in the lives of women in the areas where the plans are implemented. However, one plan alone cannot change the structural problem of poverty. Poor people are not without the capacity to develop; they are poor because they do not have opportunities to develop.

Worsening rural poverty is caused by many factors; simply throwing money at the problem does not have a positive effect. Rural residents may very likely take out loans to pay for food, places to live, or other pressing needs, and not on economic production. In addition, people in rural villages commonly lack skills for economic production and management. Without improvements in these areas, the development of rural villages is difficult to sustain and can easily result in economic losses. When loan recipients cannot pay back their loans, these debts create more of a burden for rural residents and end up having a negative effect.

Currently, UNICEF is working together with some nongovernmental organizations (NGOs) on a microloan project in rural villages in southwestern China to help women earn incomes. Households or women who receive the loans must participate in programs that involve comprehensive rural development, such as literacy and technical training, sending children to school, and family planning.[7] This approach, it is hoped, will not only increase the incomes of rural households and women but also improve women's capacity to develop themselves.

The national government needs to adopt four interventionist methods. First, strengthening the economic participation of poor women and improving their productivity would provide the material basis for social equality between men and women. In Bangladesh, for example, providing poor women with microcredit to increase their incomes has been an outstanding success. Helping poor women to break free of poverty improves living conditions for the women themselves and their families and gives women opportunities for self-development.

Second, having access to water nearby and a plentiful supply of fuel would make it easier for girls to go to school and for women to get involved in production activities that earn incomes. Measures should start with improving ways of accomplishing household tasks through providing drinking water and fuel. The state should assist poor areas in building roads, installing water and electricity facilities, and improving other infrastructures in order to improve living conditions for women.

Third, women must be guaranteed equal opportunities for education, including technical education. This is crucial to raising women's status in the economic sphere. Research on developing countries shows that every additional year of education received by a woman increases her future income by 15 percent.[8] Education for women not only raises their productivity, increases their incomes, and improves their quality of life; it also has tremendous social benefits. According to a report from the World Bank, a close relationship exists between women's education and social development. Well-educated women better understand the importance of medical care and personal hygiene. Education for women raises their level of knowledge about healthcare and reduces the average number of pregnancies, thereby reducing the dangers of pregnancy and childbirth.[9] Although women's education is not a panacea that will eliminate the world's disasters, there are close relationships among women's education, healthy families, and expanding economic growth and democracy.

Fourth, basic hygiene and health conditions guarantee women's participation in development. In poor rural villages without healthcare personnel and facilities, women do not receive appropriate care during pregnancy or childbirth and afterward. With regard to nutrition, although women gather and prepare food for their families, malnutrition is more common among women than among men.

In sum, then, for women to participate fully in the work of development, they must have adequate and equal opportunities to receive healthcare, nutrition, and other social services, including family-planning services and child-care facilities. More important, for women three critical areas need attention: education, childbearing and healthcare, and credit resources.

NOTES

1. Leishan County Health Department, "Qiandongnan 1994 nian weisheng gongzuo mubiao guanli zeren shu" (Management Responsibility Document for Public Health Work for Southeastern Guizhou), 1994.

2. Information provided by the Poverty Assistance Bureau of Leishan County.

3. "Zhongyang fupin kaifa gongzuo huiyi zhaokai" (Central Government Convenes Conferences on Poverty Assistance and Development Work), *Renmin ribao* (People's Daily), 24 September 1996.

4. Leishan County, Guizhou Province Project, "Shijie yinhang daikuan xiangmu jianbao (1991–1997)" (Brief Report on the World Bank Loan Project [1991–1997]), 1992.

5. Leishan County, Guizhou Province Project, "Lianheguo erjihui yuanzhu xiangmu shishi qingkuang ji xiaoyi baogao (1991–1995)" (Report on the Implementation and Benefits of the United Nations Children's Fund Assistance Project [1991–1995]), November 1995.

6. Michael P. Todaro, *Economic Development in the Third World*, trans. Yu Tongshen and Su Rongsheng (Beijing: Zhongguo renmin daxue chubanshe, 1988), 483. [Orig. pub., London: Longman, 1977]

7. United Nations Children's Fund, "Project Framework Document, Social Development Project for Poor Areas, Chinese Government . . . United Nations Children's Fund Cooperative Project 1996–2000."

8. United Nations, *Human Development Report 1995* (New York: Oxford University Press, 1996), 118.

9. L. H. Summers, *Investing in All the People: Educating Women in Developing Countries*. Economic Development Paper series No. 45 (Washington, DC: World Bank, 1994), 11–18.

LEAVING HOME AND COMING BACK: EXPERIENCES OF RURAL MIGRANT WOMEN

Tan Shen

Beginning in the mid-1980s, young people from China's rural villages began a migration to cities and industrially developed regions. At first there were several million, but by the 1990s their numbers had grown to tens of millions. The census in 2000 put the total at almost 90 million. Within this large group of migrants, approximately one-third are women, totaling around 26 million. They come primarily from undeveloped inland provinces and poor rural villages. Most of them seek employment opportunities in cities and towns within their own province, but 20 to 40 percent leave their provinces and go to cities or industrially developed regions along the east coast.[1]

In contrast to men who migrate, approximately two-thirds of the women leaving home are unmarried; for men the rate is nearly half. When women leave their home provinces, their destinations tend to be places with high concentrations of other migrants. Half of them go to the export-processing centers of Guangdong province, primarily the Pearl River Delta region. One-quarter of them go to coastal cities, with relatively sparse distribution in other regions. Men, however, usually spread out over a wider area, perhaps in relation to work opportunities. The primary jobs for migrant women are as workers in processing industries; as hired labor in the service sector, including restaurants, retail stores, and hotels; and as domestic help. These jobs are mainly concentrated in industrial regions and large cities. The jobs men take are often in construction and shipping, and thus their distribution is more scattered. But there is a trend of family migration. Some data show that over 40 percent of migrants run their own businesses. It is estimated that most of these are husband-and-wife operations, spread throughout cities and towns, and this may explain why the disparity in the proportion of male to female migrants is not wider.[2]

The large number of rural women leaving home to find work has become a social phenomenon that is attracting attention. What does it mean for the women themselves? What does it mean for society? People are paying attention to and interpreting these questions from different perspectives. My primary area of concern is the influence of women's migration on gender structures during this specific period of China's history. For ten years my partners and I have conducted a number of surveys of migrant women in their most important destinations—the Pearl River Delta region in Guangdong province and their hometowns in Sichuan and Hunan provinces. I study women workers in the processing factories and, at the same time, organize research teams of colleagues to study two other important occupations held by migrant women from rural villages—as domestic hired labor and in the sex trade.[3]

The focus of discussion in this chapter is not theoretical. Rather, it offers a description of typical situations for rural migrant women, followed by discussion of some of the controversial topics that have attracted attention in recent years. In my descriptions I am interested in interpreting these topics through the perspective of gender consciousness.

REASONS FOR LEAVING HOME

Why leave home? While motivation was an important topic of study during the 1990s, two issues need to be re-examined: First, researchers usually interpret people's motives, including women's motives for leaving home, from a strictly economic perspective, ignoring social reasons. Second, too much emphasis has been placed on the traditional influence of the Chinese family. For example, scholars have assumed that "family strategy" entirely dictates decisions about whether someone should leave home and who this person should be, without further analysis of the different roles and attitudes within the family and the personal opinions of the ones leaving.

From our surveys and from those done by others, we learned that the main reasons people give for leaving home are "to earn money" and "to help the family get out of poverty." However, ranking just behind these are "to see the world" and "to seek opportunities for development," along with other noneconomic personal motivations. Men's "self-development" is seen as consistent with the goals of the family, because traditionally, at some point, a man will continue the family's name. For a woman, however, the situation is different. If she is married, her personal development may conflict with the responsibilities traditionally assigned to her by marriage. If she is unmarried, she is in a transition within her parents' home, and her responsibilities depend upon the family's circumstances. If she is an older daughter and the other sisters are still young, she faces a heavy responsibility in helping her parents support the family until she marries, especially if the family's economic situation is poor. If she does not need to take on such a burden at home, then she has a greater degree of freedom. Surveys show that decisions to leave home are rarely made by the head of household or as a result of family negotiations. Most women make the decision on their own and then seek the consent of their parents or husbands. Some women leave home without such consent, and still others leave "to escape family strife," hardly a "family strategy."

My conclusion is that the large number of rural women do not leave home to look for work entirely because of industrialization and urbanization. For one thing, this phenomenon represents a breakdown of the old system. During much of China's history cities and rural villages were isolated from each other. National systems and policies severely limited the free mobility of rural people. During that time, rural people who wanted to use work to change their status or position had very few possibilities open to them, and most of the opportunities were given to men. Women could change their circumstances only through the even more limited opportunities offered through marriage. Since China's reforms and opening to the outside world, leaving home to find work has provided rural people with a variety of choices and possibilities. But, of course, the social system changes slowly. Hence those who leave home may face a series of difficulties later in life, particularly with regard to planning for the future.

Furthermore, because of women's liberation under socialist revolution and the promotion of the idea of gender equality, there have been changes in the mechanisms of severe repression toward women. Rural women are not forced into absolute obedience in rural households. Since the reforms, family relationships and power have shifted toward the axis of husbands and wives and the younger generation, giving young married women more autonomy. Migration also promotes the growth of individualism as legal and reasonable, manifested most clearly in the case of unmarried women. However, in marriage, the traditional structure of "the man decides and the woman follows" has remained basically unchanged, and women who have developed their individuality, especially those who have achieved some success in work, face more conflicts in their families than do men.

CHANGES BROUGHT ABOUT BY LEAVING HOME TO FIND WORK

After migrants arrive at their destination, they immediately enter a labor market that is divided in two ways. First, the labor market is split between locals and migrant people. The jobs open to outsiders are the physically demanding, low-wage jobs that the locals are unwilling to do. Second, the labor market is divided on the basis of gender. Employment advertisements clearly state gender requirements. In the Pearl River Delta region where I conducted surveys, many employment advertisements posted on the streets and on factory gates read: "Seeking skilled female workers." There it is easier for young women, especially women with a certain amount of work experience, to find jobs than it is for men.

However, in general, men's incomes are higher than women's and men hold higher positions. Within the same factory, the higher the position, the fewer women there are. The fact is that the kind of unskilled, labor-intensive jobs most available for women are monotonous, strictly managed, and poorly paid. If a woman wants to earn a certain income, she must work even harder. Women working on factory assembly lines frequently work ten hours or more a day. When there is a rush to fill an order, women commonly work more than ten hours straight or all night long on overtime. Stressful work over long periods of time, combined with poor nutrition, leads many women workers to faint on the job.

Faced with this harsh market, migrant women initially experience tremendous psychological pressures, and their feelings of being adrift and of missing home are often intense. Some women who are psychologically more fragile find it difficult to cope with such feelings. In many places we visited we heard about incidents of migrant women committing suicide. Although there are no statistics, we believe that suicide rates for migrant women must be higher than for the general population.

Except for the minority that returns home, however, most women stay. They slowly adjust to life away from home, and they learn methods of coping and resistance, such as expanding their social networks and switching jobs frequently. As they become more skilled, their incomes gradually rise and become more stable, which bolsters their self-confidence. Some women with stronger aspirations for development begin to take training courses in the hopes of finding new opportunities.

THE SIGNIFICANCE OF MARRIAGE

If an unmarried woman of eighteen leaves home, after two or three years she typically starts to think about getting married. For rural young men and women alike, leaving home raises their expectations with regard to love and marriage. Love and marriage are another career for them, in addition to work. The cultural environment of migrant life, which is so clearly different from that of the village, causes young people who leave home to formulate concepts of love and marriage vastly different from those of the older generation. We have divided women who leave home into four categories based on their experience of emotions and marriage.

The first category is the steady type and represents the majority. The woman loves a man from her home area, and their parents accept their selection easily. This type faces virtually no obstacles. In comparison with villagers who do not leave home, this woman has more opportunities to express her feelings, both toward her parents and her prospective husband. She is more autonomous and receives more respect. As the saying goes, "She doesn't want a country bumpkin." In addition to "knowing the other's background thoroughly," these women who have left home also require that their mates too have left home. Men who have left home do not require women to leave. Women who leave home generally demand that their spouses at least have the same experience, in other words, be equal to them.

The second large category is the troubled type. When we talked with women who had left home, we discovered that their most common problems are with love and marriage. They do not know how to handle conflicts between their ideals and reality. Many of their problems stem from the fact that their lovers are from other places. Although emotionally things may be fine, the practical difficulties are hard to overcome, and their parents usually do not support their choices. In this situation many women have had to give up their relationships. Couples with good economic prospects establish families in the places to which they have migrated. For a while, this will solve their problems, but eventually they will face again the question of "where to settle."

In recent years the phenomenon of women migrants getting married away from home has attracted a lot of attention. These women do not constitute a large proportion of migrant women, but their total number is significant. The local population in the migrant's destination views young women from the outside as having a significant impact on the local marriage market. In some villages in the Pearl River Delta, local people claim that, among the newly married in recent years, one-third involve one party from outside, mostly women marrying local men. The women who attract the attention of the local men are usually above average and are considered to be "the lucky ones." However, their background as outsiders usually exposes them to discrimination and misunderstandings.

The third category is the marginal type. Some women experience emotional frustration or find it difficult to find an ideal mate, and their youth slips away, leaving them rural spinsters. This category of women appears everywhere, and they are marginalized both spiritually and in terms of their social position. They have a bigger problem than their counterparts from the cities because they cannot return to their home villages, and they do not have stable positions in the cities. This is an unhappy group of wanderers.

The fourth category is the sexually "delinquent" type. Places where migrants gather usually have a greater incidence of sexual problems. The victims in nonmarital sexual relationships are nearly all women. They may become pregnant and have abortions. In many hospitals in areas with high migrant populations, women migrants account for large proportions of abortions. Even without these consequences, nonmarital sexual relationships are the greatest obstacles to future marriages for women in this category. They must try to hide their past or find husbands who understand—and this is very difficult. In summary, the social culture still considers the nonmarital sexual relationship a "shame," and such women have no choice but to bear these unfair pressures on their own.

Clearly, a migrant woman's work, life, and psychological history are closely connected to her life cycle—a situation that does not hold true for migrant men. Regardless of which category a woman falls into, she is always at a disadvantage. Leaving home raises women's economic status, but it does not change the patriarchal structure and patterns of marriage or social life and expectations. Even if men regard the selection of a mate and marriage as important life events, a man's choice of a woman has relatively little impact on his social status and personal development. The higher his status, the more autonomy he has in selecting a mate and in marriage. For women the case is quite different: An increase in a woman's personal status actually shrinks the range of mates available to her, since a man's status usually defines the upper limits for a woman's. If the wife's status and development exceed her husband's, the result may be instability in the marriage. Thus, for women, the issue of marriage is not merely one of emotions and lifestyle, but a fundamental question that determines her prospects for self-development in the future.

RETURNING HOME

The so-called migrant population refers to people who leave their place of residence and temporarily work or live elsewhere. Due to the distribution of China's material and social resources on the basis of region and sector, as "outsiders," migrants do not have the right of permanent legal residence and do not enjoy any welfare benefits in their new destinations. Workers who leave rural villages are all migrants, and during the late 1980s and early 1990s when the migration began to occur on a large scale, migrants were aggressively excluded wherever possible. Later, people came to accept migration as a fact but continued to assume that once rural migrants had earned enough money, they would go home.

After more than ten years, it is clear that these assumptions have not held. According to surveys, the proportion of those returning to their home villages after leaving accounts for only a few of the migrants. Approximately 20 to 30 percent of migrants return to a neighboring city or town. We will refer to both of these as "returnees." What do migrants think about going home?

In our surveys we found three categories of returnees. One were the failures, who returned home after encountering frustrations they could not overcome. Generally speaking, they do not leave again. Another group, usually husbands and wives working together, accumulated some money working in business and then returned home. A third group returns home out of necessity, such as for childbirth, a shortage of labor at home, or a child who needs care. Most of the returnees in the third category are women. Surprisingly, the results of our surveys showed that these women were not willing to stay at home permanently. At least half of them stated firmly that they would leave home again. The reasons they gave included the following: They were no longer accustomed to rural life and its conditions; they found caring for the family very burdensome; and their family still needs money.

Both the government and society at large have already recognized that it is impossible for all rural people who leave home to return. The government is currently preparing to offer household registrations in small cities and towns so that a large number of people can set up residence there. As researchers, we are interested in those who return home to their villages, those who settle in the small cities, and the changes that may take place in their marital relationships and the division of labor in the family. These are questions we will address in the future.

THE RIGHTS AND INTERESTS OF RURAL MIGRANT WOMEN

Rural women who take jobs in factories in their chosen destinations are called "outsiders." In the export-processing enterprises throughout the Pearl River Delta, "outsiders" account for over 70 percent of the total number of workers, and more than 90 percent of them are on assembly lines. In the regions of China where the export-oriented economy is most developed, migrant rural women workers make up the main labor force. They number at least six million.

China's labor laws and the local labor statutes in Guangdong clearly regulate labor contracts, working hours, labor protection, minimum wage, and social insurance, but according to our survey as well as those of other researchers, the rights and interests of migrant women workers are frequently violated. We believe that there are three serious problems. One is occupational safety and health. In July 2000 the State Economic and Trade Commission reported to the State Council on safety in production nationwide, stating that the highest number of accidents occurred in village and township enterprises, in privately operated individual enterprises, and in "three types of export-processing" enterprises, and that most of those killed or injured were agricultural and migrant workers.[4] According to incomplete statistics from the city of Shenzhen, at least twelve thousand industrial accidents occur each year, killing over eighty people.[5]

Occupational diseases are another important negative aspect of the lives and health of migrant workers. A survey by the Ministry of Health showed that varying degrees of occupational hazards existed in over 82 percent of village and township industrial enterprises; nearly 30 percent of workers were engaged in toxic and dangerous occupations, and that more than 10 percent of workers were suspected to be suffering from occupational diseases.[6] Toxic and dangerous occupations exist in 40 percent of the industrial enterprises in Shenzhen, affecting more than half of the workers.[7] In 1994 we conducted surveys of migrant workers in six cities in the Pearl River Delta and found that one-third of the migrant workers believed that the noise, dust, and toxic fumes in the workshops were seriously harmful. As mentioned earlier, labor that exceeds a worker's strength damages the worker's health. Women workers frequently experience fainting and disruptions in their menstrual periods. It is also not unheard of for workers to die suddenly on the job.

Further, there are problems with wages and fees. Our 1994 survey showed that the monthly income for migrant workers was less than half that of local employees; in addition, migrant workers do not enjoy the same benefits beyond the nominal wages as local workers. Also, migrants pay various fees because of their status. For the more than two-thirds of migrant workers living in extreme poverty, these fees can take up to half their wages.[8] In recent years, incomes of local people in the Pearl River Delta have risen tremendously, but there has been no similar increase in the wages of migrant workers. In addition, certain problems appear to be intractable: They include businesses that are slow to pay wages or that are embezzling funds from workers' wages. Since China established an arbitration system for labor disputes, such cases have become most numerous. In addition, local governments and agencies collect fees and penalties under all kinds of pretexts. Migrant workers often say, "It's difficult to find money when one is away from home." Such problems have been exposed by the media and reported on by researchers. In 1996 many locations began to implement a minimum wage system. Recently, the State Planning Commission decided to cancel seven types of fees collected from migrant workers in different locations.[9]

SPECIAL PROBLEMS FACING MIGRANT WOMEN

In addition to occupational hazards. low wages, and uneforced labor regulations, special problems face migrant women that are specific to their gender.

Sexual Harassment

In our surveys we found that sexual harassment of young migrant women could come in the form of physical harassment by a boss or manager. One respondent wrote on her survey, "Women workers who have been targeted by the boss can't get away." This type of harassment based on power is almost the same as that experienced by white-collar women. Most of the harassment, however, is verbal and humiliating, coming from managers and local young men in the workplace. Chinese researcher Tang Can believes that, when analyzing the quality of sexual harassment experienced by migrant women, one must assess the status and position of the victim of the harassment. As "outsiders" and "peasants," migrant women are considered to have the lowest status, and thus they are easy targets for bullying. The harassment directed toward them is savage and destructive.[10]

The Sex Trade

In recent years, with an increasingly mobile population and economic development, the sex trade industries have grown rapidly in mainland China. These industries are found throughout cities and towns on the coast and inland. At the same time, a large number of new sex workers have appeared. Most of these women are migrants from rural villages. This issue has caused tremendous controversy. The official mainstream opinion argues that prostitution, an ugly social phenomenon that corrupts social decency and causes the spread of sexually transmitted diseases, should be strictly prohibited. Some scholars, however, believe that, since prohibiting it would not end its existence, it would be better to legalize it in a limited way in order to control it. Some local government officials believe that the existence of this industry benefits the local investment environment. The common theme in these opinions is their attention to the social effects of the existence of the sex trade. Little attention has been paid to the lives and problems of the "girls"—the women who do the work. Why do they enter so disreputable an occupation? What impact will engaging in this occupation have on their futures?

The research of the renowned Chinese sexual sociologist Professor Pan Suiming presents still another perspective. He has conducted long-term observations and interviews with sex workers engaged in the trade and with their associates, and he has documented that both the girls and their madams (the girls' managers, although there is no relationship of personal dependence between them) are usually migrants. Like their sisters who have left home to find work, these women are also common people—though they face harsh prejudices. Professor Pan has described in detail their working and personal lives, and points out, "They are at the lowest level of our society, the weakest and most hopeless people," and they should at least receive equality and assistance.[11]

As a woman scholar, I agree. However, I also wonder why they become "the lowest level . . . the weakest and most hopeless people." Perhaps we should look at two aspects of the problem: first, the exclusion of these women by the ideology and systems of mainstream culture, mainly when they are working; and, second, the exclusion of these women by male ideology and the male-dominated system of marriage after they leave the profession and want to marry. What kind of gender relationships and structures does this kind of dual exclusion reflect? Since the sex workers understand the consequences of engaging in this kind of work, how do they plan for the future, and how do they cope with the many disadvantages? Currently there are many limitations to conducting this kind of research, and for the time being we can only wonder about such questions.

Educating the Children of Migrants

As rural migrant workers begin to live for longer periods of time in cities, questions about how to deal with their children, especially with regard to education, become more apparent and urgent. As the current Compulsory Education Law states, "The implementation of compulsory education is the responsibility of local government, with management on different levels." Local governments in places where migrants work do not want to assume the fiscal burden of educating the children of migrants. Although some public schools allow the children of migrants to attend, the high tuition is difficult for low-income migrant workers to afford. In this situation, a new market— schools for migrant children—has sprung up. Researchers in Beijing have visited one hundred of these schools, and it is said that there may actually be more than three hundred of them. These schools are illegal and can be forced to disband at any time.[12]

From what we have learned, of the more than two million migrants in Beijing, one hundred thousand are children between the ages of six and fourteen. Except for a small porportion who can attend local schools on a temporary basis, at least twenty thousand of them go to schools for migrant children, and the remaining large numbers of children are usually deprived of an education. Individual surveys have discovered that many children help their parents make a living in Beijing, especially girls. When a reporter interviewed the father of an eleven-year-old girl and asked him why he did not let his daughter go to school, the father's response was, "It's no use for girls to go to school, because when we go back home in the future they're just going to get married." According to sampling surveys of the urban migrant population, there are approximately two million school-age migrant children throughout the country.[13] The problems found in Beijing exist everywhere in the country, and this has become a major issue for researchers and the media.

NOTES

1. Tan Shen, "Nongcun laodongli liudongdi xingbie chayi" (Gender Differences in Rural Labor Migration), *Shehuixue yanjiu* (Sociological Research), Vol. 1, 1997; Ministry of Labor and Social Guarantees, Office of Training and Employment, "Nongcun laodongli liudong jiuye zhuangkuang yu yuce" (The Employment Situation and Forecast for Rural Labor Migration) (Beijing: International Forum on Rural Labor Migration, 2001).

2. Hu Ying, "2000 nian Zhongguo nongcun liudong renkou kin tezheng" (New Features of China's Rural Migrant Population in 2000) (Beijing: China Statistics Information Network, 2001) (www.stats.gov.cn).

3. Project Team, Institute of Sociology, Chinese Academy of Social Sciences, "Study on Rural Women Who Leave Home for Work," *Nongmin liudong yu xingbie* (Peasant Migration and Gender) (Zhengzhou: Zhongyuan nongmin chubanshe, 2000). Most of the material in the paper came from surveys conducted by our project team.

4. Liu Yu, "Anquan shengchan huhuan jianquandi guanli fagui" (Safe Production Calls for Comprehensive Management Statutes), *Fazhi ribao* (Legal Daily), 24 July 2000.

5. Sun Fuhai, "Shenzhen bufen wailai laowugong laodong anquan qingkuang shenyou, qunian shangcan wanyu re, siwang 80 duo ren" (Some Migrant Workers in Shenzhen Fear for Their Safety on the Job; Last Year More Than 10,000 Were Injured or Disabled and over 80 Died), *Gongren ribao* (Workers' Daily), 31 March 1999.

6. Feng Lei et al., "83% xiangzhen qiye cunzai zhiye weihai, quanguo renda chang-weihui jiajin shenyi 'zhiyebing fangzhi fa caoan'" (Occupational Hazards Exist in 83 Percent of Township Enterprises, the Standing Committee of the National People's Congress Will Accelerate Deliberation on the "Draft of the Occupational Disease Prevention and Treatment Law"), *Nanfang dushi bao* (Southern Metropolitan News), 6 September 2001.

7. Sun Fuhai, "Shenzhen."

8. "Zhujiang sanjiaozhou baogao zhiyi" (One Report from the Pearl River Delta), in Project Team, Institute of Sociology, Chinese Academy of Social Sciences, *Nongmin*.

9. "Guojia jiwei he caizhengbu xuanbu quxiao wailai laogong renyuan qi da feiy-ong" (The State Planning Commission and the Ministry of Finance Announce the Cancellation of Seven Major Fees for Migrant Workers), *Renmin ribao* (People's Daily), 15 November 2001.

10. "Xing saorao wenti" (The Problem of Sexual Harassment), in Project Team, Institute of Sociology, Chinese Academy of Social Sciences, *Nongmin*.

11. Pan Suiming, *Shengcun yu tiyan* (Survival and Experience) (Beijing: Zhongguo shehui kexue chubanshe, 2000).

12. Zhang Yongqiang, "Liudong ertong ruxue nan" (The Difficulty of Attending School for Migrant Children), *Fazhi ribao* (Legal Daily), 14 August 2000.

13. Shen Yan, "Yuan 'liudong xuexiao' buzai liudong" (Hoping That "Migrant Schools" Will Not Migrate Again), *Renmin ribao* (People's Daily), 30 August 2000.

Part VI

Women
and
the
Future

HALF THE SKY: A TELEVISION PROGRAM FOR WOMEN

Shou Yuanjun

Ban bian tian (Half the Sky) is China's only television program that champions equality between men and women. It uses the perspective of gender to observe society and analyze people, and reports mainly on women. First aired on 1 December 1994, the program began formal broadcasting on New Year's Day 1995. As one of its founders, I remember clearly the circumstances surrounding its creation.

For more than forty years China Central Television (CCTV) had been producing special programs for children, preteens, adolescents, youth, the elderly, workers, peasants, the military, ethnic minorities, the handicapped, and others, but not for women, fully half of China's massive population. In early March 1994, three female writer-directors discussed airing a television program for women, though they could not predict that their idea would become a reality.[1] The initial motivations for the program arose out of these women's personal feelings about gender. They were also inspired by the countless number of women from all walks of life whom they had met and learned about during the course of their work, but who were of no interest to the media. These women believed that, to correct the unfairness of having no special program about women, CCTV should establish at least one women's program. Thus the process of preparing *Half the Sky* reflected the budding of gender consciousness among female writer-directors for television and broader thinking on the part of decision-makers. The timing—just prior to the United Nations' Fourth World Conference on Women in Beijing in 1995, when women were of increasing interest to media-makers—was perfect to launch this television program for women.

After *Half the Sky* aired nationally, some ten provincial, municipal, and local television stations in China started their own programs for women. Although they had different names and varied in quality and length of time on the air, they all had in common women writer-directors who initiated, developed, and promoted them. In 1995 many female writer-directors expressed great enthusiasm for their work, and it seemed as though in their efforts to bring consciousness to the screen, female writer directors were a force to be reckoned with. But after the Fourth World Conference, the interest in women's programs flagged, and these programs were canceled one after another. Some lasted only a few months, while others struggled on for three or four years. Ultimately the only one that remained was CCTV's *Half the Sky*.

Although the reasons behind the decline of women's programs are complex, analysis of the programs themselves points to one common underlying factor: The producers of the programs were influenced by traditional culture and thus accustomed to viewing women from the perspective of patriarchy. These programs had not fully reflected women as active in many different social roles. As Liang Bing writes,

> The images and value of women were limited to their age and the physical characteristics of their appearance. Their interests were focused on makeup, clothing, and jewelry. Their domain was limited to the home, and their existence to being mothers and wives. Their relationships with men were characterized by obedience, submission, service, and sexual attraction. Their intelligence was confined to the pursuit of fashion, love, and pleasure.[2]

And, as I wrote elsewhere, "These programs were not substantially different from such nonwomen's programs as soap operas, programs on household management, and fashion. This could be said to be their fatal flaw."[3] Clearly, if one asks, "What is women's media?" these programs do not fit the definition.

According to Bu Wei (see "Chinese Women and the Mass Media: Status Quo, Interventions, and Challenges" in this volume), the most important missions and responsibilities of women's media are, "(1) to help women recognize the value of their own independent existence and to empower women; (2) to influence social consciousness and public opinion in order to establish a gender-equal culture; (3) to influence policy-makers, so that they make gender consciousness part of the mainstream and promote gender equality in the society."[4] At the time of *Half the Sky*'s inception, the producers of programs at the provincial, municipal, and local television stations lacked awareness of these issues. Even CCTV's *Half the Sky* went through a process of moving from "superficial knowledge" to "profound knowledge."

The Chinese are accustomed to looking at things from the perspectives of class and politics, but before the 1995 World Conference on Women, even intellectuals had never heard of "gender perspective" or "gender consciousness" and had no idea what these terms meant. The Chinese participants at the 1995 conference went through a large-scale gender training exercise. Because of this, many new ideas, concepts, and perspectives on gender equality gradually came into people's view. For many Chinese, steeped in feudal culture, these ideas were strange and difficult to accept. Some people believed that Chinese women had gained equal status with men long ago and saw no point in talking about sexual discrimination. Others felt that Chinese women had already lost their "femininity" and worried that if discussions on gender equality continued, there would be no distinction between men and women; life would have no more meaning.

Faced with this sociocultural complexity, the newly created women's program *Half the Sky* was at first both naive and immature. On the one hand, it foregrounded images of women who had made contributions in various fields. It made women who on other programs were merely embellishments, accessories, or foils into the main subject of the program. On the other hand, it conveyed a great deal of information related to women but not related to gender consciousness. Concepts from traditional culture created gender blind spots, and the show unwittingly broadcast episodes taking the perspective of male-dominated culture. For example, on 30 June 1995, a report on female prostitution aired under the title "Women, Please Respect Yourselves!" The title announced the program's critical view of women prostitutes; nowhere did it address the social causes that lead women into prostitution, such as poverty, a lack of resources and information, or sexual discrimination in employment, love, or marriage. The program castigated women for "not respecting themselves" and turned a "women's problem" into "problem women." It attributed the lack of equality suffered by women in society to their own poor character and encouraged women to respect and strengthen themselves on their own. The episode took the popular perspective that views everything in terms of male-centered culture and is an example of how women's media unwittingly becomes a vehicle for sexual discrimination.

Following that episode, *Half the Sky* began to grow step by step through the producers' experiences, their views of other programs, and their reflections on their own lives. The producer's consciousness about equality continually increased, until they were able to define the program's mission as "promoting social gender consciousness in keeping with the trends of social development, involving people as subjects in gender roles and gender relationships, removing and overturning outmoded gender patterns that violate the fundamental national principle of male-female equality, and promoting the advancement and development of women."[5]

Thus a female perspective, in addition to gender consciousness, gave *Half the Sky* its special insight. The producer's ability to see the many hidden factors that lie behind a myriad of complex phenomena in society gave *Half the Sky* its uniqueness and character. With competition among television programs intensifying daily, the program not only survived but also became quite popular. According to a survey conducted during the first quarter of 2000 by the

CCTV polling center, of the twenty-two specialty programs in the survey, *Half the Sky* ranked first in popularity, second in quality, and sixth in terms of audience satisfaction. In a 2000 UN report, Secretary-General Kofi Annan said, "The CCTV program *Half the Sky* that airs regularly is extremely influential and specializes in reporting on topics relating to women."[6]

INCREASING THE GENDER CONSCIOUSNESS OF HALF THE SKY

Before *Half the Sky* appeared, most television programs about women were broadcast around the time of International Women's Day on 8 March. They usually showed women celebrating their holiday by holding meetings or receiving bouquets of flowers from children. Most central, provincial, and municipal television stations broadcast cultural extravaganzas celebrating the day. The audience was treated to representative images of outstanding women: selflessly devoted mothers, model women workers, sophisticated women teachers, and women officials. Women gathered together to watch and applaud the performances of women. When one of them faced the camera and talked about contributing her talents to society and to other people, she would usually get teary-eyed and take herself to task before her children, husband, and the older generation for not being a good mother, a good wife, and a good daughter. After *Half the Sky* began to air, this television phenomenon started to change. Creating images of contemporary women, showing their lives, their spirit, their fate, and the special character and charm of contemporary women was a responsibility *Half the Sky* would not shirk. Discovering that women could display their true selves on television was the glory of *Half the Sky*.

In creating new images of contemporary women, *Half the Sky* advocates independent character and autonomy, diversity, and community. Based on these principles, *Half the Sky* presents over three hundred women every year, and it has shifted the focus away from the celebrities the mass media is fond of covering. Instead, *Half the Sky* turns the camera on laid-off female workers, rural women, migrant female workers, young women who have been kidnapped and sold, girls deprived of education, people with AIDS, the disabled, pregnant women, and others, providing the audience with a broad view and communicating human values. Second, it shatters the old pattern of thinking that equates women only with the family.

Many people believe that "woman" equals "mother." In traditional Chinese culture women are seen as tools for procreation. Tradition claims that "of the three unfilial acts, not having descendants is the worst," and this concept persists to the present day. For example, the slogan proposed for the Spring Buds Plan to help impoverished girls go to school was "Today's girls, tomorrow's mothers." Much of the mass media does not take seriously the value of women as independent people with unique personalities, emphasizing only their value as carriers of the next generation. For example, some reports continue to say, "When you educate a boy, you cultivate only one person, but when you educate a girl, it has a bearing on the entire race, because girls are future mothers."[7] Some people say, "Because women can become mothers, a woman's biological function is what makes her significant, and rearing children becomes her profession." The "vocation of motherhood" does not allow a woman the opportunity or possibility of doing other things. As a result, this so-called vocation becomes a method of oppressing women.[8] Actually, the way toward helping impoverished girls lies in their right to an education. It is important that a girl be helped regardless of whether or not she is going to bear children after she grows up.

Interestingly, the family is not among the twelve urgent areas listed in the Platform for Action of the 1995 World Conference on Women. The writers of that document sought to encourage women to participate in social development and to resist the defining of women solely through the family. Furthermore, the Platform for Action points specifically to the importance of the media: "There exist in the media images of women that perpetuate outmoded patterns and demean women. . . . [And yet] the mass media has great potential to promote the equal status of men and women. It can break down outmoded ideas and use varied and balanced ways to portray images of men and women."[9]

In principle *Half the Sky* is not opposed to reporting on mothers, but they are different from the teary-eyed, selflessly devoted mothers who say, "I suffer so that the rest of the family can be happy." They are members of a family and, at the same time, they take on important responsibilities in the community. Our reports advocate equal relationships among members of the family and mutual respect for each member's character. They portray a variety of images, including mothers from intact families, single mothers, and mothers who have adopted children not biologically related to them. They also show respect for a woman's choice not to have children. These women embody the idea that husbands and wives share the responsibility for educating children and that a father's love is just as important as a mother's. They encourage contact between children and fathers after a divorce. The mothers portrayed do not have a pathological love for their children or sacrifice their entire lives for their children. They respect the autonomy of grown children.

From 8–13 October 1998, *Half the Sky* aired a series of episodes titled "A Mother's Concerns," which showed mothers expressing their personal opinions on social issues. For example, writer Chen Danyan used her daughter's experiences crossing the street while going to and from school to discuss how public infrastructure can ensure the safety of children. Lu Qi, an attorney, talked about the problems her daughter encountered in writing compositions and how to respect the innocence of children and their childish language. Poet Wang Xiaoni used her relationship with her son to talk about how to make friends with a child going through puberty.

From 11 to 14 December 1998, another series of episodes aired titled "Inside a Single Parent Household," which attempted to defuse the exaggerated media accounts of single-parent families as miserable, resentful, and helpless. These mothers and their children had passed beyond the shadow of divorce and were now living normal happy lives.

In creating images of women, *Half the Sky* must guard against certain stereotypes: the out-of-touch "strong woman" and the coquettish, spoiled "girlish woman." Around the time of the Cultural Revolution (1966–1976), television, newspapers and periodicals, films, novels, and the arts created a huge number of images of stoutly built, loud-talking, tanned, and ruddy "iron girls." Genderless and devoid of individuality, they were a product of that special era. Although the Cultural Revolution ended long ago, when reporting on accomplished women, media-makers often consciously or unconsciously adhere to this old stereotype. When describing these women in business and public affairs, the media emphasizes that they have sacrificed close feelings with their families, thus setting up an opposition between devotion to one's work and love for one's family. In reality, audiences do not believe in this kind of person, and content producers have no appreciation for them; it's simply a matter of following the well-trodden path.

Running counter to the genderless woman is the "girlish woman," who serves as a marketing device. Packaged by business interests, she is held in high esteem by the mass media and has become the character that greets women from the pages of fashion magazines, magazines on family and marriage, and the lifestyle and housekeeping sections of newspapers. The "girlish woman" is notable for a single-minded emphasis on her femininity. The banner she holds up and the slogan she shouts can be summarized as follows:

> Women must be feminine. This femininity is, above all, beautiful and tender on the outside and good at understanding other people's needs on the inside. In addition, she must be clever, good at putting on makeup, dressing up, shopping, keeping house, complimenting her husband, and taking care of children. If she is over forty she must be sacrificing and patient. If she is under twenty she must be coquettish and show off her cleverness. If she is around thirty she must be mature and sexually charming.[10]

In reality, a woman must also have her own work, her own struggles and aspirations. She must participate in and contribute to the community outside the home. In contrast to the essentially washed-up "strong woman," the stereo-type of the "girlish woman" is more difficult to overcome. She constitutes a type of cultural invasion that is breaking down and consuming the indepen-dent autonomous consciousness of many women. In contrast to other media, in its images of women, *Half the Sky* is wary of depicting this type of weak "girlish woman" who indiscriminately looks to men to protect her.

Another feature of *Half the Sky* is its insistence on using gender conscious-ness to analyze social phenomena. During the past two years, *Half the Sky* has presented discussions on such social phenomena as men going to work while women give up work to stay home; the notion that a woman is long on hair but short on savvy; women who are forced to leave the home merely because they bear a daughter; schools that do not accept ugly girls; the idea that women are for use in bed; domestic violence; the high value placed on women's virginity; the idea that women's level of participation in politics is low because they are not qualified; women who are fired after they get pregnant; the ten major rea-sons dogs are considered better than women; weight loss; breast augmentation; eyelid surgery; and osteotomies (a kind of orthopedic surgery) to increase height. Moreover, the program has expressed its own assessment of these issues. We will discuss three of these episodes.

On 20 February 1999, during Chinese New Year, *Half the Sky* aired an episode titled "Public Restrooms Are Important Places, so Please Pay More Attention to Them." The media frequently airs reports on public restrooms, but most focus on sanitation or on the hard work of environmental sanitation work-ers. This program broke new ground by referring to a survey of twenty-seven public restrooms in the Xidan commercial zone in Beijing that compared the space given to men's and women's restrooms, the number of stalls, and the amount of time men and women spent in the restroom. Reporters then discov-ered from the "Survey and Implementation Report to Revolutionize Public Restrooms in the Capital," prepared by the Beijing Municipal Office of Philosophy and Social Science Planning, that serious gender discrimination existed in the city's public facilities. The size of restrooms and corresponding facilities were all based on the needs of men, and the physiological characteris-tics and special needs of women were not given any attention at all. The pro-gram included interviews with women, who had numerous complaints. They said, for example, that they were afraid to drink water before going out, since at restrooms, they had to wait in long lines, thus damaging their bodies and even leading to incontinence. When women get their menstrual periods, they may experience uncomfortable leakage because they cannot change their sanitary pads in time. There were no dividers between the stalls, so there was no privacy. There were also no handrails, so the elderly, pregnant women, children, and those with joint problems had nothing to hold on to, to support themselves while squatting. There are no hooks for hanging one's belongings, making it difficult to go about the business of elimination. In summary, facilities designed for males cause great physiological inconveniences for women, even leading to fear and anxiety.

The program ended by introducing humane international designs for restrooms and a Chinese woman designer who is using gender consciousness to draw up a design plan for public restrooms. *Half the Sky* intentionally scheduled this program to air during the Chinese New Year holiday so that a larger audience would see it. It had a great impact on the audience, who for the first time discovered that men's and women's experiences and feelings about this commonly overlooked area of life could be so different. It was undoubtedly a kind of gender enlightenment for the audience and city facility designers.[11] For *Half the Sky* it was an excellent example of integrating gender consciousness into the program and set the benchmark for future programs. The creator of the program was a male writer-director, which showed that men as well as women can possess gender consciousness.

After producing "The History of Chinese Women in the Twentieth Century," *Half the Sky* aired a special program during prime time on 8 March 2000 celebrating International Women's Day, titled "Our Century." The concept of this program was entirely different from that of the traditional March 8 extravaganzas. Most impressive was a lively discussion—by a female presenter, a female scholar, a male intellectual, a young woman who had undergone plastic surgery, and several male and female members of the studio audience—about whether or not footbinding and eyelid surgery were conceptually the same thing. In contrast to the mass media, which is saturated with articles and advertisements promoting breast augmentation, nose jobs, eyebrow tattoos, eyelid surgery, osteotomies to increase height, weight loss, and procedures to repair the hymen, *Half the Sky* focused on gender equality and criticized the glorification of "a women who will beautify herself for one who loves her." The program pointed out that promoting such aesthetic standards actually diminishes women's development.

On 12 March 2000, an episode titled "Now That Male Teachers Are in Kindergartens" aired. In February and March 2000 a number of reports appeared in the Beijing media claiming that boys were becoming more timid and that it would be difficult for them to serve as pillars of society. According to the analysis in some articles, the problem lay in the fact that all kindergarten teachers are female. *Half the Sky* sent a reporter to kindergartens to investigate, which led to the production of this episode. The reporter first went to a fairly upscale kindergarten in the Fengtai district of Beijing. The female director of the kindergarten believed that male teachers could make the children tougher and braver, and so the school hired male teachers. The reporter then went to the gymnasium, where a male teacher was teaching martial arts to a group of boys. The reporter asked why there were no girls in the class, and the teacher replied, "Martial arts are suitable for boys, but not for girls." Outside the gymnasium window a group of girls was peering inside. When the reporter asked them why they did not go in to learn martial arts, the answer was, "The teacher won't let us." The reporter asked, "What does the teacher let you do?" Their answer, "Play house or play mommy."

The reporter interviewed two male students who were majoring in the education of young children and about to graduate from the Dongcheng Professional Teachers Center in Beijing. They both asserted that boys and girls should be taught different things. One of them introduced a curriculum he had designed for male students, which included giving the boys hands-on experience with computers, teaching them science and technology, and allowing them to build some things on their own. The other student said that girls are more gentle and quiet and suited to learning embroidery, paper cutting, and so on. At the end of the program a female teacher from a city-run kindergarten in Beijing was interviewed. In her opinion boys and girls are the same, and there should be no distinctions between them in the curriculum. She did not agree that boys would develop a weak character because of female teachers. She said that female teachers were also brave and tough, and she went further to pose the question: If boys are the future pillars of the society, then what are girls?

A third feature of *Half the Sky* is its use of the female perspective to understand men. Traditional roles harm women, but they harm men as well. Therefore, promoting gender equality has become an important component of a development strategy for breaking free of poverty and raising living standards for all people. In 1996 *Half the Sky* proposed to evolve into a program in which both women and men participated. In discussions of social issues, men were not barred from participating, and the women's program was not turned into a place where women monopolized the conversation. As long as their viewpoints were justifiable, both men and women could participate in the program, creating a greater interplay of viewpoints and avoiding a situation in which one side's opinion serves as the conclusion. After 1999, the show established a section called "Investigating Men," which boldly used a female perspective to report on, learn about, and analyze men. This showed the audience that a gender perspective was not only the privilege of women, but was also an asset held in common by both sexes in civilized society. The elimination of gender prejudice requires the concerted efforts of both men and women. Obviously, this feature of *Half the Sky* attracted the attention of many men. After programs about ED (erectile dysfunction), breast cancer in men, and caring for husbands going through the change of life were aired, letters and calls from male members of the audience increased markedly. One man from Heilongjiang wrote in a letter: "I love watching *Half the Sky*. I truly appreciate the way you give a whole picture of everything, making us see that the Earth is round, and that the sky is also round."

THE OPERATIONAL MECHANISM OF HALF THE SKY

Gender is different from the physiological sex people are born with, in that it is acquired, is socially constructed, and can change. In order for the program's producers to possess gender awareness and gender sensitivity to ensure the general direction of the program, *Half the Sky* organized gender training for the entire staff in November 1997, September 1998, and December 2000. At the first session, in November 1997, two female scholars came to *Half the Sky* to present the results of their research using a gender perspective to study images of women in advertising. The study was not well received by the producers and the great majority of writer-directors. The two scholars claimed that images of women in advertisements presented women only in outmoded patterns reflecting male superiority and other stereotypes. In response, some thought these statements unfounded, while others believed that the scholars were simply argumentative, and a lengthy debate ensued.

One year later, three speakers were invited (one of whom was a man) to conduct gender training with the program's writer-directors and producers. This time everyone was very interested in the participatory and interactive style of the training. The tone of discussion was moderate and enthusiastic throughout. One of the female writer-directors recalls, "The first time they just shoved things down our throats, and I couldn't accept it. The second time my gender consciousness began to awaken." Another male writer-director said, "I'm very interested in gender consciousness. I used to live in a small city, and there the men frequently beat their wives. They think it's their god-given right. I also beat my wife. After the gender training, I understood what domestic violence is. Beating your wife is shameful behavior, and I apologized to my wife." Another male writer-director said, "Since the training I have not only been able to use gender consciousness to examine my own shows, but I can also discover the hidden discrimination in other television shows."

Half the Sky holds biweekly meetings chaired by the editor-in-chief to select topics. Producers, hosts, and writer-directors attend. Policy planners—scholars and colleagues in the media who possess gender consciousness and humane ideas—are also invited. Topics that might be produced as an episode within the given time frame are discussed, and the unsuitable ones are discarded. This is an important step in ensuring the direction and quality of the program, and it frequently uncovers some outmoded concepts of which the writer-directors are unaware. For example, in the summer of 2000 an advertisement appeared in

Chengdu showing a drawing of a man underneath a pair of high-heeled shoes. The advertisement caused protests among men in Chengdu, who believed it insulted the image of men. As one writer-director described it, if insulting women is not allowed, then one should not allow the insulting of men, and he proposed to make a show about this topic. After analyzing it, the editor-in-chief wrote the following recommendation: "Please think about why people don't even notice the many advertisements that discriminate against women, but when an advertisement involves men, it stirs up such a controversy in Chengdu." An agreement was then reached to place the incident in the context of the more prevalent social phenomena, the discrimination against women in advertisements. There was to be no discussion on the program of the specific incident in Chengdu, since that would make it appear as though *Half the Sky* supported the complaints of the men, without pointing out the wrong done to women by the advertising industry.

Half the Sky has established close connections with scholars in women's studies and other colleagues who are sensitive to gender. When the program needs to express an opinion about a particular phenomenon, event, or issue (such as men going out to work while women give up work and stay at home or what to do when a friend develops AIDS), it invites scholars and experts with different opinions to appear on air. This not only makes the shows livelier but also allows the results of scholarly research to reach a broader audience, creating a bridge linking scholars, television, and the audience to facilitate exchanges of information. At the same time, scholars with gender consciousness bring more and deeper concepts of gender equality to *Half the Sky*, renewing the program's concern for the advancement and development of women. The viewpoints of other experts have also broadened *Half the Sky*'s perspective.

In early 1999, a new title that was completely unfamiliar to Chinese audiences—gender consultant—suddenly appeared in the credits of *Half the Sky*.[12] The establishment of this position was a first not only for Chinese television but also for other fields. Once again *Half the Sky* pioneered a fundamental policy to promote male-female equality.

In May 1994, when CCTV approved the establishment of *Half the Sky*, it granted the program considerable autonomy. Except for shows on major topics, which had to be submitted to superiors for final approval, the authority for making day-to-day decisions about the program was given to *Half the Sky*. At a time when most media workers did not understand and appreciate gender consciousness, this was very important for *Half the Sky*. For example, in December 1998, a writer-director recorded an interview with a male film and television star. This celebrity made many witty remarks on camera and talked about his three marriages, conveying the idea that, in marriage, women are dependant and subordinate. He championed the outworn idea that "women are like clothes," and that a man can change them at will. The producers decided not to air the episode.

Beginning at the end of 1994, *Half the Sky* established a system of awards for the program. Awards are a way of encouraging outstanding work and also a type of guiding force that reminds those involved in creating the program of its goals. The writer-editor of the episode mentioned previously, "Women, Please Respect Yourselves!" submitted it for prize selection. It received zero votes because it approached its topic—female prostitution—from a male perspective.

The goals of *Half the Sky* would be impossible to reach if the decision-makers for this program that promotes gender consciousness were without it themselves, since all the mechanisms for the program must be acted upon by them. In the past seven years, there have been three producers at *Half the Sky*. The first producer served for two years and established the brand during the difficult initial period. The second producer held the job for five years, creating many high-quality and socially influential episodes. This was the period of maturation for the program. The third producer has not been in the position very long.

Women have dominated the decision-making positions, including the editor-in-chief, producer's assistants, and heads of the creative team. But although gender is important, the key is gender consciousness. Some female decision-makers are not necessarily capable of promoting gender equality in news reporting. The most serious test facing women's media is remaining vigilant to prevent allowing traditional consciousness, commercial culture, and consumerism to permeate women's media. The key to eliminating these influences lies in the determination of decision-makers in women's media to promote gender equality.

NOTES

1. These three female writer-directors were the general producer of CCTV's *Half the Sky*, Sun Suping; CCTV senior editor and artistic director of *Half the Sky* Shou Yuanjun, who became editor-in-chief of *Half the Sky* in October 1996; and CCTV senior editor Wang Xian, who served as the artistic director of *Half the Sky* from October 1995 to May 1997.

2. Liang Bing, "Dui nüxing xuanchuan daoxian di yixie sikao" (Some Thought on Guiding Women's Propaganda), *Zhongguo jizhe* (China Reporter), Vol. 10, 1997.

3. Shou Yuanjun, "Ban bian tian di meili—Xingbie shijiao" (The Charm of *Half the Sky*—Gender Perspective), *Zhongguo funü bao* (Chinese Women's Gazette), 10 August 2000.

4. Bu Wei, *Meijie yu xingbie* (Media and Gender) (Nanjing: Jiangsu renmin chubanshe, 2001), 77.

5. Shou Yuanjun, speech presented at the "Chinese Women's Theoretical Seminar to Commemorate the Fifth Anniversary of the World Conference on Women in Beijing."

6. United Nations, "Review and Appraisal of the Implementation of the Beijing Platform for Action," Document No. E/CN.6/2000/PC/2 (2000).

7. Bu Wei, "Guanzhu meijie xingbie, shi ge weishenma" (Ten Reasons for Being Concerned About Gender in the Media), in Women's Media Monitoring and Testing Network, ed., *Shei shi bawang shei shi ji* (Who's the King and Who's the Concubine) (Beijing: Zhongguo Funü chubanshe, 2001), 256.

8. Shen Rui, "Zhuli Miqieer tantao funü de lingdi" (Julie Mitchell Explores Women's Leadership), *Zhongguo funü bao* (Chinese Women's Gazette), 24 September 2001, 3.

9. Feng Yuan, "Nan nü you bie? Zhudao baozhi zhong di liang xing shijie" (Is There a Difference Between Men and Women? Two Gender Worlds in Leading Newspapers), in *Shei shi bawang shei shi ji?*, 183.

10. Feng Xiaoshuang, "Jiyu *Ban bian tian*" (Letters to *Half the Sky*), in *Ban bian tian '95* (Half the Sky 1995) (Beijing: Zhongguo Funü chubanshe, 1997), 416.

11. The Jinan Environmental Sanitation Bureau in April 2000, the Beijing Environmental Sanitation Bureau in September 2001, and the Guangzhou Environmental Sanitation Bureau in October 2001 announced to the public that, when public restrooms were remodeled, consideration would be given to gender, and the problem of having more toilets for men than for women would be addressed to increase convenience for women.

12. The consultant was Liu Bohong, Research Fellow, Women's Research Institute of the National Women's Alliance.

CHINESE WOMEN AND THE MASS MEDIA: STATUS QUO, INTERVENTIONS, AND CHALLENGES

Bu Wei

Like Chinese men, Chinese women are today seen as an "audience" for mass media. However, I believe that male and female audiences are quite different. Under the influence of traditional feudal culture and commercialization, women are disadvantaged as they attempt to use information for four reasons. First, Chinese women do not have as many opportunities in their daily lives for personal development as men do, and their social status is lower. Although women's media needs differ from those of men, those who control the media and dominate the culture usually ignore the masses of women, particularly those of the lower classes. Second, numerous stereotypes of men and women in the media reinforce the cultural traditions of gender discrimination. Third, women are usually not considered users, sources, or creators of information but, rather, only potential "consumers." Fourth, the media tends to use women's bodies or appearance as "selling points." Since the founding of new China in 1949, although people no longer openly oppose the "equality of the sexes," the phenomena described above unconsciously demean and marginalize women as a group.

Prior to 1995, neither activists nor researchers in media studies, women's studies, or gender studies paid much attention to the issue of the media and gender.[1] Because of the United Nations' Fourth World Conference on Women, held that year in Beijing, not only has the media become a hot topic in the field of gender studies, but gender has gained some attention in the field of media studies. Some women working in the news industry, women's nongovernmental organizations (NGOs), gender researchers, and women activists have realized that the gender inequality in the flow of information creates adverse effects on women's development and social policy. For this reason, they have begun to intervene actively in the flow of information in the media, attempting to create "interactions" with the mass media. In such circumstances women not only are the "audience," passively receiving what is broadcast, but also enter the mainstream media, expressing the independent voices of women.

Women and the Mass Media

This essay discusses the developing relationship between women and the media from 1995 to 2001, the interventions of women, and future challenges.

This paper uses the traditional model of the process of media transmission (see below) to describe the current situation of women and the media:

Creation   Transmission
Initiators → Message → Vehicles → Audience → Effect or influence

According to partial statistics, nearly 200,000 people in mainland China currently work in the news industry, reporting, editing, translating, proofreading, broadcasting, and hosting programs. There are a total of 87,000 news professionals, of which 28,000 or 33 percent are women. In the newspaper industry, women account for 27.5 percent of all reporters and editors. In the radio and television industries, women are 37.3 percent of the workforce, and women make up 29.2 percent of the staff at news agencies. The average age of women working in the news industry is thirty-five, and more than 80 percent have university or professional degrees.[2] At present there are no statistics to show how many women encounter obstacles to entering the news media profession, but during the late 1980s and the 1990s such obstacles were common. An invisible barrier has always blocked women from becoming 50 percent of the media industry workforce.

A 1995 survey of female news workers across the nation showed that women made up 4.4 percent of the personnel at the highest decision-making levels (editor-in-chief, deputy editor-in-chief, chief of staff) and 9.6 percent of midlevel decision-making personnel. If we examine all news-related jobs, the statistics show a remarkable difference. Women hold only 8.5 percent of the positions at the highest decision-making levels and 17.8 percent of midlevel decision-making positions. There are several main reasons for this: First, although equality of the sexes is guaranteed by law, "the tendency to exclude women exists in society's subconscious," a statement affirmed by 84.1 percent of women news workers surveyed. Second, 60.5 percent of women news workers believe that "There are few women in some departments, and selecting and promoting women is difficult." Third is the issue of women's self-consciousness, which means that women are unwilling to take the decision-making positions. Of the women news workers surveyed, 54.2 percent maintained, "Women like to do professional work"; "They are not willing to lead." In addition, 41.7 percent of women news workers believe that "Women have a stronger sense of responsibility for the family and are afraid that taking on leadership roles will affect their family lives."[3] Social culture exerts an invisible pressure on women when it comes to assuming leadership.

In the news organizations where they work, women journalists are mainly engaged in reporting on economic, social, cultural, and educational issues. In comparison to male reporters, fewer women report on economics, politics, and sports, and the contrast is dramatic.[4] Obviously, in news organizations, male reporters tend to report the "hard news," while female reporters focus on the "soft news." Another study conducted by the media monitoring and testing network provided new evidence for this. The researchers gathered statistics on signed news items that appeared in China's eight largest mainstream newspapers during 1996 and discovered that of the 18,619 signed news items, excluding those where the sex of the author was unclear, approximately 80 percent of the news items on politics, economics, science and technology, international affairs, and other important areas of reporting had male bylines. On the signed news items relating to women, as much as 67.6 percent of the bylines were male.[5]

The 1995 nationwide survey of women news workers showed that, in the area of gender equality, most were satisfied that their opportunities were equal to those of men in the areas of promotion and salaries, the selection of outstanding news pieces and programs and the awards given for them, the selection of outstanding news workers, the distribution of assignments, access to healthcare benefits, and child care. However, more than 25 percent of women news workers believed that in the following important areas they did not have equal opportunities with men: advanced training (26.7 percent), trips abroad (48.9 percent), housing allocations (38.4 percent), reporting assignments in other locations (35.2 percent), and decision-making postitions (46.0 percent).[6]

Discussions of the relative proportion of men to women in the media imply a set of assumptions, one of which is that increasing the number of women in the profession, especially the number of women at decision-making levels, will raise the status of women in the media. If women have a higher status, they can assume conscious leadership, and this will improve reporting on women and promote gender equality through the media. However, for at least two reasons, sometimes having equal status may not mean having an equal effect. First, whether or not an "effect" is achieved is determined not merely by the proportion of women but by whether women news workers and women decision-makers possess gender awareness. To a certain extent, gender consciousness determines these women's concern for and sensitivity to women's issues and further determines how much and in what way they will report on women's issues. Currently, there are no specific data that can measure the gender consciousness of women in the news media. Although Chinese women—since the founding of new China—have enjoyed the right to work, autonomy in marriage, and other rights, unlike Western women, they did not struggle to gain these rights. For this reason alone, women news workers may lack gender sensitivity. But since the 1995 Fourth World Conference on Women, we have seen a marked change in the gender consciousness of some female and male news workers.

Second, and more important, the guiding policies and operational mechanisms developed by the media determine whether an "effect" is achieved. Women reporters or women decision-makers working under mechanisms that do not promote women's development may have gender consciousness, but the time and space they have to express independent voices are limited. Thus, unless efforts are made in other areas, simply increasing the number of women will not necessarily achieve the effects of improving reporting on women and promoting gender equality.

THE CONTENT OF MEDIA TRANSMISSIONS

What content does the mass media transmit that either benefits or detracts from women's development? This chapter cannot conduct a systematic content analysis of China's three hundred–plus television stations, three hundred–plus radio stations, two thousand–plus newspapers, and eight thousand–plus magazines, as well as audio and video products. However, based on more than one hundred reports of content analysis and critiques of the media, and the analyses done for a seminar held on the fifth anniversary of the 1995 World Conference on Women, 13 May 2000, which was cosponsored by the Chinese Women's Research Council and the United Nations gender task force, we can make a preliminary assessment.[7] Since 1995, as a result of the concerted efforts by the news media and women's groups, mass media reporting has made progress in the following areas:

1. Reflecting the accomplishments and contributions made by Chinese women in their participation in social development, showcasing the developmental milestones achieved by women in the process of reform and opening to the outside, as well as demonstrating women's creativity and initiative, and their promotion of the national policy of equality of the sexes.
2. Exploring the problems encountered by women during this period of social transformation, such as the issues of re-employment for laid-off women workers and young migrant women.
3. Protecting the basic rights and interests of women in accordance with the law.
4. Meeting a variety of women's needs by providing knowledge, information, and entertainment to women.

However, in other respects, obstacles to gender equality in mass media transmissions still exist. There are several aspects of this problem. The media does not fully report on women and the women's movement and issues.

Women's news has difficulty making it into mainstream news. The mainstream media's reporting rarely covers news items of significance such as women's poverty, women's health, women's employment, mechanisms for gender equality, domestic violence, and violence against women in ethnic conflicts. The media lacks the sensitivity it should have toward this type of news.

Second, the mass media continues to reproduce many stereotypical images of male and female roles, including generalizations about "the female personality" or character and women's abilities. Some television advertisements, women's magazines, popular songs, films, and literary works reinforce the traditional view that "women are the subordinate sex." Third, the commercial culture and consumerism of the mass media, including women's publications and some websites for women, mislead women into blindly striving for thin bodies, "makeovers," and molding themselves into something that pleases successful men. Some of the media continues to display negative or humiliating images of women.

MEDIA FOR WOMEN

Of the thirty-two central, provincial, and municipal television stations, only seven, or 22 percent, had established programs specifically for women as of October 1998. These programs include China Central Television's (CCTV) *Ban bian tian* (Half the Sky; see the chapter by Shou Yuanjin in this volume), Beijing Television's *Jinri nüxing* (Today's Women), Fujian Television's *Nüren shijian* (Women's Time), Guangdong Television's *Nüxing xin shijiao* (New Women's Perspective), Shandong Television's *Nüxing huati* (Women's Topics), Hunan Television's *Shengyu shenghuo* (Childbearing Life), and Liaoning Television's *Nüxing shijie* (Women's World). The remaining 78 percent of television stations had no programming especially for women.[8] The program *Jinri nongcun* (Today's Rural Village) on CCTV's Channel 7 includes segments on "rural women," but because Channel 7 has low viewership, the influence of this program is small. Altogether, the seven stations provide 470 minutes, or approximately 8 hours, of women's programming every week. According to a 1995 survey conducted by the CCTV consultation center, the number one prime time slot for female viewers is 7:00–8:00 PM (nearly 50 percent of the female audience). The second prime time slot is 8:00–9:00 PM (approximately 28 percent of the female audience), and the third most popular time slot is 5:00–7:00 PM (more than 9 percent of the female audience). A 1998 survey revealed, however, that very few women's programs air during these prime viewing times.[9]

A small number of women's media outlets exist for Chinese women. According to statistics, in 1996 there were forty-two women's magazines in

China.[10] Among these, the ones with the largest circulation are *Zhiyin* (Bosom Friends), published by the Hubei Women's Federation, whose circulation grew from 1.28 million copies in 1996 to 4.269 million copies in 2000; *Nüyou* (Women's Friend), from the Shaanxi Women's Federation, whose circulation grew from 850,000 copies in 1996 to 466,000 copies in 2000; *Funü shenghuo* (Women's Lives), from the Henan Women's Federation, whose circulation grew from 580,000 copies in 1996 to 560,000 copies in 2000; and *Zhongguo funü* (Chinese Women), from the All-China Women's Federation, whose circulation was 340,000 copies in 1996.[11] Statistics from the National News Publishing Headquarters from 1996 show that there were a total of three women's newspapers at the national, provincial, autonomous region, and municipality levels.[12] In 2000 there were four such newspapers, *Zhongguo funü bao* (China Women's News), *Shanxi funü bao* (Shanxi Women's Gazette), *Funü zhi sheng bao* (Women's Voice Gazette), and *Jinri nü bao* (Today's Woman Gazette), with an average of 507,300 copies per issue. The circulation of these newspapers accounts for less than 1 percent of the average circulation of 55.41 million copies per issue published by China's 322 newspapers.[13] Women's newspapers do not enjoy as large a market share as women's magazines.

Due to the influence of the Fourth World Conference on Women in 1995, some media, represented by CCTV's *Ban bian tian* (Half the Sky), and the *Zhongguo funü bao* (Chinese Women's News) published by the All-China Women's Federation, improved the situation of news reporting in China in the areas of promoting gender equality and protecting women's rights. These media played an important role in opposing gender discrimination in all fields and promoting equality of the sexes in society.

In order to meet the development needs of the masses of rural women, in 1992 *Zhongguo funü bao* created a pocket-sized publication called *Nongjiafu baishitong* (The Rural Woman's Guide to Everything). This was the only magazine in China targeted to rural women. More than 60 percent of the articles in the guide came from rural women. The magazine also developed a series of small projects to promote and influence the progress and development of China's rural women, such as literacy classes, microloans, a "working women's house" in Beijing, and training schools where rural women could learn practical skills. There are at least 400 million rural women in China, and the *Rural Woman's Guide* has empowered these women, allowing them to enjoy the right to information.

WOMEN AS AN AUDIENCE

Television reaches 90 percent of China's population of 1.2 billion. If everyone in the areas where television is available watches television, China's female television audience is around 600 million people. Little is known about the viewing interests and behavior of this audience, and only one national survey has been conducted to analyze the female audience. Influenced by the Fourth World Conference on Women in 1995, CCTV used the national television ratings network to conduct a large-scale survey of the female audience (N = 9,294, weighted). The survey discovered that Chinese women watch an average of 2.6 hours of television per day and that 87.4 percent of women watch television between 5:00 and 9:00 PM.[14] This means that approximately four million Chinese women watch television in the evening. The survey also showed that, as with male audiences, the favorite programs among women are *Zongyi daguan*, a combination travelogue/game show; *Xinwen lianbo*, joint news broadcasts; *Jiaodian fangtan*, focus interviews and discussions; *Zhengda zongyi*, another combination travelogue/game show; and *Quyuan zatan*, talk about Chinese folk arts. The difference between the male and female audiences is that women rank *Zongyi daguan* (the travelogue/gameshow) first, while men rank *Xinwen lianbo* (the joint news broadcast) first. According to the survey, 68.4 percent of women know about the program *Ban bian tian* (Half the Sky), and 21.8 percent of women watch it regularly.[15]

Research institutions and the news media have conducted hundreds of audience surveys since 1982, and every survey includes the female audience. However, as Song Xiaowei, deputy researcher at the Institute of Journalism and Communication of the China Academy of Social Sciences points out:

> In the questionnaires and forms created by those conducting the surveys, the first item in the survey is usually the sex of the respondent. This is probably because sex is one of the most natural and basic population features. In marked contrast to this, the reports that are later prepared about these surveys pay little attention to analyzing the gender characteristics and differences in audience psychology and behavior. Surveys and studies that specifically target audience gender characteristics are very rare.[16]

Between 1990 and 2000 the "audience survey" column of *Zhongguo guangbodianshi nianjian* (Yearbook of Chinese Radio and Television) published ninety-one survey reports. From 1990 to 1996 these were surveys of television audiences; reports from 1997 to 1999 included surveys of television and radio audiences. Very few of these surveys, however, mention gender differences in access to media or interest. None of the reports conducted gender analyses (see Table 1). The "mention" of gender in the survey reports is limited to simple statements such as, "housewives hope to learn cooking from television," but there are no specific analyses about gender or from a gendered perspective. The "mention" of gender typically refers to the "gender composition" of the viewing or listening audience, or to the differences between what men and women prefer to watch or listen to. For example, the "Chongqing Cable Television Audience Survey Report" explains that, in watching television programs, men prefer current events programs, while women prefer soap operas and entertainment programs.[17]

Table 1
GENDER IN SURVEY REPORTS ABOUT CHINESE RADIO AND TELEVISION

Year	No. of published surveys	Mention of gender differences	Gender analysis	Data source
1990	4	1	0	*1991 Zhongguo guangbo dianshi nianjian* (Yearbook of Chinese Radio and Television; hereafter *YCRT*)
1991	4	0	0	*1992–1993 YCRT*
1992	10	0	0	*1992–1993 YCRT*
1993	4	0	0	*1994 YCRT*
1994	4	1	0	*1995 YCRT*
1995	4	0	0	*1996 YCRT*
1996	6	2	0	*1997 YCRT*
1997	20	4	0	*1998 YCRT*
1998	16	1	0	*1999 YCRT*
1999	19	4	0	*2000 YCRT*

Survey reports that do mention gender differences show that, in comparison to men, women are at a disadvantage in terms of receiving information. The 1997 "Central People's Broadcasting Station Audience Survey Report" points out: "The proportion of loyal listeners is higher among the urban population than the rural population, higher among men than women, higher among the elderly than among young people, higher among people with higher levels of education than among those with lower levels of education, and higher among people with higher incomes than among those with lower incomes."[18] The "China Central Television Program Ratings Annual Report" from the same year also indicates that the audience for CCTV–1 news programs includes a higher proportion of male and urban viewers.[19] The 1997 "Henan Television Audience Sampling Survey Analysis Report" is the only report to provide a cross-analysis of gender differences and differences between urban and rural areas, showing that the researchers took seriously the issue of access to the media by weaker groups. This report states that over 90 percent of those who answered that they "never" or "rarely" have access to television were rural peasants. (Of course, economic development in rural villages lags behind that in cities.) In addition to working outside the home, women must also bear the burden of housework and looking after children, and thus the frequency with which they have access to television, radio, and newspapers is lower than that of men. In the male audience, 31.7 percent report that they watch television nearly every day, while for the female audience the rate is only 20.6 percent, eleven percentage points lower. The authors point out that a considerable portion of the male audience watches television news at a certain time each day. With regard to the lower newspaper readership among women (see Table 2), the authors attribute this to a lower level of female education. According to 1990 data from the National Bureau of Statistics, the rate of illiteracy among urban women in Henan province was 18 percent, while for men it was 6 percent. Illiteracy rates for rural dwellers were 35 percent and 16 percent for women and men respectively.[20]

Table 2
GENDER DIFFERENCES WITH RESPECT TO HOW OFTEN THE HENAN TELEVISION AUDIENCE READS THE NEWSPAPER

Gender	Never	Rarely	Sometimes	Often	Almost every day
Male	6.3%	32.7%	35.2%	19.5%	4.5%
Female	14.6%	32.3%	25.7%	10.4%	2.3%

In summary, the data above indicate that men have more access to information than women do. Moreover, the type of information favored by men (such as news) helps them to improve their social awareness. Since those researching Chinese audiences lack gender consciousness, they generally ignore the issue of gender in their research, and the needs of a female audience are thus lost in a sea of statistical data. Another important issue is rural women's limited access to media, information, and knowledge. To date there have been no studies on rural women's use of the media (including traditional media and mass media). We have no studies about how much of China's media is targeted to rural women, the types of media needed by rural women, how much of the information in the media satisfies the needs of rural women, and how much space the media provides for rural women to express themselves. When we speak of female audiences, we are usually referring to urban women. Surveys of rural populations rarely distinguish between the sexes, and, as a result, the needs of rural women with regard to the media are largely ignored. This gap in the field of study not only indicates the existence of a gender blind spot in media studies, but also makes manifest the cultural dominance of urban life.

INTERVENTION—WOMEN'S NGOS AND THE MEDIA

A small number of outlets, such as the newspaper *Zhongguo funü bao* (China Women's News) and the CCTV program *Ban bian tian* (Half the Sky) deserve applause for protecting the rights of women and promoting gender equality by transmitting women's voices. But they do not control the rest of the media, its content, and its audience. The current situation in China is summarized below in a table of those who intervene in several forms to promote gender consciousness (see Table 3).

Table 3
OVERVIEW OF INTERVENTION

Intervening institution	Content of intervention	Method or strategy of intervention
All-China Women's Federation	Monitor and encourage creators, promote fair reporting of both genders	Conferences/study sessions/seminars
Capital Association of Women Reporters	1. Monitor and encourage creators to pay attention to women	Study session/classes
	2. Ask the media to invite women to create programming for March 8	Write proposals
	3. Host discussion classes for rural women and women reporters	Seminars, discussions, etc.
Women's Media Monitoring and Testing Network	1. Monitor and test media content	Establish newspaper columns to comment on issues in the news
	2. Develop research on media and gender	Open discussion in the media of important news events
		Establish monitoring and testing hotlines
		Develop training about gender Negotiate with media on the creation of gender equal programming, etc.
Gender researchers/ Women activists	1. Unequal gender treatment in the media, etc.	Write articles or speeches

In 1994 the Women's Research Institute of the All-China Women's Federation organized researchers from local women's federations, scientific research institutions, and the media to develop studies of images of women in the media. They discussed the issue of gender in the media and how to implement intervention by publicizing the results of research in the media. On 13 May 2000, the Chinese Women's Research Council held a media forum during a seminar marking the fifth anniversary of the 1995 World Conference on Women. The media forum recommended that the All-China Women's Federation invite editors-in-chief from the major central media to study further implementation of the measures in the Program of Action and to inform the editors-in-chief of important information from the UN's "Beijing Plus Five" conference. The All-China Women's Federation implemented this recommendation. *Guangming ribao* (Guangming Daily) and other media invited experts to write articles on the topic. The All-China Women's Federation has been active in promoting equal gender reporting in the media.

The Capital Association of Women Reporters, founded in 1986, is a non-governmental organization (NGO). The association organized a media forum during the 1995 Fourth World Conference on Women and, in May 1998, conducted follow-up activities on the program of action by convening the seminar "Challenges, Opportunities, Developments—Chinese Women Reporters and the Twenty-First Century." The seminar addressed the current status of the media and gender and invited representatives from the Propaganda Department and other leading departments in charge of the media to listen to the opinions of women reporters in order to raise the status of women within and outside the media. On 24 February 2000, the Capital Association of Women Reporters presented a proposal to news organizations in the capital based on the idea of "giving women news workers a gift for International Women's Day—the right to decide media content," responding to the UNESCO proposal for 8 March as a day on which "women create the news." The association stated: "It is our hope that, based on the situation within each news organization, leaders in the media will allow qualified women news workers the right to edit an entire issue, page or column, or to serve as editor-in-chief for the day. This would allow women news workers the right from various positions of leadership to provide women with news coverage of International Women's Day." Many newspapers responded to this proposal, including *Renmin ribao* (People's Daily), *Nongmin ribao* (Peasants Daily), and *Zhongguo qingnian bao* (China Youth Daily). The Capital Association of Women Reporters also discovered that Chinese peasant women account for more than half the agricultural labor force, yet they are an "unseen group" in the media. In order to improve media reporting on this group, the association held a seminar titled "Gender, Media, and Development—Peasant Women and Women Reporters," held 16–19 March 2001. Through communication and exchanges, this seminar raised awareness of media participation by rural women and also raised the level of concern for rural women's development on the part of reporters.

The Women's Media Monitoring and Testing Network was established on 25 March 1996 as a subunit of the Capital Association of Women Reporters. The network's members come primarily from research institutions and the media, including *Zhongguo funü bao* (Chinese Women's Gazette). This network encourages the media to portray diverse images of women in a balanced manner; to monitor and resist mass media reports that demean women, deny their independence, or strengthen stereotypical images; to negotiate with the media to ensure that women's needs and issues of concern are appropriately reflected; and to advance a supportive climate of public opinion for advancing equality of the sexes. The network's main activities have included participation in a number of international and domestic monitoring activities over the past five years, such as monitoring television programs for women in the Asia-Pacific region in 1998, global audiovisual media news in 2000, news reporting in eight leading media organizations, and images of women in television advertising. In addition, by using columns such as "Funü luntan" (Women's Forum), "Nüxing yu shehui" (Women and Society), and others, which appear in *Zhongguo funü bao*, the network has created a platform for publicizing important ideas and organizing discussions on such critical topics as the issue of women's chastity. In 2001, the China Women's Press published *Who's the King and Who's the Concubine?*, a collection of essays that challenges the traditional view, strengthened by the media, that women are "the subordinate sex." The network also sponsors training for the media on gender consciousness by helping television stations to produce gender equal programs, working with a number of media outlets to discuss images of women in the media, and promoting the idea that the mass media should present balanced reflections of women's images and resist outmoded stereotypes of women's roles. Lastly, the network develops research about the media and gender.

Obviously, the main force behind intervening in the media comes from grassroots NGOs. The All-China Women's Federation is a special NGO because of its close connection to several state agencies. The federation has played an important role in encouraging the media to implement gender equality in reporting and to promote women news workers to leadership positions. The Women's Media Monitoring and Testing Network is an NGO with no government ties and concentrates on monitoring media content. Its main weapon is the theory of gender. In China, this grass-roots monitoring network is only five years old, so further exploration is needed to determine the strategies for and strengths of grass-roots organizations. Through its activities, however, the monitoring network has already encouraged the media to reflect on the issue of gender in reporting and has promoted the popularization of gender equality among media personnel and the public. Women's NGOs, gender researchers, and women activists might have started out as mere audiences, but with these acts of intervention they are actively disseminating news and serving as sources of information.

FUTURE CHALLENGES

When discussing the issue of the media and gender, we often overlook pre-existing assumptions about the topic, the first being that society can provide adequate information and support changes in attitudes. The second assumption is that all groups in society have equal opportunities to receive information broadcasts. The third is that the people who decide which information (or relevant policies) is broadcast represent the interests of all people. Actually, society cannot provide adequate information or support changes in attitudes (an example is the difficulties rural women encounter obtaining information concerning reproductive health); different social groups do not have equal opportunities to receive information broadcasts (for example, radio and television in China reach approximately 90 percent of the population, but nearly 100 million people do not have access to television; print media resources available to rural women are extremely scarce, etc.); and the people making the decisions about information broadcasts usually represent the interests of the dominant social group or the cultural elite (for example, television, the most widely marketed media, focuses on cities). For these reasons, we pose the following challenges:

1. Current broadcasting regulations and policies lack gender consciousness, and the media lacks self-discipline and standards for reporting. These factors prevent the media from offering an accurate portrayal of women and discussing women's issues from a perspective of gender equality. The government should be urged to enact broadcasting policies that possess gender consciousness and to make gender consciousness a part of mainstream policy-making. Media policy-makers at all levels should take reporting on women's issues seriously and should set down editorial principles that advocate equality of the sexes.

2. In news organizations, the editorial board has the decision-making authority over the broadcast content. In order to implement gender equity in our nation's news industry, more women should be encouraged to join editorial boards. Specialized training courses in news broadcasting for women should be held with the help of institutions of higher education, professional organizations, and other institutions.

3. The government and relevant departments should be encouraged to enact policies that develop women's media, particularly media targeted at rural women, and should encourage the media to develop special columns and pages devoted to rural women, while monitoring their progress. When planning its reporting, the media should pay attention to meeting the needs of women at all levels of society. The media should encourage participation by women of all social levels, especially rural women, and should include the voices of women from the lower classes.

4. The media should be monitored and encouraged to eliminate gender bias

and stereotypical images in its content, and to portray diverse images of women in a balanced manner.

5. A larger and more efficient media monitoring network should be established. First, nongovernmental media monitoring activities are uniquely independent, and therefore media monitoring networks must maintain their NGO character. Second, the existing network should be used as a base to expand network-monitoring activities, including the establishment of routine monitoring teams in different locations, regular announcements, and the enlisting of support from male news professionals. Working together with the government, the network can inform the media of the monitoring situation by organizing contacts through the All-China Women's Federation and the Chinese Women's Research Council.

6. The propagation of large numbers of stereotypes and gender bias in the mass media are related to the fact that media creators generally lack gender consciousness. Women's organizations must promote gender consciousness among decision-makers in the media. Training courses and lectures should include a component on gender consciousness. All planning of education and training related to news broadcasting must include the establishment of curriculum related to gender, and gender consciousness training must gradually be developed into a system. The target of gender consciousness training should not be limited to news professionals but should also include all professionals in mass media, including those in advertising, television, theatre, and film.

7. Women should be viewed as active participants in the news process and not merely the recipients of media broadcasts. For this reason, appropriate training and discussions should be organized to encourage women as individuals, as well as women's organizations and women's NGOs, to participate in media decision-making and media broadcasts, utilizing the mass media to broadcast the voices of women. At the same time, another challenge facing us in the twenty-first century is how to utilize new communications technology to strengthen women in expressing their opinions and participating in the decision-making process. This challenge also presents an opportunity.

NOTES

1. Bu Wei, *Meijie yu xingbie* (The Media and Gender) (Jiangsu: Jiangsu renmin chubanshe, 2001), 70.

2. Task Force on the Current Situation and Development of Chinese Women News Workers, "Zhongguo nüxinwengongzuozhe xianzhuang yu fazhan diaocha baogao" (Survey Report on the Current Situation and Development of Chinese Women News Workers), *Xinwen yu chuanbo yanjiu* (News and Broadcasting Research), Vol. 2, 1995, 1–6.

3. Ibid., 5.

4. Ibid., 3.

5. Feng Yuan, "Nan nü you bie? Zhudao baozhi zhong di liang xing shijie" (Is There a Difference Between Men and Women? Two Gender Worlds in Leading Newspapers), in Women's Media Monitoring and Testing Network, ed., *Shei shi bawang shei shi ji* (Who's the King and Who's the Concubine) (Beijing: Zhongguo Funü chubanshe, 2001), 191–195.

6. Task Force, "Zhongguo," 4–5.

7. See Bu Wei, *Meijie*; Women's Media Monitoring, *Shei*; Chinese Academy of Social Sciences, Institute of News and Broadcasting, "Xinwen yu chuanbo yanjiu" (News and Broadcasting Research); and All-China Women's Federation, *Funü yanjiu luncong* (Collected Essays on Women's Studies), for reports on the media and gender.

8. For survey samples and methods, see Bu Wei, "Zhongguo dianshi funü jiemu yanjiu" (Research on Chinese Television Programs for Women), in *Meijie*, 169–170.

9. Ibid.

10. No data for this have been formally announced by the government. Statistics here are based on studies by the All-China Women's Federation.

11. *Zhongguo chuban nianjian* (Yearbook of Chinese Publishing), 1996; data for 2000 comes from News Publishing Headquarters Office of Planning and Finance, *Zhongguo xinwen chuban tongji ziliaohui* (Statistical Data for Chinese News Publishing) (Beijing: Zhongguo laodong shehui baozhang chubanshe, 2001), 182, 183, 186, 187.

12. *Zhongguo chuban nianjian*, 1996.

13. News Publishing Headquarters, *Zhongguo*, based on data appearing on pp. 178, 182, 183, 186, and 187. The 322 newspapers include only newspapers of the central, the provincial and the municipal levels. The Headquarters has their circulation data.

14. Zhang Lingzhen, "Zhongguo funü wenti diaocha baogao" (Survey Report on Chinese Women's Issues), in Hu Yungfang, ed., *1995 Zhongguo funü wenti diacha baogao yu lunwen xuanji* (Collected Reports and Theses on Chinese Women's Issues, 1995) (Beijing: Zhongguo shehui chubanshe, 1995).

15. Hu, *1995 Zhongguo*, 29–33.

16. Song Xiaowei, "Tantan woguo shouzhong meijie jiechu yu shiyongzhong di xingbie chayi" (Discussing Gender Differences in the Way Chinese Audiences Access and Use Media), *Xinwen yu chuanbo yanjiu* (News and Broadcasting Research), Vol. 2, 1995, 36.

17. "Chongqing youxian dianshi guanzong wenzhuan diaocha baogao" (Chongqing Cable Television Audience Questionnaire Survey Report), in *Zhongguo guangbo dianshi nianjian 2000* (2000 Yearbook of Chinese Radio and Television), 253.

18. "Zhongyang renmin guangbo diantai tingzhong diaocha baogao" (Central People's Broadcasting Station Audience Survey Report), in *Zhongguo guangbo dianshi nianjian 1998* (1998 Yearbook of Chinese Radio and Television), 298.

19. "Zhongyang dianshitai jiemu shousilü niandu baogao" (China Central Television Program Ratings Annual Report), in *Zhongguo guangbo dianshi nianjian 1998* (Yearbook of Chinese Radio and Television), 301.

20. "Henan dianshi guanzhong chouyangdiaocha fenxibaogao" (Henan Television Audience Sampling Survey Analysis Report), in *Zhongguo guangbo dianshi nianjian 1998* (1998 Yearbook of Chinese Radio and Television), 317.

CLASS AND GENDER IN CONTEMPORARY CHINESE WOMEN'S LITERATURE

Dai Jinhua

During the 1990s in China, as the processes of social transformation and advancing globalization moved ahead, a process of dramatic class division also began to take form. In this process, women were unconsciously chosen as the social group that would bear the major sacrifices. Since the 1990s, as social issues and cultural statements, the tightly interwoven rewriting and restructuring of class and gender have become topics that conceal and suppress each other. Discussions of gender seemingly imply a social stance that supersedes other social issues (especially class) and thus cannot directly address hardships experienced by women, particularly women in the lower strata of society in the process of social transformation. Especially when a certain "imported" view of gender resistance has found a valid corresponding Chinese view, a certain type of women's survival and resistance then becomes the entirety of women's issues. Expressions by women of feminism unexpectedly become a kind of cover for the social survival of women.

For example, during the 1990s, a specific type of women's writing and a kind of literary criticism about this type of women's writing became a recognizable feature in the cultural landscape. The praise or defense of the "I–my self–my monster–my body" style of contentious women's writing may have covered up the far more complex and sad reality of what happened to women and women's bodies in China during that period.[1] When we argue the case for "women's writing about their bodies"—expressions of the physical experiences of women, their desires and sexual experiences—do we at the same time address the women workers who suffered in the fire at the Zhili toy factory in Shenzhen in 1993?[2] In that incident women workers burned to death locked behind metal doors. The charred remains of those who perished and the survivors, some of whom were permanently disabled, were shipped back home with only paltry compensation.[3]

We become indignant over the rage and sniping incurred from the male-dominated society by certain kinds of self-revealing expressions about women's bodies, but how do we handle the other facets of women's culture and social outlooks? For example, how do we react to the ads for breast enhancement cream plastered everywhere that read "being a full-figured woman is great" or "you can't let a man get it all in one handful"? What do we make of the reports of "antiprostitution" campaigns that slyly reveal the physical experiences of working girls who provide seminude or nude sexual services?

Against a backdrop of feminist critical logic that views the world in terms of active/passive, observer/observed, how do we deal with the male-dominated capitalist logic that has been crowned supreme by official position and money? Can capitalist logic be effectively interpreted and critiqued only through the issue of class? Closely associated with the "my body, my self" expressions is another aspect revealed in women's writing, which is the use of one's own body (especially the "virginal body") as one's only "capital" in order to "strike it rich in the flourishing special economic zones." This undoubtedly displays a kind of logic in which the woman is the actor—an idea that the logic of male-dominated culture refuses to address. But does the discovery of this actor imply the end and conclusion of this issue?

Such cultural discussions of reality actually occur on two different but related levels. First, however complex and multifaceted, one discussion is still the effective construction of a new mainstream ideology and mass culture built from the top down, in which gender becomes a "minority" or "secondary issue," used consciously or unconsciously to shift focus away from increasingly sharp class distinctions. If it becomes too apparent that, in the course of social transformation, social crises have been dumped on women as a group, and if these social problems can no longer be avoided, mainstream ideology and mass culture transform the discussion into one of specific social gender roles and the division of labor between the sexes. It is abundantly clear that not only do the "unemployment shock waves" in society underscore the problem of laid-off women workers, but the discussion of laid-off women workers then becomes one about miraculous "re-employment stars" and "female entrepreneurs."

More interesting still is the issue of laid-off women workers who have been deprived of their right to work, which has been quietly reformulated into arguments for "full-time wives" and "professional mothers." Stories about these fortunate full-time wives are always about "white-collar beauties" or suburban housewives. One exception is a popularized advertisement for laundry detergent, which has the unusual feature of a young girl's voice narrating off screen. The girl says, "Recently Mom is always unhappy." The scene shows a gloomy young woman trudging along, staring in exhaustion at employment ads posted on a wall. When she returns home, she finds a pile of neatly folded, clean laundry on the sofa and her daughter sound asleep next to it. The mother tearfully embraces her daughter. The ad then promotes a brand of detergent. Although this is the first time that the image and problem of laid-off women workers have appeared in a commercial advertisement, it undoubtedly hints at the widespread nature and depth of this problem. More important, the ad suffuses images of the home, mother, and daughter with a "middle-class" flavor. Thus, the culture of advertising removes the focus from issues of survival, poverty, and class that accompany this problem, presenting it instead as a temporary difficulty experienced by individuals and their families.

At the turn of this century, at the same time as this ad for laundry detergent appeared, in many sentimental television soap operas leading female characters suffered layoffs, and in all cases the representations and images were similar. The heroines in soap operas are young, beautiful, and well-educated, and have specialized skills, and for this reason they effectively cover up the reality of laid-off women workers—middle-aged and elderly who at the same time face pressure and discrimination on account of their age and educational background. In contrast to this, when official statements draw on classic socialist aphorisms concerning the working class, attempting in a veiled way to mobilize and unify the society, the working class is cast in the image of men.

On another level, the issues of class and gender are topics that began to emerge in the 1990s as targets of concern and theorizing by critical intellectuals concerned about social equality and integration. Again, these issues tended to obscure each other. Let us put aside for a moment the fact that many male intellectuals (even the so-called critical intellectuals) similarly discount or ignore the complexities and harsh reality of gender issues in Chinese society today. Let us focus instead on the more general issue of class. Let us also lay aside the fact that the theoretical and critical resources used by feminists carry the obvious overtones of the white European middle class. For this reason, when feminists look at the topic of gender, the extent to which they can grasp the reality of women's survival and social issues is quite limited. As far as the topics and discourse on class and gender are concerned, the way these two issues support and conceal each other reveals profound theoretical and linguistic misunderstandings and contradictions.

Although, in this author's view, class divisions and the reconstruction of a gendered social order are also the most prominent and harshest realities of Chinese society in the 1990s and beyond, these two issues are intertwined in profound and complex ways. Teasing them apart becomes very difficult. Even when we direct our attention to the gradually marginalized lower strata of the population and at women as a group, we are bound to encounter the same difficulty in both theory and discourse. Instead of highlighting each other, discourse on class and gender obscure one another. When we go back to theoretical Marxist sources and look again at the exploitation of the lower strata of society and the hardships the increasingly invisible lower-class masses endure, we may, in formulating a new description and summary of society based on class, obscure the factor of gender that went into choosing who would make the sacrifices in this process of reconfiguring society. We may also overlook the ideological and practical implication that the restructuring of a gendered order legitimizes the reality of class.

By contrast, when we attempt to use the perspective of gender to reveal the survival and cultural realities of the dramatic setbacks suffered by women as a group in the name of progress, we either cover up or ignore vast differences in class. In the name of gender or of women, we may occasionally highlight or gather information on the homes that wealthy men have set up for their mistresses all over the special economic zones, the thriving sex trade and the "contributions" the women engaged in it make to the local economy, "laid-off women workers" and "full-time wives," the struggles of "white-collar beauties" and the blood and tears of "girls from the outside" (factory workers from rural areas), the "absolute privacy" of female entrepreneurs and the cases of rural women being abducted and sold into slavery. But since class consciousness is usually absent when this information is collected, what it reveals is trivial and spurious. When we protest the fact that laying off women workers causes a dramatic drop in the percentage of female workers making up the staff at large and medium-sized enterprises, do we at the same time look at the large numbers of rural women workers and child workers consumed by joint venture enterprises and foreign subsidiaries?

When books such as *Siren shenghuo* (Private Lives) or *Yige ren de zhanzheng* (An Individual's War) appear, both of which draw on and confirm feminist theories and furthermore step on the sore toes of male-dominated culture, in our support and affirmation do we tacitly acknowledge, consciously or unconsciously, that in women's literature of the 1980s and 1990s, urban, quasi-middle-class, and intellectual women served as the subject of the great majority of these works, if not all of them?[4] When we applaud the fact that from the 1970s to the 1980s, women as a social group finally broke free of the oppression of class and again "emerged from the horizon of history," do we recognize that, at the same time, the survival, experiences, and realities of lower-class working women were gradually sinking beneath the surface?[5]

Still another example of an author who represents the 1970s is Wei Hui. Her book *Shanghai baobei* (Shanghai Baby) is full of women's material desires, middle-class imagination, and the worship of things Western in the name of alternative culture or feminism.[6] At the turn of the twenty-first century, while women's "physical writing" exhibits women's bodies and desires in literature, these same physical features are also manifested in performance art in the marketplace, such as a female author selling men's underwear imprinted with a photo of herself[7] or people shouting at book signings, "look at *Shanghai Baby*'s beautiful chest!"[8] What is a feminist to make of this kind of writing and what can she say about it when it expresses a worship of Paris and Henry Milleresque fantasies and when it expresses a wish to experience sadistic mistreatment, or the frustration of idle dissolute women who frequent seedy urban bars?

In 2000, Wei Hui (and the rock and roll singer Mian Mian), although slightly faded, were still the number one fads in the fairly downsliding literary market. They received heavy coverage from the media and were regarded as representations of youth culture. They were among the most fashionable topics in Internet culture and hot topics in discussions of women and feminism. On the other hand, virtually all feminists or critics of women's literature maintained a cautious silence about these two authors. If we say the reason was that Wei Hui and Mian Mian constitute some kind of weird pop trend that has little to do with "women's literature," women's writing, or feminism, then can we ignore the online controversy that occurred, summed up by the statement "It's all trouble stirred up by beautiful women"?[9] This statement resulted in an extremely complex but real confrontation of the sexes and torrents of male chauvinistic statements.

Can we ignore the fact that *Shanghai baobei* was ultimately banned and that the publisher was required to seize the books, destroy the printer's proofs, and was furthermore ordered to "cease operations indefinitely pending inspection"?[10] Although subtle political realities were undoubtedly at work here, this incident reflected real outrage on the part of male-dominated culture. However, in spite of the ban on the book and the subsequent threats of a "harsh crackdown," Wei Hui's other works have sold very well, and the online version of *Shanghai baobei*, which was unscathed, took off like a rocket. The attraction of a banned book made it impossible to prevent pirated copies from being sold everywhere. All sorts of imitations, such as *Xiaocheng baobei* (Small Town Baby), also have cropped up.[11]

Another interesting aspect of this cultural phenomenon is the media excitement caused by appearances of these popular female authors, Mian Mian and Wei Hui. Although Mian Mian, who dressed the part, often appeared onstage with Wei Hui to "soak up the spotlight," discussions of trends, women, and "physical writing" did not touch on another, maybe more truthful aspect of Mian's works. In these, she reveals usually invisible aspects of life in the 1990s: her life experiences as a "troubled young woman," a member of the rock-and-roll generation, and a twice-reformed drug addict who had sunk to rock bottom (or you could say was just dust in the wind), the so-called "living witness to the filthy underside of Chinese society." She not only represents the anonymous urban youth culture of the "generation who left home after hearing the rock and roll of Cui Jian," but, for the first time in fashionable and women's writing, she allows us to witness the lower strata of society for ourselves. However, amid all the media frenzy and controversy, with quotations such as "the face of an eighteen-year-old and the sexual organs of an eighty-year-old" being cited repeatedly, the importance of her combined experiences of class and gender was completely lost.

A feud between Mian and Wei also caused great excitement in the male-dominated media and on the Internet. When Mian sniped at Wei, "You're not even from Shanghai (are you just an adventurer from a small town?)," Wei retorted, "You have no creditable education whatsoever." The excitement in the media and on the Internet about the animosity between the women similarly obscured their real conflict. In China today, class conflicts are frequently manifested as or shifted to geographical conflicts. In this context, *Xiang Wei Hui nayang fengkuang* (As Crazy as Wei Hui) is a more representative work than *Shanghai baobei*.[12] This novel portrays a woman in the image of "youth from the provinces" in the 1990s rather than craziness, a story of one slightly different individual's struggle and "panning for gold."

The prejudices these two women publicly expressed in the media revealed in a certain way a type of historical and pragmatic pattern. The strict system of household registration during the Mao era drew virtually uncrossable boundaries between urban and rural areas. Moreover, a clear hierarchy of key cities, marginal cities, and small and medium-sized towns was set up. The university entrance examination system served as a modern version of the imperial examinations and became the only possible means of crossing social barriers. When the system changed and capitalism developed, the status people held in the old socialist system rapidly became in some circles an intangible asset. Legal residency in a key city also became an asset for moving up the social ladder. If Wei Hui's prestigious education and "Fudan [University] complex" express the significance of education as symbolic capital in the new social structure, they also serve as stepping-stones to changing her "family background" and entering the new upper class. Mian Mian's retort is full of local/class arrogance. However, in the enthusiastic cultural performances of sex and gender, expressions of socially symptomatic factors are absent.

One very strange phenomenon in the structure of Chinese cultural ideas from 1990 to the present demonstrates that, if political correctness is required, the correct expressions of class and gender are mutually exclusive. Expressions of a clear class consciousness and social rebellion are nearly always accompanied by profound and open, albeit possibly unconscious, gender bias, or at least prejudice. On the other hand, women's resistance and the awakening of a profound gender consciousness are seemingly limited to intellectual women of the urban middle class. By contrast, in mass culture, the discourse on class and gender allows richer and freer interplay between the two issues. Focused only on class, social criticism, however, doubles or more than doubles the amount of oppression and sacrifice forced upon women.

One clear example of this is the play *Che Guevara*, which was first performed in April 2000 and created a considerable cultural sensation in Beijing.[13] In a certain respect, this play can be said to be the first "revolutionary play" of the twenty years of "reforms and opening to the outside" that does not present the official view. It could even be considered a far cry from what officials would like to see. The play revisits the theme of "revolution" by invoking the name of Che Guevara and discusses the confrontation between rich and poor in today's China in a fresh vigorous (while at the same time crude, simple, and brutal) way. The play addresses the inequities of distribution, social inequalities, and factors of injustice and the reason they exist in such a grand and blatant way. Setting aside for a moment the play's artistic or historical reflections and other factors, the play can be considered something quite rare today, a politically correct work on the levels of class consciousness and pragmatic resistance. But it is also clear that, while the play speaks in the name of revolution, in the name of class, and in the name of Che Guevara, it is undoubtedly laden with a prejudiced and discriminatory gender consciousness. This prejudice is even one of the basic elements in the idea of the play.

At the rear of the stage is a backdrop with the famous portrait of Che Guevara, who gazes down on the stage. The dramatic structure of the play uses an argumentative style in which the good guys, the revolutionaries, are played by three men, while the bad guys, the ruling powers who have all the advantages, are played by four disguised women. In this way, the opposition between oppression and resistance, counterrevolution and revolution, social prejudice and social justice is transformed on the stage into conflict and confrontation between images of men and women. Nevertheless, the bad guys' appearance, behavior, and cultural logic are undoubtedly characterized by male mainstream culture. This type of latent gender representation does not end here. Mocking feminism (or attacking it) has clearly become a new fad in drama. During the play the bad guys say,

> I think it must be because they're too fucking poor! We're not afraid of poverty—we can play the stocks, play the futures, play around in brothels, play on the Internet! We can do women's rights, feminism, womanism, female-ism! We can do postmodernism, premodernism, pre-postmodernism, post-premodernism! If none of that works, we'll do rock and roll, experimental, avant-garde, racy literature. We'll go running around stark naked in front of our foreign friends! There are a million things to do in the world. Why must they have a revolution?!

It should be pointed out that on the landscape of Chinese elite or mass culture during the 1990s and beyond, expressions of a class posture or standpoint are actually very rare. But, by the same token, the rewriting of gender and prejudice is found everywhere. The images of women during the 1990s are two extremes: the hysterical, unreasonable woman and the committed, serious woman who is willing to endure humiliation in order to carry out an important mission. In both women's writing and men's writing we can discover many works with an active woman's consciousness and consciousness of resistance. However, we can say categorically that these works are all about the survival of urban, middle-class or quasi-middle-class, intellectual women (or at least women with some characteristics of the typical intellectual woman). Writers of these works and their female protagonists never focus on women of the lower classes, much less identify with them.

This type of writing that both highlights and conceals women as a social group is most prominent in the literature and women's writing of Guangzhou and the surrounding special economic zones. Through her unique works, the female author Zhang Mei looks at the lives of the new "full-time wives" to reveal the process of "marital alliances" and trading places that take place among the communist and moneyed elite.[14] Zhang Mei examines the "painless groan" that escapes from these relatively privileged women.

One of the most successful writers of popular novels in the early 1990s is Zhang Xin. She was the first to portray realistically and in detail in her urban romance novels the vague but poignant bitterness experienced by the urban middle class during the wave of commercialization that swept the early part of the decade. Moreover, unlike in conventional romance novels, Zhang always has the heroine sacrifice love in order to preserve feelings of sisterhood.[15] The stories of the "painless groans" of upper-class women written by female authors in the special economic zones reproduce a version of women's lives, leaving invisible the hardships experienced by the working women of the open ports on the coast.

With the reform of the economic system, changes in the system of ownership, and the restructuring of large and medium-sized state-run enterprises, class divisions have become an important fact in society, but statements of a rickety and outmoded ideology obscure the process of class division in Chinese society. The legitimization of class divisions and of the existence of classes lurks within the socialist ideology of destroying class, social exploitation, and oppression and all forms of inequality and injustice. This legitimization became an important component of mainstream Chinese ideology in the 1990s. In spite of the adoption of the social rhetoric of economic pragmatism and consumerism, and in spite of the empty promises made by proponents of development (such as "allowing some people to become wealthy first" will make the society better off as a whole; in other words, creating a society dominated by the middle class), socialist ideologues are simultaneously forced to and unable to come to terms with the profound and intense conflicts the increasingly dramatic class divisions present to classical socialist ideology. Socialist ideology is still the basis of legitimacy for the ruling powers, but is also a factor in the social culture that must be rescripted or repressed, because otherwise it could become a ready-made spiritual resource and weapon of resistance for the lower classes, who have been sacrificed in the process of class division.

During the 1980s, China successfully transformed the historical and cultural "bidding farewell to the revolution" by the elite and intellectuals into a kind of social consensus that could be termed a "cultural hegemony." However, the lower classes (workers from formerly state-run enterprises and the masses of peasants who left the rural areas during the process of shifting the economy away from agriculture), facing the realities of exploitation, abandonment, and poverty, can still use the socialist aphorisms they know by heart to compete for their own interests. Thus, statements on the reality and existence of class became an important part of ideological legitimacy in the 1990s, but they confronted the virtually impossible limits of "respecting" and conforming to the old socialist ideology. By exposing and writing about the reality of class divisions and the hardships experienced by the lower classes, intellectuals who take the position of struggling against or criticizing society run the risk of breaking the political taboos imposed by the strictly controlled ideology. Faced with a political regime that calls itself socialist but cannot simply return to classical Marxism, the social critics refuse to identify with the "official doctrines" either of the past or the present and thus cannot provide effective solutions to social problems. Instead, they create different forms of social aphasia on the issue of class division. For these reasons, statements on class division became invisible writings everywhere in Chinese society during the 1990s and occasionally relied on different methods of cultural transference. The topics of gender and women have become one of the important ways of doing this, highlighting and concealing the existence of class reality.

A rhetorical method commonly used in the mainstream media and mass culture in China during the 1990s and beyond has put a feminine face on a widespread social problem. For example, "laid-off women workers" has become synonymous with the large number of unemployed people who have virtually no system of social benefits. "Girls from the outside" is a term that "resonates" with the rural migrant workers whose numbers far exceeded those of laid-off workers. A relatively widespread social problem was confined to the special circumstances experienced by a particular gender, and thus, in the picture of "progress" based on capitalist history, the problem could be described and interpreted as "a process" or "labor pains." The compassion and pity of "great humanism" could be invoked to divert people's attention from the harsh reality. For example, in an advertisement for public benefits for laid-off workers, the Chinese character for "person/man" is superimposed on the upside-down character for "job." The prominent tag line reads, "Be a laid-off worker who pulls himself up by his own bootstraps!" In another ad for public benefits, a female worker has been taking her time finding a job in the labor market, unable to accept the "re-employment" choices offered to her. When she walks by a school and sees the children getting out for the day, she thinks of her own child and "resolutely" sets out again and takes a job in "social service."

An even more typical example is the film *Piaoliang mama* (Pretty Mother; released as *Breaking the Silence* in the United States), which was a box office flop but created a stir in the media and became well known.[16] The film was widely known because the internationally famous star Gong Li portrayed a laid-off woman worker in it, but the character was "laid off by choice," motivated by her tremendous love for her son. The male director Sun Zhou said, "I hope to cause some thinking about feminism,"[17] adding that "in a woman's beauty and radiant smile there are obstacles that men never have and never will be able to surmount."[18] Here, a mother's love and self-sacrificing spirit conceal the penalties exacted by society on women and the lower classes, and the fact that they have no choice but to make sacrifices.[19]

Examining the media coverage of *Piaoliang mama*, we can catch glimpses of the reality it conceals. First, Gong Li was awarded the prestigious honor of being named the "Love Heart ambassador" to the United Nations because of her portrayal of a great mother, not as a lower-class woman. Still, this honor was nothing compared to the distinction she gained by serving as "image ambassador" for L'Oréal, the women's cosmetics company. Second, when the film was released, to promote it, Gong and the boy who played her son in the film were housed together in Beijing, and the child's "real mother" became a shadowy background figure.[20] Third, there was the coverage of Gong Li's discussions with the women workers of state-run enterprises. Deeply moved by the film, these mothers told her their own heart-rending stories.[21] Although the coverage was obviously carefully edited, it still disclosed that the hardships experienced by these not-so-pretty "pretty mothers," were similar to what the soap opera characters suffered. The media passed these hardships off as part of a mother's love, but it is more accurate to say that they were struggling to survive. It is interesting to note that, although we can find large numbers of male "Little Red Cap" workers moving through the streets and alleys every day, their social existence is completely concealed beneath the mask of women and mothers' love. Thus, the circumstances of laid-off workers, the class realities and age discrimination of both men and women are buried even deeper in darkness. Fourth, while *Piaoling mama* was being intensely promoted in the Chinese film market, the media and websites feverishly reported the selection of "ten most beautiful mothers" in Hollywood.[22] In this way "beautiful mothers" reverted to extremely splendid and noble "women of privilege and beauty." Their "eternally enchanting" story has little bearing on the harsh reality of Chinese society and takes place in the lofty heights far above the reality experienced by lower-class women.

Naturally, the topics of class and gender do not fully cover all the social problems facing contemporary China. Statements on race and nationality appear in even stranger forms, which, along with the blatant age discrimination that accompanies the process of class division and the rewriting of gender roles, undoubtedly reveal the complex social reality of China in the 1990s. These are issues this chapter cannot set aside or ignore. However, the importance of class and gender as issues lies not only in their implications for the exploited or sacrificed majority, but also in the strange ways in which class and gender are expressed from the 1990s forward, which reveal social and cultural symptoms of critical importance in China during the 1980s and 1990s. At the complex intersections and historical evolution of strong/weak and mainstream/marginal, these issues and their connections to the various power centers undoubtedly have direct connections to the history of the Mao era and to what this writer means by "historical legacy and debts" of contemporary China. Dealing with these issues is thus an important method and basic means of exposing and criticizing the legacy and debts of the past.

Thus, expressions of class and gender are intertwined in China's specific historical framework and give rise to cultural performances on many levels. Women serve as a social symbol, puppets that carry the notions of gender, appearing in all sorts of social dramas. In the complex circumstances of globalization, during a time when the scenery and frames of reference are changing, representations of women and feminism have been revealed as factors in a certain type of cultural performance. For this author, this implies critical thinking at many latitudes and on two levels. First is the revelation and criticism of mass culture and the process by which mass culture, serving as a carrier for mainstream ideology, utilizes the cultural construction of women. Second, it is also a self-reflection and criticism by one who is herself in the difficult position of being a Chinese feminist critiquing the situation.

NOTES

1. In her work *A World of Difference* (1987), American feminist Barbara Johnson specifically discusses the issue of autobiography in women's writing. A portion of this work was translated into Chinese under the title "My Monster/My Self" and appears in Zhang Jingyuan, ed., *Dangdai nüxingzhuyi wenxue piping* (Contemporary Feminist Literary Criticism) (Beijing: Beijing daxue chubanshe, 1992). In the 1990s most feminist critiques of autobiography (also called "personalized writing" or "physical writing") in women's writing used Johnson's viewpoints for their analysis.

2. The literary work of women writers in the 1990s was dominated by autobiographical novels. Most of these depicted women's physical experiences, desires, and sexual experiences.

3. In 1993, there was a terrible fire at the Hong Kong–owned Zhili toy factory in Shenzhen. The factory did not meet fire safety requirements, but was certified for safe production. In order to prevent workers from leaving the workplace, doors and windows were locked and the factory was surrounded by a chain-link fence. As a result, the workers had no way to escape when the fire erupted. Eighty-four people died in the fire, and more than one hundred were injured. This incident was reported in many newspapers.

4. Chen Liang, *Siren shenghuo* (Private Lives) (Beijing: Zuojia chubanshe, 1996); Lin Bai, *Yige ren de zhanzheng* (An Individual's War) (Neimenggu renmin chubanshe, 1996).

5. Meng Yue and Dai Jinhua, *Fuchu lishi dibiao—Xiandai zhongguo funü wenxue yanjiu* (Emerging from the Horizon of History—Studies of Contemporary Chinese Women's Literature) (Zhengzhou: Henan renmin chubanshe, 1989).

6. Wei Hui, *Shanghai baobei* (Shanghai Baby) (Shenyang: Chunfeng wenyi chubanshe, 1999).

7. In May 1995, an international avant-garde art exhibit was held in Shanghai. Wei Hui was the only author to exhibit a work. Her piece was seven pairs of men's underwear imprinted with her photograph and a paragraph from her novel. Apparently, these items "were immediately snapped up by buyers."

8. According to the article "Dajieshang di tuoyiwu" (Strip Tease on the Street), *Tianfu zaobao* (Tianfu Morning News), 5 April 2000, Wei Hui said during a promotional event in Chengdu, "let them take a look at Shanghai Baby's chest." See also Lu Yan, "Wei Hui Is as Crazy as It Gets," *Jingpin gouwu zhinan* (Buying Guide), 11 April 2000. A number of newspapers later reported on the story, using the headline "Kankan Shanghai baobei di piaoliang rufang" (Take a Look at Shanghai Baby's Beautiful Chest).

9. After Wei Hui's short novel was published, the piece "Ni shi meinü ma? Dang zuojia quba" (Are You a Beautiful Woman? Then Be a Writer), by Li Fang appeared in *Zhongguo qingnian bao* (China Youth Daily), 13 March 2000, resulting in the controversy over "beautiful women writers." Several websites based in mainland China ran columns titled "It's All Trouble Stirred Up by Beautiful Women," causing an intense online debate.

10. In May 2000, "due to its descriptions of female masturbation, homosexuality, and drug use," the Beijing news media and cultural management departments cited *Shanghai baobei* as "corrupt, decadent, and tainted with Western culture," and banned the book. The national news publishing administration placed the book on its list of banned books, and Chunfeng Arts Press, the publisher of the book, was required to destroy or return the books. The publisher was then ordered to "cease operations indefinitely pending inspection."

11. After *Shanghai baobei* was banned, it became a best-seller at book stalls, and before long there were pirated copies in a variety of forms and imitations with such names as *Beijing baobei* (Beijing Baby), *Guangzhou baobei* (Guangzhou Baby), and

Chengdu baobei (Chengdu Baby). *Xiaocheng baobei* (Small Town Baby) was published under the name *Ba Yi* by the New Era Press.

12. Wei Hui, *Xiang Wei Hui nayang fengkuang* (As Crazy as Wei Hui) (Zhuhai: Zhuhai chubanshe, 1999).

13. *Che Guevara*, "a play of history and poetry for the stage," written by Huang Jisu and directed by Zhang Guangtian. It was first performed at the Beijing People's Arts Theater in April 2000. It then toured Beijing, Guangzhou, Shanghai, and other cities.

14. ee Zhang Mei, *Jiu hou de aiqing guan* (Views of Love after Drinking), in *Xin zhuangtai xiaoshuo wenku* (Collection of New Novels), Vol. 1, February 1995.

15. See Zhang Xin, *Ai you ruhe?* (What About Love?) (Beijing: Huayi chubanshe, 1995).

16. *Piaoliang mama* (Pretty Mother) (2000), directed by Sun Zhou, starring Gong Li and Gao Xin. Screenplay by Liu Heng, Sun Zhou, and Shao Xiaoli. A joint production of the Zhujiang Film Studio and the Three-Nine Film Studio.

17. When talking about his motivation in creating *Piaoliang mama* during an online interview (http://ent.sina.com.cn, 24 February 2000, 7:30 PM), director Sun Zhou said, "I cannot abandon my principles toward this woman in order to placate the audience. I wanted to replicate the real life of a woman. I wanted to let people see how a real woman solves her own problems. I hope that this film will inspire some thinking about feminism."

18. Director's quote from poster advertising *Piaoliang mama* to the Chinese market.

19. One piece of news that was both very interesting and symptomatic of the times appeared in *Jinling wanbao* (Jinling Evening News) on 3 March 2000 under the headline "Piaoliang mama 'san ba' weiwen xiagang nügong" (*Piaoliang mama* to Cheer up Laid-off Female Workers on March 8). Later *Nanjing ribao* (Nanjing Daily) also reported the story under the same headline. The text read, "As March 8, International Women's Day approaches, older state-run movie houses in Nanjing plan to give free tickets to over 400 laid-off women workers to see the outstanding Chinese-made film *Piaoliang mama*. This highly artistic film should give these women more passion for life and encourage them to pull themselves up by their own bootstraps."

20. Cheng Tieliang, photo essay, "Piaoliang mama qianshou long'er" (Pretty Mother Holds Hands with Her Deaf Son), *Beijing qingnian bao* (Beijing Youth Daily), 20 April 2000.

21. Xie Yanchen, "Gong Li daishang xiaohongmao" (Gong Li Wears a Little Red Cap), *Beijing qingnian bao* (Beijing Youth Daily), 23 April 2000, special report.

22. Netease, sina.com, and other websites reported that on Mother's Day, 15 May 2000, the ten "most beautiful mothers" chosen by the U.S. media were announced in Hollywood. Netease began its report of the story by noting that "the new Gong Li movie *Piaoliang mama* had recently made the topic of beautiful mothers extremely popular. Many people do not realize that the film "piaoliang mama" has also become a popular trend in the U.S." (17 May 2000).

SUGGESTED READING

Andors, Phyllis. *The Unfinished Liberation of Chinese Women, 1949–1980.* Bloomington: Indiana University Press, 1983.

Barlow, Tani E., ed. *Gender Politics in China: Writing and Feminism.* Durham, N.C.: Duke University Press, 1993.

———. With Gary J. Bjorge. *I Myself Am a Woman: Selected Writings of Ding Ling.* Boston: Beacon Press, 1989.

Bray, Francesca. *Technology and Gender: Fabrics of Power in Late Imperial China.* Berkeley: University of California Press, 1997.

Cahill, Suzanne. *Transcendence and Divine Passion: The Queen Mother of the West in Medieval China.* Stanford, Calif.: Stanford University Press, 1993.

Cass, Victoria B. *Dangerous Women: Warriors, Grannies, and Geishas of the Ming.* New York: Rowman and Littlefield, 1999.

Chang, Kang-I Sun. *Women Writers of Traditional China: An Anthology of Poetry and Criticism.* Stanford, Calif.: Stanford University Press, 1999.

Chang, Pang-mei Natasha. *Bound Feet and Western Dress.* New York: Doubleday, 1996.

Chow Rey. *Women and Chinese Modernity: The Politics of Reading Between West and East.* Minneapolis: University of Minnesota Press, 1991.

Croll, Elisabeth. *Changing Identities of Chinese Women: Rhetoric, Experience, and Self-Perception in Twentieth-century China.* London: Zed Books, 1995.

———. *Chinese Women Since Mao.* London: Zed Books, 1983.

———. *Feminism and Socialism in China.* London: Routledge and Kegan Paul, 1978.

Davin, Delia. *Women Work: Women and the Party in Revolutionary China.* New York: Oxford University Press, 1997.

Dikotter, Frank. *Sex, Culture, and Modernity in China: Medical Science and the Construction of Sexual Identities in the Early Republican Period.* Honolulu: University of Hawaii Press, 1995.

Dooling, Amy D., and Kristina M. Torgeson, eds. *Writing Women in Modern China: An Anthology of Women's Literature from the Early Twentieth Century.* New York: Columbia University Press, 1998.

Ebrey, Patricia Buckley. *The Inner Quarters: Marriage and the Lives of Chinese Women in the Sung Period.* Berkeley: University of California Press, 1993.

Entwisle, Barbara, and Gail E. Henderson, eds. *Re-drawing Boundaries: Work, Households, and Gender in China.* Berkeley: University of California Press, 2000.

Evans, Karin. *The Lost Daughters of China.* New York: Jeremy P. Tarcher/Putnam, 2000.

Feng Xu. *Women Migrant Workers in China's Economic Reform.* New York: St. Martin's Press, 2000.

Furth, Charlotte. *A Flourishing Yin: Gender in China's Medical History, 960–1665.* Berkeley: University of California Press, 1999.

Suggested Reading

Gilmartin, Christina K., Gail Hershatter, Lisa Rofel, and Tyrene White, eds. *Engendering China: Women, Culture, and the State.* Cambridge, Mass.: Harvard University Press, 1994.

Guisso, Richard W. L., and Stanley Johannesen, eds. *Women in China: Current Directions in Historical Scholarship.* New York: Philo Press, 1981.

Hershatter, Gail. *Dangerous Pleasures: Prostitution and Modernity in Twentieth-Century Shanghai.* Berkeley: University of California Press, 1997.

Hershatter, Gail, Emily Honig, Susan Mann, and Lisa Rofel, eds. *Guide to Women's Studies in China.* Berkeley, Calif.: Institute of East Asian Studies, 1998.

Hom, Sharon K., ed. *Chinese Women Traversing Diaspora: Memories, Essays, and Poetry.* New York: Garland, 1999.

Honig, Emily. *Sisters and Strangers: Women in the Shanghai Cotton Mills, 1919–1949.* Stanford, Calif.: Stanford University Press, 1986.

Honig, Emily, and Gail Hershatter. *Personal Voices: Chinese Women in the 1980s.* Stanford, Calif.: Stanford University Press, 1988.

Jaschok, Maria, and Suzanne Miers, eds. *Women and Chinese Patriarchy Submission, Servitude and Escape.* London: Zed Books, 1994.

Jin Yihong. *Chinese Women Organizing.* Oxford: Berg Publishers, 2001.

Johnson, Kay Ann. *Women, the Family, and Peasant Revolution in China.* Chicago: University of Chicago Press, 1983.

Judd, Ellen R. *Gender and Power in Rural North China.* Stanford, Calif.: Stanford University Press, 1994.

Knapp, Bettina L. *Images of Chinese Women: A Westerner's View.* New York: Whitston, 1992.

Ko, Dorothy. *Teachers of the Inner Chambers: Women and Culture in Seventeenth-Century China.* Stanford, Calif.: Stanford University Press, 1994.

Kung, Lydia. *Factory Women in Taiwan.* New York: Columbia University Press, 1994.

Lang, Olga. *Chinese Family and Society.* New Haven, Conn.: Yale University Press, 1946.

Lau Siu-kai, ed. *Inequalities and Development: Social Stratification in Chinese Societies.* Hong Kong: Chinese University of Hong Kong, 1994.

Levy, Howard. *The Lotus Lovers: The Complete History of the Curious Erotic Custom of Footbinding in China.* New York: Prometheus, 1992.

Li, Chenyang, ed. *The Sage and the Second Sex.* Chicago: Open Court, 2000.

Li Shuzhuo and Zhu Chuzhu. *Research and Community Practice on Gender Difference in Child Survival in China.* Beijing: China Population Publishing House, 2001.

Liu, Dalin, Man Lun Ng, Li Pingzhou, and Erwin J. Haeberle. *Sexual Behavior in Modern China: Report on the Nationwide Survey of 20,000 Men and Women.* New York: Continuum, 1997.

Mann, Susan. *Precious Records: Women in China's Long Eighteenth Century.* Stanford, Calif.: Stanford University Press, 1997.

Ono Kazuko. *Chinese Women in a Century of Revolution, 1850–1950.* Stanford, Calif.: Stanford University Press, 1989.

Pruit, Ida. *A Daughter of Han.* Stanford, Calif.: Stanford University Press, 1945.

Rofel, Lisa. *Other Modernities: Gendered Yearnings in China After Socialism.* Berkeley:

University of California Press, 1999.

Salaff, Janet. *Working Daughters of Hong Kong: Filial Piety or Power in the Family?* New York: Columbia University Press, 1995.

Salaff, Janet, and Mary Sheridan, eds. *Lives, Chinese Working Women*. Bloomington: Indiana University Press, 1984.

Smedley, Agnes. *Portraits of Chinese Women in Revolution*. New York: The Feminist Press, 1976.

Spence, Jonathan D. *The Death of Woman Wang*. New York: Penguin Books, 1978.

Stacey, Judith. *Patriarchy and Socialist Revolution in China*. Berkeley: University of California Press, 1983.

Stockard, Janice E. *Daughters of the Canton Delta: Marriage Patterns and Economic Strategies in South China, 1860–1930*. Stanford, Calif.: Stanford University Press, 1989.

Tao Chunfang and Jiang Yongping. *Review of the Social Status of Chinese Women*. Beijing: New Word Press, 1995.

Tao Chunfang and Xiao Yang. *Research on Women's Reproductive Health in China*. Beijing: New Word Press, 1995.

T'ien, Ju-kang. *Male Anxiety and Female Chastity: A Comparative Study of Chinese Ethical Values in Ming-Ch'ing Times*. Leiden: E. J. Brill, 1988.

Tierney, Helen, ed. *Women's Studies Encyclopedia*. Westport, Conn: Greenwood Press, 1999.

Tung, Jowen R. *Fables for the Patriarchs: Gender Politics in Tang Discourse*. New York: Rowman and Littlefield, 2000.

Gulik, R. H. Van. *Sexual Life in Ancient China: A Preliminary Survey of Chinese Sex and Society from ca. 1500 B.C. till 1644 A.D.* Leiden: E. J. Brill, 1961, 1974.

Wang Ping. *Aching for Beauty: Footbinding in China*. Minneapolis: University of Minnesota Press, 2000.

Wang Zheng. *Women in the Chinese Enlightenment: Oral and Textual Histories*. Berkeley: University of California Press, 1999.

Watson, Rubie S., and Patricia Bukely Ebrey, eds. *Marriage and Inequality in Chinese Society*. Berkeley: University of California Press, 1991.

Weidner, Marsha Smith, ed. *Flowing in the Shadows: Women in the History of Chinese and Japanese Painting*. Honolulu: University of Hawaii Press, 1990.

West, Jackie, Zhao Minghua, Chang Xiangqun, and Cheng Yuan, eds. *Women of China: Economic and Social Transformation*. New York: St. Martin's Press, 1999.

Widmer, Ellen, and Kang-I Sun Chang, eds. *Writing Women in Late Imperial China*. Stanford, Calif.: Stanford University Press, 1997.

Wolf, Margery. *Revolution Postponed: Women in Contemporary China*. Stanford, Calif.: Stanford University Press, 1985.

———. *Women and Family in Rural Taiwan*. Stanford, Calif.: Stanford University Press, 1972.

Wolf, Margery, and Roxane Witke, eds. *Women in Chinese Society*. Stanford, Calif.: Stanford University Press, 1975.

Xie Bingying. *A Woman Soldier's Own Story*. New York: Columbia University Press, 2001.

Xinran. *The Good Women of China: Hidden Voices*. New York: Pantheon Books, 2002.

Yang, Mayfair Mei-hui, ed. *Spaces of Their Own: Women's Public Sphere in Transnational China.* Minneapolis: University of Minnesota Press, 1999.

Young, Marilyn B., ed. *Women in China: Studies in Social Change and Feminism.* Ann Arbor: Michigan Papers in Chinese Studies, 1973.

Young, Marilyn B., Sonia Kruks, and Rayna Rapp, eds. *Promissory Notes:Women in the Transition to Socialism.* New York: Monthly Review Press, 1989.

Zhang, Yingjin. *City in Modern Chinese Literature and Film: Configurations of Space, Time, and Gender.* Stanford, Calif.: Stanford University Press, 1996.

Zhong Xueping, Wang Zheng, and Bai Di, eds. *Some of Us: Chinese Women Growing up in the Mao Era.* New Brunswick, N.J.: Rutgers University Press, 2001.

Zhu Chuzhu, Li Shuzhuo, Qiu Changrong, Hu Ping, and Jin Anrong, eds. *The Dual Effects of the Family Planning Program on Chinese Women.* Xian: Xian Jiaotong University Press, 1997.

Zito, Angela, and Tani E. Barlow, eds. *Body Subject and Power in China.* Chicago: University of Chicago Press, 1994.

CONTRIBUTORS

Bu Wei, born in 1957, is an associate researcher at the Institute of News and Broadcasting of the Chinese Academy of Social Sciences, and director of the Research Center for Media Broadcasting and Youth Development. She is engaged in research on the influence of the media on children, the media and gender, the social influence of the Internet, and methods of studying broadcasting. Her published writings include *Shehui kexue chengguo jiazhi pinggu* (A Values Assessment of the Results of Social Science, 1999*)*, *Meijie yu xingbie* (The Media and Gender, 2001), *Dazhong meijie dui ertong di yingxiang* (The Influence of Mass Media on Children, 2002), and others. She has written over eighty articles and research reports.

Chen Mingxia was born in August 1940. She is a graduate of the Law Department of Peking University and a researcher at the Law Institute of the Chinese Academy of Social Sciences. From 1987 to 1988 she was a guest researcher in the Law Department of Tokyo Metropolitan University in Japan. Her primary areas of research are civil law, marriage and family law, women's law, and inheritance law. She has participated in the drafting and revision of statutes on marriage law, women's law, laws protecting mothers and infants, inheritance law, and adoption law. She is currently engaged in a research project to study intervention in domestic violence. She has authored, coauthored, and translated ten books and written more than one hundred research papers.

Dai Jinhua was born in 1959 in Beijing. She previously taught in the Department of Film Literature at the Beijing College of Film and is currently a professor and graduate advisor at the Institute of Comparative Literature and Comparative Literature Research at Peking University. She holds a concurrent professorship at Ohio State University in the Department of East Asian Studies. She researches the history of film, women's literature, and mass culture. She is the author of *Fuchu lishi dibiao—Xiandai Zhongguo funü wenxue yanjiu* (Emerging from the Horizon of History—Studies of Contemporary Chinese Women's Literature, 1989), "Cinema and Desire: A Feminist Marxism and Cultural Politics" in *Dai Jinhua's Works*, and more than ten other essays.

Han Jialing received a Ph.D. from Peking University in 1997 and is currently an associate researcher and director of the Center for Migrant Population Education and Training at the Beijing Academy of Social Sciences, Department of Sociology. As a member of Zigen Fund, an NGO, she participated in development projects in China's poor areas, including Guizhou, Yunnan, Guangxi, Shanxi, Shaanxi, Gansu, and Inner Mongolia beginning in 1991. The projects included basic education, basic medical care and hygiene, environmentally friendly technology, agricultural training, microloans to poor women, and income-generating projects for women. From 1997 to 1999 she completed postdoctoral research at the Peking University Institute of Sociology and Anthropology, where her topic of research was poverty. Her thesis, *Cong yige shili kan zhongguo xibu piikun diqu funu de fazhan* (Study of the Progress of Development of Women in China's Poor Rural Villages—Case Study from Leishan County, Guizhou Province), won top honors in the Second National Youth Award for Outstanding Results in Sociology.

Gail Hershatter is professor of history and director of the Institute for Humanities Research at the University of California, Santa Cruz. She is author of *The Workers of Tianjin, 1900–1949* (1986), co-author of *Personal Voices: Chinese Women in the 1980s* (1988), and co-editor of *Engendering China: Women, Culture, and the State* (1994), *Remapping China: Fissures in Historical Terrain* (1996), and *A Guide to Women's Studies in China* (1999). Her most recent book is *Dangerous Pleasures: Prostitution and Modernity in Twentieth-Century Shanghai* (1997; Chinese edition, 2003). Her current project is entitled "The Gender of Memory: Rural Chinese Women and the 1950s."

Huang Yufu, Ph.D., was born in 1945. She is a senior research fellow and director of the Department of Research at the Center for Documentation and Information of the Chinese Academy of Social Sciences (CASS), chief editor of *Social Sciences Abroad*, director of the Editorial Department of *Contemporary Korea*, and a member of the Standing Committee of the Center for Women's Studies of CASS. Her publications include *Ren yu shehui—meiguo de shehuihua wenti* (Human Beings and Society: Socialization in America, 1986); *Xifang xingjiaoyu* (Education in the West, 1989); and *Jingju, qiao, he zhongguo de xingbie guanxi, 1902–1937* (Peking Opera, Qiao, and Chinese Gender Relations, 1902–1937, 1999).

Jiang Yongping was born in 1953. She is an associate professor and director of the Department of Policy and Law at the Women's Studies Institute of China. For many years she led research on issues related to the status of Chinese women in society. Her research areas include women and urban employment, women's social guarantees, women's occupations and occupational development in work, women and the economy, and women's societal position. She is a member of the Sociology Association of China and has published many articles about women and sociology.

Jin Yihong is a professor at the Jinling Women's College of Nanjing Normal University and director of the Women's Center at Nanjing Normal University. Her primary areas of research include rural women and women's labor and employment. She is author of *Fuquandi shiwei—Jiangnan nongcun shehui bianqianzhongdi xingbie yanjiu* (The Decline of Paternal Authority—Gender Studies on Socially Changing Rural Southern China, 2000) and *Hunlian chongtuzhongdi nüren* (Women in Conflict in Love and Marriage, 1998), coauthor of *Zaihun jiating yanjiu* (Study of Remarried Families, 2002) and *Suxingzhongdi nüwa—Nüxing yishi xinlun* (Nüwa Revived—A New Theory of Women's Consciousness, 1990), and coeditor with Liu Bohong of *Shijizhi jiaodi Zhongguo funü he fazhan* (Chinese Women and Development at the Turn of the Century, 1998).

Lily Xiao Hong Lee was born in China and studied in Hong Kong, southeast Asia, the United States, and Australia. She lectures on Chinese literature at the Chinese Department of the University of Sydney and is the author of *The Virtue of Yin* and coauthor of *Women of the Long March*. She coordinates a project that aims to compile a comprehensive dictionary about the women of China and is the coeditor of this four-volume work. Her two-volume *Biographical Dictionary of Chinese Women* has recently been published. Throughout her career, she has also written numerous articles and papers on Chinese women and the literature and history of the Wei-Jin period (265–420).

Danke Li holds a Ph.D. from the University of Michigan and is currently an assistant professor of history at Fairfield University. Her research interests include women's education and popular culture and revolution in China. Her article "Gender Inequality in Access to Knowledge in China" appeared in *China Review*, April 2002.

Li Xiaojiang (b. 1951) is professor and director of the Center for Gender Studies at Dalian University. Her major works include *Jiedu nüren* (Interpreting Women, 1999), *Guanyu nürendi dawen* (Questions and Answers on Women, 1997), *Zouxiang nüren* (Walking Toward Womanhood, 1994), *Nüxing shenmei yishi tanzheng* (An Exploration of Women's Aesthetic Appreciation and Awareness, 1990), *Xing gou* (Gender Gap, 1989), and

Xiawadi tansuo (Exploring Eve, 1988). She was editor of *Funü yanjiu congshu* (Compendium of Women's Studies Series, 1987–1992, 15 volumes), joint editor *Xingbie yu Zhongguo* (Gender and Engendering China Series, 1994–1999, 4 volumes), *Ershi shiji funü koushushi congshu* (Compendium of Chinese Women's Oral History in the Twentieth Century, 2003, 4 volumes), and *Xingbie luntan* (Gender Studies Forum, 2000–2002, 4 volumes).

Liu Ying, born in 1932, has been a researcher with the Institute of Sociology, Chinese Academy of Social Sciences, and is former director of the Office of Family Studies. She is currently a member of the board of directors for the Chinese Academy of Social Sciences Center for Elder Studies and the board of directors of the Chinese Academy of Social Sciences Center for Theoretical Research on Women. Her major writings include *Zhongguo chengshi jiating—Wuchengshi jiating diaocha* (Chinese Urban Households—A Survey of Households in Five Cities), *Zhongguo hunyin jiating yanjiu* (Research on Marriage and Family, 1987), *Zhongguo nongcun jiating—13 shengshi diaocha* (Chinese Rural Households—A Survey of Thirteen Provinces and Municipalities, 1992), *Jiating deyu yu zinü chengcai* (Moral Education in the Home and the Achievement of Children), and *Funü jiuye yu jiating* (Women's Employment and the Family). She is currently engaged in research primarily on elderly women.

Lu Meiyi, born in 1944, graduated from the History Department of Beijing Normal University in 1968 and is currently a professor in the History and Archeology Department of Zhengzhou University. She is primarily engaged in teaching and research on contemporary Chinese history. She is a member of the Chinese Women's Research Council. Her major works on the history of women include *Zhongguo funü yundong (1840–1921)* (The Chinese Women's Movement [1840–1921], 1990), *Jindai Zhongguo funü shenghuo* (The Lives of Women in Contemporary China, 1993), and *Zouchu zhongshiji—jindai Zhongguo funü shenghuodi bianqian* (Walking Out of the Middle Ages—Changes in the Lives of Women in Contemporary China, 1996). She has published dozens of scholarly papers.

Ma Wanhua is currently associate professor at Peking University College of Education. In 1992 she received a master's degree and in 1997 a Ph.D. in education from Cornell University. She has participated in and chaired the United Nations Development Programme, UNESCO, and Ford Foundation research projects on issues of gender and education. The current focus of her research is the internationalization of higher education, gender and women's education, and the pedagogical reform of higher education.

Shirley L. Mow is a U.S.-based educational consultant. She recently served as associate director of the Educational Partnership Center at the University of California, Santa Cruz. Prior to that she was the executive director of the Westchester Education Coalition, executive assistant to the president of Hunter College of the City University of New York and associate dean of University College of Pace University. She was also an American Council of Education Fellow and a research fellow at Educational Testing Service. She has conducted research and written extensively on student achievement and educational reform. Dr. Mow holds an A.B. from Hunter College, an M.A from Columbia University Teachers College and a Ph.D. from Columbia University. She serves on the Board of Directors of the Feminist Press at the City University of New York, the Board of Trustees of the Lingnan Foundation, and the Advisory Board of the Center on Chinese Education at Teachers College, Columbia University.

Shou Yuanjun graduated from the Journalism Department at Renmin University of China in 1961. She is a senior editor at CCTV and a member of the board of directors of the Chinese Women's Theoretical Seminar. She is a founder of the CCTV programs *Women zhei yidai* (Our Generation), *Shier yanboshi* (Studio Twelve), and *Ban bian tian* (Half the Sky). Her major writings include *Dianshi ertong jiemu de teshuxing* (The Special Nature of Television Programs for Children), *Dianshi jizhe di xianchang tiwen* (On-Site Interviewing for Television Reporters), *Ban bian tian de sange fazhan jieduan* (The Three Stages of Development of *Half the Sky*). She is also coauthor of *Zhongyang dianshitai fazhan shi* (The Developmental History of CCTV).

Tan Shen is senior editor of *Shehuixue yanjiu* (Sociological Research), the journal of the Institute of Sociology at the Chinese Academy of Social Sciences. She serves on the Standing Board of Directors of the China Women's Seminar as a permanent member of the China Women's Studies Association. She is responsible for the Labor Project at the Center for Contemporary Chinese Studies at Qinghua University. Her primary research projects include "Rural Migrant Working Women," 1998, through the Chinese Academy of Social Sciences, Institute of Sociology; research with the Ford Foundation concerning rural migrant working women and supporting projects; the "Labor Studies Series" through the Center for Contemporary Chinese Studies at Qinghua University; and the survey "Groups of Rural People with the Experience of Leaving Home," a subproject of the "Second National Survey on the Social Status of Women," a cooperative project by the National Women's Alliance and State Bureau of Statistics.

Tao Jie is professor of English and deputy director of the Women's Studies Center at Peking University. She has translated into Chinese works by William Faulkner, Robert Penn Warren, Alice Walker, and other American writers. She edited *Fukena duanpian xiaoshuoji* (Selected Short Stories by William Faulkner, 2001); *Yingyu meiwen 50 pian* (Fifty Best English Essays [in Chinese and English], 2002); and *Yuwai funu* (Women Abroad, 1995). Her research interest is in twentieth-century American fiction, especially Southern literature and women's writing.

Wang Qingshu was born in December 1927. She graduated from the Nanjing Central University Law Department in 1949. She has served as director of the Peking University Institute of Dialectical Materialism and of the Institute of Aesthetics and Literary and Artistic Theory. She also held positions as the deputy editor-in-chief of People's Press, secretary of the All-China Women's Federation Secretariat, and president of the China Women's Managing Cadre College. She currently serves as advisor to the Chinese Women's Research Society.

Wang Xingjuan, born in January 1931, is a graduate of the Chinese Department at Jinling University, Nanjing. She has been engaged in journalism and publishing for many years and began studying women's issues in the early 1980s. She has written papers on women's political participation, marriage and the family, domestic violence, and women's psychology. She edited *Zhongguo funü canzhengdi xingdong* (Actions for Chinese Women's Political Participation), *Dianhua xinli zixun xinli zixundi lilun yu shiji* (The Theory and Practice of Telephone Counseling and Psychological Counseling), *Zaishequ, shei guan jiating wenti* (Who Manages Family Problems in the Community?), and other books, and wrote major chapters on these topics.

Xia Xiaohong was born in 1953. She holds a master's degree in literature and is currently a professor in the Chinese Department at Peking University. Her research focuses on contemporary Chinese literature and society, as well as the history of women during the late Qing dynasty. Her major works include *Wanqing shehui yu wenhua* (Society and Culture During the Late Qing, 2001), *Wanqing wenren funüguan* (Perspectives of Men of Letters Toward Women During the Late Qing Dynasty, 1995), and *Jueshi yu chuanshi—Liang Qichao di wenxue daolu* (Enlightening the World and Passing It Down to Later Generations—The Literary Path of Liang Qichao, 1991).

Xiong Yu was born in 1932. In 1958 she graduated from the People's University Department of Statistics. She is currently a researcher at the Institute for Population Studies of the Chinese Academy of Social Sciences, a member of the board of directors of the China Urban Anthropology Society, a member of the Standing Committee of the Center for Women's Studies of the Chinese Academy of Social Sciences, and a member of the board of directors for the Center for Elder Studies. She is the former director of the Chinese Academy of Social Sciences Office for Studies on Population and Society of the Institute for Population Studies. Her major writings include *Dangdai Zhongguo funü jiating diwei yanjiu* (Study of the Status of Contemporary Chinese Women in the Family, 1995), *Mianxiang ershi shijidi xuanze— Dangdai funü yanjiu zuixin lilun gailan* (Choices in Facing the Twenty-First Century—Overview of the Newest Theories in Contemporary Women's Studies, 1993), *Zhongguo laonian renkou shehui* (The Society of China's Elderly Population, 1991), *Lun shengyu wenhua yu renkou kongzhi* (On the Culture of Reproduction and Population Control, 1994), *Zhongguo shaoshu minzu renkou yanjiu* (Population Studies of China's Minority Nationalities, 1988), and *Woguo shaoshu minzu renkou siwanglü fenxi* (Analysis of the Death Rates of Our Nation's Minority Populations , 1987).

Zhao Liming, born October 1948, holds a Ph.D. in history from Qinghua University, where she is a professor and director of the language teaching and research section of the Chinese Department. Her fields of study include the history of Chinese, the study of Chinese characters, and anthropology. She has conducted numerous field studies and discovered and researched the women's script, writing systems of the Miao and Dong ethnic minorities, and grammatical symbols used for the primitive language of the Yao people. In recent years she has studied changes in the transmission of Chinese characters and comparative philology. She is the author or coauthor of over ten published works and has published dozens of papers. Her most important works include *Nüshu—yige jingrendi faxian* (The Women's Script—A Startling Discovery), *Zhongguo nüshu jicheng* (Collection of the Chinese Women's Script, 1992), *Nüshu yu nüshu wenhua* (The Women's Script and the Culture of the Women's Script, 1995), and *Hanzi bianyizhongdi bianyi yanjiu* (Studies on Variations in Chinese Characters).

Zheng Bijun was formerly professor in the History Department and director of the Women's Studies Center at Peking University. She served as advisor to the Chinese Society for Women's Studies, vice president of the Beijing Society for Women's Studies, and president of the Haidian Society of Women's Theories. Her research focuses on ancient Chinese history, ancient Chinese women's history, and contemporary Chinese women's studies. Her publications include *Huai Gu Lu Jiao Zhu* (Annotations to The Book of Nostalgia) as well as numerous articles on her research topics in key Chinese journals and in *Contemporary China*, published by the Free Berlin University Press.